People and Computers XII

Springer-Verlag London Ltd.

H. Thimbleby, B. O'Conaill and
P.J. Thomas (Eds)

People and Computers XII

Proceedings of HCI '97

 Springer

Harold Thimbleby
Middlesex University
Bounds Green Road
London N11 2NQ, UK

Brid O'Conaill
Hewlett-Packard Research Laboratories
Filton Road
Stoke Gifford
Bristol, BS16 6QZ, UK

Peter J. Thomas
Centre for Personal Information Management
University of West of England
Coldharbour Lane, Bristol BS16 1QY, UK

ISBN 978-3-540-76172-3

British Library Cataloguing in Publication Data
People and computers XII : proceedings of HCI '97
1. Human-computer interaction - Congresses
I. Thimbleby, Harold II. O'Conaill, Brid III. Thomas, Peter J. IV. British Computer Society
004' .019
ISBN 978-3-540-76172-3   ISBN 978-1-4471-3601-9 (eBook)
DOI 10.1007/978-1-4471-3601-9
Library of Congress Cataloging-in-Publication Data
A catalog record for this book is available from the Library of Congress

Typesetting: Camera-ready by author

34/3830-543210 Printed on acid-free paper

Contents

The HCI'97 Conference Committee

Conference Chair	Peter Thomas, UWE Bristol
Technical Programme Chair	Harold Thimbleby, Middlesex University
Technical Programme Committee	Brid O'Conaill, Hewlett-Packard Peter Thomas, UWE Bristol
Committee Administrator	Annette Brune, UWE Bristol
Demonstrations Chair	Clive Frankish, University of Bristol
Doctoral Workshop Chair	Judith Ramsay, South Bank University
Industry Day Chair	John Cato, Software Design and Build
Organisational Overview Chairs	Chris Roast, Sheffield Hallam University Andrew Stratton, University of Sheffield
Panel Chair	Peter Brown, University of Kent, Canterbury
Poster Chair	Frank Maddix, UWE Bristol
Short Paper Chair	Alan Dix, Staffordshire University
Tutorial Chair	John Dowell, City University
Video Chair	Paul Kearney, Sharp Laboratories of Europe

Advisory Committee Members

Bob Anderson, Xerox
Dick Bolt, MIT Media Lab
Bill Buxton, Alias / Wavefront
Peter Cochrane, British Telecom
Ken Dye, Microsoft
David Frohlich, Hewlett-Packard
Greg Garrison, Reuters
Simon Hakiel, IBM
Brenda Wroe, Usability Services NatWest Group UK

Conference Management and Liaisons

Auditing	Nicholas Pearce, Nicholas Pearce and Co. Bristol
A / V Equipment	David Lees, UWE Bristol
BCS-HCI Liaison	Gilbert Cockton, University of Northumbria, Newcastle
Conference Dinner Liaison	Constance Fleuriot, UWE Bristol
Co-operating Societies	Anne Morris, Loughborough University
CyberCafe	Lefteris Kanavas, UWE Bristol
Delegate Pack	David Cartwright, UWE Bristol
European Liaison	Morten Borup Harning, Copehagen Business School
Hewlett-Packard Liaison	Erik Geelhoed, Hewlett-Packard
Identity	Paul Arrowsuch, Consultant
IEE Liaison	Claire Coleshill, IEE
Local Co-ordinator	Steve Jones, UWE Bristol
OZCHI Liaison	Steve Howard, Swinburne University, Australia
Press Liaison	Hazel Lacohee, UWE Bristol
Proceedings	Duncan Reed, UWE Bristol
Publicity	Robert Macredie, Brunel University
Publisher Liaison	Dan Diaper, Bournemouth University
Secretariat	David Withers, UWE Bristol
Site Visits	Mike Bartley, SGS Thompson
Social Programme	Jules Tuckett, UWE Bristol
Sponsorship	John Meech, UWE Bristol
US Liaison	Sarah Douglas, University of Oregon

The Reviewers

Hans-Juergen Hoffmann (*Darmstadt University of Technology, Germany*)
Andrew Monk (*University of York, UK*)
Alfred Attipoe (*Aerospatiale Protection Systemes, France*)
Alison Crerar (*Napier University, UK*)
Andy Dearden (*University of York, UK*)
Anker Helms Jorgensen
Nektarios Georgalas (*UMIST, UK*)
Bob Anderson (*RXRC Cambridge, UK*)
Bob Fields (*University of York, UK*)
Brian Shackel (*Loughborough University, UK*)
Carys Siemieniuch (*Loughborough University, UK*)
Chris Roast (*Sheffield Hallam University, UK*)
Claire Dormann (*Technical University of Denmark*)
Clive Warren (*British Aerospace plc, UK*)
Donald Day (*The University of New South Wales, Australia*)
Damon Clark
Darren Van Laar (*University of Portsmouth,, UK*)
Darryn Lavery (*University of Glasgow, UK*)
Dave Usher (*InterAction of Bath Ltd, UK*)
David Benyon (*Napier University, UK*)
David Bonyuet <*Dunklee@tenet.edu*>
David Haw (*Harlequin Limited, UK*)
Lisa Tweedie (*Imperial College, London, UK*)
Ann Blandford (*Middlesex University, UK*)
Chaomei Chen (*Glasgow Caledonian University, UK*)
Robert Macredie (*Brunel University, UK*)
Ghassan Al-Qaimari (*RMIT, Melbourne, Australia*)
Hans Dybkjaer (*Roskilde University, Denmark*)
Hirohide Haga (*Doshisha University, Japan*)
Ian Franklin (*Occupational Psychology Division, Employment Service, UK*)
Ismail Ismail (*University College, London, UK*)
Jarnail Chudge (*MPR Extensys Inc., BC, Canada*)
Jean Vanderdonckt (*The University of Namur, Belgium*)
John Seton (*BT Labs, UK*)
Jon May (*University of Sheffield, UK*)
Chris Kelly (*Defence Evaluation and Research Agency, UK*)
Kenton O'Hara (*RXRC, Cambridge, UK*)
Alwyn Lewis (*BT Labs, UK*)
Licia Calvi (*University of Antwerp, Belgium*)
Lorna Love (*University of Glasgow, UK*)
Lorna Uden (*Staffordshire University, UK*)
Lorraine Johnston (*University of Melbourne, Australia*)

Mike Dooner (*University of Hull, UK*)
Maggie Williams (*Usability Editor, PC Magazine*)
Michael Smyth (*Napier University, UK*)
Berardina De Carolis (*Universita' di Bari, Italy*)
Nick Rousseau (*Employment Service, UK*)
Nigel Bevan (*National Physical Laboratory, UK*)
Nikos Prekas (*UMIST, UK*)
Owen Daly-Jones (*National Physical Laboratory, UK*)
Philippe Palanque (*University Toulouse, France*)
Uma Patel (*City University, UK*)
Paul Luff (*University of Nottingham, UK*)
Phil Gray (*University of Glasgow, UK*)
Phil Turner (*The MARI Group*)
R.M.Webster (*Electric Paper Limited*)
Reinhard Oppermann (*GMD FIT, Germany*)
R. Moyse (*Harlequin Ltd*)
Sandrine Balbo (*CSIRO-MIS, Australia*)
Scott McRae (*BT Labs, UK*)
Stefania Errore (*CO.RI.N.T.O., Italy*)
Stephen Brewster (*University of Glasgow, UK*)
T J Anderson (*University of Ulster, UK*)
Willemien Visser (*INRIA, Rocquencourt, France*)
John Meech (*UWE, Bristol, UK*)
Hazel Lacohee, (*UWE, Bristol, UK*)
Frank Maddix (*UWE, Bristol, UK*)

Making Passwords Secure and Usable

Anne Adams[1], Martina Angela Sasse[2] & Peter Lunt[3]

[1] Department of Computer Science, UCL, Gower Street, London.
WC1E 6BT
Tel no:- +44 171 419 3462
Fax no:- +44 171 387 1397
Email :- A.Adams@cs.ucl.ac.uk

[2] Department of Computer Science, UCL, Gower Street, London.
WC1E 6BT
Tel no:- +44 171 380 7212
Fax no:- +44 171 387 1397
Email :- A.Sasse@cs.ucl.ac.uk

[3] Department of Psychology, UCL, Bedford Way,
London. WC1E 6BT
Tel no:- +44 171 387 7050 ext. 5401
Email :- p.lunt@ucl.ac.uk

To date, system research has focused on designing security mechanisms to protect systems access although their usability has rarely been investigated. This paper reports a study in which users' perceptions of password mechanisms were investigated through questionnaires and interviews. Analysis of the questionnaires shows that many users report problems, linked to the *number of passwords* and *frequency of password use*. In-depth analysis of the interview data revealed that the degree to which users conform to security mechanisms depends on their perception of *security levels*, *information sensitivity* and *compatibility with work practices*. Security mechanisms incompatible with these perceptions may be circumvented by users and thereby undermine system security overall.

Keywords : Security, Passwords, Grounded Theory, Organisational Factors

1   Introduction

Most organisations try to protect their systems from unauthorised access, usually through passwords. Considerable resources are spent designing secure authentication mechanisms, but the number of security breaches and problems is still increasing (DeAlvare, 1990; Gordon, 1995; Hitchings, 1995). Unauthorised access to systems, and resulting theft of information or misuse of the system, is usually due to hackers "cracking" user passwords, or obtaining them through social engineering. System security, unlike other fields of system development, has to date been regarded as an entirely technical issue - little research has been done on usability or human factors related to use of security mechanisms. Hitchings (1995) concludes that this narrow perspective has produced security mechanisms which are much less effective than they are generally thought to be. Davis & Price (1987) point out that, since security is designed, implemented, used and breached by people, human factors should be considered in the design of security mechanism. It seems that currently hackers pay more attention to human factors than security designers do. The technique of social engineering, for instance - obtaining passwords by deception and persuasion - exploits users' lack of security awareness. Hitchings (1995) also suggests that organisational factors ought to be considered when assessing security systems. The aim of the study described in this paper was to identify usability and organisational factors which affect the use of passwords. The following section provides a brief overview of authentication systems along with usability and organisational issues which have been identified to date.

1.1   Background

Confidentiality is a key element in information security, with user authentication as the main mechanism to obtain this (Parker, 1992). Authentication procedures have traditionally been divided into two different stages. *User identification* (User ID) initially identifies the user interacting with the system. As it is merely a means of specifying who the user is, this id does not have to be secured. At the second - *user authentication* stage - the user has to be verified as the legitimate user of the ID; the *password* used as the means of authentication has to be secret.

Originally, passwords were *system-generated* to ensure users employed "secure" combinations of characters. Most users, however, found these passwords hard to remember, and therefore tended to write them down. Furthermore, security risks were identified in the distribution of system-generated passwords. Both of these reasons have lead to *user-generated passwords* as the most widely used process for password production. In addition to one-word passwords, there are a number of other authentication mechanisms currently in use:

- Passphrases (phrase required instead of a word);
- Cognitive passwords (question-and-answer session of personal details);
- Associative passwords (a series of words & associations) and
- Personal Identification Numbers (PINs).

This paper investigates user-ID and user-generated passwords, the most widely-used password mechanisms. The level of security provided by this can vary greatly, depending on the individual user's password design expertise and security awareness. The US Federal Information Processing Standards (FIPS, 1985) suggest that there are several criteria that should be used to assure different levels of password security. *Password composition,* for example, relates the level of a password's security to the size of the character set from which it has been chosen. An alpha-numeric password is therefore more secure than one composed of letters only. Short *password lifetime* - i.e. changing passwords frequently - is suggested to reduce the risk associated with undetected illicit use of a "compromised" password. Finally, *password ownership* is noted as an important aspect of its security. The FIPS suggest that individual ownership:

- increases individual accountability;
- reduces illicit usage;
- allows establishment of system usage audit trails;
- reduces the requirement for frequent password changes dues to group membership fluctuations.

There is indeed evidence that many users do not follow secure password construction. DeAlvare (1988) found that once a password is chosen, a user is unlikely to change it until it has been shown to be compromised. This research was continued in 1990 to show that, if allowed, most users will tend to construct passwords that contain as few characters as possible. These observations cannot be disputed, but the conclusion that these observed behaviours are due to users being inherently careless and therefore insecure ought to be reconsidered. Security departments try to counteract users' "inherently insecure" behaviour with system-based mechanisms such as password expiry and construction restrictions, assuming that forcing users to comply with security measures will reduce insecure behaviour. Again, the notion that desired behaviour can be enforced may work in a military environment, but this fits less well with modern organisations and work practices.

The guiding principles of system security have determined the type of security problems identified and their approach to possible solutions. The tendency is to respond to security problems by enforcing more restrictive authentication regimes, such as:

- increasing change regimes (change password once a month);
- longer and more complex passwords (alpha-numeric & required length);
- reduction in allowed input error rates.

Whether these mechanisms have resulted in more secure user behaviour has not been empirically confirmed. Anecdotal evidence suggests that their effect may be the opposite of what was intended: the more restrictive mechanisms are, the more likely it is that users will circumvent them, resulting in behaviours which are even less secure. The reason for this apparent paradox is usability as more restrictions in authentication mechanisms create more usability problems. Carroll (1996) pointed out that the very characteristics which make a password more secure also make it less memorable. This has produced efforts to identify mechanisms for generating memorable yet secure passwords (DeAlvare, 1988; Barton and Barton 1988). The impact of these recommendations seems to have been limited; most users do not seem to be aware of them.

1.2   Usability issues in password systems

The aim of this study is to identify human and organisational factors which impact on the security and usability of password systems. *Security* is defined as reducing unauthorised access to information or systems; *usability* in the password domain is defined in terms of memorability and perceived overheads. The study was conducted in two parts. In the first part of the study, a detailed questionnaire on security and usability of password authentication systems was designed to elicit descriptions of user behaviour and problems related to the use of passwords. The web-based questionnaire was completed by 139 respondents, half of which were employees in Organisation A, the other half were Internet users from around the world. The questionnaire results are reported and discussed[1] in Section 2. The quantitative research seeks to identify relationships between users password memorability, frequency of password usage, automaticity in entering a password and perceptions of the need for security levels. The issues most frequently raised in the questionnaires were followed up with in-depth semi-structured interviews with 30 users, 15 from Organisation A and 15 from Organisation B. Section 3 explains how the interviews have been analysed using a qualitative method from social sciences called grounded theory, and presents the resulting model of system and organisational factors along with their impact on security and usability. Implications of the findings are discussed in Section 4 and recommendations made for improving authentication processes.

---

[1] Further relationships were reviewed but few of any interest were found.

2 Questionnaire study

2.1 Method

2.1.1 Participants

139 responses were received, half of which were from organisation A. The other half from organisations throughout the world. Participants were recruited via email and web interest groups which could be argued restricted subject sampling to technologically biased respondents. It should be noted however that respondents were varied in both computer (less than 1 year to 10 years) and password (1 to over 10 passwords - some stating over 30 passwords) experience. For security reasons, participants' personal details were automatically anonymised and personal detail sections of the questionnaire were not always completed.

2.1.2 Instruments

As there has been little previous research on this particular issue, a pilot questionnaire was used to obtain initial quantitative and qualitative data. Although this questionnaire took a broad approach to the subject area, it focused on password related user behaviours, in particular memorability problems. Results from the open ended sections of the questionnaire, however, suggested that this narrow approach was not addressing key problems with password usage as a user authentication device.

2.1.3 Procedure

The questionnaire was placed on the web and once completed was anonymised before being automatically returned, via email, for analysis.

2.2 Results

The significant relationships observed in the study are summarised in Table 1. There is a significant (P<0.05) correlation between *"infrequently used passwords"* and *"frequent memory problems"* with the same password, and between *"frequently used passwords"* and *"infrequent memory problems"*. There is also a significant (P<0.005) correlation between *"have to think first"* (before password recall) and *"frequent memory problems"* with the same password. The opposite end of this relationship is between *"automatic"* (password recall) and *"infrequent memory problems"*. An interesting point is the significant (P<0.05) correlation between *"desire to decrease security"* and *"frequent memory problems"* with the same password.

	Responses	Correlation Coefficient	Significance
Password usage by Memory problems	137	-.2204	P<0.05
Automaticity by Memory problems	136	-.6338	P<0.005
Required security changes by Memory problems	122	-.2079	P<0.05

Table 1: Mean correlation coefficients[2] between automaticity, memorability and frequency of password usage.

50% of respondents wrote their passwords down in one form or another. It was also found that 50% of respondents using more than one password had produced a method to construct "related" passwords, i.e. all or most of their passwords had a common theme or domain. In fact, this applied to all users who answered these question - almost half left these questions blank.

The results clearly suggest that password memorability is partially reliant on frequency of use, which produces automaticity. This would tie in with observations on *encoding specificity* and the *implicit vs. explicit* memory models (Graf and Mandler, 1984; Graf and Schacter, 1985). Encoding specificity suggests that to retrieve information efficiently, the form of password construction should match the retrieval procedure; a semantically meaningful password should be retrieved semantically). The explicit *vs.* implicit memory model suggests that semantically stored passwords (those that have a meaning) are best for explicitly retrieved material (thinking about the item to be recalled). However, if a password is frequently used and therefore automatically (implicitly) retrieved, a structural construction (the shape of the word or the position of keys on the keyboard) is more effective for retrieval purposes.

The open-ended sections of the questionnaire suggested there were other factors which influenced user behaviour or led to user problems. It was concluded that further qualitative analysis was required to comprehensively investigate relevant issues.

3   Qualitative analysis

3.1   First-pass analysis: method

The first set of 15 semi-structured in-depth interviews lasted approx. 30 minutes and were conducted with users in Organisation A. Respondents had varying levels of password expertise, both over period and frequency of use. Participants were asked a series of semi-structured questions that covered issues of password

---

[2] (All variables in above analysis are means for all password systems using a 2-tailed Significance using a Spearman's Rho test for ordinal related data)

generation and recall along with more general system and organisational factors. The interview format allowed participants to introduce new issues to the discussion that they regarded as important.

3.2   *First-pass analysis: results*

The initial analysis of the interviews and free-format answers in the questionnaire was guided by *frequency* and *fundamentality* of the issues raised by the users. This produced 4 factors influencing effective password usage. Problem areas for password usability were *multiple passwords, password content, users' perceptions of security* in the organisation and *information sensitivity*.

3.2.1   *Multiple passwords*
Many users have to remember *multiple passwords*, i.e. they have to use different passwords for different applications and/or change password frequently because of password expiry mechanisms. A high number of passwords reduces memorability, increases insecure work-practices (e.g. writing passwords down) and poor password design (e.g. using *password* as their password), as illustrated in the following quotes:

> *"Constantly changing passwords results in very simple choices which are easy to guess or break within seconds of using 'Cracker*[3]*. Hence there is no security."*

> *"But basically because I was forced into changing it every month I had to write it down."*

Many users devise their own method for beating memorability problems such as *related passwords* - linking their passwords via some common element. Such methods are devised in response to password expiry mechanisms, and by users who have to have different passwords for different applications. Many of these users consciously implemented their own security by varying elements in these linked passwords (e.g. *tom1, tom2, tom3*). However the results show that, rather than improving memorability and security, this decreases password memorability. This has been identified as due to the within-list interference (Wickens, 1992) of related passwords which causes users to write passwords down which in turn reduces password security levels.

---

[3] A password dictionary checker

3.2.2   Password content

Password content is defined here as the character content of the password reviewed in terms of its memorability and security. Initial results found that users' knowledge of secure password design was very inadequate. This leads users to create rules and judgements on password design strategies which are anything but secure. Words contained in the dictionary and names are the most vulnerable form of password. These results showed that many users do not realise this:

> *"I mean I would have thought that if you picked something like your wife's Christian name or something then the chances of a complete stranger guessing ********* in my case were pretty remote."*

3.2.3   Security perceptions

Analysis of the results revealed that users perceptions of security levels and potential threats was a key element in motivating their work-practices. Without clear feedback from the organisation, users construct their own model of *security threats* and *importance of security*. The two extracts below illustrate users' misconceptions in their perceptions of both organisational security and possible breaches:

> *"I don't think that hacking is a problem I've had no visibility of hacking that may go on. None at all."*

> *"I think that security problems are more by word of mouth than computer problems"*

3.2.4   Information sensitivity

The study identified that users' security behaviour often depends on their perceptions of the *information sensitivity*. Users identified certain systems as worthy of secure password practices, whilst others were perceived as "not important enough". In the absence of guidance, users concluded that confidential information about individuals (personnel files, email) was sensitive; but commercially sensitive information, such as customer records and financial data, were often not regarded as sensitive. Some users stated that they liked the classification of printed documents (e.g. *Confidential, Not for Circulation*). This indicates that users need guidance on information sensitivity and rules for levels of protection.

3.3   In-depth analysis: grounded theory

The initial approach to the qualitative analysis ignored a wealth of information in the data. Further analysis using *grounded theory* methods (Glaser & Strauss, 1967; Strauss & Corbin, 1990) enabled us to resolve apparent contradictions and inconsistencies in users' statements. This analysis of the qualitative and quantitative data was then used to build a model of users' password behaviour.

Social science methodologies have been used for some years in HCI particularly in the field of CSCW (Suchman, 1987; Fafchamps, 1991). Unlike other social science methodologies, 'grounded theory' (Strauss & Corbin, 1990) provides a more focused, structured approach to research (closer in some ways to quantitative methods) which is why it has been termed a post positivistic method (Stevenson & Cooper, 1997). We have not found any published examples of its application to HCI problems, but found it matched the requirements of this study for a number of reasons:-

1. This study uncovered a complex web of variables interacting to produce users' password behaviour. Grounded theory was able to descriptively relate these variables in a way that enabled possible intervention points to be identified.
2. In a field where there has been little previous research, the direction of the study could be biased by the researcher. Grounded theory enables research to be grounded in the data obtained so that the validity of the theories produced are increased.
3. The structured format of grounded theory encourages the building of a framework and theories that are grounded in the data which then improves the external validity of the research conducted.

The analysis provided a step-by-step account of password usage problems and possible intervention points. A framework of password usage was produced which was substantiated by a further 15 in-depth interviews in organisation B. As the findings from the various studies are too numerous to discuss in detail, we only provide a top level diagram of the model (see Figure 3) and a description of it through a detailed walk-through (see Table 2). Items that are of particular interest in the efficiency of password usage are also presented (Sections 3.4.1 & 3.4.2).

3.4 In-depth analysis: results

3.4.1 Security perceptions: solving apparent contradictions
Several of the interviews show users identifying one perception of their behaviour and then later stating the opposite. Such contradictions make it hard to establish relationships between factors which influence user behaviour. Contradictory statements could be caused by users' being unsure of their own descriptions, or discussing complex issues which involve several factors. The application of grounded theory techniques for analysing the free-format statements on the questionnaires and the interview data identified the latter as the case. An example of an apparent contradiction is shown in Figure 1.

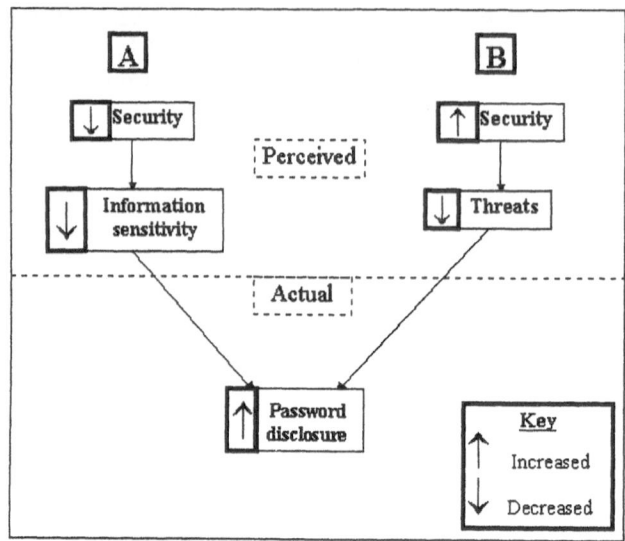

Figure 1: User behaviours produced by perceptions of security levels

(A) If users perceive the organisation's general security level as low (decreased), this decreases their perception of how sensitive the information protected is. This, in turn, increases insecure work procedures such as password disclosure. (*"Well, if the information isn't important, why make a big fuss about keeping your password secret?"*)

(B) If users perceive the organisation's general security level as high (increased) this then decreases their overall perception of threats to the information. This, in turn, also increases insecure work procedures such as password disclosure (*"Well, security for getting into the site is so tight, there's no harm in writing down my password and leaving it on my desk."*)

3.4.2   Work practices: the full story

The analysis revealed the importance of compatibility between work practices and password procedures. Organisation A forced users to have individually owned passwords for group working. This was perceived as incompatible with working procedures whilst *shared passwords* for teams, with shared information, was considered a compatible replacement (see section A in Figure 2). Further research with users in a comparative organisation (see section B in Figure 2) revealed almost the opposite problem and yet the same cause: Enforced group passwords for individual personal information were passionately rejected by users, perceived as incompatible with the nature of the work and information involved in it.

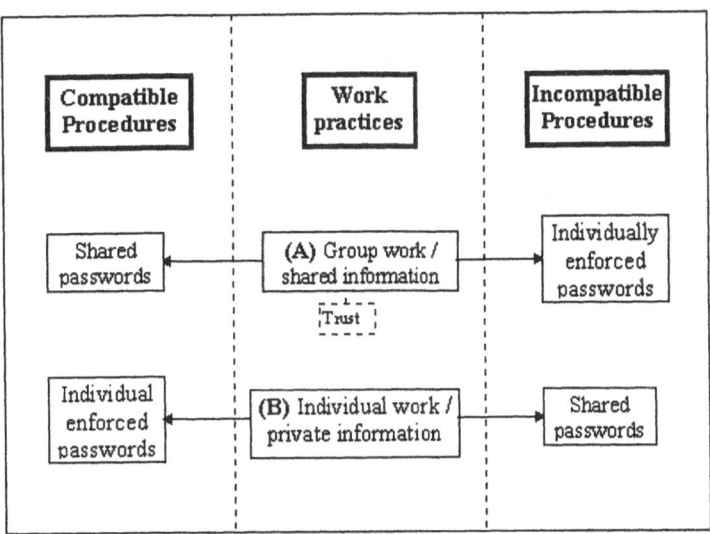

Figure 2: Users perceptions of work practices & system procedures compatibility. This analysis using the grounded theory approach has enabled detailed models of password usability and security to be formulated (see Figure 3). Table 2 provides a rule-based version of the model represented in Figure 3.

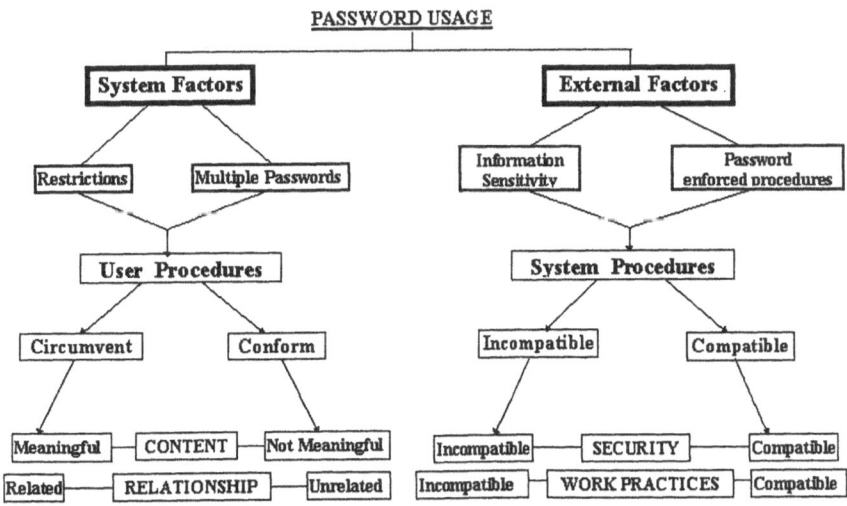

Figure 3: High level story-line of password usage

Table 2: Password Usage [High Level Story-line - Walkthrough].

1. SYSTEM FACTORS

    A) ARE:-

        1. Password restriction mechanisms

        2. Passwords for multiple applications and multiple changes over time.

    B) Have USER PROCEDURES that:-

        1. CONFORM with system factors to produce:-

            a) UNRELATED PASSWORD CONTENT these are:-

                I. Non-words

                II. Words that contain unrelated elements and that are not automatically meaningful.

            b) MULTIPLE PASSWORDS which are:-

                I. Passwords that are totally independent and not related in anyway to one another.

        2. CIRCUMVENT system factors to produce:-

            a) RELATED PASSWORD CONTENT these are:-

                I. Meaningful words either personally or generally identifiable.

                II. Related content within the password (e.g.abc123)

            b) RELATED PASSWORDS (JOINED PASSWORDS) these are:-

                I. Related elements across multiple passwords. Either across passwords for applications or across changes in passwords for a single application or both.

2. EXTERNAL FACTORS

    A) ARE:-

        1. Information's perceived sensitivity or importance.

        2. Enforced password practice so that passwords are perceived to be allocated to the individual or the group.

    B) Have ORGANISATIONAL PROCEDURES that are:-

        1. COMPATIBLE with users perceptions to produce:-

            a) COMPATIBLE SECURITY these are:-

                I. Where sensitive information has a high security where there are high perceived threats

II. Where unimportant information has a low security where there are low perceived threats.

b) COMPATIBLE WORK PRACTICES these are:-

I. Where employees work individually with personal or sensitive information and have individual passwords.

II. Where employees work in groups sharing information and have group or shared passwords.

2. INCOMPATIBLE with users perceptions to produce:-

a) INCOMPATIBLE SECURITY that is:-

I. INSECURE

i) Where sensitive information is poorly secured with low security levels.

ii) Where Perceived threats are also high with non-sensitive information and low security.

II. SECURE

i) where non-sensitive information is well secured with high security levels. With perceived threats being high or low.

b) INCOMPATIBLE WORK PRACTICE that are:-

I. Where group work with shared information has perceived individual enforced passwords.

II. Where individual work with personal or sensitive information has perceived group enforced passwords.

4   Discussion

This analysis has identified two main problem in password usage; *password mechanisms* that users perceive as forcing them to produce behaviours that circumvent them and *organisational factors* that are perceived as incompatible with working procedures. These problems are due to a lack of communication between security departments and users - users do not understand security issues and system departments lack an understanding of users' perceptions, tasks and needs. Resulting perceptions (by security departments) of users' as 'inherently insecure' and of security mechanisms and procedures (by users) as illogical are then increased, de-motivating naturally secure user behaviours. In this section we examine the consequences of this in detail and discuss intervention points for improving communications.

4.1   Users lack security knowledge

Parker (1992) points out that a major doctrine in password security, adopted from the military, is the *need-to-know principle*. The assumption being that the more known about a security mechanism, the easier it is to attack. Part of the defence is therefore to information only to those who "need to know". A similar approach to security is taken by many business organisations today: those responsible for system security argue that explaining the rationale behind security mechanisms increases its vulnerability. Many security departments see users as "inherently insecure" which produces a tendency to tell users as little as possible. One clear finding from this study is that "insecure" user behaviour is often caused by a lack of understanding. This can be seen in a number of user observations with password content, security perceptions and information sensitivity (see 3.2).

In many organisations, system-generated passwords have been replaced by user-generated ones. This means that the responsibility for creating secure passwords has been shifted to the users; but the "need-to-know" policy of many security departments means that known rules for creating secure passwords are rarely communicated to users. Many users are being asked to complete a skilled design job without adequate training and little on-line guidance. Our data shows that, lacking basic knowledge, users make their own judgements about which practices are secure, and these judgements are often wildly inadequate.

The grounded theory analysis also revealed that many users confused user identification (user ID's) and the password sections of the authentication process. Without knowledge of the authentication process, users assumed that these ID's were another form of password to be secured and recalled in the same manner. This maybe due to the fact that many user ID's are often non-words without meaning. Even if the user ID's are related to the users' name, they differ in format for the varying applications used. This in turn increases users' perceived mental workload associated with passwords. Lack of understanding here increases the perceived overhead, which in turn reduces users' motivation to comply with suggested behaviour.

Finally, users have a poor understanding of password security breaches and risks. Users perceived threats to be low because of a lack of visible risk feedback. Users' lack of understanding also lead to the general misconception that password cracking was completed on a personal basis: perceptions of threats were found to decrease as they perceived their insignificance in the system.

4.2   A lack of user-centred design in system security

This study has identified that many mechanisms designed to improve system security can in practice decrease it. Lack of communication with users also leads to a lack of a user-centred design of security mechanisms. Many mechanisms create overheads for users or require user behaviour which is unworkable. It is hardly surprising to find that many will try to circumvent such mechanisms.

Change regimes are employed to reduce the impact that an undetected security breach could have on an organisation. However, our findings suggest that change regimes reduce overall password security. Users required to frequently change their passwords were found to be producing passwords with less secure content and disclosing their passwords more frequently. Requiring users to have a large number of passwords (for multiple applications and change regimes) creates serious usability problems. Reduced memorability causes password disclosure and crackable passwords (see Section 3.2.1). Many users feel they are forced into circumventing security procedures which decreases their security motivation. Hackers using social engineering techniques rely on a lowered security motivation among users to breach security mechanisms.

Ultimately, a lack of user-centred design in password mechanisms forces users to circumvent procedures. Users are aware that their behaviour is insecure and it is this awareness that decreases their security motivation. The grounded theory model has identified that this can then lead to a spiralling decline in users secure behaviour (*"oh well my behaviours are not secure anyway so it doesn't really matter how lax I become."*)

4.3   *Motivating users security awareness*

The analysis revealed that users' perception of security threats was motivating or de-motivating as far as their security behaviour was concerned. A lack of organisational feedback on security issues was also found to de-motivate users' security awareness. However, one of the major factors de-motivating users was a lack of user-centred design in security mechanisms.

It has been suggested by the US Federal Information Processing Standards (FIPS, 1985) that individual ownership of passwords increases accountability and decreases illicit usage of passwords, because of the possibility of audit trailing - a by product of authentication. We found, however, that most users are not aware that auditing of system use can be linked to passwords. Further evidence shows that this is probably for the best, since those users who did realise this possibility circumvented auditing by using another person's password - not necessarily because their actions broke rules, but *"just in case, so someone else gets the blame if things go wrong"*. FIPS (1985) states that shared passwords for groups are insecure. However, our results indicate that they should be used if work is carried out by a team. If a password mechanism is incompatible with users' work practises, they perceive the security mechanism as "not sensible" and will circumvent it (e.g. by disclosing it to other group members). This can lead to a perception that all password mechanisms are "pointless", and are therefore circumvented.

It is important to challenge the view that users are never motivated to behave in a secure manner. Our results show that the majority of users were security-conscious, as long as they perceive the *need* for these behaviours e.g. because of obvious external threats or information sensitivity. These findings are supported by research within Organisation B, where both physical and computer security levels were low and security threats were evident. In this situation, users demonstrated exemplary behaviour with their own passwords. We would argue that the "need-to-know" policy ought to be reconsidered and users ought to be told of past or existing (attempted) breaches of security.

5   Conclusions

5.1   *Increase communication between users and security experts*

The technical bias towards security mechanism has produced a simplistic approach to user authentication: restricting access to data by identification and authentication of a user. This simplistic approach may work well in military environments, but limits usable solutions to the security problems of modern organisations which seek to encourage work practices such as teamwork and shared responsibility. Such organisations require support for *trust* and *information sharing*. The authoritarian approach has also led to security departments' reluctance to communicate with users. Informing users about security mechanisms and threats is seen as lowering security by increasing the possibility of information leaks. Ultimately, this has lead to a two fold problem:-

1. Users' lack of security awareness.

2. Security departments' lack of knowledge about users produces security mechanisms and systems which are not usable.

These two factors lower users' motivation to produce secure work practices. This then reinforces security departments' belief that users are "inherently insecure" and leads to the introduction of stricter mechanisms. Communication between security departments and users is therefore often restricted to "ticking off" users caught contravening the rules. This type of relationship is not suitable for modern distributed and networked organisations which encourage communication and collaboration. This vicious circle needs to be broken by improving communication between security departments and users, along with training and user-centred design of security mechanisms.

5.2   *Users and password behaviour*

Insecure work practices and low security motivation have been identified by information security research (DeAlvare, 1990; Ford, 1994; Gordon, 1995) as a major problem which must be addressed. There is, however, no identification by those same researchers as to the cause of these user related problems. Instead, the blame has been squarely placed on the user with a lack of security motivation as the reason. It is assumed that users naturally lack security motivation and that this state will not be changed until they have been made aware of, or forced into completing, secure actions. This assumption, however, suggests that humans start, as do computers, from a blank sheet that is programmed into a certain action. The truth is that human behaviour is far more complex than simple conditioned responses. Forcing users to complete an action, may only make them circumvent the whole procedure giving the *appearance* that they have completed that action.

The results from this study suggest that if users show insecure security behaviours and have a low security motivation, it is often due to the security mechanisms employed. These mechanisms have not been assessed in terms of their compatibility with users' work practices, organisational strategy and usability - factors which we would expect to be considered during the design and implementation of most systems today. Designers of security mechanisms must realise that human and organisational factors are a key issue in security design. Social engineers understand this and have used it to their advantage, increasing system security breaches. Unless security departments understand how their mechanisms are used in practice, they will always be doomed to produce mechanisms which look secure on paper but fail in practice.

5.3   Recommendations

The construction of secure passwords can be assisted by the recommendations given below under "content" and "password relationships". Users' motivation to apply these relies on the recommendations set out in "security perceptions" and "work practices".

Password Content

- Give on-line instruction and training on how to construct usable/secure passwords. This will show users that they need not circumvent security mechanisms in order to construct memorable passwords.
- Give on-line feedback to users on what constitutes an insecure password. This will hopefully aid in users' knowledge of what not to use in their password design procedures.

Password Relationships between Multiple Passwords

- Multiple passwords decrease overall security and memorability which in turn increases users' overheads.
- If multiple passwords have to be used, a maximum of 4 or 5 is recommended to reach the extent of most users' memory abilities for totally different multiple passwords. This number is reduced if passwords are used infrequently.

- If more passwords are needed, then users should be advised that they can join the passwords (produce several passwords that have related content) to reduce the number. They should also be advised that this could cause memory interference problems unless joint passwords are identical which will increase memorability and security (by reducing password disclosure). A possible solution could be presented in a physical format with smart card technology giving a second barrier of security which could be used for various systems.

Security Perceptions

- Give on-line feedback to users of how crackable their password is. This will identify for users the importance of constructing secure passwords and help them to identify those more highly crackable.
- Relay to users the possible threats to the organisations system and information. This will increase the users' concept of perceived threats and thus the need for security measures. *This measure is especially necessary on sites where security is high and the site is isolated. Users perception of threats to security is especially low under these conditions.*
- State the role that password security plays in combating perceived threats.
- Make explicit the level of sensitivity that different information has. This will reduce the degree of arbitrary judgements made by users.
- State how security levels relate to information sensitivity. This will indicate how well the security conforms to organisational procedures.

Work Practices

- Relate enforced password practice to organisational procedures. This will mean that users will identify how relevant security is to their working practices with shared information having shared passwords and individual work having personal passwords. If this is not to be adhered to, reasons must be given to the user as to why it is necessary for the security mechanisms to circumvent working procedures.

References

Barton, B.F. & Barton, M. S. (1984) "User-friendly password methods for computer-mediated information systems. *Computers and Security*, **3**, 186 - 195.

Carroll, J.M (1996) "Computer Security" 3rd ed. Butterworth-Heinemann, MA.

DeAlvare, A. M.(1988) "A Framework for Password Selection" *Unix Security Workshop II*. Portland. Aug 29 - 30

DeAlvare, A. M.(1990) "How Crackers Crack Passwords OR What Passwords to Avoid" *Unix Security Workshop II*. Portland. Aug 27-28

Davis, D. and Price, W. (1987) "Security for Computer Networks" John Wiley & Sons, Chichester.

Fafchamps, D (1991) "Ethnographic workflow analysis: Specifications for design." In Bullinger, H. J. (eds). Human aspects in computing: Design and use of interactive systems and work with terminals, Elsevier, pp. 709-715.

FIPS (1985) "Password Usage" Federal Information Processing Standards Publication. May 30.

Ford, W.(1994) "Computer communications security: Principles, standard protocols and techniques" Prentice Hall. NJ

Glaser, B. & Strauss, A. (1967) "The discovery of grounded theory". Aldine, Chicago.

Gordon, S.(1995) "Social Engineering: Techniques and Prevention", *Computer Security*, 1995

Graf, P. & Mandler, G. (1984) "Activation makes words more accessible, but not necessarily more retrievable." *Journal of Verbal Learning and Verbal Behavior*, **23**, 553-568.

Graf and Schacter (1985) "Implicit and explicit memory for new associations in normal and amnesic subjects" *Journal of Experimental Psychology: Learning, Memory and cognition*, **11**, 385 - 395.

Hitchings, J. (1995) "Deficiencies of the Traditional Approach to Information Security and the Requirements for a New Methodology." Computers & Security, **14**, 377-383.

Parker, D. B. (1992) "Restating the foundation of information security" in "IT Security: The Need for International Co-operation" G. G. Gable & W.J. Caelli (eds). Elsevier Science Publishers, Holland.

Strauss , A. & Corbin, J. (1990) "Basics of qulitative research: Grounded theory procedures and techniques" Sage, London.

Stevenson, C. & Cooper, N. (1997) "Qualitative and Quantitative research." The Psychologist: Bulletin of the British Psychological Society, April. 159-160

Suchman, L. (1987) "Plans and Situated Action: The problem of Human-Machine-Communication" Cambridge Univerity Press. Cambridge.

Wickens, C.D (1992) "Engineering Psychology and Human performance" (2nd ed.) Harper Collins, NY.

Strategies for organising email

Olle Bälter

Department of Numerical Analysis and Computing Science
Royal Institute of Technology
SE-100 44 STOCKHOLM
SWEDEN
Phone: +46 8 790 91 57
Fax: +46 10 24 77
Email: balter@nada.kth.se

With the increasing flow of email, strategies for organising email messages become more important. Research describes various strategies used for archiving and retrieving messages. Categorising these strategies is important to identify special needs, problems and solutions for users of each strategy. This study extends earlier categories by grouping users after folder usage and cleaning frequency. Conclusions are that the strategies are affected by the choice of mail tool and number of incoming messages, but no influence by the work task or position could be found. Some advice on interface design to support the different strategies is given.

Keywords: Electronic mail, email, organisation, archiving, folder, cleaning, strategy.

Introduction

With the increasing flow of email, practical strategies for organising email messages become more important. Research describes strategies based on managing incoming messages and how to archive messages for subsequent use (Mackay 1988), as well as strategies based on usage of folders and frequency of cleaning (Whittaker & Sidner 1996). This paper describes a case study of a company, here named MainframePC, where all users have access to and use at least one of three email systems. The focus is on how users organise their email messages, based on an extended version of the categories described in Whittaker & Sidner (1996). The purpose is to identify special needs, problems and solutions within these groups, and especially factors that may influence the choice of strategy.

Organisation of email messages is a complex task. The Utopia of email organisation would probably be a folder structure with well-defined names of all folders that clearly state the nature of all messages in each folder, only relevant messages that need to be retrieved later are stored, and although all other messages are deleted, not a single one of these was deleted by mistake and needs to be retrieved. Few email users reach this Wonderland, and those who do are soon expelled by demands from other tasks: time pressure, changing conditions that make deleted messages indispensable and stored messages obsolete, a new email tool incompatible with the old, vacation or other absence from the mail tool that causes incoming email messages to stack up. How do users handle this situation?

Ann Lantz (1995, 1996), in a study of heavy users of email, concluded that users do not have a defined strategy for archiving email messages, instead the folder structure evolves over time. By studying users it might become possible to identify strategies that the users themselves are unaware of. When strategies are identified, they can be compared and users can be given advice on which strategy to use depending on their situation. Also, each strategy has advantages and disadvantages. The disadvantages could be reduced by improved interfaces or functionality in the mail tools.

Whittaker & Sidner (1996) identified three strategies based upon the two criteria folder usage and cleaning frequency. Two of their strategies are used in this study as well (frequent filer and spring cleaner), but their third category "no filer" (person using few or no folders) is in this study divided in two categories resulting in a total of four categories, as displayed in table I.

	Use folders	Few/No folders
Clean often	Frequent Filer	Folderless Cleaner
Clean occasionally	Spring Cleaner	Folderless Spring Cleaner

Table I: Strategies based on usage of folders and frequency of cleaning.

A "frequent filer" uses folders and makes at least weekly passes to archive messages in folders or delete them. A "spring cleaner" uses folders, but does clean-ups more seldom than weekly. The two remaining categories of users do not use folders and are divided into "folderless cleaner" for those that clean at least weekly and "folderless spring cleaner" for those that clean more seldom. Our objective is to examine the distinguishing features of users in these four groups in order to answer the question "Why have users, deliberately or un-deliberately, chosen one of these strategies?"

Related research

Filtering is a process where rules are defined for how to prioritise, sort and delete messages. Filtering rules can be applied both to sort incoming messages in different folders before they are read, and to messages already read and stored in different folders. Suggestions for filtering based on user defined rules have been made by e.g. Jeffries & Rosenberg (1987) and Westergren (1989). Mackay, Malone, Crowston, Rao, Rosenblitt & Card (1989) describe how people used rules to prioritise messages before they read them and to sort messages already read. Delete rules were used primarily to filter out messages from low-priority distribution lists.

Malone, Lai & Fry (1987) describe problems with *excessive filtering*: the rules can be used to filter out messages that are personally addressed, users of such a rule could become less responsive to information from other people in the organisation; *imperfect finding*: people may have difficulties knowing what they want and do not know that they want to see a message until they have seen it; and *conflicts of interest*: an advertiser that has a message that most people would filter out may send messages with a popular topic to trick people to read them.

A complement to user defined filtering rules are intelligent agents that draw conclusions from the way the user reads and sorts messages. After a while the agent tries intelligent guesses on how the user wants to have the messages organised (Sheth & Maes 1993; Kilander 1995).

There are several experimental email systems that address the problems of filtering and organising messages: Messages (Borenstein & Thyberg 1988 and 1991), Information Lens (Malone, Grant, Turbak, Brobst & Cohen 1987, Object Lens (Lai & Malone 1988), and Oval (Malone, Lai & Fry 1992).

Jones, Bock & Brassard (1990) describe that users felt overwhelmed by the amount of mail they received, and were uncertain of the structure of the folders they had created. A direct manipulative interface was superior for organising messages by making the organisational structure visible, but also created new problems with synchronisation when several windows were opened at the same time.

Mander, Salomon & Wong (1992) studied how users organise papers and other physical objects of information in real life. A conclusion is that users like to group items spatially and often prefer to deal with information by creating physical piles of paper, rather than immediately categorising it into specific folders.

Mackay (1988) interviewed researchers at a laboratory as a pre-study of an introduction of Information Lens. In her study it was found that the feeling of being overloaded varies a lot among people, independent of the number of messages they send and receive. Persons who feel overloaded had, according to Mackay, some of the following characteristics:

- subscribe to many distribution lists,
- try to read all of their mail but do not always succeed,
- save hundreds of messages in their inbox,
- often do not reach the bottom of their inbox,
- want to save a large part of their mail,
- maintain many folders on different topics where mail is saved,
- have difficulty finding messages.

The next section describes the studied company and the method for this study. The results are then presented, divided after folder usage, cleaning habits and the combination (i.e. the four groups in table I). Finally, a discussion about strategies for organising email follows including a comparison with Whittaker & Sidner (1996).

MainframePC

MainframePC's business concept is to provide customised computer solutions with everything from batch jobs such as monthly payment of salaries to development of applications. The company has approximately 600 employees and is mainly located at two sites approximately 120 km (75 miles) apart. One site is in a major city, the other in a country side village. Both sites are roughly the same size.

The company has traditionally used mainframe computers, but with the growth of the PC market, the focus of the business has gradually shifted towards personal computers. The backbone of the electronic communication within the company is electronic mail handled by two different mainframe systems, one at each site, here named MMM and MMC. The reason for this is that the country side site was bought a decade ago and continued to use the already established email system (MMC). All employees had access to at least one of the two mainframe mail systems. A substantial amount of the employees work mainly or solely with mainframe computers and will do so for years to come.

Before this survey, a pilot study had been made with the conclusion that Lotus Notes could be a solution to the problems at MainframePC. With the growing PC market in mind they decided to use Notes as a common platform for the company's communication. The global mother company had announced a switch to Notes within a year or two. At the time of the study, a few departments had transferred to Notes completely. Individuals that claimed they had a need of Notes were allotted a license and the appropriate hardware. A plan was made to provide licenses, hardware and servers for the remaining mainframe email users.

Method

The purpose of the present study was to investigate the strategies used to organise email messages before the complete transfer from the old mainframe systems to

Notes. This study is a part of a more extensive study of the transfer from the old mainframe systems to Notes described in Bälter (1997a, 1997b).

In order to gather background information as a basis for a survey; a set of initial interviews was made with the group responsible for the introduction at MainframePC. Six employees were selected to achieve a diversity regarding usage of mail system (Notes or one of the mainframe mail systems), position (manager or not) and location (main or country side site). The respondents also answered preliminary versions of the questionnaire during the interviews. I also made some participatory observations by taking internal classes in usage of the mainframe systems and Notes. The results of the pre-study are here described together with the results of the survey.

The 14 page questionnaire covered five general topics:

- Work situation: Describe work tasks, your position, how and what kind of information you share with others.
- Communication: How often do you communicate, with whom and why, and which media are used?
- Computer system: What operating systems and applications do you use and for what? What are your opinions about your systems and applications?
- Email system: How long experience do you have of email, how do you use email, where and when do you use it and who do you send them to?
- Email handling: How do you save, organise, delete, and search your email messages? How many messages do you have today?

When answering questions about "how often", the respondents were asked to use a scale "never", "once a year", "quarterly", "monthly", "weekly" and "daily". One fifth of the questions were open-ended. The respondents had the possibility to write open-ended comments to all questions.

The questionnaire was sent to 116 people with more than six months of employment at the company and in total, 81 people responded (70%).

Results

The employees of MainframePC are here divided in two different ways: according to position and main work task, in order to investigate the impact of position and work task on their filing strategy.

Divided by position, they form four groups: employees, project managers, group managers, and high rank managers. In table II the distribution of the respondents is displayed. The two project managers that also were group managers are classified as group managers.

Employee	Project manager	Group manager	High rank manager
39	18	18	6

Table II: Position, number of respondents.

From open-ended questions about work situation and computer usage the respondents were categorised in main work task categories according to table III.

Work task	Total
Management	27
Mainframe system	18
Customer contact	9
PC-system	9
Others	7
System (PC and/or mainframe)	6

Table III: Respondents' main work tasks.

It seems to be a diversion between formal position and perceived main work task. All high rank managers considered management as their main work task, but only two thirds of the group managers and half of the project manages. Also, one employee considered management as his main work task. From table III it is clear that mainframe systems still were the main product at MainframePC. The division into the strategy groups displayed in table I are based on answers to three questions:

> How many folders do you have totally today?
> How many of your folders are currently not used or useful?
> How often do you normally clean (delete old messages, file messages in folders) among your email messages?

Subjects that had more than four useful folders were categorised as "folder users", those that cleaned among their messages at least weekly were categorised "clean often". The limit "four" is a compromise between the average of 6.8 useful folders among the no filers in Whittaker & Sidner (1996) and "two" where the problems with deciding which folder to use begins. The distribution is displayed in table IV.

	Folder users	Few/No folders
Clean often	Frequent Filer 10	Folderless Cleaner 13
Clean occasionally	Spring Cleaner 37	Folderless Spring Cleaner 20

Table IV: Strategies based on usage of folders and frequency of cleaning.

Managers were more likely to use folders, but the differences were insignificant with one exception: Folderless cleaners were less likely to be managers (Chi^2 (1 df)=3.9, P-value 0.05). No other significant difference could be found in the choice of strategy based on position (table II) or main work task (table III).

The choice of folder and cleaning strategy may be influenced by available time, therefore we asked the respondents:

How long may email messages normally remain before they are completely handled, in other words: How long is your backlog?

The answers are presented in table V, together with data for number of email messages. No significant difference could be found between the different strategies regarding the backlog. Further comments to the number of messages follows below.

Strategy	Backlog (days)	Incoming messages per day	Messages sent per day
Frequent Filer	2.0	12.3	7.5
Spring Cleaner	2.3	15.8	12.5
Folderless Cleaner	1.7	6.8	3.6
Folderless Spring Cleaner	1.5	9.8	7.8

Table V: Backlog and message flow.

Usage of folders

Usage of folders to archive email messages can be viewed as a mapping from the real world's files, bindings and folders. Folders may simplify overview of messages, but at the same time cause problems with archiving messages: folders must be properly named and messages must be manually moved. Kidd (1994) describes filing as a cognitive difficult task. One of the interviewees expresses a problem with folders:

> There is always a risk that if you cannot remember the name [of the folder], you write a slightly different name, and then you have two [folders] that are almost identical.

Therefore we asked the respondents of the survey to give examples of their problems with filing/categorising their incoming messages. Of the 51 respondents that used folders, 21 reported problems with classification of email messages. In table VI the answers are displayed.

Problem	#
1. Message belongs to several folders	9
2. Finding the appropriate folder	5
3. No/unclear strategy for classification	4
4. Disk space shortage	2
5. Sub-folders not visible	1

Table VI: Problems with classification of email messages.

The problems with filing messages in folders is cognitive, but users could be better supported for the mentioned problems in several ways: aliases for messages make filing in several folders possible, without increasing the number of actual messages; filtering messages to suggest folders for storage; identifying strategies that will work for a user even though the number of messages increase.

Since folders are used to archive messages for subsequent usage, the folder users were expected to search for messages more often, and this study supports this hypothesis: Folder users searched for their archived messages in median weekly, compared to monthly for the others. Divided into those who searched at least weekly a Chi^2-test (1 df) gives a P-value <0.025.

The respondents' answers to questions about size of the email flow, how often they accessed their mail tool and electronic bulletin boards indicate that folder users were using email and other computer based messaging systems more intensely than others: they received more messages (mean 15 a day, compared to 9, t-test P-value 0.028), accessed their email system more often (continuously, compared to several times a day), and read more electronic bulletin boards (mean 5.8 a day, compared to 2.5, t-test P-value 0.0021). The folder usage did not affect the time spent per message; no statistically significant differences could be found.

The importance of email is also confirmed by the answers to the question:

How often do you need to read your email at other places than your normal work site?

Folder users had more often a need to read email at other places than their original work place (mean every other day, compared to once a week, t-test P-value 0.017), despite that there were no correlation between the number of incoming messages and the frequency of this need. They also sent a larger percentage messages abroad (mean 3.8 a day, compared to 0.4 , t-test P-value 0.084).

One problem mentioned in the pre-study of the company was the "cc-disease", when messages were sent as carbon copies "just in case" to managers, despite the fact that advice had been distributed to limit the number of carbon copies. In this company the cc-problem may partly be explained by the SYA (Save Your Ass) attitude. The three letter acronym was generally known in the company, and employees often sent messages with cc to managers. If anything went wrong later, the manager became partly responsible since "he was informed". Also, there was no spoken policy for what messages that should be distributed via email or via an electronic bulletin board. Therefore we asked

How large amount (in percent) of your email consists of messages that are not necessary for you to read (e.g. unnecessary carbon copies (cc), information that arrives too late or too early)?

and

How large amount (in percent) of your incoming email do you believe that it would be better to distribute in another way (e.g. an electronic bulletin board)?

The answers to the two questions above give certain information about the possibilities to reduce the number of incoming messages, but it must be clear that the answers are opinions, not facts. Under the assumptions that:

- the email habits are possible to change,
- the unnecessary messages and the messages that it would be better to distribute in another way are independent,
- the time to handle incoming messages is one eight of the time it takes to write and send a message (Bair 1979),

only six respondents would save more than five minutes a day, the person that would save most 19 minutes a day. The conclusion is that this is not an efficient way to reduce the email flow. Filtering rules in the email tool may be one solution, but as Hiltz & Turoff (1985) put it:

Overload, within the context of an organisation, is essentially a behavioural phenomenon. It makes more sense to address inappropriate behaviour through social norms and sanctions than to obscure the problem with software.

Also, filtering may cause problems with awareness of the arrival of messages. In the study reported in Bälter (1995) some users wanted incoming messages to be stored directly into folders, some wanted this sorting only to be a suggestion for where to store the message after reading.

The tool may affect the choice of folder usage, the MMC users were less likely to use folders (Chi^2 (1 df)=18.7, P-value <0.001). An explanation may be that MMC has a maximum limit of the number of both messages and folders; this forces the users to use fewer folders.

Cleaning habits

Cleaning simplifies searching among the remaining messages, but is not always an advantage: the user must make a choice for each message whether to delete the it or not. Also, messages can be deleted by mistake, or deleted for perfect reasons at the time, but then other things change and the deleted message ought to be retrieved after all. Some users clean their mailboxes to get a sense of well-being (Bälter 1995):

If the inbox grows up towards 40 messages, then I start to feel sick about it.

Cleaning habits may not be the choice of the user as some systems limit the users' disc space and force users to delete messages. In this study, respondents that cleaned at least weekly were categorised as "cleaners". On average this group cleaned their mailboxes nearly once a day, the "non-cleaners" once a month. Cleaners spent less time on email (mean 35 minutes a day, compared to 64 for those that cleaned seldom, t-test P-value 0.028), probably due to their tendency to send fewer messages (mean 4 a day, compared to 11, t-test P-value 0.060). They also received slightly fewer messages than non-cleaners, but the difference was insignificant (mean 9.3 a day, compared to 13.7, t-test P-value 0.15).

There might be a relation between different strategies for message archiving and the reasons why messages are stored. Therefore we asked:

Why do you store email messages? Please state the percentage for the different reasons. The sum does not have to be 100%.

To be certain of what has been written. ____ %

The messages contains information I probably need later. ____ %

I store messages just in case I will need them. ____ %

I use the messages as a "to do" list. ____ %

Other reasons_____ ____ %

As expected, cleaners saved a larger percentage of their messages to store information (mean 62 %, compared to 40 %, t-test P-value 0.0087). They also had a tendency to store a smaller percentage of their messages "just in case"(mean 12 %, compared to 4 %, t-test P-value 0.097).

Again, the strategy is related to the mail tool: MMC users were more likely to clean often (Chi^2 (1 df)=6.4, P-value <0.05), and they also had fewer messages in their inbox (mean 30, compared to 108, t-test P-value 0.026). Once again, the maximum limit of the number of messages and folders in MMC may force the users to clean more frequently.

Those that used only MMM cleaned more seldom (Chi^2 (1 df)=9.4, P-value <0.005). This is more difficult to explain, but one reason may be that in MMM new messages are added to the top of the message list, compared to the bottom in the other tools. This "top adding" may facilitate for users to ignore older messages, since there is no need for scrolling down a long list to find the new messages.

Cleaning may affect the possibilities to search manually among the messages, but search tools were used by cleaners as often as by no-cleaners, neither did cleaning affect the time spent per message; no statistically significant differences could be found.

In summary: besides the mail tools, no distinct features related to cleaning habits could be found. The cleaners are below divided after their folder habits into frequent filers and folderless cleaners.

Frequent filers

Frequent filers are cleaners that use folders. The small number of frequent filers in this study (10) makes it difficult to identify characteristic features, but as expected their habit to delete messages frequently reduce the percentage of messages saved "just in case" (mean 1.7 %, compared to 13.6 % for the spring cleaners, t-test P-value 0.049).

The respondents were asked to describe how often they communicate about, among other things, projects. The Frequent filers had a tendency to communicate more often about projects than the others (a t-test gives a P-value of 0.088). The influence from the mail tool is clear: All frequent filers used Notes. Notes' modern interface may facilitate folder usage and deleting messages compared to the older mainframe mail tools. Also, the groupware possibilities in Notes may be more useful for those that were involved in projects.

Folderless Cleaners

Folderless Cleaners are cleaners that do not use folders. The cleaning decreases the size of the inbox, where folderless cleaners had a mean of 18 messages, compared to 64 for others (t-test P-value 0.05).

This strategy may be optimal for a limited usage of email. A third of the folderless cleaners had an experience shorter than 6 years, compared to less than a tenth of the others. They were also less likely to be managers and handled fewer messages than others (mean 9 a day received and sent, compared to 24, t-test P-value 0.049). Also, all other categories of users claimed that they accessed the mail tool continuously as median, while the folderless cleaners accessed their mail tool several times a day, a small but subtle difference. One explanation may be the fewer incoming messages. The folderless cleaners had a tendency to spend more time per message (mean 8.3 minutes, compared to 5.4, t-test P-value 0.061). This may partly be explained by the shorter experience of email – the folderless cleaners do not handle their email flow in the same pace as more experienced users.

Again, the strategy is closely related to the tool: all folderless cleaners but one used MMC (Chi^2 (1 df)=9.1, P-value <0.005). The maximum limit of messages and folders in MMC may force users to clean more frequently and use fewer folders.

Spring cleaners

Spring cleaners are folder users that clean more seldom than once a week. Spring cleaners are characterised by an extensive use of email: they sent more messages than others (mean 12 a day, compared to 6.7, t-test P-value 0.039), used more time for email (mean 73 minutes a day, compared to 40, t-test P-value 0.0055), and had a greater need to use email at other sites than their main work site (mean every other day, compared to once a week, t-test P-value 0.023).

Spring cleaners extensive usage of email affect the number of incoming messages addressed to the receiver only. They receive a smaller percentage of these messages (mean 34, compared to 63, t-test P-value < 0.0001).

Once again, the choice of strategy is affected by the choice of mail tool: Spring cleaners were more likely to use MMM (Chi^2 (1 df)=13.2, P-value <0.001), and less likely to use MMC (Chi^2 (1 df)=18.2, P-value <0.001), and Notes (Chi^2 (1 df)=4.0, P-value <0.05). MMM was mandatory at the main site, MMC at the country side site. The only choice of Notes usage was to start use it now or later.

The reasons for this may be complex, but for MMM users, as stated before, one reason may be that new messages arrive "on top" of older messages and facilitates for a spring cleaner to ignore older messages that a frequent filer would have deleted. MMC users have their limited number of folders, and many Notes users must scroll through a list of messages to reach the new items at the bottom (the order is user tailorable in Notes, but this option was default at MainframePC).

Folderless spring cleaners

Folderless spring cleaners do not use folders, and clean less often than once a week. It seems as these users are forced to clean partly due to the limited disk space. Several comments to the cleaning question in the survey mentioned the disc space as a reason:

> Yearly, or when the disc is full.

This group is similar to the "no filers" in Whittaker & Sidner (1996), but the only statistically significant characteristic in this study was that they were more inclined to use MMC (Chi^2 (1 df)=5.7, P-value <0.025). Yet again, the maximum limit of folders in MMC forces users to use fewer folders. Also, the smaller number of incoming messages (compared to the spring cleaners) allows these users to ignore cleaning for a longer time, until the MMC maximum limit of messages is reached.

Discussion

We have presented a survey of a company where all employees had access to at least one of three email systems and had a long experience of it. The study has illustrated consequences of, and possible explanations for, different strategies for organising email messages based on usage of folders and frequency of cleaning. The choice of strategy is affected by the tool and by the number of incoming messages. No support could be found for connections between filing strategy and work task. Neither did we find any support for a relation between strategy and work position, which confirms findings in Whittaker & Sidner (1996). Other statistical significant results that are in line with their study are:

- Managers received more messages than others (t-test P-value 0.0026).
- The number of failed folders (here defined as folders not in use, Whittaker & Sidner defined them as folders with fewer than 3 items) was correlated with the

total number of folders (r_{44} = 0.73, P-value <0.001). Whittaker & Sidner's explanation for this is that the problems of remembering folder name definitions increases with the number of folders and time.

Also in line with their study, but not statistically significant were the results that frequent filers had fewer messages per folder and fewer "failed" folders than others, and that spring cleaners were less likely to be managers and had more failed folders.

The only result in this study that contradicts Whittaker & Sidner is that the spring cleaners here received more messages than others (t-test P-value 0.035). The difference may be explained by the different methods used and the diversity of mail tools at MainframePC; as the choice of mail tool clearly affects which strategy users have. Whittaker & Sidner were able to gather quantitative data by taking a "snapshot" of each users mailbox. The users at MainframePC that were overloaded with email and other tasks may be underrepresented in this study. However, the answer frequency from managers were 81% compared to 61% for others.

Folder users were more intense users of email and other electronic communication than no-folders as they sent and received more email messages, searched for stored messages more often, and read more electronic bulletin boards regularly. The cleaning habits in this study were only related to which tool the user had. In table VII, the four subgroups are displayed together with a typical profile for a user.

Strategy	Typical profile
Frequent Filer	Intense email user. Involved in projects. Uses Notes.
Spring Cleaner	Relies heavily on email. Uses MMM.
Folderless Cleaner	Limited email usage. Uses MMC.
Folderless Spring Cleaner	Uses MMC.

Table VII: Strategies and their main causes.

Why do the users, deliberately or un-deliberately, choose a certain strategy to organise their email messages? One hypothesis is that user behaviour evolves with time (Bälter 1995; Lantz 1996). A user new to email will probably start without folders, that is to the right in figure I. Whether the user cleans often or occasionally may be a more individual attitude towards organisation of messages and cleaning. With time the number of incoming and stored messages increases, and a folderless cleaner may take an active decision to start using folders and transform into a frequent filer, or give up cleaning and become a folderless spring cleaner. A folderless spring cleaner may start to use folders, and become a spring cleaner. Once the decision is made and folders are created, few users voluntarily go back to the folderless state. A frequent filer overloaded with messages may due to time shortage give up the deleting and filing and become a spring cleaner. These transitions are displayed in figure I.

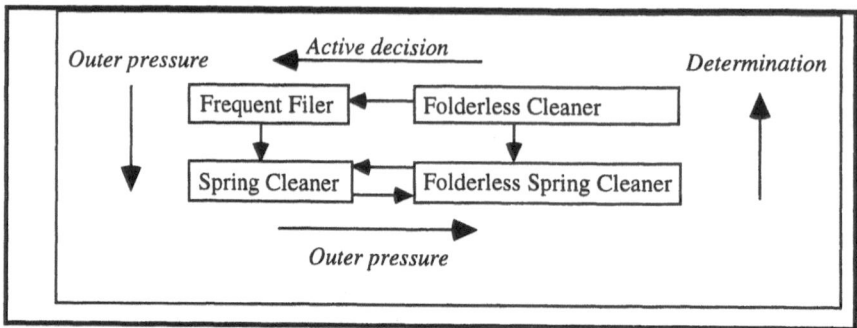

Figure I: Expected main transition of users and forces for changes.

The outer pressure that push users down and right consists of other tasks that limits the available time for handling email messages, but also of the stream of incoming messages. A large number of messages makes the organisation time consuming. The only thing that makes a user move up in figure I is persistent determination to clean mailboxes frequently, in combination with available time to do this. An intermittent clean-up will transfer the users to the top states only for a short period of time. The outer forces in figure I may be influenced by giving the users time to handle their email (if this is desirable).

There are certain data that suggest that the evolution of a user mainly is counter clockwise in figure I. The number of email users is increasing and with it the number of email messages. The respondents in this study that used email most were also folder users (to the left in figure I). Therefore it is important to support folder users with their specific problems. In Whittaker & Sidner (1996) the group named "No filers" had given up the efforts to keep an order of their email messages. The Folderless spring cleaners in this study uses a similar strategy, but had fewer incoming and stored messages. A possible explanation is that their no filers is an end state for users with a large number of incoming messages (average 58 messages a day in their study compared to 10 in this for the folderless spring cleaners), that do not have time to archive and delete old messages.

The identification of different strategies is important to understand the nature of email organisation. The transition between the different strategies indicated in figure I cannot be followed by a single study during a short period of time; users must be studied for a long consecutive time to identify the reasons for transitions between the different strategies. The tools had in this study a strong influence on the strategy for organisation of messages. According to Lantz (1996) most users do not have a defined strategy for archiving messages. A defined thoroughly considered strategy may be better than an ad hoc version that has to be redefined with time. The tools must therefore provide support for several strategies.

Design suggestions

In order to support folder users, it would be nice to have the possibility to store aliases of a message in several folders, as this is the most frequent problem for folder users in this study. This will make it possible to add comments to the message in one folder, that will be visible in the other folders as well (i.e. there exists only one message, but is visible in several folders).

Also, a warning for creating new folders with names that are similar to old folder names could reduce the number of "failed folders". The functionality is closely related to the spelling checkers in word processors.

The problems of finding the correct folder for a message could be supported by clustering (see e.g. Söderberg 1995 or Whittaker & Sidner 1996), where a distance between messages in a multi-dimensional space, with each word as a dimension, is used to define messages as "closely related" to each other. New messages are then sorted into the same folder as the most closely related message(s). A slightly more straight forward way is to allow the user to characterise each folder with some keywords. When a new message arrives, the mail tool could suggest a few folders for the message, based on clustering or these keywords. If the tool only suggests the folder instead of automatically placing the message in a folder, the user would still be in control and have the possibility to accept or override suggestions from the mail tool. Further investigations with user studies are necessary.

For spring cleaners, more support for deleting messages might be useful. Some users do not want to delete messages because they might delete the wrong message, or might regret the decision to delete later. If deleted messages were moved to a waste-basket, the user would be assured that the messages are possible to un-delete in the future, not only during the current session. In systems that automatically backup files, this would give enough time to store the messages on backup tape and thereby allow the user to un-delete a message even after several years. The messages could then automatically be removed from the waste-basket after a user specific time, e.g. a week or a month. When asked in this study, a third of the respondents were positive or very positive to such a functionality.

In a system that keeps records of when a message is opened, it becomes possible to delete e.g. all messages not opened for a certain period of time, e.g. two years. These messages could be listed separately first in order to give the user complete control over messages that should be deleted.

Barreau & Nardi (1995) describes how the information in a users file system can be divided into ephemeral, working and archived. This is highly applicable for email, but the email systems of today lack support for handling this information in different ways. For example by providing the user with possibilities to organise email messages spatially (which is possible today in all file systems with a graphical interface) or handling dialogues. Some email messages are ephemeral, for example messages that informs about meetings and service messages from the system. When the time for the meeting or the service is over, these messages are of no interest for many users. These messages could be provided with a "use before" date, to simplify deleting. Within an organisation the senders of messages could give this "use before" date, or there could be a short default date. This would provide the sender with a gain (the message would be kept longer) for her work (changing the default time), see Grudin 1988. The receiver should have the same possibilities to mark messages when they are read for automatic deletion after a certain date.

Future studies

To identify different strategies and the reasons for them is important to understand the factors that influence the organisation of email messages and to adapt the tools and education of users to their needs and work situation. It would be interesting to know if it is economically sound to give staff time to organise email messages in the same way as time and money is devoted to cleaning floors. Why should order in the real world be more essential than order on the computer?

Acknowledgements

I would like to thank my contacts at MainframePC for their co-operation, all the employees that participated, Kerstin Severinson-Eklundh at the Royal Institute of Technology, and Katarina Augustsson at the Karolinska Institute for valuable comments on the study.

References

Bair J. (1979): The Impact of Office Automatisation, The Office of the Future, Uhlig, Farber, Bair, North-Holland.

Barreau D. & Nardi B. (1995): *Finding and Reminding, File Organisation from the Desktop.* SIGCHI Bulletin, **27** (3) pp39-43.

Borenstein N. & Thyberg C. (1988): Cooperative Work in the Andrew Message System, Proceedings of CSCW 88, pp 306-323.

Borenstein N. & Thyberg C (1991).: Power, ease of use and cooperative work in a practical multimedia message system. International Journal of Man-Machine Studies, 1991, 34, pp 229-259.

Bälter O. (1995): *Electronic mail from a user perspective: Problems and remedies.* Licentiate thesis. IPLab report 100, NADA, Royal Institute of Technology, Sweden.

Bälter O. (1997a): *Kommunikation i ett teknikföretag* (in Swedish). IPLab report 128, NADA, Royal Institute of Technology, Sweden.

Bälter O. (1997b): *Experience cannot be neglected.* Forthcoming IPLab report, NADA, Royal Institute of Technology, Sweden.

Hiltz S.R. & Turoff M. (1985): Structuring computer mediated communication systems to avoid information overload. In Communications of the ACM. vol. 28, No. 7, (pp 680-689).

Jeffries R. & Rosenberg J. (1987): Comparing a Form-Based and a Language-Based User Interface for Instructing a Mail Program. Proceedings of CHI+GI 1987, pp 261-266.

Jones S., Bock G. & Brassard A.(1990): Using Electronic Mail: Themes Across Three User Interface Paradigms.SIGCHI Bulletin Jan. 1990, Vol. 21, No 3 pp 45-48.

Kidd A. (1994): The marks are on the knowledge worker. In *Proceedings of CHI'94 Human Factors in Computing Systems*, ACM Press, New York, pp 186-191.

Kilander F. (1997): *Intelligent Filtering of Computer-Mediated Human Communication*. http://www.dsv.su.se/~fk/if_Doc/IntFilter.html.

Lai K.-Y. & Malone T (1988): Object Lens: A "Spreadsheet" for Cooperative Work, Proceedings of CSCW 88, pp 115-124.

Lantz A. (1995): "Tunga" användare av datorpost. (in Swedish) IPLab report 90. NADA 1995, Royal Institute of Technology, Stockholm, Sweden.

Lantz A. (1996): *"Heavy" Users of Electronic Mail; An Interview Study*. IPLab report 101. NADA 1996, Royal Institute of Technology, Stockholm, Sweden.

Mackay W. (1988): More Than Just a Communication System: Diversity in the use of Electronic Mail. Proceedings of CSCW'88, pp 215-218.

Mackay W., Malone T., Crowston K., Rao R., Rosenblitt D. & Card S. (1989): How do Experienced Information Lens Users Use Rules?, Proceedings of the ACM conference on Human Factors in Computing Systems, April 1989.

Maes P. (1993): *Learning Interface Agents*. ACM-SIGCHI International Workshop on Intelligent User Interfaces, January 1993.

Malone T., Lai K.-Y. & Fry C. (1992): Experiments with Oval: A Radically Tailorable Tool for Cooperative work. Proceedings of CSCW'92, pp 289-297.

Malone T., Grant K., Turbak F., Brobst S. & Cohen M. (1987): Intelligent Information sharing systems. Communications of the ACM, Vol. 30, No 5, May 1987, pp 390-402.

Mander R., Salomon G. & Wong Y. Y. (1992): A 'Pile' Metaphor for Supporting Casual Organization of Information. Proceedings of CHI'92. pp 627-634.

Sheth B. & Maes P. (1993): Evolving Agents for Personalized Information Filtering. Proceedings of the Ninth IEEE Conference on Artificial Intelligence for Applications.

Söderberg J. (1995): *Classifying email.* Master Thesis TRITA A_E9543. NADA 1995, Royal Institute of Technology, Stockholm, Sweden.

Westergren A. (1989): Elektroniska meddelande och konferenssystem. (in Swedish) UNINF 163.89, ISSN 0348-0542. Institute of Information Processing, University of Umeå, Sweden.

Whittaker S. & Sidner C. (1996): *Email overload: exploring personal information management of email.* Proceedings of CHI'96, pp 276-283.

Navigating Telephone-Based Interfaces with Earcons

Stephen Brewster

Glasgow Interactive Systems Group, Department of Computing Science, University of Glasgow, Glasgow, G12 8QQ, UK.
Tel: +44 (0)141 330 4966,
Email: stephen@dcs.gla.ac.uk
Web: http://www.dcs.gla.ac.uk/~stephen/

Non-speech audio messages called *earcons* can provide powerful navigation cues in menu hierarchies. However, previous research on earcons has not addressed the particular problems of menus in telephone-based interfaces (TBI's) such as: Does the lower quality of sound in TBI's lower recall rates, can users remember earcons over a period of time and what effect does training type have on recall. An experiment was conducted and results showed that sound quality did lower the recall of earcons. However, redesign of the earcons overcame this problem with 73% recalled correctly. Participants could still recall earcons at this level after a week had passed. Training type also affected recall. With 'personal training' participants recalled 73% of the earcons but with purely textual training results were significantly lower. These results show that earcons can provide excellent navigation cues for telephone-based interfaces.

Keywords: Earcons, telephone-based interfaces, auditory interfaces, non-speech audio, navigation.

1   Introduction

Previous research has shown that structured non-speech sounds can provide powerful navigation cues in menu hierarchies for non-visual interfaces (Brewster *et al.*, 1996a and Brewster *et al.*, 1996b). However, this work did not consider the particular problems of telephone-based interfaces (TBI's). This paper describes an experiment to investigate the ability of non-speech sounds to provide navigational cues in such interfaces.

TBI's are becoming an increasingly important method for interacting with computer systems. The telephone is an ubiquitous device and is many people's primary method of entry into the information infrastructure. Access to an increasing number of services is being offered over the telephone, such as voice-mail, electronic banking and even Web pages. The rapidly increasing use of mobile telephones means that people access these services at many different times and places. Telephones themselves are now also incorporating greater functionality (such as multi-party calling or call forwarding). The provision of this extra functionality may be rendered useless if usability issues are not considered (Maguire, 1996). The work described here will improve the usability of TBI's.

The telephone itself allows only a limited form of interaction. There is no graphical display (although some do have small LCD displays) so output is limited to speech and simple sounds. Users provide input via the keypad (although speech recognition is sometimes used). These techniques are limited and reduce the usability of telephone-based systems (Schumacher *et al.*, 1995).

One common problem when interacting in TBI's is that users get lost in the hierarchy of menus that they must go through to reach an option or function (Rosson, 1985 and Wolf *et al.*, 1995). For example, in a telephone banking system users might call their bank and navigate through a hierarchy of voice menus to find the service required. However, they may get lost in the menu structure before they get to the option they want. As Yankelovich *et al.* (1995, p 369) say: "These {telephone-based} interfaces, however, are often characterised by a labyrinth of invisible and tedious hierarchies which result when menu options outnumber telephone keys or when choices overload users' short-term memory". After analysing a similar TBI, Rosson (1985, p 251) concluded: "It is important to note that the information needed to convey position in the hierarchy was implicit in the content of the utterances users heard". Feedback confirming that one had moved from the top to the middle level of the hierarchy was available only by understanding a category/sub-category relationship. She suggested that this caused many of the usability problems.

Why is navigation information not given? Because it gets in the way of the information the user is trying to access with the TBI. The more navigation information that is given the more it obstructs the actual information the user is trying to get at. Speech is also serial and slow (Slowiaczek & Nusbaum, 1985). The lower quality of sound over the telephone system makes it hard to attend to more than one speaker at once, especially if the speech is synthesised or constructed from poorly concatenated samples. It is suggested here that many navigation problems occur because current TBI's are limited to using speech alone. Speech is forced to perform two tasks: Information and navigation. Designers choose to present information to users as that is what they are using the system to find. This means that navigation cues are not provided.

As a solution to the problems of navigation Rosson suggested using more speech. However, any extra speech is likely to make the problem worse instead of better. If navigation cues are given in speech then it will obstruct the information the user is trying to access. It is suggested here that speech cannot provide the necessary feedback. As an alternative, non-speech sounds can give the navigation cues (Brewster *et al.*, 1996a). A hierarchical system of sounds could be used to represent a menu hierarchy. The sounds would play continuously (but quietly) in the background at each level, giving location information. Users could listen to the current sound and from it work out their location in the hierarchy. The sounds would make explicit the differences moving from level to level or across the same level because the sounds would be related in different ways. The sounds could do this without interfering with the speech presenting information (just as one can simultaneously listen to the music and lyrics of a song). This is a similar approach to that taken by Stevens (1996) and Stevens *et al.* (1994) in the Mathtalk system. This system displays algebra to blind mathematicians. Non-speech sounds give the listener information about their location in a mathematical structure. They do this without interfering with the synthetic voice presenting the mathematics. The cues are also much shorter than an equivalent voice message.

Little use has been made of structured non-speech sound in TBI's (apart from the standard dial tone, engaged tone, etc.). For example, guidelines for the design of TBI's (Maguire, 1996 and Schumacher *et al.*, 1995) include nothing about the use of non-speech sound. The use of such sounds, in addition to speech, will increase the bandwidth of communication between the system and the user, allowing a richer interaction. These 'multimedia' telephone interfaces will be more usable than their speech-only counterparts. Sound has many advantages. For example, it is good for communicating information quickly (Brewster, 1994). Unlike speech, non-speech sound is universal; the user is not tied to one language, which is important for the increased international use of computer systems. There is also great potential for the results of this work in other non-graphical interfaces such as those for visually disabled people and those where working conditions or protective clothing mean that a screen cannot be used. This paper will investigate some important questions about the use of non-speech sound for navigation cues in TBI's.

2   Earcons

The non-speech sounds used for this investigation were based around structured audio messages called *Earcons* (Blattner *et al.*, 1989 and Brewster, 1994). Earcons are abstract, musical tones that can be used in structured combinations to create sound messages to represent parts of an interface. Detailed investigations of earcons by Brewster *et al.* (1993) showed that they are an effective means of communicating information in sound.

Earcons are constructed from motives. These are short rhythmic sequences that can be combined in different ways. The simplest method of combination is concatenation to produce *compound earcons*. By using more complex manipulations of the parameters of sound (such as timbre, register, intensity, pitch and rhythm) *hierarchical earcons* can be created (Blattner *et al.*, 1989) which allow the representation *of hierarchical structures.*

APPLICATIONS DIRECTORY

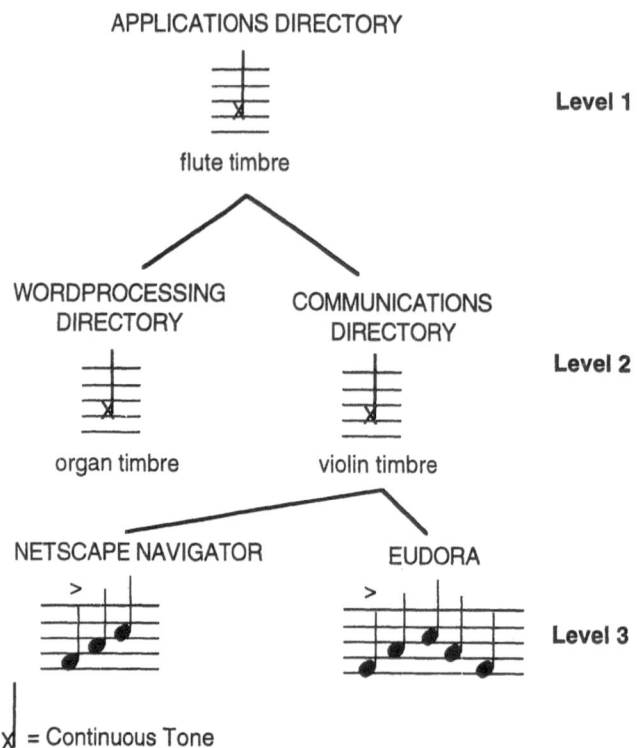

Level 1

flute timbre

WORDPROCESSING
DIRECTORY

COMMUNICATIONS
DIRECTORY

Level 2

organ timbre   violin timbre

NETSCAPE NAVIGATOR   EUDORA

Level 3

= Continuous Tone

Figure 1: A hierarchy of earcons representing a family of applications.

Figure 1 shows a simple example hierarchy of earcons based on one possible family of applications. Each earcon is a node on a tree and inherits the properties of the earcon above it. The different levels are created by manipulating the parameters of earcons (for example, rhythm, pitch, timbre). In the diagram the top level of the tree is a neutral earcon. It has a neutral flute timbre played continuously at middle C. The structure of the earcon from Level one is inherited by Level two and then changed. At Level two there is still a continuous flute sound but new timbres are added to play alongside it. At Level three a rhythm is added to the earcon from Level two to create a sound for a particular application. This rhythm is based on the timbre from the level above. In the case of Netscape Navigator there would be a continuous flute sound with a three note rhythm played on an organ accompanying it. Other levels can be created by using parameters such as tempo or effects.

Using earcons, this hierarchy is easily extensible. For example, to add another major category of applications all that is needed is a new timbre. To create a new type of communications application only a new rhythm is needed and it can be added to the existing hierarchy. Therefore earcons provide a very flexible system for representing telephone-based menu structures. The structure could be extended and users would not require retraining. Wolf *et al.* (1995) confirm the usefulness of this approach and suggest that this might be a solution to some of the problems they had with their combined voicemail and email speech interface system: "Replacing much of the text-to-speech feedback with brief distinctive earcons would make traversal of the mailbox more efficient".

2.1 Previous attempts to use earcons to present hierarchy information

There is little work on the use of sound to represent hierarchical structures. There has only been one previous study of the use of non-speech sounds for navigation information. This was performed by Brewster *et al.* (1996a,1996b). In this experiment we tried to represent a medium sized hierarchical structure of four levels and 25 nodes. Figure 2 shows the hierarchy used.

We created a set of 25 earcons on four levels based around fixed rules. These rules described the sound at each of the nodes. For example the rule for Level three used three different rhythms to indicate whether the node was a left, centre or right one (for more on the rules see below - in our current experiment Levels 1-3 of the hierarchy used the same rules as this previous experiment). Users were trained by the experimenter describing and playing each of the sounds. They were then given five minutes to use the system to learn for themselves.

Users had to identify their location by listening to an earcon and indicating their position in the hierarchy. Results showed that participants could identify their location with over 80% accuracy (see bar marked 'Control' in Figure 6), indicating that earcons were a powerful method of communicating hierarchy information. Participants were also tested to see if they could identify where previously unheard earcons would fit in the hierarchy. These new earcons were constructed using the same rules as the other earcons. If the users had learned the rules for earcon construction then they should have been able to work out their location from these new sounds. The results showed that they could do this with accuracy equal to the sounds they had heard before. These results showed that earcons were a robust and extensible method of communicating hierarchy information in sound. However, this work attempted a general solution for representing menu structures in sound and was not aimed particularly at TBI's.

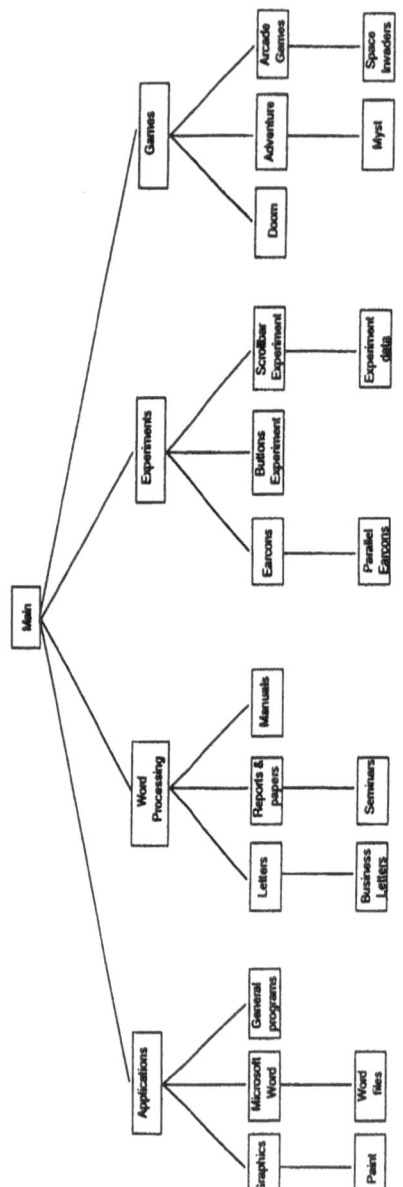

Figure 2: The heirarchy used by Brewster et al (1996a) and in the current experiment.

2.2   Problems with the previous experiment

The experiment by Brewster *et al.* gave a strong indication that earcons could provide navigational cues in TBI's. However, there were important question left unanswered:

- The earcons used were of CD quality (16bit 44kHz) - sounds played over the telephone are of much lower quality due to the narrow bandwidth of telephone equipment. This could have a significant affect on recall rates for the earcons.

- The earcons made use of stereo information to differentiate one from another. Again, stereo information is not available over the telephone so this might affect the usability of the earcons because position information is a very powerful cue.

- The sounds from Level 4 of the hierarchy were not recalled well, with 72% of all of the errors coming from this level. Tempo was used for this level and it may not have been a good indicator. Improvements were needed to reduce these errors.

- In Brewster *et al's.* experiment there was no measure of the ability of participants to recall the earcons over time. In fact, in none of the previous work on earcons has any investigation been done on this. It is important for TBI's because a user might not use the system frequently. He/she would have to be able to remember the earcons over time otherwise he/she would have to be retrained each time the system was used, which would be unacceptable.

- The training in the previous experiment was highly personal. The experimenter trained each participant individually. This would be impossible to do in a real telephone interface because of the high cost to the provider of the service. Therefore an investigation is needed into alternative, more practical training techniques.

These five points motivated the research described in this paper. With answers to these questions the usefulness of earcons for TBI's would be established and our understanding of earcons in general would also be greatly enhanced.

3   The experiment

The aim of the experiment described here was to investigate the five problems described above. Figure 2 shows the hierarchy used. This was the same as that used by Brewster *et al.* (1996a) so there was consistency between the experiments and the results could be directly compared. The hierarchy had 25 nodes on four levels.

3.1   Hypotheses

The first hypothesis was that the reduction in sound quality and lack of stereo information would reduce recall rates. With poor quality sounds it would be harder for participants to identify the earcons. This should be shown by comparison with the recall rates of Brewster *et al.'s* previous experiment.

Redesign of the Level 4 earcons should improve recall rates. In the previous experiment most errors came from this level. Redesign should result in increased recall rates in Level 4 as compared to the previous experiment.

Participants should be able to recall earcons equally as well a week after they were trained on them as they could when first trained due to the simplicity of the rules describing the earcons at each level. This would be shown by similar overall recall scores from testing presentation session 1 to session 2.

Different training techniques should reduce the recall rates of the earcons with personal training giving the best recall rates and written training giving the worst rates.

3.2   Participants

Forty-eight volunteer participants were used, split into four groups of twelve. They were computer science students and staff from University of Glasgow. All were familiar with computers and computer file systems.

3.3   Sounds used

The earcons were based on those from Brewster *et al.* (1996a) to maintain consistency. They were designed using the guidelines proposed by Brewster *et al.* (1995) . The sounds were all played by HyperCard on an Apple Macintosh computer through a telephone handset (to simulate the output of a real telephone). The sounds were generated on a Yamaha TG100 sound synthesiser and recorded by a Macintosh at a sampling rate of 8bit 11kHz (sounds with this sampling rate played over the telephone handset were of telephone quality). Each sound played for 7.5 secs. The sounds used at each level of the hierarchy will now be described. For Levels 1 to 3 the sounds were the same as for Brewster *et al's* previous experiment except stereo position was not used. For more details on these sounds see the previous paper.

Level 1: For the top level of the hierarchy ('Main' in Figure 2) a constant sound with a flute timbre was used (see Table 1). It had a pitch of D_3 (261Hz).

Level 2: Each family was given a separate timbre and register. Table 1 shows these. Register was lowest on the left and highest on the right following the conventional musical pattern.

Nodes	Timbre	Register
Main	Flute	D_3
Applications	Electric organ	C_4
Word Processing	Violin	C_3
Experiments	Drum/synthesiser	C_2
Games	Trumpet	C_1

Table 1: The timbre and register for Levels 1 and 2 of the hierarchy.

The continuous sound was inherited from the Level 1 earcon but the instrument and pitch were changed.

Level 3: At this level rhythm was used to differentiate the nodes. Each left node had one rhythm, each centre node another rhythm and each right node another. Figure 3 shows the rhythms used. For example, from Figure 2 'Graphics', 'Letters', 'Earcons' and 'Doom' all had the left node rhythm. Each of these rhythmic groups repeated continuously once every 2.5 seconds. As Figure 3 shows, the first note in each group was accented. The last note of each group was also lengthened slightly. These two help make each group into a complete rhythmic unit (Brewster *et al.*, 1995).

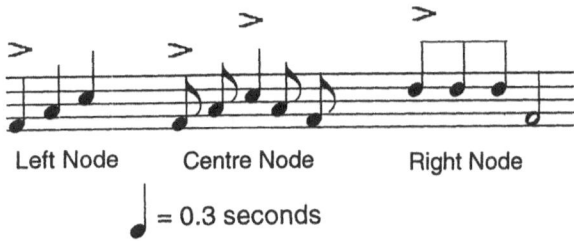

Left Node   Centre Node   Right Node

♩ = 0.3 seconds

Figure 3: The rhythms used for Level 3 of the hierarchy.

At this level the earcons inherited timbre and register from Level 2. This meant, for example, that 'Graphics' used the left node rhythm described in Figure 3 and it was played with an electric organ timbre in the register of C_4.

Level 4: In the previous experiment by Brewster *et al.* (1996a) 72% of the recall errors came from Level 4 earcons. A faster tempo was used to differentiate the items at this level. The errors occurred because Level 4 was the bottom of the hierarchy so participants had to remember the most sound manipulations to work out their location. For the current experiment it was decided to try an alternative method of presenting the Level 4 information to make it clearer to participants. The Level 3 earcons were used again at Level 4 but a 0.3 sec. sitar note was played before each of the repeating rhythmic units. A sitar timbre was used as it sounded recognisable when played over the telephone and was also distinctly different to the other timbres used. This acted as a Level 4 identifier to reinforce the switch to this level. The note was played once for a left node, twice for a centre and three times for a right node (see Figure 4). It was hoped that this would provide stronger information to the participants that they were on Level 4.

Centre Node

Figure 4: An example of a Level 4 centre node (for example Word files). The first two notes were played on the sitar.

3.4   *Training*

One of the main aspects of this experiment was the investigation of different training techniques. In the previous experiment training was done by the experimenter. This would not be practical in a real world TBI due to cost. Therefore an investigation of alternative techniques and their effect on recall was needed. This would also give us insight into the training of users to use sounds in other types of interfaces. Participants were randomly assigned to one of four groups. Each group investigated a different training technique. The techniques are summarised in Table 2.

Group / Training Type	Method	Sounds in Part 1	Part 2 Training
Group A	Personal	yes	yes
Group B	Online tutorial	yes	yes
Group C	Online tutorial	no	yes
Group D	Online tutorial	no	no

Table 2: The different training techniques used in the four groups.

Group A: In this group training had two parts. For the first part, participants were given personal training by the experimenter. He showed the participant each of nodes of the hierarchy in turn and played the associated earcon. This was done once only. The structure of the earcons at each level was fully explained. In the second part of the training participants were given five minutes to learn the earcons by themselves with no help from the experimenter. They did this using the HyperCard stack. This was the 'best case' training. This condition allowed us to compare directly our results with those of Brewster *et al.* (1996a).

For a TBI this would be the equivalent of the telephone service provider sending a training officer to show new subscribers how to use the system. The subscribers would then get five minutes of free call time to try the system.

Group B: The training was the same as Group A except that the participants received an on-line tutorial explanation of the sounds rather than personal training. The tutorial fully explained the structure of the sounds and the participants listened to the sounds as they worked through the tutorial. Figure 5 shows an example of the on-line tutorial for this group.

This type of training is equivalent to the telephone service provider giving a tutorial to their system on a training video or over the Web. Again the subscriber is allowed five minutes of free call time to try the system.

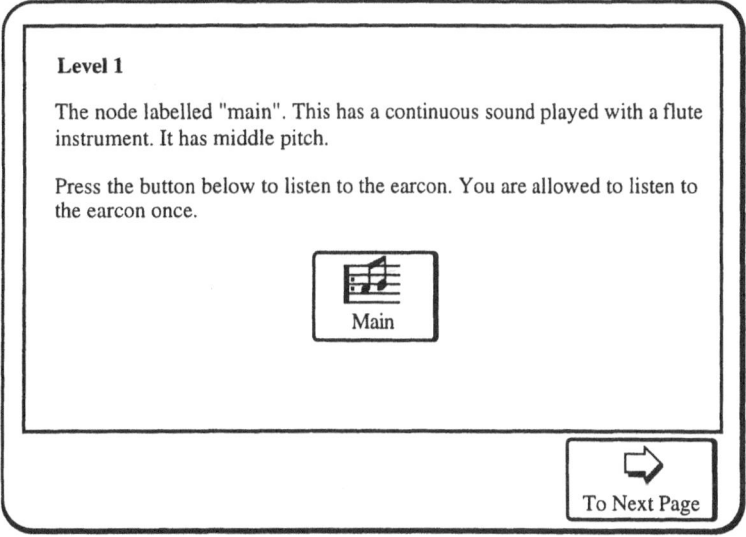

Figure 5: Training screen for the earcon 'Main' in Group B.

Group C: Training for this group was similar to Group B except that the on-line tutorial did not allow the participants to listen to the sounds. In all other respects the on-line training for this group was the same as that shown in Figure 5. Participants still heard the sounds in part two of the training.

For this group the training is equivalent to the service provider sending a training brochure to new subscribers with instructions on how to use their new system. Again they are given five minutes of free call time.

Group D: This final group was similar to Group C except that participants did not get part two of the training. This meant that the participants did not hear any of the sounds before the experiment started; they just read once through a description of their structure. This was the 'worst case' training condition.

For this group the training is equivalent to the service provider sending a training brochure to new subscribers with instructions on how to use their new system. No free call time is given. The training in the four groups decreases in cost from Group A which is the most expensive to Group D which is the least. The important question to be answered was: What effect would this have on the recall rates of the earcons (and therefore their usability as navigation cues)?

During the training participants could look at a map of the hierarchy (similar to Figure 2). The aim of the experiment was not to test the participants' abilities to learn hierarchies but to test their ability to learn the earcons. Instructions were read from a prepared script.

3.5   Testing

The participants heard twelve earcons during testing. These were randomly selected from all of the sounds in the hierarchy (and were the same as those used in the previous experiment to maintain consistency). The same set of earcons was presented to each of the participants. An earcon was played and the participants then had to say where the it fitted into the hierarchy.

Testing was done in two sessions. The first presentation session was done directly after the training and the second a week later. No further training was given before the second testing session. This allowed an investigation of the ability of participants to recall the earcons over a period of time, which would be essential for the real-world use of earcons for navigation cues in TBI's.

4   Results

4.1   Comparison with previous results

The first comparison undertaken was to compare the results of Group A(1) with the previous results of Brewster *et al.* (here called the Control Group). Group A(1) had the same training method as the previous experiment. The only differences were the sound quality, lack of stereo information and construction of level 4 earcons. The results are shown in the first two bars of Figure 6. A one-factor ANOVA showed no significant difference between the score from the previous experiment and the current one ($F_{1,22}$=1.11, p=0.301). The results showed that five participants in Group A(1) obtained scores equal to or higher than members of the Control Group.

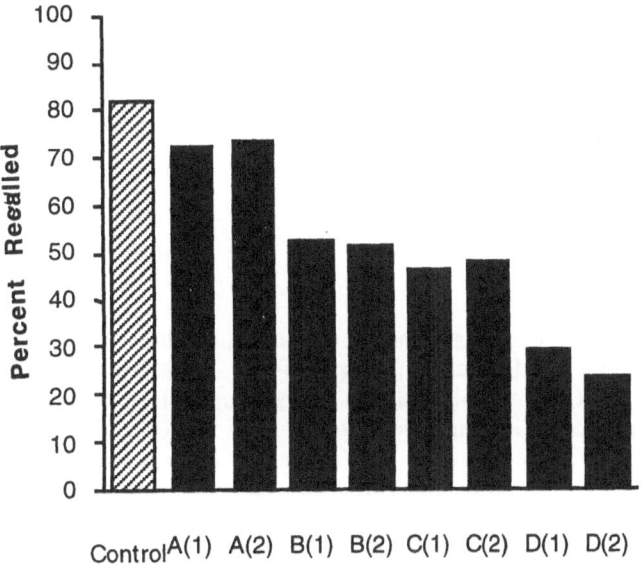

Groups

Figure 6: Recall rates for each of the groups for both presentation sessions. (1) shows results of the first testing session and (2) the second. The Control Group shows the results from the previous experiment by Brewster *et al.* (1996a). This group appears once because there was no re-testing in that experiment.

In Brewster *et al.'s* previous work, 72% of the errors occurred with Level 4 earcons. In this experiment the Level 4 sounds had been redesigned to help reduce this error rate. Was the redesign successful? Examination of the data showed that Level 4 earcons now accounted for only 41% of the errors. This indicated that improvements to the Level 4 earcons had been successful. The Level 4 sounds became no harder to recall than any of the other levels.

Although the Level 4 error rate had been reduced the overall recall rate was not significantly different. The effect of lower sound quality and lack of stereo information was to distribute errors more uniformly throughout all levels. In Brewster *et al.'s* previous work 28% of the errors came from Levels 1-3, in this experiment it was 59%. There were now significantly more errors in Levels 1-3 (T_{12}=4.4, p=0.0008). Therefore improvements in the Level 4 earcons offset the problems due to reduced sound quality and lack of stereo information. The end result was no significant difference between the recall rate in this and the previous experiment.

4.2   Recall over time

The next investigation undertaken was to compare the results of the participants after the first testing session with those after the second. This would indicate how well participants could remember earcons over time. Figure 6 shows the overall results for groups A-D, presentation sessions one and two. As can be seen from the figure the differences between the scores were small. T-tests showed no significant differences between any of the groups in presentation session one and two (for example D(1) vs. D(2) T_{11}=1.24, p=0.24. In D(2) four participants had equal or greater scores than in D(1)). This indicates that participants could recall earcons well over time.

4.3   *The effects of training*

One of the most important aspects of the experiment was to investigate the effect of training type on the recall of earcons. Again, Figure 6 shows the results. As discussed above, the Control and Group A used the same training techniques. There were no significant differences between these so analysis will concentrate on the differences between Groups A-D. There were also no significant differences between the scores obtained from presentation session one and two, therefore data from presentation one in each of the groups will be used to simplify analysis.

A one-factor ANOVA between Groups A-D showed a significant main effect ($F_{3,44}$=5.3, p=0.003). In order to find out where the main effect occurred Tukey HSD tests were carried out between each of the groups. This analysis showed that the only significant difference was between Groups A and D (Q_{44}=43.5, p=0.01). This indicated that training type did have a significant effect on recall but only between Groups A and D.

A more detailed analysis of the D(1) scores was undertaken to find out what information participants managed to extract in this condition. Results showed that participants got the level of the earcon correct 67.3% of the time (where 25% would occur by chance, so they were performing significantly better than chance).

5   Discussion

5.1   *Comparison with previous results*

Results from Group A(1) showed no significant differences to those of Brewster *et al.* (1996a). Recall rates of 72% suggest that earcons can provide good navigation cues in telephone-based systems. Users of such systems can listen to an earcon and from it work out where they are in the hierarchy of menus. This then allows them to avoid becoming lost, one of the major problems in such systems (Wolf *et al.*, 1995 and Yankelovich *et al.*, 1995). After Brewster *et al.'s* previous work there was still a question about the ability of earcons to provide good navigation cues when the quality of the sounds were reduced to those of the telephone system. The results described here show that this is not a problem.

There was an increase in errors due to reduced quality of the sounds and the lack of stereo information. However, this was offset by the greatly improved recognition of earcons at the bottom of the hierarchy. These results show that the problems caused by sound quality can be overcome by better design of the earcons. In future experiments earcons at Levels 1-3 of the hierarchy will be improved so that recall rates will hopefully again increase.

The results show that earcons can indicate position in a hierarchy of information very successfully. In a real system using earcons, a move to a new node would cause a new sound to play. The user would listen to this sound and from it work out his/her location, therefore avoiding becoming lost in the hierarchy. This and our previous experiment have shown that earcons can provide good navigation cues. The next stage of this work is to incorporate earcons into a real telephone-based system and evaluate their effectiveness in real-world conditions.

5.2   *Recall over time*

The results here are the first to demonstrate the recall of earcons over time. In Brewster *et al.* (1992) and Brewster *et al.* (1993) detailed investigations of earcons were undertaken. Brewster *et al.* tested recall over very short periods of time (approximately 15 - 20 mins. after training). The results showed there were no significant differences after this short period. However, only a small set of sounds (9 earcons) were tested and over a very short period of time. This was not characteristic of the use of earcons in everyday applications. The results presented here show that a large set of earcons can be recalled well over the period of one week. One reason for this is that the construction rules are simple and clear making them easy to remember. These results show that the participants understood the rules by which the earcons were constructed and could apply them again a week later. This is an important result for earcons in general but is particularly important for their use in TBI's. It means that users of a TBI would not need to be retrained if they used the system infrequently.

5.3   *The effects of training*

Training type did have a significant effect on recall rates. Personal training by the experimenter gave the highest rates with the lowest coming from the purely textual training. The results showed that the only significant difference was between Groups A and D. However, there was much within-group variance which may have masked some potential differences. By looking at Figure 6 we can see three groupings in the results: The Control Group and Group A, Groups B and C, and finally group D.

As expected, good results were obtained in the Control Group and Group A. Personal training was very effective. However, this type of training would be the most expensive for a telephone service provider. There was a 20% difference in recall from Group A to B where the only difference was an on-line tutorial rather than personal training.

There was little difference between groups B and C which indicated that the use of sounds in part one of the training did not help recall. More important was to let users use the system themselves. This 'active learning' seems to help them remember the sounds better than reading about the sounds and then hearing them together.

Group D shows that if users cannot hear any of the sounds before they use the system then recall rates are likely to be poor. However, even though the overall analysis presented in Figure 9 showed low recall rates, participants were able to extract some useful navigation information from the earcons. In fact, they were get the correct level in the hierarchy 67.3% of the time. According to Rosson (described above), many navigational problems came from mistaking switches to different levels in a hierarchy. Therefore, purely textual training can provide a reasonable solution to this problem. It may also be possible to increase recall by improving the design of the textual description. Remember that the participants were only allowed to read the training documentation once. If they were allowed to read over the document several times (which is more likely to happen in a real world use of earcons) then we might be able to improve rates (this would also apply to the other groups).

The current results indicate that there is no significant difference between Groups A, B and C. This would suggest that training of type C could be given and high recall rates achieved but with only a low training cost.

6   Conclusions

The experiment described here has answered many fundamental questions about the use of earcons in general and in particular about their application as navigation cues within telephone-based interfaces (TBI's). Brewster *et al.* (1996a) showed that earcons could be used as navigation cues but left many unanswered questions about their usefulness under the restricted   conditions of the telephone. The research in this paper has shown that reductions in the quality of sound that occur with telephone systems can be offset by improvements in the design of earcons, thus making earcons a good method for providing navigation cues in TBI's.

This research was also the first investigation into the memorability of earcons over time. This is important for earcons in general and also for their use in TBI's. If users do not use the system frequently then they must be able to remember the sounds in order to use them as navigation cues. Results here showed that there was no difference in the recall of earcons a week after their first presentation. This shows that they are a robust method of presenting navigation information.

Results showed that training techniques do affect the recall rates of earcons. Training techniques are a cost to the provider of a telephone service. The provider must ensure that users can use the sounds whilst minimising the amount spent on training. Results here indicate that an on-line tutorial plus a short period of free call time can enable users to reach high recall rates without much training cost. Now that these fundamental questions have been answered, designers of telephone services can use earcons to provide navigation cues to greatly enhance the usability of their systems.

Acknowledgements

Many thanks to Ayotunde Aboaba who helped greatly in this project as part of his MSc. in Information Technology at Glasgow. Thanks to Phil Gray for proof-reading and comments.

References

Any references by Brewster (along with sound samples and further information) are available electronically from http://www.dcs.gla.ac.uk/~stephen/

Blattner, M., Sumikawa, D. & Greenberg, R. (1989). Earcons and icons: Their structure and common design principles. *Human Computer Interaction*, **4**, 11-44.

Brewster, S.A. (1994) *Providing a structured method for integrating non-speech audio into human-computer interfaces*. PhD Thesis, University of York, UK.

Brewster, S.A., Raty, V.-P. & Kortekangas, A. (1996a). Earcons as a method of providing navigational cues in a menu hierarchy. In Sasse, Cunnigham & Winder (Eds.), *Proceedings of BCS HCI'96*, (pp. 169-183), London, UK: Springer.

Brewster, S.A., Raty, V.-P. & Kortekangas, A. (1996b). *Using earcons to provide navigational cues in a complex menu hierarchy* (Technical Report No. TR-1996-24). Department of Computing Science, University of Glasgow.

Brewster, S.A., Wright, P.C. & Edwards, A.D.N. (1992). A detailed investigation into the effectiveness of earcons. In Kramer (Ed.), *Proceedings of ICAD'92*, (pp. 471-498), Santa Fe Institute, Santa Fe: Addison-Wesley.

Brewster, S.A., Wright, P.C. & Edwards, A.D.N. (1993). An evaluation of earcons for use in auditory human-computer interfaces. In Ashlund, Mullet, Henderson, Hollnagel & White (Eds.), *Proceedings of ACM/IFIP INTERCHI'93*, (pp. 222-227), Amsterdam: ACM Press, Addison-Wesley.

Brewster, S.A., Wright, P.C. & Edwards, A.D.N. (1995). Experimentally derived guidelines for the creation of earcons. In Kirby, Dix & Finlay (Eds.), *Adjunct Proceedings of BCS HCI'95*, (pp. 155-159), Huddersfield, UK

Maguire, M. (1996). A human-factors study of telephone developments and convergence. *Contemporary Ergonomics*, 446-451.

Rosson, M.B. (1985). Using synthetic speech for remote access to information. *Behaviour Research Methods, Instruments and Computers*, **17**, 250-252.

Schumacher, R.M., Hardzinski, M.L. & Schwartz, A.L. (1995). Increasing the usability of interactive voice response systems. *Human Factors*, **37**, 251-264.

Slowiaczek, L.M. & Nusbaum, H.C. (1985). Effects of speech rate and pitch contour on the perception of synthetic speech. *Human Factors*, **27**, 701-712.

Stevens, R. (1996) *Principles for the Design of Auditory Interfaces to Present Complex Information to Blind people*. PhD Thesis, University of York, UK.

Stevens, R.D., Brewster, S.A., Wright, P.C. & Edwards, A.D.N. (1994). Providing an audio glance at algebra for blind readers. In Kramer & Smith (Eds.), *Proceedings of ICAD'94*, (pp. 21-30), Santa Fe Institute, Santa Fe: Santa Fe Institute.

Wolf, C., Koved, L. & Kunzinger, E. (1995). Ubiquitous Mail: Speech and graphical interfaces to an integrated voice/email mailbox. In Nordby, Helmersen, Gilmore & Arnesen (Eds.), *Proceedings of IFIP Interact'95*, (pp. 247-252), Lillehammer, Norway: Chapman & Hall.

Yankelovich, N., Levow, G. & Marx, M. (1995). Designing SpeechActs: Issues in speech user interfaces. In Katz, Mack & Marks (Eds.), *Proceedings of ACM CHI'95*, (pp. 369-376), Denver, Colorado: ACM Press, Addison-Wesley.

Do Users Always Benefit When User Interfaces Are Consistent?

David A. Caulton and Ken Dye

One Microsoft Way
Redmond, WA 98052
USA

Do users always learn a new program faster if its UI is consistent with a previously learned user interface? Most UI style guides claim they do. A study is described that refutes this claim by demonstrating a case where a version of Microsoft Project that is less consistent with Microsoft Office is more usable to expert Office users than one that is more consistent with Office. It is proposed that the inconsistent version is more usable because Microsoft Project is a different class of application – more vertical – and thus different UI techniques are appropriate. It is argued that users benefit from consistent interfaces where programs perform similar functions over a wide range of user goals, but in more vertical applications and where the user's goals are different, appropriateness to purpose is more important than consistency.

1   Introduction

User interface designers must satisfy a large number of often-conflicting design constraints. As a result designers are often faced with tradeoffs. One common tradeoff is choosing between consistency with existing interfaces and appropriateness to the user's goals. Each approach has advantages. If users have learned one program's interface, an unfamiliar but consistent program can be more readily learned. On the other hand, different programs have different uses and types of users, and their user interfaces should be optimized for those users' goals.

Prior to the mid 1980s, learning a new program was much like learning a new computer system is today; each program had an entirely original UI. This has changed, and today personal computer applications tend to favor consistency. The Apple Macintosh and Microsoft Windows GUIs have helped users by enforcing consistent use of window elements and menus. Consistency is now properly considered to be one of the most important aspects of usability (Nielson, 1989), and software interfaces widely reflect this. For example, nearly all mainstream business applications now feature a File and Edit menu and have scrollbars along the right and bottom sides of windows.

There is some empirical evidence that emphasizes the importance of consistency. For example, Polson (1988) demonstrated several examples where consistent interfaces took advantage of transfer-of-learning to improve user performance. However, it is not difficult to find extremely broad endorsements of consistency, such as:

> "...a programmer's new solution that precisely matches a particular situation should be set aside in favor of a slightly less effective but more commonly used solution. In most cases, consistency should be valued above idiosyncratic cleverness." (Apple Human Interface Guidelines: The Apple Desktop Interface, 1988)

Is it possible to go to extremes with this philosophy? Can inconsistent - but suitable to task - interfaces provide benefits that justify violations of consistency? In particular, how do we avoid designing "least-common denominator" interfaces, in which all the UIs are shackled with the problems of each of the applications? Empirical examples (such as in Polson, 1988) where consistency is helpful are intriguing, but they do not necessarily demonstrate a user interface "law" that must be applied everywhere.

Others have asked this question. In particular, Gruden (1989) discussed a number of examples where consistency might work against users. In addition, he provides a useful discussion of some general principles that might guide the application of consistency as a design principle. This paper adds specific, empirical evidence to this argument.

A specific example where it may be of value to violate consistency would be when designing a project management (PM) application. If we know that a high percentage of the PM users also use a spreadsheet, we might look to the spreadsheet UI and attempt to maximize consistency with it. However, the spreadsheet's UI faces challenges not shared by the PM's UI. Might this unnecessarily constrain our design in response to problems we need not face? A spreadsheet must allow an overwhelming variety of users to accomplish many different goals. The best UIs are designed around user goals – but what is the typical spreadsheet users' goal? To answer this question, we must know what the "typical spreadsheet user" is, and there is probably no such beast. Spreadsheets are used for *thousands* of unrelated tasks and goals, and designing around one user's goal would confound other users. In response to exactly this problem, the Microsoft Excel UI is built around very generic goals such as inserting things, viewing things, formatting things, etc....

In contrast, a PM application is a more vertical, or single-use application. What do most users want to do the first time they sit down with a PM application? *Plan and manage a project.* What's more, we can identify definite stages towards this goal: Planning the project in advance, tracking it while in progress, communicating with others, etc.... These are categories that all users, even those who are not professional project managers, will understand. The UI might be better if it was structured around these stages and goals. However, if we blindly adhere to the spreadsheet for our UI, we lose this advantage. Of course, the PM application is just one example; the same argument could be applied to a personal finance program, email client, or any of countless other vertical applications.

In practice, can an interface that is specialized for a vertical application (and thus is idiosyncratic) be better than a consistent interface that maximizes transfer of learning between applications? To answer this question, we compared task performance among Microsoft Office users while they learned to use one of two versions of Microsoft Project. One version had menus that were identical to those in Microsoft Office. The other violated consistency but was designed around the stages in the project management process. If it is more beneficial to Microsoft Office users for other applications to be consistent with Microsoft Office, then the consistent menus should facilitate better performance. If suitability-to-task is more beneficial, then the opposite should be true.

2 Method

2.1 Subjects

The subjects were 29 managers who reported using Microsoft Word 95 and/or Excel 95 for more than 2 hours every day, but who had never seen or used Microsoft Project. In return for their participation, subjects were given the Microsoft software package of their choice.

2.2 Materials

2.2.1 Microsoft Project 95
A vertical application was needed for the test, and Microsoft Project was chosen. Microsoft Project is a project management application, and is used to organize large amounts of complex information about tasks and employees. It allows users to plan and keep track of who is doing what, when they are going to do it, and how much it will cost. The application was run under Microsoft Windows 95 on a 90 MHz Pentium-based PC.

2.2.2   The Menu Designs

Figure 1 illustrates the menus shipped in Microsoft Project 95, which we will refer to as the Office-consistent menus. These menus are identical to those in the Microsoft Office 95 applications (Microsoft Word and Excel 95).

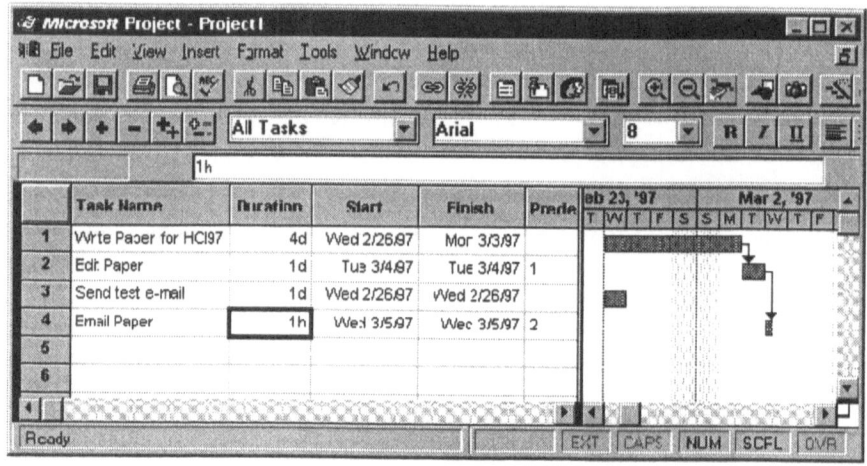

Figure 1: The Office-Consistent menus.

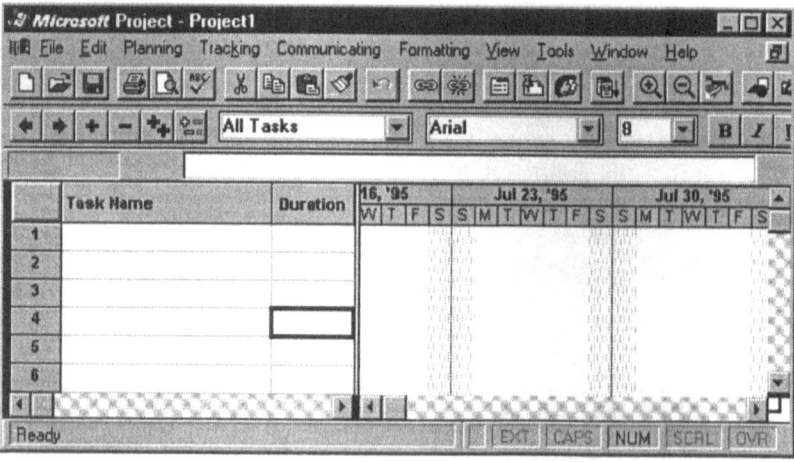

Figure 2: The Experimental Goal-Based menu.

The goal-based menu prototype (GBM, figure 2) added four new menus to Microsoft Project 95. The new menus (Planning, Tracking, Communicating, and Formatting) corresponded to various goals that users have when they use Microsoft Project. The new menus (Figure 3) contained features that were relevant to those goals. No changes were made to the File, View, Window, or Help menus.

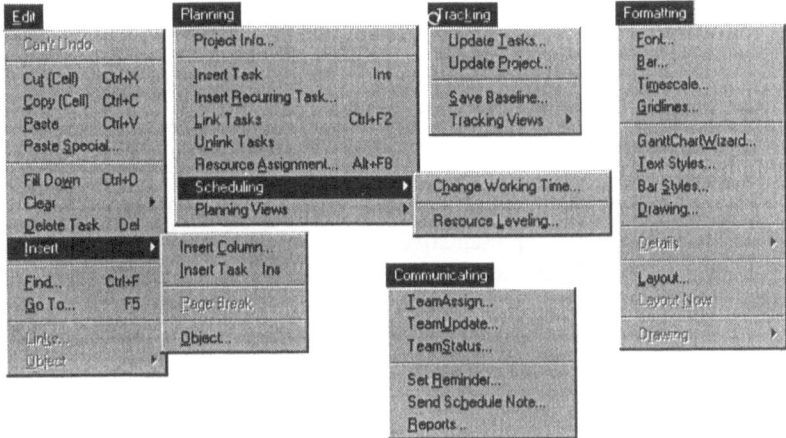

Figure 3: The Contents of the Modified GBMs

We predicted that two aspects of the GBM would affect user performance:

- For reasons discussed above, the Office-consistent menus categorize features in a very generic way. This design allowed the same menus to be used in all the Office applications. The GBM is organized around the stages of the project management process and user goals, which even beginning users should understand. This should make it easier for subjects to find features that map to basic PM goals.
- Wider, shallower menus provide better categorization of features into categories than deeper, narrower menus. By breaking the features out into more "root" menus, the GBM should make it easier for users to find the features they need to accomplish the tasks.

2.2.3 Procedure

The experiment tested whether users could accomplish tasks more quickly and successfully using the GBM than the Office-consistent menus. Users were asked to perform eleven tasks in one of the versions of Microsoft Project. Sixteen of the subjects attempted to perform the tasks using the GBM, and 13 used the Office-consistent menus.

The GBM prototype was designed to identify *only those improvements that resulted from the menu restructuring.* No other aspect of the interface was modified. We can thus be certain that any usability differences resulted from the restructuring. In particular:

- The GBM contains all of the items that the Office-consistent menus do. Thus, if usability improves, it isn't because the number of features has changed.
- The names of the menu items the same in the two conditions, so if users do better, it isn't because of any labeling improvements.

The subjects were handed an 11-page booklet that listed tasks they were to accomplish in Microsoft Project. Each page included a Task Instruction and a color image of what Microsoft Project should look like at the *end* of the task. The tasks are summarized in Table 1.

After completing these tasks, subjects had created and used their first project. The tasks were selected to be a representative sample of the features in Microsoft Project. Note that tasks #2 and #5 could not be accomplished using the menus. These tasks served as a "check" on the experiment – if there were consistent differences between the GBM and Office-Consistent-menu groups on these tasks, then the sampling or methodology in the study would be suspect.

Each user was scored as succeeding or failing at each task. If the user failed a task, they were instructed to shut down Microsoft Project and open a file in which that task had been completed. This ensured that all subjects began each task in the same state (with the results of all previous tasks completed) and that failure on one task did not impede performance on subsequent tasks.

Two measures were taken in the experiment: Successful task completion time and Success/Failure rates. A subject was scored as successful if they completed the task, and their time to completion was recorded. The first time a subject indicated they gave up on a task, they were prompted to continue. The second time they gave up, the subject was scored as failing the task. Time to failure was not used in the analysis. If the GBM is really more usable than the Office-consistent menus, we would expect some or all of the following results:

- Because the GBM is goal-based, wider, and shallower, GBM users will more rapidly accomplish tasks.
- For the same reasons, GBM users will be more successful at accomplishing the tasks.

#	Task instruction
1	Enter some tasks as shown below. Note that the project starts on February 2, 1997. Try to set this date for the whole project at once, not just by setting each task to a new start date.
2	Enter durations as shown below
3	Link the tasks as shown below
4	Outline the tasks as shown below (note that the bold tasks are called "summary tasks")
5	Add 3 resources (people who will work on the project)
6	Assign resources to tasks as shown below
7	Change the Gantt to another style as shown below. This can be done without explicitly changing each bar and font, so try to do all the changes in one step.
8	Format the fonts in the project to be the "times new roman" font. Your goal is to change all the text – both in the chart and on the sheet. This can be done all at once without doing each column or view separately.
9	There is a quick way to make all the "summary tasks" bold, italic 11-point Arial *in one step*. Please do this as illustrated below.
10	Now you decide that you want to tell your resources (people) what they need to be doing, and when they need to be doing it. Can you find a way to send this information from within project (electronically)
11	You decide you would like it if Project could automatically adjust your schedule so it happens in the quickest possible time without overworking any of your people. Can you find a feature that will let you do this?

Table 1: The eleven tasks that were tested in the study.

3   Results

3.1   Time and Success Rates

The speed and success rate results generally supported the contention the GBM was more usable than the Office-consistent menus. Table 2 shows the speed and success rate data from the experiment in detail. For each measure (time or success rate) the table shows mean values across subjects for the GBM and Project 95 menus, and the difference (Δ) between the two. Positive Δs indicate a better score for the GBM. To determine statistical reliability, one-tailed t-tests against the hypothesis that the GBM was better were performed, and * indicates $p < 0.05$, ** indicates $p < 0.01$.

	Task	Times (min:sec)			Success Rates		
		GBM	Proj95	Δ	GBM	Proj95	Δ
1	Enter Tasks & set project start date.	6:27	7:20	0:53	0.63	0.38	.24
2	Enter durations	2:03	2:14	0:11	1.00	1.00	0
3	Set up links	2:50	2:09	-0:41	0.94	0.77	.17
4	Outline the tasks	3:35	7:43	4:08**	0.38	0.31	.07
5	Add 3 resources	1:39	2:17	0:38	0.88	0.85	.03
6	Assign resources to tasks	2:58	4:24	1:26*	1.00	0.77	.23*
7	Format the Gantt using the GCWiz	3:46	3:17	-0:29	0.81	0.46	.35*
8	Format all fonts using Text Styles	2:01	3:22	1:21*	0.75	0.77	-.02
9	Fmt summary tasks using Text Styles	1:59	2:02	0:03	0.69	0.77	-.08
10	Send a TeamAssign	1:56	5:22	3:26**	0.94	0.31	.63**
11	Level the Project	2:21	4:35	2:14*	0.75	0.46	.29
	Total Time/Average Success Rate	31.6	44.8	13.2**	0.80	0.63	.17**

* (p<0.05)
** (p < 0.01)

Table 2: Time to Completion and Success Rates for the two menus.

Overall, the GBM users were 17% more successful and 13 minutes faster at the test. It is unlikely that these differences are due to sampling or methodological errors because neither of the tasks that did not involve menus (#2 and #5) showed reliable differences between the groups.

4   Conclusions

The results of this study clearly demonstrate one case where a violation of consistency produced in increase in usability. Of course, this should not be taken as a criticism of consistency in general. This represents a special case where an inconsistent UI improved usability, and it is instructive to consider why this occurred.

As discussed previously, first and foremost is the fact that Microsoft Project is a vertical application while the Office applications are not. This allowed the UI for Microsoft Project to be designed specifically for its narrow class of users and their goals – at the expense of consistency with Microsoft Office. The fact that the subjects in this study were experienced Office users means that they have a shared knowledge base – they already know how to use Office. But they also share more relevant domain knowledge: Project Management. By being consistent with Office, we tap into the former. By being inconsistent, we tap into the latter, demonstrably more important experience.

Another reason why inconsistency might improve usability would be if the UI for one application were inappropriate for the other. This may have been the case in the current study. The menus for Office were optimized for Office, not for Microsoft Project. This may have resulted in a "shoehorning" of features into a suboptimal interface. One particularly salient example is the Tools menu in

Microsoft Office vs. Microsoft Project. Microsoft Excel and Word are primarily document creation tools, and this is reflected in their feature sets. Most of the Office applications' features involve document manipulation (editing, viewing, inserting, etc...), and thus most of Word and Excel's features fit into the Office menu scheme. Microsoft Project, on the other hand, is a planning, tracking, and analysis tool – and thus has many features that do not fit into the Office menu scheme. Figure 4 shows the resulting distributions of features across menus. Project's Tools menu has a huge number of items, those features that did not fit into one of the other menus. This makes locating and identifying those features more difficult than in the more specialized GBM.

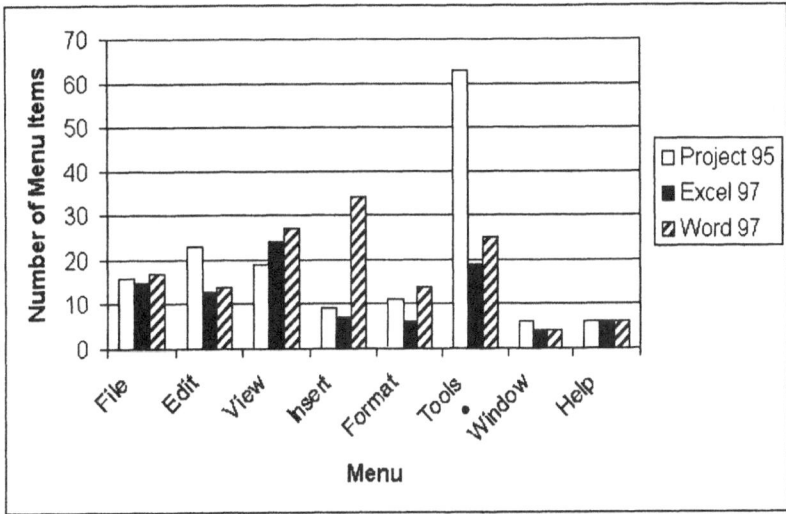

Figure 4: The distribution of menu items in various software products.

It is important to note that we are not claiming that the GBM is simply a better UI than the Office UI. It is trivial to say that we should not maintain consistency with a *bad* user interface. This would not argue that Office and Project should be inconsistent, rather it would argue for using the GBM *consistently* in both Office and Project. We do not claim that the GBM would be better than the Office menus for Excel (although these data do not address this question). We are claiming is that the GBM was a better UI *for Microsoft Project* and the Office UI is a better UI *for Microsoft Office*, and thus that the optimal solution is for Project and Office to be inconsistent.

The fact that the GBM violates consistency, yet improves usability does not mean that consistency is a bad thing. In many – perhaps most – cases, consistency will improve usability. It does mean that when considering the design tradeoffs, appropriateness to purpose may be more important for vertical than for large domain applications. Indeed, there are many areas where Microsoft Office and Microsoft Project are *and should be* consistent. For example, the Microsoft Project "Gantt Chart" (Figure 1) has two basic screen regions: A sheet of task names, durations, etc... on the left and a chart on the right. Microsoft Project users reasonably expect that the sheet will work like an Excel spreadsheet, and that the chart will work like an Excel chart. This expectation is reasonable because (a) they look like Excel sheets and charts and (b) the user wants to do the same things as in Excel sheets and charts.

The results of this study refute global claims that "consistency is good", and "we should always prefer consistency". They argue that in some cases consistency wins out, and in others it does not – a much more complex conclusion that mandates more work for designers. The discovery of guiding principles for when consistency is best is beyond the scope of this paper. However, I will close with a speculation on this issue. While these results do not argue against the use of consistency, they do argue against the simplistic application of consistency everywhere. Consistency is better than inconsistency when *all other things are equal*, which they nearly never are. Instead of valuing consistency over all other attributes, we should perhaps value suitability-to-task. Where a pre-existing application performs the same functions as a new one, the user will benefit from a consistent UI. Where they differ, they will not. Application UIs will naturally be consistent where the users' goals and tasks are the same, and different where their goals and tasks are different.

References

Apple Computer, Inc. (1988). Apple Human Interface Guidelines: The Apple Desktop Interface. Addison-Wesley, Reading, MA.

Gruden, J. (1989). The case against user interface consistency. Communications of the ACM, 32, 10, 1164-1173.

Nielson, J. (1989). Coordinating user interfaces for consistency. SIGCHI Bulletin 20, 63-65.

Polson, P. (1988). The consequences of consistent and inconsistent user interfaces. In *Cognitive Science and its Applications for Human-Computer Interaction*. Lawrence Erlbaum. Hillsdale, N.J.

Conceptual Design Reconsidered: The Case of the Internet Session Directory Tool

Louise Clark & M. Angela Sasse

University College London
Gower Street
UK - London WC1E 6BT
Email: L.Clark@cs.ucl.ac.uk
Email: A.Sasse@cs.ucl.ac.uk

We report a case study in which conceptual design was applied to create a user interface of an innovative software tool. The Session Directory Tool (sdr) allows users to set up and participate in real-time interactive multimedia events on the Internet. To make this functionality available to users who are not familiar with the underlying network technology and videoconferencing, we identified a metaphor which could be extended into a design model (Electronic TV Listings Guide), and communicated this model through linguistic and structural features of the user interface. Evaluation results indicate that this effort was largely successful: new users handled sdr competently after a short training session and 5 days' practise, and articulated their knowledge of the tool in terms related to the design model. The case study demonstrates the potential of conceptual design, integrated with tangible HCI design techniques, for developing user interfaces to innovative technology.

Keywords: conceptual design, mental models, users' models, Internet conferencing

1   Introduction

Over the past 5 years, the Internet has developed from a research network - used mainly by academic researchers to transfer files - into a global network used by the general public. Thanks to innovations in network and compression technology, parts of the network are now capable of supporting interactive real-time multimedia traffic. Users can watch remote broadcasts, hold meetings or job interviews, and even stage remote parties, concerts and arts events - provided they know how to set up and join such events. Software tools have been developed to support these activities, but they assume technical knowledge of networking and multimedia. The challenge is to make this technology available to users who not only lack detailed knowledge of the underlying technology, but also have no conception of a real-world task which the tool supports. This paper reports on an attempt to apply conceptual design to create a user interface which facilitates access to this novel technology.

1.1   Conceptual Design

Conceptual design as proposed by Norman (1986) is based on the assumption that users construct internalised *users' models* (often referred to as *mental models*) of computer systems, and that appropriate users' models result in successful user-system interaction. Users' models are formed as a result of user-system interaction, but can also be influenced by instruction. The process of conceptual design starts with the construction of a *design model*: an accurate, consistent and complete representation of system functionality. The design model is communicated through the user interface (or *system image*). If this process is successful, users interacting with the system should develop an appropriate *users' model* (see Figure 1). This process seems straightforward enough. Conceptual design is included in all modern HCI textbooks, and research publications on this topic reflect a general consensus that users' models exist and are important for successful user-system interaction. Yet, there is a dearth of reported cases in which conceptual design has been successfully applied to the design of user interfaces.

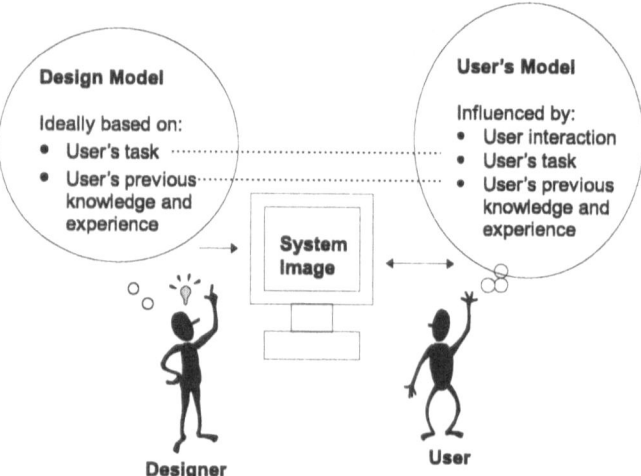

Figure 1: Conceptual Design

1.2   Problems in Applying Conceptual Design

Tognazzini (1991), an eminent user interface designer who subscribes to the idea of conceptual design, reports from experience that formulating a design model and communicating it through the system image, does not necessarily result in the user's model and user behaviour intended by the designer. Firstly, other factors (mainly users' *previous knowledge and experience*) influence the model-building process. Secondly, constructing a "good" design model and communicating it through the user interface is not necessarily a straightforward process. Norman (1986) suggests that

> *"Ideally, the model is based on the user's task, requirements and capabilities [and] must also consider the user's background, experience and the powers and limitations of the user's information processing mechanisms." (p. 47)*

The notion of grounding the design in the *user's task* is central to conceptual design. HCI has produced a number of techniques for analysing and representing users' tasks, but it is not clear how a designer can turn the output into a design model. Due to the lack of guidance as to how users' tasks should be analysed and represented, it is often the *designer's model of the user's task,* rather then the *user's model of the task,* on which the design model is based.

Early HCI literature (e.g. Carroll & Carrithers, 1984) often argued that users are experts at the real-world tasks they are trying to complete (and should not be expected to be experts in electronics and programming as well). Assuming that users have a "perfect" model of the real-world tasks may, however, provide an unrealistic starting point for a conceptual design model, and thereby cause a conceptual design approach to fail. With innovative technology, users may have no conception of a real world task at all for designers to draw on as a starting point for the design model. This leaves users' existing knowledge and experience as a starting point: designers should identify an existing knowledge structure which can be used as a metaphor and function as a design model. There is little guidance on how to identify suitable models, so designers tend to select metaphors they themselves are familiar with. Even when a metaphor is drawn from users' knowledge and experience, many designers do not appreciate that metaphors can facilitate access to and provide a starting point for users' models, but the process of adapting and extending a metaphor into an appropriate user's model needs to be supported for the metaphor to be successful (Wozny, 1989).

Finally, there is little guidance on how to communicate a design model through the user interface; guidance here is limited to generalisms such as *"Design user interface objects which encourage and facilitate user behaviour that is consistent with the design model"* (Tognazzini, 1991).

We have thus identified three problems which user interface designers who are trying to put conceptual design into practice, are likely to encounter:

1. How to construct a design model on the basis of the users' tasks.
2. How to identify users' existing knowledge and experience which provides a basis for a design model.
3. How to communicate a chosen design model through the user interface in a manner which supports the construction of an appropriate users' model.

In section two, we present two simple methods we have developed to assist designers in overcoming the last two problems: a method for identifying appropriate models from users' existing knowledge and experience, and using linguistic elements of the user interface to cue and communicate design models.

1.3   The Session Directory Tool (sdr)

Sdr is a tool for advertising and joining real-time multimedia sessions on the Internet.   Sessions are either broadcasts or interactive meetings, using a combination of audio, video and shared workspace tools. Sdr is presently being used to advertise meetings, ranging from weekly meetings of geographically distributed researchers to NASA broadcasts of space shuttle launches; there are also Internet "radio" and "TV" stations. The functionality provided by sdr can be distinguished into 4 high-level tasks:

1. Seeing what sessions are available.
2. Joining sessions - sdr automatically starts up the relevant audio, video and shared work space tools for the session.
3. Setting up and advertising sessions.
4. Making quick private multimedia "phone calls" to other sdr users.

Like many other new applications which are taking advantage of the new possibilities that the Internet offers, sdr represents a new concept in communication. Explaining what sdr does requires explaining an entire new concept in communication — sdr provides, among other facilities, functions which support Internet telephony, videoconferencing and selecting radio and TV-type broadcasts. Sdr therefore makes an interesting candidate for trying out conceptual design.

2   Applying conceptual design to sdr

Our approach to supporting conceptual design is based on the belief that language plays an important part in forming people's mental models. Johnson-Laird's (1983) theory of mental models identified procedural semantics as the process through which models are constructed, and Manktelow & Jones (1987) state that *"verbal material can be used to evoke existing schemata [mental models] or direct memories"*. Likewise, "verbal material" like everyday talk can be used to elicit people's mental models (Anderson & Alty, 1995). Aitchison (1994) argues that every word is associated with a mental model which in turn brings up associated mental models. For example, if someone hears the word *cat,* she will not only think of a cat in its strictest sense as in a dictionary entry, but probably also think of a particular cat that she used to play with as a child. Depending on her previous experiences with cats, words like *cuddly* or *smelly* might surface as well. Furthermore, there is a good chance that the word *dog* will come to mind as the two words are often used together.

Different people form different mental models of the same thing, and the words that they associate with a particular word will be different from person to person. Our mental models are shaped by cultural factors and individual experiences. Cultural differences can appear between different nations around the world, or different departments in the same company. In this case we are worried about the differences between software designers and users. An expert on networks and multimedia communication will invariably have a different user's model of an application like sdr than a user who has no knowledge of networks.

It was important to try and bridge this gap between the designer and the users by choosing a design model, in this case a metaphor, that could help users form correct users' models of the application. Furthermore, it was important to make the language, i.e. the labels and any instructions (tutorial and help system) linguistically consistent with the design model.

Redesigning the user interface of sdr involved three stages:

1. Identifying a suitable basis for a design model;
2. Applying the design model to sdr;
3. Communicating the design model through the user interface.

2.1   *Identifying a design model*

To find a suitable metaphor to use as a design model, we interviewed existing users of sdr at University College London, and sent out questionnaires to existing users at other sites in the UK and Europe. Our aim was to establish

- which tasks existing users apply sdr to
- which existing functions were most frequently used
- which existing functions users felt were most useful

The responses showed that the most common use of sdr was to see what multimedia events are taking place on the Internet. 11 out of the 16 users who answered the questionnaire use sdr to see what sessions are on more than 3 times a week. 7 users join a session from sdr more than 3 times a week, and only 3 users set up sessions more than 3 times a week.

We also asked existing users how they would explain sdr to a user who was new to Internet conferencing and sdr. Two metaphors emerged from the explanations:

- "Radio Times", a weekly TV listings guide, and
- "Yellow Pages", a telephone directory for businesses.

We compared both metaphors to sdr and decided that the "Radio Times" covered most of its core functionality. The broadcasting domain of the "Radio Times" - selecting or locating TV or radio programmes, and maybe recording them - is more closely related than the telephony domain; for instance, sdr has a strong notion of *time* built into it which is not covered in the Yellow Pages metaphor. Since the task most existing users apply sdr to, is seeing what sessions take place and when they take place, this is a key element that the model needs to cover.

Anderson et al. (1994) suggest that for an interface metaphor to be effective, the features of the metaphor must not differ too much from the features of the application. The core features of the system should be supported by the metaphor. At the same time, the metaphor should not have too much *conceptual baggage* - i.e. a high proportion of features that *do not apply* to the system compared to the amount of features that the metaphor and application have in common. Metaphors with too much conceptual baggage make inefficient design models.

If we look at the core features of sdr and compare them with the actual programme guide in the "Radio Times", we shall see that the main functions of sdr are supported well (see Table 1).

Sdr	"Radio Times"
• Seeing what is on	• Main purpose of "Radio Times"
• Joining sessions	• The "Radio Times" provides the necessary information to watch a programme
• Setting up sessions	• N/A

Table 1: Comparison of sdr and "Radio Times".

And if we look at conceptual baggage, i.e. the features of the "Radio Times" that are not relevant to sdr, we find that the conceptual baggage is, in fact, very small. For each programme in the "Radio Times" the following are listed (see Table 2):

"Radio Times"	Sdr
• time of broadcast	• supported by sdr
• name of program	• supported by sdr
• PDC (video code)	• supported by sdr; sessions can be recorded by the press of a button (not yet implemented)

Table 2: Comparison of "Radio Times" programme listings and sdr.

Furthermore, the following information about the programme may appear after the description (see Table 3):

• stereo	• sdr gives information about the formats of the different media
• subtitled	• not supported by sdr
• repeat	• not supported by sdr
• write to...	• sdr provides details of who to contact about a session
• video plus code	• supported by sdr; sessions can be recorded by the press of a button (not yet implemented)
• reference to a page where more information about the program can be found	• a link to a web page containing more information can be given in sdr
• film ratings	• not supported in sdr
• if the program is a film or a choice, it will have an icon showing one or the other in the corner	• each sdr session is categorised as a test, broadcast or a meeting. This information is shown as a small icon in the session information window

Table 3: Comparison of "Radio Times" programme information and sdr.

If we disregard the journalistic parts of the "Radio Times" with articles about certain topics, programmes or actors/actresses, we can see that the conceptual baggage is minimal as nearly all features in the "Radio Times" are matched in sdr. Furthermore these common features constitute a large part - and the most used part - of sdr.

The major difference between the "Radio Times" and sdr is that the "Radio Times" is printed on paper and sdr is electronic, so rather than using the "Radio Times" as a design model, we extended the metaphor to encompass features of an "Electronic Radio Times".

2.2 Applying the design model

As stated above, we believe that labels and terms which appear in the user interface are an important vehicle for communicating the design model through the user interface and supporting the construction of a user's model. We therefore wanted to establish the terms the "Radio Times" metaphor would evoke in potential new users of sdr. Does a TV programme have a *name* or a *title*? What is the bit underneath the name called - *summary, review, description*? We also considered general broadcasting terminology in an attempt to make the entire user interface linguistically consistent with the metaphor. Another issue was how to deal with the fact that the design model is an *"Electronic Radio Times"*, something which does currently not exist. To find answers to these questions, we interviewed 14 potential users recruited from UCL staff and students, and employees of a major UK bank, representing a diversity of people as prospective sdr users would be, and none of them with previous multicast conferencing experience. The interviews were recorded on tapes and partially transcribed.

From the interviews we identified the words and terms in which users described the "Radio Times." We also found that those users who are familiar with hypertext systems easily imagine an electronic version of the "Radio Times" and the functionality it might provide. The interviewees had many ideas of what features they would like that only an electronic listings guide could provide them with, such as:

- being able to see what was on at a particular time on all the channels;
- a list where only the programme names showed and by clicking on the name, more information about the programme could be obtained;
- program their video recorders by pressing a button in the "Radio Times".

Many similar suggestions were made, and most of the suggested features are already supported in sdr. Users who were not familiar with hypertext systems, on the other hand, were not able to imagine such innovative functionality for an "Electronic Radio Times".

Sdr consists of four main windows: The Main Window lists the sessions alphabetically (see Figure 2). The default setting is a list of all sessions that have been announced. In the next version of sdr to be released, users will be allowed to choose to have sessions listed according to their category - meetings, broadcasts, tests etc. This particular feature was on the wish list for an "Electronic Radio Times": People wanted to be able to list garden programmes or films for the following week.

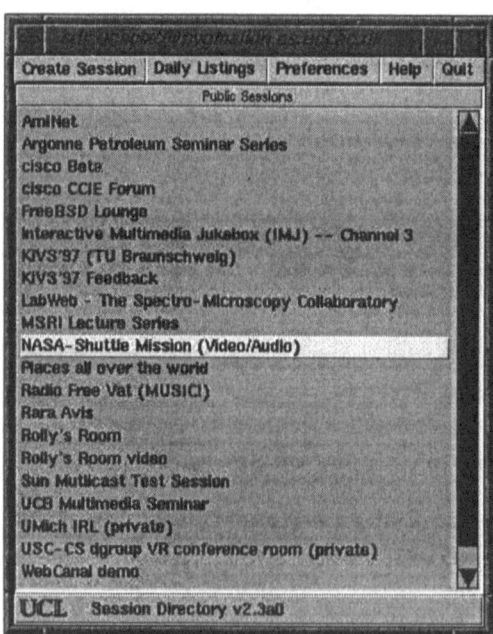

Figure 2: Main Window

From the main window it is possible to open a calendar where the user can see what sessions have been scheduled to take place at any particular day and at what time (see Figure 3). This feature is very similar to the "Radio Times". The only major difference is that the "Radio Times" lists programmes according to which channel they will be broadcast on and within each channel, the programmes are listed in order of appearance. In multimedia communication on the Internet, there are no channels, each session just takes up a certain amount of bandwidth, so the sessions in the calendar are listed alphabetically. But the graphical representation makes it easy to see what sessions are on at any particular time.

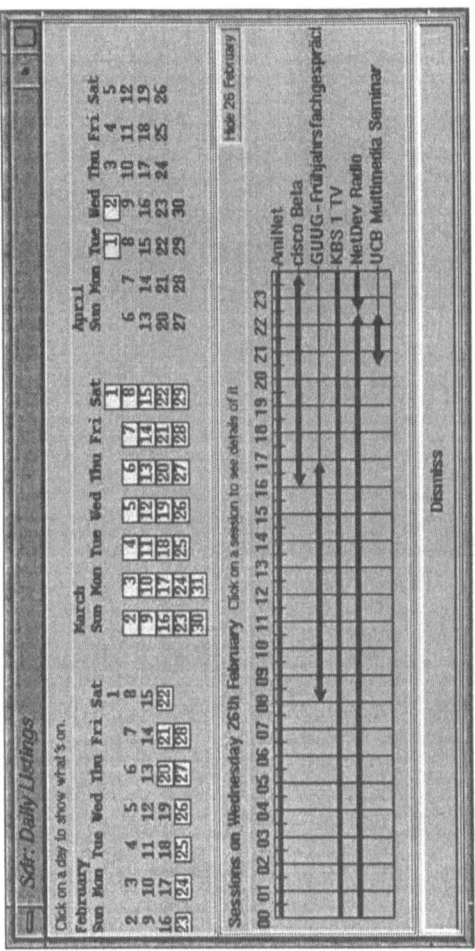

Figure 3: Daily Listings Window.

By clicking on a session in either the Main Window or in the Daily Listings Window, a Session Information Window with more information about the session can be opened (see Figure 4). The window will say when the session is scheduled take place; it might contain a link to a web page; it tells the user who is responsible for the session, or who set it up; which tools or media the session makes use of, audio, video, whiteboard and/or text; the user can invite other people to take part

in the session and finally, the user can join the session. By pressing *join*, sdr will
start up the relevant tools for that particular session.

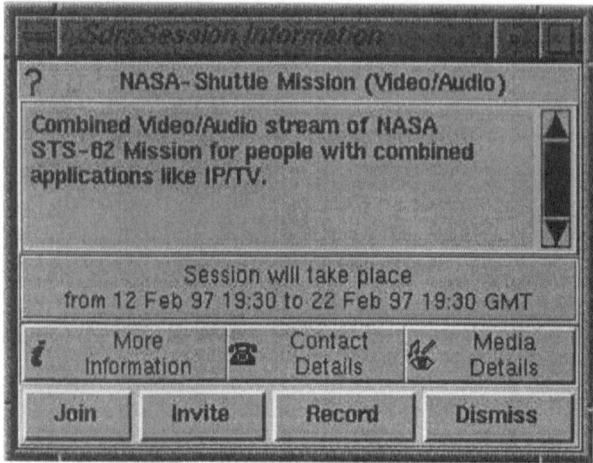

Figure 4: Session Information Window

The last of the main windows allows the user to create and advertise sessions of his
own (see Figure 5). This basically means inputting the information that will
appear in the session information window.

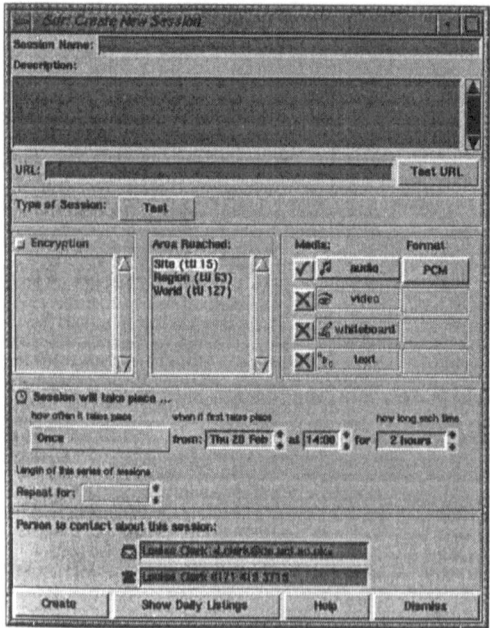

Figure 5: Create New Session Window

2.3   *Communicating the design model*

In this section we describe the main changes which application of the design model to sdr necessitated.

Table 4 lists the main changes to sdr, followed by bullet points describing the changes in further detail.

Original interface	New interface

Main Window
    Calendar
    New
	Main Window (see Figure 2)
	    Daily Listings
	    Create Session

Calendar
    Bookings for...
	Daily Listings Window (see Figure 3)
	    Sessions on...
	    \<Help texts added\>

Session Information Window
    Lifetime/active
    Start All
	Session Information Window (see Figure 4)
	    Session will take place
	    Join

Create New Session Window
    Security
    Scope
    Session   will   be
active...
	Create New Session Window (see Figure 5)
	    Encryption
	    Area Reached
	    Session will take place...

Table 4: Main changes to sdr.

- Daily Listings used to be called Calendar in the original version of sdr. We changed it because we wanted to make it clear that Calendar is the "Radio Times" part of sdr. "Radio Times" was referred to as "programme listings" "programme guide" and "programme directory" by the people interviewed about the "Radio Times". The Calendar corresponds very closely to the "Programme Guide" section in the "Radio Times". However, as "programme guide" and "programme directory" are synonymous, it would not make sense to have the main window called "Session Directory" and then a button called "Session Guide". We therefore settled on "Daily Listings" which is a label that clearly signals that the sessions will be listed daily rather than alphabetically.
  Ideally, we would have liked an initial window in which users would have to choose between *seeing what sessions are available* and *creating sessions*. In this way we could have maintained "session guide" for seeing what sessions are on, and thereby signal linguistically which part of sdr the "Radio Times" metaphor applies to.
- We decided to maintain the word *sessions* to signify that there is a difference between sessions and TV programmes. TV programmes are broadcast, whereas sessions are often interactive with shared workspaces.
- The other major change was to the concept of "lifetime" and "active" which existed in the original version of sdr. "Lifetime" referred to the length of time a session was announced, whereas "active" referred to the time when something

was actually happening in the session. If a user were to set up a session today to
take place every Wednesday between 14.00 and 16.00 for four weeks, the
session's "lifetime" would be from the first Wednesday at 14.00 till the end of the
last of the four sessions. The session would be "active" for four Wednesdays
between 14.00 and 16.00. This information was conveyed both implicitly and
explicitly: A session would appear in the list of sessions in the Main Window
from when it was set up and throughout its "lifetime", whereas it would only
appear in the Calendar on the days where it was "active". Explicitly, this
information could be found in the Session Information Window, where by default
the "lifetime" would be displayed, and the "active" times could be seen by
clicking a button labelled *Detailed Times*. However, for a one-off session,
"lifetime" equals "active" time, and the *Detailed Times* button would not appear
in the Session Information Window.

The notions of "lifetime" and "active" are not covered by the "Electronic Radio
Times" design model, where programmes are either "on" or "not on" at a specific
point in time. We decided after many discussions with sdr's designer to combine
the explicit information, so now the Session Information Window only contains
one box, saying when the session will take place. For recurrent sessions it will
say, for instance, "session will take place every Wednesday at 14.00 for two
hours between 1st February and 26th February". The reason why a session now
"takes place" rather than "being on" is that some sessions are meetings rather
than broadcasts and meetings are not "on". "Take place" was the compromise
that we made with the designer between "lifetime" and "on".

- The last major change was to change the balloon help to be consistent with the
labels in the user interface and to reinforce the design model.

- The changes to the user interface resulted in longer labels (for instance
"Calendar" is 8 characters long, "Daily Listings" is 14 characters long). This
proved a problem for frequent users who have sdr running on the screen all the
time. They want the sdr window as small as possible without it looking
"squashed". The solution to this was to introduce a customisable interface where
users can choose between long and short labels.

- We also performed a heuristic evaluation and did some general "tidying up" to
make the user interface consistent.

3   Evaluating the new interface

The goal of the evaluation was to determine if users who were new to sdr would
form users' models based on the "Electronic Radio Times" design model. We
were, in other words, not only looking for competent performance on a set of tasks,
but also aimed to detect the users' models of sdr. We were looking for linguistic
evidence of the "Electronic Radio Times" design model, as correct completion of
tasks does not necessarily mean that the user has a correct user's model, i.e. the
user might do the right thing for the wrong reasons. Having a correct user's
model, i.e. doing the right thing for the *right* reason, is important in situations like
error recovery etc. In other words, possession of a correct user's model is a
prerequisite for effective use of a system. Sasse (1996) reviewed empirical work
on users' models and concluded that performance results alone may not be reliable
indicators of users' models, and strongly recommends using verbal protocols in

addition. So we were looking for ways of making the users verbalise their thought processes in a natural way. One way of doing this is to have the user to teach someone else about the application (Miyake, 1986). But first we had to introduce the users to sdr and give them time to consolidate a user's model. In the following section we describe the training and evaluation procedure.

3.1   Methods for eliciting mental models

To enable us to compare users' models, we studied both the existing and the new interface. The new user interface was evaluated with 12 users who had never used sdr before (new users), and the existing user interface was tested with 12 users who had been using the original version of sdr (existing users). The reason for evaluating the original as well as the new interface was to provide a control group that we could compare with when eliciting the new users' models. The study was divided into three parts:

Task completion. Users were asked to complete six tasks while thinking aloud. They were told that we would prefer them work out how to do the tasks themselves, but if they got irreversibly stuck, they could ask for help. The tasks were scored, based on whether the subjects had successfully completed the tasks without help or not, and problems that the users had completing the tasks were noted.

Mindmaps. Users were given paper copies of the four main windows of sdr, a large piece of paper, a pen and some glue, and asked to glue the windows onto the piece of paper and draw arrows from one window to another if they thought they could get from one window to the other in sdr. The arrows from the mindmaps were listed in tables and added up to see if there were any differences in the mindmaps of the new users and old users.

Teach-back. Users were asked to teach sdr to a contrived co-learner, whom they were told was new to sdr. In fact, the co-learner knew sdr well and prompted users to explain sdr functionality and behaviour of the user interface. The teach-back sessions were transcribed to supply data in which to look for linguistic evidence of users' models. As mentioned earlier, words are linked together in a semantic network, i.e. words which are closely related will tend to be present at the same time. When looking for evidence of "Electronic Radio Times" based users' models, we were therefore not only concerned with the actual words "Radio Times" and "Daily Listings" but also words closely related to the entire concept of TV and broadcasting.

Existing users performed all three parts in one session. New users did the first part one week and the second and third the following week. The first part the tasks was performed as a practice session for the new users, but they were also asked to use sdr in the week between the first and the second session to familiarise themselves with it. Part one and three were recorded on videotapes and transcribed. The videotapes contain an overlay of two images. One is a frontal image of the users, recorded with a video camera next to the workstation. A camera is an integral part of a multimedia workstation and is a necessary accessory when using sdr and it should therefore not be extraordinarily intrusive to the user. The other image was the screen the users were looking at. By overlaying these two images, and recording them onto a videotape, it is possible to see and hear the user as well as see what the user is doing on the screen, all at the same time.

3.2   Results

The Calendar, or Daily Listings Window as it is now called, was one of the key areas of change to the user interface, and where we expected to find the biggest differences between existing and new users' models. The results show major differences in the mindmaps: 9 of the new users had made the link from the Daily Listings Window to the Session Information Window where sessions are joined from; only 4 of the existing users connected the two windows and only 2 had the arrow pointing the right way. All the existing users had an arrow directly from the Main Window to the Session Information Window, whereas only 9 of the new users had that. This shows that the new users are to a much larger extent aware of the Calendar/Daily Listings Window.

The transcripts from the teach-back sessions show that 8 of the new users began with showing the Calendar/Daily Listings Window to the co-learner, whereas only 1 of the existing users did that. The use of language also differed considerably between the two groups: Half of the new users explicitly used the "Radio Times" metaphor to explain certain features of sdr (mainly the Daily Listings Window), but even new users who did not explicitly mention the "Radio Times" used language belonging to the "Electronic Radio Times" design model. They referred to different "stations" or that sessions were "on" etc. Existing users stated that sessions would be "active".

The change from "lifetime" and "active" to "Session will take place" also evoked differences between the two groups. Most of the existing users had in one way or the other been involved in the development of tools relating to multimedia conferencing. They are very knowledgeable about the technical aspects of sdr, but only one of them could confidently explain the difference between "lifetime" and "active/detailed times". Typically, an existing user would state that a session with a "lifetime" of two months, would be "active" for two months. None of the new users had any problems finding out when the sessions were on. The fact that new users with less knowledge of the domain developed an accurate representation of the functionality where users experienced in the domain had a misrepresentation is a very encouraging result.

Results indicate that 8 of the new users had few or no problems teaching sdr to the co-learner. 5 users communicated models clearly based on the "Electronic Radio Times" design model. (We suspect that the number could have been 7, had it not been for a software bug in the Daily Listings Window which caused some sessions not to appear in the Daily Listings Window, despite the fact that they were "on" — this appears to have disturbed the construction of their users' models, particularly because the sessions that did not appear in the Daily Listings Window, were "exciting" ones like the NASA shuttle launches and a Canadian Internet TV station.)

We analysed the transcripts from the teach-back sessions for "Electronic Radio Times" based users' models. All users successfully completed all main tasks for sdr. However, they all encountered problems at some time during the session. These problems were divided into major and minor problems. The users who successfully completed all tasks without any major problems, were categorised as having successful task performance.

The criteria for determining whether users had an "Electronic Radio Times" based user's model were:

- Users who had no major problems, or one major problem unrelated to the listing of sessions, and who explicitly used words like "Radio Times", "TV guide" or "TV listings" to explain the functionality of the Daily Listings Window and who implicitly placed importance on the Daily Listings Window by, for example referring to it often or pointing out that to them the Daily Listings Window was an important feature of sdr, showing the Daily Listings Window as the first thing to the co-learner etc., or simply using "Radio Times" related language were classified as having "Electronic Radio Times" based users' models (4 users).

- Users who did not explicitly mention "Radio Times" but who implicitly indicated that it was the foundation of their user's model as described above, were also classified as having "Electronic Radio Times" based users' models (1 user).

- However, users who explicitly mentioned the "Radio Times", but did not show any implicit evidence, were *not* classified as having "Electronic Radio Times" based users' models (2 users).

#	STP	ERT	Comments
1	+	+	Goes straight to the Daily Listings Window and calls it *"the sort of Radio Times in that it tells you what's on when"*
2	+	+	About sdr, *"sdr is a multimedia tool which enables you basically to network between various persons and stations throughout the Internet"*. "Stations" is a word belonging to TV more than networking. Later, when the co-learner asks about the time information in the Session Information Window, *"Imagine, if you will, the analogy of the Radio Times, which gives you listings of when a program is going to be and you switch on at that time to watch the program..."*
3	+	-	No problems, but very little "Radio Times" related language. He says about the Daily Listings Window, *"If you wanna check what's on"* which is different from most existing users who use language like "active" and "up and running" rather than saying that sessions are "on"
4	-	-	Has got a couple of major problems, in particular concerning the difference between the listings in the Main Window and the Daily Listings Window. We believe, however, that this is because of the software bug in the Daily Listings Window.

5	-	+	Has got a major problem in relation to the different media that sdr sessions make use of. About the Daily Listings Window, "*From there you can go and see what else is on...not this one* [main window], *but the Radio Times sort of daily listings.*"
6	+	+	Starts out with, "*...it's like a TV guide, Radio Times, something like that, and within you can find out what sort of programmes, in quotes, are being run every moment on the multicast backbone of the Internet*" and later on, "*and this* [points to the Daily Listings button] *is where you find out what's going on. That's the real Radio Times, if you will, so you can click on that and you'll get a window.*"
7	+	+	Goes straight to the Daily Listings Window, "*We might as well go straight for the daily listings to find out what's happening today*"
8	-	-	Has similar problems to user number 4.
9	-	-	Has several major problems. However, makes use of the "Radio Times" metaphor in an hitherto unused context, "*OK, like this is description* [points to the description box in the Create Session Window] *like, you know, in the Radio Times there are sometimes movies and they will refer you to so and so and they will give you a little summary, so that is what that is, what the session is going to be about*"
10	+	(-)	Starts off by saying, "*sdr is like a Radio Times*", but does not pursue the metaphor. Has a good understanding of sdr, but without the metaphor. We believe that this might be due to the software bug, as she enjoys watching the CBC Newsworld session which does not show up in the Daily Listings Window.
11	+	-	Has in a conversation later told us that she did not understand the metaphor until halfway through the teach-back session...
12	+	(-)	Shows some indirect evidence of having an "Electronic Radio Times" based user's model, but not quite enough. Like user 10, his favourite session, the NASA shuttle launch, did not appear in the Daily Listings Window.

\# (user number), STP (Successful task performance) ERT ("Electronic Radio Times" based user's model)

Table 5: Successful task performance and users' models of new users

Table 5 shows a list of users with an indication of whether they had successful task performance (STP) and "Electronic Radio Times" based user's models (ERT), followed by a few examples as to why they were categorised as such.

4   Conclusions

The paper reports a case study of applied conceptual design to create a user interface for a tool with novel functionality; results indicate that users' models of the tool were successfully shaped through:

- identifying a suitable metaphor from users' existing knowledge and experience;
- adapting the metaphor into a suitable design model;

- communicating the design model through the user interface through structural and linguistic features.

The evaluation results show that new users, without prior experience with multimedia- or videoconferencing, competently performed a set of tasks after a short period of training and practice. Linguistic evidence indicates that many (7 out of 12) were drawing on the design model when describing sdr, whereas a comparison group of existing users did not. The design model was communicated via the labels in sdr's interface. This indicates that the linguistics elements of the user interface are very important in cueing the construction of users' models, and that careful engineering of these elements can support the construction of the desired user's model. Our next step will be to engineer the visual elements of the user interface in a similar manner. Visual elements, such as icons, are already widely employed to communicate metaphors, but we would argue that they would be more effective if their selection and use would follow a procedure similar to the one employed for the linguistic elements in this study.

When constructing the design model, it is of paramount importance to start from the users' view of the task, or existing knowledge and experience. If potential users have no experience with videoconferencing, for instance, there is little point in using this as the basis for the design model. Likewise, ensuring linguistic consistency within the metaphor in the interface is an important part of supporting users building a correct and useable user's model. Both of these tasks are painstaking and piecemeal work, but we feel encouraged to persist in developing conceptual design in this manner. By adding more concrete techniques for identifying, adapting and communicating design models, we can develop the idea of conceptual design into an applicable method through which designers can support users in the construction of appropriate users' models. The emphasis must be on techniques which help designers to identify and build on users' tasks and knowledge and experience. In our experience, designers often reject suitable models as "too simple" or "wrong"; this assessment is made on the basis of their own knowledge and experience, and that of their peers. The results from this study illustrate that simpler models can be extremely useful if they are selected and implemented with care; the resulting user interface may enable users without knowledge of the underlying domain to use applications as competently as experienced users with knowledge of the domain.

Acknowledgments

We would like to thank Mark Handley, the designer of sdr; for his co-operation in the design and implementation of the new user interface. We would also like to thank Anne Adams who acted as the contrived learner in the study. Finally, we would like to thank all users who took part in the study as users. For more information about where to obtain sdr etc. see http://www-mice-nsc.cs.ucl.ac.uk/mice-nsc/ For more technical details of multicasting on the Internet, see Handley & Jacobson (1996) and Macedonia & Brutzman (1994).

References

Aitchison, J. (1994): Words in the Mind. Oxford, UK: Blackwell.

Anderson, B. & Alty, J. L. (1995): Everyday Theories, Cognitive Anthropology and User-centered System Design. In Kirby, M. A. R., Dix, A. J. & Finlay, J. E.: *People and Computers X - Proceedings of HCI'95*, Huddersfield, pp 121-135.

Anderson, B., Smyth, M., Knott, R. P., Bergan, M., Bergan, J. & Alty, J. L. (1994): Minimising Conceptual Baggage: Making choices about metaphor. In Cockton, G., Draper, W. W. & Weir, G. R. S.: *People and Computers IX - Proceedings of HCI'94*, Glasgow, pp 179-194.

Carroll, J. M. & Carrithers, C. (1984): Blocking Learner Error States in a Training Wheels System. *Human Factors*, 26(4), 377-389.

Handley, M. & Jacobson, V. (1996): SDP: Session Description Protocol, Internet-Draft.

Johnson-Laird, P.N. (1983): Mental Models. Cambridge, England: Cambridge University Press.

Macedonia, M. & Brutzman, D. (1994): Mbone provides audio and video across the Internet. In *IEEE Computer Magazine*, April 1994.

Manktelow, K. & Jones, J. (1987): Principles from the Psychology of Thinking and Mental Models. In: Gardiner, M. M. & Christie, B. [Eds.]: *Applying Cognitive Psychology to User-Interface Design*. Chichester: Wiley.

Miyake, N. (1986): Constructive interaction and the iterative process of understanding. *Cognitive Science*, 10, pp 151-77.

Norman, D. A. (1986): Cognitive Engineering. In Norman D. A. & Draper S. W. [Eds.]:*User-Centered System Design: New perspectives in human-computer interaction*. Hillsdale, NJ: LEA.

Sasse M. A. (1996): Eliciting and Describing Users' Models of Computer Systems. Unpublished PhD Thesis, School of Computer Science, The University of Birmingham.

Tognazzini, B. (1991): TOG on Interface. Reading, MA: Addison-Wesley.

Wozny, L. A. (1989): The Application of Metaphor, Analogy and Conceptual Models in Computer Systems. *Interacting with Computers*, 1, 273-283.

Computer Anxiety and the Human-Computer Interface

Donald Day[1] & Päivi Mäkirinne-Crofts[2]

[1]*School of Information Systems, The University of New South Wales, Sydney NSW 2052 Australia*
Tel: +61 (0)2 9385 4760
Fax: +61 (0)2 9662 4061
Email: d.day@acm.org

[2]*Lately of:* [1]*Centre for Study of CAD, Cheltenham & Gloucester College of Higher Education, Pittville Campus, Albert Road, Cheltenham GL52 2JG UK*

Despite widespread PC use in recent decades, many users remain anxious about their ability to cope with computers. This paper reports a study evaluating how interface features contribute to computer anxiety. Key constructs include cultural and individual differences, interface quality, self-efficacy, ease of use, user attitudes and intended usage behaviour. Findings indicate that anxious users prefer innovative I/O devices, experience low self-efficacy, and dislike inconsistent status messages and blocked-option menus. Intended usage behaviour appears to be inversely related to levels of computer anxiety. These findings provide moderate support for a modified Technology Acceptance Model proposed by the study.

Keywords: computer anxiety, interface quality, self-efficacy.

1 Introduction

The venue is Nottingham, the famous haunt of Robin Hood, in days of old. It is 1811. Masked men are shot down by their employer during a pre-dawn raid, for trying to attack textile machines that are felt to threaten jobs and families. A mass trial ends with several Luddites hanged in public and others "transported" to Australia (Reid, 1986; Rosengarten & Smith, 1981).

Five generations pass. In the United States, on a continent far removed from Nottingham, disenchanted postal workers pour honey onto data entry devices (Henderson, Deane & Ward, 1995, citing Dickson, Simmons, & Anderson, 1974). And, an intellectual known for his work in human creativity laments that "It will be a sinister day when computers start to laugh, because that will mean they are capable of a lot of other things as well" (DeBono, 1969).

The link between 19th Century Luddites, and 20th Century postal workers and intellectuals, is their aversion to new technology. Contributing to their fear is the fact that terminals, word processors and PCs have reached the same per capita level of penetration in a few decades that it took the telephone 75 years to achieve (Gardner, Young, and Ruth, 1989, citing Gantz, 1986). Incredible as it may be, 40 percent of individuals who use computers may be "computer anxious" (Gardner, Young, and Ruth, 1989; Weil, Rosen, and Wugalter, 1990). The persistence of anxiety reactions may be due in part to computing's very ubiquitousness, as spreading technology continues to force new groups of initiates into computer use for the first time.

2   Computer Anxiety

Before examining the role that interface design plays in the fear of computers, it is important to define the key construct "computer anxiety" and to examine its context.

Computer anxiety may be considered "...a function of fear and apprehension, intimidation, hostility and worries that one will be embarrassed, look stupid, or even damage the equipment" (Heinssen, Glass and Knight, 1987).

Sheridan (1980) identifies seven "factors in alienation" which also may contribute to computer anxiety:

- feelings of inferiority and threatened obsolescence,
- isolation from end processes or products,
- de-skilling and re-skilling,
- access to information and power by the technologically literate,
- mystification of the workings of computers,
- fear of catastrophic failure, and
- fear that machines will replace people.

All seven factors threaten the atmosphere of trust that is important to a productive relationship between users and machines. This relationship occurs within the context of ethical and social concerns that often escape the notice of computer professionals (Huff and Finholt, 1994).

Research has shown that breakdowns in trust may be triggered by common locus of control and computer reliability problems (Rosen and Weil, 1995), and by feelings of intimidation (Shore, 1985). The uneasy state of trust between users and machines also may be due to the perceived threat of computers to human identity (Mruk, 1987). As automated systems have assumed roles and capabilities which for ages have been the sole province of humans, it has become increasingly difficult for some to distinguish the actions of people from those of automated tools.

This blurring of boundaries is especially distressing to craftspeople such as fashion designers. For them, the introduction of automated design and manufacturing represents a serious interruption of the symbiotic relationship between them and their traditional tools. Fashion designers consider such tools to be extensions of self. The use of computers isolates the creator from the created -- a profoundly disturbing estrangement in which tactile properties are ignored and an impoverished 2-D representation is substituted for the infinitely richer 3-D world. Many creative users feel that computers interfere with private cognitive processes such as incubation and gestation that are vital to their work. For example, interference takes place as computers force premature extrusion of designs under construction from mind to machine (Mäkirinne-Crofts et al, 1995; Godwin, Mäkirinne-Crofts, & Saadat, 1996; Aldrich, 1992). To a fashion designer, the computer is an obstacle that stresses process over product -- not a partner.

The extent of frustration with technology experienced by creative users is demonstrated by the following anecdote describing a student in fashion school, contributed by the second author.

> `I recall a girl in college with a knitting machine, frustrated and under stress, tearing the sharp, long needles out of the needle bed; her bare hands bleeding, swearing and crying with pain. Usually one has a tool to remove the latched needles. It was no good for the work or the knitting machine, but it got her fury out.'

Some people respond to computer fears by adopting *anthropocentrism.* Anthropocentrism is "the tendency of individuals to perceive the world from a human-centred perspective", espousing a doctrine that it is not acceptable for computers to fill routinised, interpretative, and personal roles traditionally held only be people (Nass et al, 1995). Anthropocentrism is in part a psychological construct. Much of the work in computer anxiety addresses the psychological impacts of change. Various authors have cited theories of individual reactance (Nelson and Kletke, 1990), expectancy (Gallo, 1986), operant conditioning (Henderson, Deane & Ward, 1995), and even early childhood experiences (Weil, Rosen & Wugalter, 1990) to explain computer anxiety.

Individual reactance proposes that individuals display resistance toward change when they perceive that the change threatens potential losses. *Expectancy* suggests that an individual would want to learn a new computer technique if he believed that only a modest amount of effort would result in learning, which in turn would lead to improved, valued productivity. *Operant conditioning* states that anxiety motivates individuals to avoid the stimulus for anxiety (i.e., computers). According to this theory, success in avoidance for long periods reinforces individuals' capacity to diminish anxiety (and to avoid computers). The importance of *childhood experiences* is based in "contagion" theory (our term) which holds that individuals assimilate negative attitudes toward technology from the people who first teach them about technology -- people who themselves are not particularly comfortable with automated tools.

Computer anxiety appears to be treatable through the use of psychologically based intervention strategies (Rosen, Sears and Weil, 1993; Nelson and Kletke, 1990). However, it might be argued that it would be better if such anxieties were avoided, rather than treated. Therefore, the object of the current study is to evaluate the extent to which features of the human-computer interface contribute to feelings of computer anxiety among users.

Why should HCI professionals be concerned about computer anxiety?

In describing what they term the "design ethic", Huff and Finholt (1994) argue that ethical concern and social awareness must be part of decision-making in computer design -- a case also made by Coldwell (1993). Huff and Finholt's argument is that because of obligations implicit in the computer professional's specialised knowledge, it is his or her responsibility to recognise the impacts that designs may have on users. Such impacts may arise from interface design. Igbaria and Chakrabarti (1990) find that the interaction between users and systems has a strong positive effect on attitudes toward computers, and that quality interface design is associated with significant reductions in computer anxiety. Furthermore, *quality* interface design appears to be *simpler* interface design (Rosen and Weil, 1994; Szlichcinski, 1983).

3   Experimental Design

3.1   Research Model

The current study is guided by a modified Technology Acceptance Model (Figure 1) based initially on Davis (1993). Davis's model specifies the relationships among system design features, perceived usefulness, perceived ease of use, attitude toward using technology, and actual usage behaviour. Its measurement validity is verified in Davis and Venkatesh (1996). In the current study, perceived usefulness has become perceived self-efficacy. Computer anxiety is added as a major intervening construct, and system quality is implemented as interface quality.

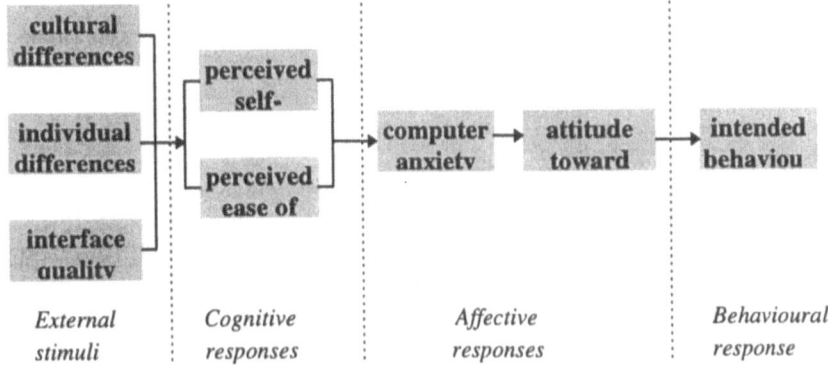

Figure 1: Research Model

3.2 Constructs in the Literature

Several of the constructs in Figure 1 have been addressed in previous work.
Weil and Rosen (1995) find that five cultural factors influence computer fear:

- public attitudes toward technology,
- general cultural characteristics,
- political climate,
- computer use in the educational system, and
- general availability of technological innovations.

For example, these authors report that Australian subjects are characterised by high experience with computers, yet exhibit medium levels of technophobia. Other cross-cultural research relevant to either computer anxiety or to interface effects is reported in Rosen and Weil (1995), Omar (1992), Allwood and Wang (1990), and Day (1996).

Igbaria and Chakrabarti (1990) suggest that demographic variables may influence attitudes (but only indirectly), via their effects on computer anxiety. Based on females' significantly higher levels of maths anxiety, Bandalos and Benson (1990) note that women may have higher levels of computer anxiety than men, as found previously by Dambrot et al (1985). In their validation of the Computer Attitude Scale, Bandalos and Benson report that older users also experience higher anxiety. However, they attribute this effect to such users' lower levels of experience with computers.

In a study of 23 countries Weil and Rosen (1995) find that experience with computers is associated significantly with reduced levels of technophobia. Handzic, Low and O'Connor (1994) find that individuals' previous computer experience affects their intention to use information technology, by influencing their beliefs about usefulness and ease of use. Igbaria and Chakrabarti (1990) propose that training may reduce computer anxiety and improve attitudes toward computers, but only as mediated by improvements in perceived self-efficacy. However, Rosen and Maguire (1990) maintain in a meta-analytic study of 81 studies that individual differences have *not* been consistently proven to be strongly associated with computerphobia.

Henderson, Deane and Ward (1995) find that self-efficacy is the best predictor of computer anxiety. Igbaria, Schiffman and Wieckowski (1994) find that acceptance is due more to perceived usefulness than to the fun perceived in using computer technology.

Kernan and Howard (1990) argue that computer anxiety and attitudes must be treated as separate constructs, and report that both anxiety and attitude have low predictive validity in terms of user behaviour. However, Fishbein and Ajzen (1975), propose that behavioural *intention* is predictive of behaviour. Gardner, Young and Ruth (1989) suggest that fear of computers has a negative impact on both user attitudes and productivity.

Constructs in the research model were operationalised by mapping them to questionnaire response items. For two constructs (self-efficacy and anxiety), items were summarised as composite scales (see "Materials" and "Procedure", below). The response items mapped to each construct are presented in Table 1.

3.3   Research Questions

The following research questions guide data analysis in the current study.

1. To what extent does interface design impact users' perceptions of self-efficacy?
2. To what extent does interface design impact users' computer anxiety?
3. To what extent does computer anxiety impact users' intended behaviour when they encounter difficult interfaces?

4   Method

4.1   Subjects

Participants consisted of 291 largely first- and second-year students in two introductory information systems subjects at The University of New South Wales (Sydney, Australia). Because the two subjects selected are required of most Commerce and Economics students at UNSW (regardless of major), a diverse group of business disciplines is represented.

4.2 Materials

Data were collected using a 37-item, three-page questionnaire including 27 five-point Likert scale questions, one response scenario, four closed-option items, and two open-ended items. Of these, those dealing with computer anxiety and self-efficacy (one-third of items in the questionnaire) had been validated in previous studies (see note to Table 1). The scale items were anchored at either end by "disagree" and "agree"; there were no labels for intermediate scale points. Respondents were provided with a sample question, to demonstrate how to answer scale questions; the instrument was headed by an introduction stressing subject anonymity and the fact that completing the form was not to be considered a test (that there were no right or wrong answers). The header also identified the researchers and their institutions.

4.3 Procedure

Participants were selected at random (only those attending lecture on arbitrarily selected days completed questionnaires). Instruments were distributed with the co-operation of lecturers-in-charge. Students were given between 10 and 20 minutes to complete the questionnaire. Due to the in-class administration, the response rate was 100 percent.

Following data entry, items were allocated to research model constructs. Perceived self-efficacy and computer anxiety scales were built from groups of items, using reliability analysis. The Cronbach alpha for the self-efficacy scale was .76; for the anxiety scale, .79. These levels are considered respectable (DeVellis, 1991). Simple descriptive statistics, Pearson correlations, cross-tabulations, and an ANOVA were generated, using SPSS-PC.

5 Results

5.1 Descriptive Statistics

Three-quarters of respondents were ages 17-20, with an additional 21.4% ages 21-24. Fifty-four percent were female. Two-thirds were in their first year at university; 22.3% in second year. Nearly half (48.5%) use a computer from 2-to-9 hours per week, and only a few (13.1%) had taken more than three computer-related subjects at university.

In terms of interface quality, respondents indicated that frequent, consistently positioned status messages and cultural familiarity promote feelings of trust in computers. Nearly two-thirds said that they often get excited about what they can do with a computer, with nearly as many reporting that their world views match those represented in computers. Although they said that the design of interfaces is not central to their level of trust in computers, respondents also reported that the more important that they feel interfaces are, the more computer anxious they tend to be (r=.33, p<.000).

When asked how they would react if ordered to use a computer at work that had a confusing interface and a hard to understand help facility, 49.6% said they would ask a colleague for help while about 23% each said they would either ask their boss for training or simply master the machine on their own. Responses suggest that a confusing interface would be more frustrating than a poor help facility.

As a sample, respondents reported somewhat low computer anxiety (mean 1.5 of 5) and somewhat high self-efficacy (3.3 of 5). However, males reported lower computer anxiety and substantially higher self-efficacy than females (males = 1.3 anxiety, 3.6 efficacy; females = 1.8 anxiety, 3.1 efficacy; p<.000).

5.2   Associative Statistics

Of most interest are the interface quality findings, which suggest that users' self-efficacy is lower if they like voice input and output, feel interface design is important to trust, and like consistently positioned, frequent status messages. Their self-efficacy also tends to be lower if they dislike menus that feature blocked selections. Computer anxiety tends to be higher the more users dislike blocked selection menus, and the more they like voice-activated interfaces.

An analysis of variance among users' behavioural intentions and their computer anxiety is reported in Table 3.

The ANOVA indicates significant differences in computer anxiety among groups, based on their intended behaviour. The most anxious are those who would damage their computers, with those who would give up and look for a new job second. The least anxious are users who would accept the interface and get on with their work.

6   Discussion

6.1   Validation of Theory

6.1.1   Research Questions

Question 1: This study finds low but significant correlations among three interface features and self-efficacy. It appears that level of concern about interface design is inverse to level of self-efficacy.

Question 2: This study also finds a low but significant correlation between interface design and computer anxiety, with anxiety varying directly with levels of concern about interface features.

Question 3: This study finds that low anxiety is associated with confident, self-supporting behaviour. Low anxiety users apparently prefer to engage technology, rather than avoiding it.

External Stimuli

Cultural Differences

24. Trusts culturally adapted interfaces more.

33. Language spoken at home during childhood.

Individual Differences

31. Age.

32. Gender.

34. Hours of computer use in a typical week.

35. Course of study at uni.

36. Year of study at uni.

37. Number of computer-related subjects taken at uni.

Interface Quality

2. Interface design determines trust or distrust.

5. Voice recognition less intimidating.

6. Consistently placed status messages lead to trust.

9. Blocked menu selections lead to distrust.

Cognitive Responses

Perceived Self-Efficacy

13. Lots of self-confidence using computers.[1]

15. Gets sinking feeling when using computers.[1]

16. Feels OK solving new problems with computers.[1]

18. Confident could learn computer skills.[2]

19. Difficulty in understanding technical matters.[2]

22. Machine responsible if subject fails at tasks.

23. Acceptance tied to degree computer controls tasks.

25. Fear of mistakes stops use of computers.[3]

Perceived Ease of Use

4. Don't use computer if must use help often.

Affective Responses

Computer Anxiety

1. Distrust computers

11. Computer hostile people are ridiculous.

12. Computers do not scare me.[1]

17. No threat when others talk about computers.[1]

20. Computers kind of strange and frightening.[2]

21. Subject not a part of the computer revolution.[2]

26. Subject afraid of damaging computer.[3]

27. Apprehensive about using computers.[4]

Attitude Toward Using

8. Computer and subject world views mismatched.

14. Often excited about computer capabilities.

Behavioural Response

Behavioural Intention

28. Action when facing difficult to use interface.

29. Impact of confusing interface.

30. Impact of useless, detailed, confusing help.

Notes: (1) Bandalos & Benson, 1990; (2) Kernan & Howard, 1990; (3) Igbaria, Schiffman & Wieckowski, 1994; (4) Heinssen, Glass & Knight, 1987.

Table 1: Response item—construct allocations.

6.1.2 *Findings Compared to Other Studies*

Rosen and Maguire (1990) assert that the influence of individual differences on behaviour is unproven. However, this study shows that there are in fact weak links among individual differences, anxiety, and behaviour. Further, it suggests that experience with computers, training, and gender influence self-efficacy, as predicted by several studies.

Weil and Rosen (1995) report that experience with computers reduces levels of anxiety. Findings here suggest that there is indeed an inverse relationship between experience and anxiety.

Igbaria and Chakrabarti (1990) say that training may lead to self-efficacy, which in turn may reduce computer anxiety and negative attitudes. This study finds a small but significant relationship between training and self-efficacy. Moreover, there appears to be a strong and significant relationship between self-efficacy and anxiety (as reported previously by Henderson, Dean, and Ward, 1995). Also, we find a substantial and significant inverse relationship between anxiety and attitude.

Kernan and Howard (1990) report that neither anxiety nor attitude can predict behaviour. However, both influences on behaviour are supported in the current study.

Finally, Gardner, Young and Ruth (1989) predict that computer anxiety influences user attitudes. This study finds an inverse relationship between these two constructs. Links among interface design, self-efficacy, anxiety and behaviour are supported, by low but significant correlations which nevertheless fall short of predictive validity.

| | *Corr* | *Signif* |
	Self-Efficacy	
Cultural Differences		
Distrust foreign interfaces	-.06	.327
Individual Differences		
Age	-.07	.221
Year at university	.03	.677
Computer use in typical week	.46	.000*
Computer-related subjects	.22	.000*
Interface Quality		
Dislike blocked menus	-.31	.000*
Like voice I/O	-.27	.000*
Importance of interface design	-.23	.000*
Like status messages	-.11	.058

	Corr	Signif.
		Anxiety
Cultural Differences		
Distrust foreign interfaces	-.01	.914
Individual Differences		
Age	.04	.474
Year at university	.02	.787
Computer use in typical week	-.41	.000*
Computer-related subjects	-.15	.012*
Interface Quality		
Dislike blocked menus	.27	.000*
Like voice I/O	.25	.000*
Importance of interface design	.33	.000*
Like status messages	.01	.816
Perceived Self-Efficacy	-.77	.000*
Attitude Toward Using		
Excited about computer	-.40	.000*
Mismatch of world view	.23	.000*

Notes (1) "*" indicates statistical significance at $p<.05$; (2) Self-Efficacy and Anxiety are combined-item scales; (3) terms shown here were selected for brevity of presentation -- they are not the actual wording used in the questionnaire.

Table 2: Self-efficacy and anxiety associations.

	N	Mean	s.d.
Intended Behaviour			
Damage computer	4	2.47	.78
Find new job	3	2.04	.40
Ask for training	61	1.60	.72
Ask for help	127	1.57	.74
Get on with job	60	1.36	.73

Notes (1) Behavioural intentions when confronted with a difficult interface;
(2) $F_{(4,250)} = 3.03$; $p=.018$).

Table 3: Intended behaviour by computer anxiety.

6.2   Instrument Refinement

Following initial data collection and analysis, the questionnaire was analysed to identify weak items and semantic biases, in preparation for expansion of the study.

A non-response analysis resulted in elimination of two scenario items which respondents tended not to answer. One question was split into two, and another totally reworded, to avoid ambiguities in answers because the questions contained more than one major referent. Two questions became one because their meaning overlapped substantially, and two new questions were added to act as filters to test for the extent of respondent's use of computers. As a result of these filters, it also was necessary to rearrange several blocks of items to ensure logical progression.

7   Conclusion

It is not likely that the control interfaces of textile machines were a significant cause of Luddite anger, but fears similar to theirs clearly are influenced by computer interfaces of today. Man is easily threatened when he feels out of control of his own environment or destiny. Fear of those, be they human or machine, who are perceived to have power, or to be associated with an influence over him, is a normal reaction. Fear frequently results in a hostile reaction, acts of aggression which can be interpreted as self-defense -- a "fight or flight" response. Are the factors surrounding the Luddites any different from factors affecting today's workforces, who must adapt faster than the processes of new learning take place? Regardless of the answer, findings of this study suggest that by enhancing or degrading perceptions of self-efficacy, interfaces affect users' computer anxiety, which in turn affects their intended behaviour.

Considerable work remains in the investigation of these effects. In particular, it may be fruitful to assess the impact of non-standard interfaces -- those without a familiar "look and feel" -- upon users' levels of anxiety, when they encounter new systems. Future work also may address users' coping mechanisms and levels of induced stress when anxiety occurs, as well as examine other interface properties that may influence anxiety.

This study established a link between the technology acceptance and computer anxiety literatures -- a link which needs to be enriched via larger studies, incorporating direct observation of user responses to various interface design features.

This research now has turned to the collection of data from non-Australian populations and from disciplines other than commerce and economics. Thus far, the refined questionnaire has been administered to students in South Africa; future data collection is planned both in other locales (e.g., England) and among non-student populations. The addition of adult subjects will strengthen findings, by lessening problems associated with students -- such as their relative familiarity with (and presumed lack of anxiety toward) computers, and their apparent lack of concern about the impact of computing in the workplace. We anticipate that comparison of such data with those reported here will add depth to the understanding of how adjustments to interface design may ease some users' computer anxiety.

Acknowledgements

The research reported here was supported in part by a Small Research Grant from the Faculty of Commerce & Economics, The University of New South Wales (Sydney).

The first author expresses his appreciation for the contributions of Päivi Mäkirinne-Crofts, who died of cancer in North Leigh, Oxon, not long after this paper was submitted for consideration by HCI'97.

References

Aldrich, W. (1992). *CAD in Clothing and Textiles: A Collection of Expert Views.* Oxford: Blackwell Scientific.

Allwood, C. & Wang, Z-M. (1990). Conceptions of computers among students in China and Sweden. *Computers in Human Behavior* 6, 185-199.

Bandalos, D. & Benson, J. (1990). Testing the factor structure invariance of a computer attitude scale over two grouping conditions. *Educational and Psychological Measurement* 50, 49-60.

Coldwell, R.A. (1993). University students' attitudes towards computer crime: a research note. *Computers and Society* 23(1-2, July), 11-13.

Dambrot, F., Watkins-Malek, M., Silling, S.M., Marshall, R. & Garver, J.A. (1985). Correlates of sex differences in attitudes toward and involvement with computers. *Journal of Vocational Behavior* 27, 71-86.

Davis, F. (1993). User acceptance of information technology: system characteristics, user perceptions and behavioral impacts. *International Journal of Man-Machine Studies* 38, 475-487.

Davis, F. & Venkatesh, V. (1996). A critical assessment of potential measurement biases in the technology acceptance model: three experiments. *International Journal of Human-Computer Studies* 45, 19-45.

Day, D. (1996). Cultural bases of interface acceptance: foundations. *Computers and People IX*, 35-47. Proceedings of the 11th BCS Human-Computer Interaction Specialist Group conference, 20-23 August 1996, Imperial College. London: Springer-Verlag.

DeBono, E. (1969), *The Mechanism of Mind.* London: Jonathon Cape.

DeVellis, R. (1991). *Scale Development: Theory and Applications.* Applied Social Research Methods Series, Vol. 26. Newbury Park, CA: Sage.

Dickson, G., Simmons, J., & Anderson, J. (1974). Behavioural reactions to the introduction of a management information system at the US Post Office: some empirical observations. In Sanders, D. (Ed.), *Computers and Management*, 2d ed., 410-421. New York: McGraw-Hill.

Fishbein, M. & Ajzen, I. (1975). *Belief, Attitude, Intention and Behavior: An Introduction to Theory and Research.* Reading, Mass.: Addison-Wesley.

Gallo, D. (1986). Expectancy Theory as a predictor of individual response to computer technology. *Computers in Human Behavior* 2, 31-41.

Gantz, J. (1986). The growing power of the telecom manager. *Telecommunication Products Plus Technology* 4, 33.

Gardner, E., Young, P. & Ruth, S. (1989). Evolution of attitudes toward computers: a retrospective view. *Behaviour and Information Technology* 8(2), 89-98.

Godwin, W., Mäkirinne-Crofts, P., & Saadat, S. (1996). Objects in transition: a spatial paradigm for creative design. In Candy, L. & Edmonds, E.A., *Creativity and Cognition 1996*, 37-44. Proceedings, 2nd International Symposium, 29 April - 2 May 1996. Loughborough, UK: LUTCHI Research Centre.

Handzic, M., Low, G., & O'Connor, M. (1994). The effect of previous computer experience on user acceptance of information technology. In *Proceedings of the 5th Australian Conference on Information Systems* ACIS'94, 621-634. Sept. 17-19, Melbourne, Australia. Melbourne: Australian Computer Society.

Heinssen, R., Glass, C., & Knight, L. (1987). Assessing computer anxiety: development and validation of the Computer Anxiety Rating Scale. *Computers in Human Behaviour* 3, 49-59.

Henderson, R.D., Deane, F.P., & Ward, M.J. (1995). Occupational differences in computer-related anxiety: implications for the implementation of a computerized patient management information system. *Behaviour & Information Technology* 14(1), 23-31.

Huff, C. & Finholt, T. (1994)(Eds.). *Social Issues in Computing: Putting Computing in its Place.* New York: McGraw Hill. Excerpted in *Computers and Society* 25(1), 12-17 (March 1995).

Igbaria, M. & Chakrabarti, A. (1990). Computer anxiety and attitudes towards microcomputer use. *Behaviour and Information Technology* 9(3), 229-241.

Igbaria, M., Schiffman, S., & Wieckowski, T. (1994). The respective roles of perceived usefulness and perceived fun in the acceptance of microcomputer technology. *Behaviour & Information Technology* 13(6), 349-361.

Kernan, M. & Howard, G. (1990). Computer anxiety and computer attitudes: an investigation of construct and predictive validity issues. *Educational and Psychological Measurement* 50, 681-690.

Mäkirinne-Crofts, P., Stokes, L., Godwin, W. & Saadat, S. (1995). Setting the record straight: computers and creative fashion designers. In Hasan, H. & Nicastri, C. (Eds.), *HCI: A Light Into the Future*, 129-134. OZCHI'95 Proceedings, 27-30 November, Wollongong, Australia. Ergonomics Society of Australia.

Mruk, C. (1987). The interface between computers and psychology: toward a psychology of computerization. *Computers in Human Behavior* 3, 167-179.

Nass, C., Lombard, M., Henriksen, L. & Steuer, J. (1995). Anthrpocentrism and computers. *Behaviour & Information Technology* 14(4), 229-238.

Nelson, D. & Kletke, M. (1990). Individual adjustment during technological innovation: a research framework. *Behaviour and Information Technology* 9(4), 257-271.

Omar, M. (1992). Attitudes of college students towards computers: a comparative study in the United States and the Middle East. *Computers in Human Behavior* 8, 249-257.

Reid, R. (1986). *Land of Lost Content: The Luddite Revolt, 1812.* London: Heinemann.

Rosen, L. & Maguire, P. (1990). Myths and realities of computerphobia: a meta-analysis. *Anxiety Research* 3, 175-191.

Rosen, L. & Weil, M. (1995). Computer anxiety: a cross-cultural comparison of university students in ten countries. *Computers in Human Behavior* 11(1), 45-64.

Rosen, L. & Weil, M. (1994). What we have learned from a decade of research (1983-1993) on "The Psychological Impact of Technology". *Computers and Society* 24(1), 3-5.

Rosen, L., Sears, D. & Weil, M. (1993). Treating technophobia: a longitudinal evaluation of the Computerphobia Reduction Program. *Computers in Human Behavior* 9, 27-50.

Rosengarten, H. & Smith, M. (1981)(Eds.). *Shirley*, by C. Brönte. Oxford: Oxford University Press.

Sheridan, T. (1980). Computer control and human alienation. *Technology Review* 83(1), 65-73.

Shore, J. (1985). Intimidation and anxiety. Chapter 1 in Shore, J., *The Sachertorte Algorithm, and Other Antidotes to Computer Anxiety.* New York: Viking.

Szlichcinski, K.P. (1983). Designing for the day after tomorrow: I. The interaction between communications system design and social change. *Behaviour and Information Technology* 2(3), 253-261.

Weil, M. & Rosen, L. (1995). The psychological impact of technology from a global perspective: a study of technological sophistication and technophobia in unversity students from twenty-three countries. *Computers in Human Behavior* 11(1), 95-133.

Weil, M., Rosen, L. & Wugalter, S. (1990). The etiology of computerphobia. *Computers in Human Behavior* 6, 361-379.

Towards a situated action calculus for modelling interactions

Alberto Faro[1] and Daniela Giordano[2]

[1] *Istituto di Informatica e Telecomunicazioni,*
Facolta' di Ingegneria, Universita' di Catania,
viale A.Doria 6, Catania, 95125 Italy
afaro@k200.cdc.unict.it

[2] *Department of Education, Concordia University,*
1455 de Maisonneuve Blvd. W., Montreal PQ H3G1M8
Canada
giord@alcor.concordia.ca

Formal modelling of situated actions and context is a worthwhile endeavor if it provides a framework for verifying requirements correctness and generates principles for building interfaces for fluid interactions. The paper argues that action sequences, rather than states, are a suitable representation for this problem, and proposes a situated action calculus based on a new material implication relation among contexts. The situated action calculus extends in two respects a story-telling theory for embedding the user requirements in meaningful contexts. First, it provides a formalism and a set of operators that allow the designer to verify that stories told by different actors generate a safe and live representation; and second, it allows partitioning such representation in a succession of scenes which can be aggregated to define for each actor an interface that unfolds with the task and the context.

Keywords situated action calculus, formal specification, requirements engineering, information systems design.

1   Introduction

In the last years many research efforts have been devoted to the problem of understanding human action and planning behavior. Developing a better understanding of this problem not only has philosophical and psychological relevance but it also brings to bear on how we approach the design of the systems we live in and interact with.

"Classic" approaches to the above problem are based on the notions of action and goal, where actions are performed in a given context, possibly according to a plan which embodies a strategy to reach a goal and therefore changes the "state of the world" (McCarthy & Hayes, 1969).

The nature of actions, plans and context and their relationships is considered more subtle and problematic by modern approaches that emphasize, respectively, the situated, social and interactive nature of action (Suchman, 1987; Goffman, 1974; Jordan & Henderson, 1995). According to Suchman (1987), actions are observable local interactions between humans and contingencies, and goals are achieved by dynamically adapting the representation of the plan to the representation of the context. According to Goffman's frame analysis (Goffman, 1974), human actions do not exist without the rules or the premises of an interpretative framework. Such framework provides a set of conventionalized "brackets" that mark off actions from the ongoing flow of surrounding events and the framing process is placed at the basis of the individual organization of experience. The insight of the situated action paradigm is that all activities, including plan generation and other forms of representations, are fundamentally situated and that context may be better characterized by mutually relating actions and real-world situations, rather than as a "container" for action (Suchman, 1993). Also Goffman's rendering of the individual organization of experience implies that framing is a situated process. However, whereas Suchman presents a view in which actors act by resorting to whatever resource (material, social, representational) they can use to reorient themselves in a position to better achieve their goal in spite of contingencies, Goffman presents a view in which a situated framing is flexibly done to create and reinforce the conditions to make sense of a social situation and play a role in it.

The main strength of the classic accounts of action and planning is their "formality"; on the other hand, the more recent ones have cogently argued that the notion of "situatedness" is fundamental for a user-centered design of interactive artifacts. Such issues have a major impact in areas such as Information Systems (IS) modelling and design, because they are central to requirements engineering and interface design.

Approaches proposed for user-centered system's design, such as participatory design (Kyng, 1995), contextual design (Holtzblatt & Beyer, 1993) and scenario-based design (Carroll, 1995), aim at taking into account explicitly the user's social conventions, local culture and work practices for a productive representation and treatment of context. However, these approaches are not formal and inevitably tend to diminish the aspects of systems' design in which some degree of formality is an asset, such as, for example, the verification of requirements' correctness.

Attempts to bridge formality and situatedness may focus either on finding formal rules to bound the definition of the state of the world in a certain instant; or on developing a formal theory for situated actions, possibly by adapting some existing calculus for interacting systems. This paper aims at contributing to the second direction and proposes a formal approach to modelling action, henceforth referred to as situated action calculus, inspired by both the frame analysis (Goffman, 1974) and the situated action paradigm (Suchman, 1987). These two approaches can be merged on the grounds that they both are based on the notion of mutually-constitutive relationship, respectively, between actions and the bracketing frames, and between actions and real-world situations; and both postulate an on-going processes of prospective/retrospective sense-making by which the framing process is explicated. In doing such merging, the paper aims at providing a unified framework to treat, still preserving the situated nature of any form of action and interaction, two fundamental needs of information systems design. The first need is that the information systems must support the aspects of social, conventionalized or proceduralized activity that makes the organization stable and intelligible to its users; the second need is that the information system must support the user that does not succeed in finding a proper framing or an "ontology" of the situation and therefore must resort to all the available resources to get out of the impasse. It must be noted that by referring to ontologies we do not imply that they have a status of independent existence, rather they are meant to exist as shared conventions. In our view, the difficulty inherent to treating the mutually constitutive relationship is at the basis of the criticism that framing, both in Goffman and in interactionist theories, is left rather vague (Turner, 1988, p.144); as such it would not be suitable for system engineering. Computability of the mutually constitutive relationship is therefore needed to overcome such vagueness and to identify the basic framings that can be a mold for design.

The paper develops as follows: first it proposes the formalization of the notion of mutually constitutive relation; this gives rise to a new material implication between contexts that replaces the classic relation of causality between actions and that allows a computational model of framing (section 2); then the paper shows the relevance of the story-telling theory proposed in (Faro & Giordano, 1995) augmented by the situated action calculus for embedding the user requirements into meaningful contexts (section 3); finally, it extends the story-telling theory (section 4) to define interfaces that support in finding a proper framing to smoothly engage in productive interactions and that avoid unnecessary breakdowns generated by different points of view and perspectives of the interacting actors.

2   The Material Implication for Contexts

In models of action based on the classical approach (McCarthy & Hayes, 1969; Hayes, 1971), actions A(t) are simply the means by which an actor H can change the current situation S(t), e.g.:

$A(t)$ *performed by H in S(t)* $\rightarrow$ *S(t+1)*   *(Eq.1)*

where $\rightarrow$ denotes the material implication. In this view the situation is a "container" for the action, clearly distinct from the action itself.

Situations S(t) may be represented by either sequences of past actions of all the participating actors or by the notion of "state". However, states are not always available for observation since they have often only a mathematical meaning and humans find it difficult to identify what variables might represent a memory of the specific activity stream that frames the context for the present action. Thus it is more plausible that actors perceive the situations in terms of patterns dynamically discovered while interacting. Resorting to the notion of pattern as a representation of a set of action sequences, opposite to the notion of state, has some drawbacks too. In fact: i) the past actions of all the actors might not be available to everybody, ii) if they were, they might well be outside the cognitive limitation of each actor, and could not be taken simultaneously into account, and iii) many of the past actions of other actors might not be of interest to actor H. More realistically, it can be assumed that each actor perceives a partition of S(t) that he/she finds useful and manageable. A first problem is therefore how to find such partition, although this does not address the fundamental issue that there is nothing to ensure that all the actors in the situation agree on what the situation is. On the other hand, in many cases cultural conventions exist and actors substantially agree on what is going on. For example, social conventions dynamically regulate interactions among actors (Goffman, 1974), and task ontologies allow sharing the meaning of job procedures (Mizogushi, 1995). Therefore we retain the notion that limited sequences of past actions are the most manageable representation of the context in which humans perform their actions, and set out to augment this sort of representation with the flexibility deriving from the framing process.

If one purports to formalize such sequences, the choice of a proper formalism must be informed by the requisite of treating encapsulated sequences of actions, i.e., action patterns. So far, most of the formal notations that have been adopted to represent action for interactive systems (e.g., State Transition Networks and CSP) have been rightly criticized for "not being encapsulated in such a way that they can be used easily by designers" (Monk & Curry, 1994). Some attempts towards encapsulation have been proposed (e.g., Faconti et al., 1994), but they treat encapsulation in spatial boundaries and not according to the spatial and temporal framing that is at the basis of the situated action paradigm. How to encapsulate actions in spatial/temporal framings is discussed in the following analysis.

When embracing a situated view of action, the causal relation between situations of Eq.1 above, cannot be reformulated for contexts tout court. If P(H,t) is the pattern of actions representing the context influencing actor H at time t, and A(a,H,W,t) is the action that H would to perform with actor W, it is easy to understand that the following relations, where A(a,H,W,t) and A(a,W,H,t) refer to the same action as seen from the two actors H and W, are not valid:

$$P(H,t) \& A(a,H,W,t) \rightarrow P(H,t+1)$$
$$P(W,t) \& A(a,W,H,t) \rightarrow P(W,t+1)$$

In fact, when H interacts with W at instant t, he/she has to know also P(W,t) to give meaning to A(a,H,W,t) i.e., transform an action into an act (Harre' et al., 1985). Thus the following relations hold between contexts:

$$P(H,t) \& A(a,H,W,t) \& P(W,t) \rightarrow P(H,t+1)$$
$$P(W,t) \& A(a,W,H,t) \& P(H,t) \rightarrow P(W,t+1) \qquad \textit{(Eq.2)}$$

This is the *material implication for contexts* at the basis of the situated action calculus outlined in section 3.3. In this characterization the context influencing H at instant t depends on the action to be performed at the same instant, because, for each actor, *P(W,t)* and *P(H,t)* are tentatively "decided" while action A is being carried out. This implication is less restrictive than the classical one, in which H should always know the contexts influencing all the actors with whom he/she might interact in the future. However, P(All Others Actors,t) generally isn't either known nor predictable, and neither are the interactions among these actors at instant t. Equation (2) expresses that actor H has to focus "only" on the pattern of actions P(W,t) that W has performed to infer what the interpretative context for the current action might be. One of the main contributions of the situated action calculus is to show how P(W,t) can be computed. With respect to equation (2) we note that actor H generally has a partial knowledge of P(W,t). Thus it seems more realistic to assume that actor H uses equation (2) "cum grano salis". In particular, the other main contribution of the situated action calculus is to show that when an activity breakdown occurs, H either executes a recovery action or aborts a limited sequence of past actions ("episode" in our terminology), instead of starting a complex diagnosis of the cause of the breakdown.

A crucial design issue is to avoid as far as possible action breakdowns due to missing information on the appropriate H and W contexts, and find ways to communicate to H the context influencing W with respect to that action and viceversa. The information disclosed by an actor H to its partners is called, in our approach, the *interface* between H and the interacting actors. Section 4 clarifies how the situated action calculus produces such notion of interface and some heuristic rules on how information can be disclosed.

3   Information systems modelling by use of stories

Approaches to requirements elicitation based on narratives or scenarios (e.g., Carroll, 1995; Potts, 1995) are driven by a concern for a rich and contextualized modelling of requirements. A story telling theory (STT) was firstly proposed to elicit information systems requirements in terms of use cases (Faro & Giordano, 1995) and then extended to support learning IS analysis and design (Faro & Giordano, 1996). What distinguishes our approach is its formality and the emphasis on the episode, typed by context information according to the categories of a template (Who, What, When, Assumptions, How, What-Can-Go-Wrong), as the key element in the story recollection process. In this paper the narration process is modeled by an appropriate calculus that allows the designer to prove safety and liveness of the system requirements. If the requirements are incorrect, the designer reevaluates them with the user, but limiting the analysis to the deadlocked or livelocked episodes. Thus   the process of requirements specifications should converge towards a correct solution after few cycles of revisions.

What constitutes an episode is not univocally defined because the bracketing of episodes is extremely flexible with respect to temporal extension, level of detail and semantics of the described actions. To deal productively with such flexibility the story telling theory introduces a first constraint in the narration process by encouraging users to "tell stories" about the system from the perspective of a specific actor at a time, and in the form of stories enacted by sequential agents, akin to the script of each actor in a scene. In this sense the story telling theory is inherently a multi-points of view and multi-perspectives approach to information systems modelling. Definitions of point of view and perspective within the calculus are provided in sect.4.

A set of stories articulated in episodes is elicited by the designer from the prospective users of the system. The heuristics of the approach is to first start from the "seed" stories, i.e., the simplest/less costly sequence of the episodes that is necessary to perform in order to reach the goal of the story. Each episode has a goal and consists of a non interruptible sequence of actions. Each action might involve a specific interaction between actors or be performed by the actor alone. The episode is atomic in the sense that an actor cannot cease his/her activity after any action of the episode, although this activity can be temporarily suspended. Rather, activity must proceed until the goal of the episode is achieved, otherwise the entire episode is aborted. However, before aborting an episode, the story telling theory encourages every actor to consider if what is gone wrong belongs to the list of "What can go wrong (*WCGW*)" actions that can be managed by activating a suitable recovery sequence. This sequence does not belong to the seed episode but behaves as an Exception Handling episode triggered by a *WCGW*-action in the context of the seed sequence.

It can be noted that the seed sequence in the *HOW* section of the story-telling template has many points of contact with the sequence model of work that is described in the contextual design approach (Holtzblatt & Beyer, 1993). Whereas in the contextual design approach it is suggested to use the sequence model with other models of work (organizational context model, physical model, and flow model) to get complementary information, STT addresses the issue by representing this complementary information only for those aspects that are relevant to the specific use case being described, in the categories Who, (for example to take into account the role being played) When, Where, Assumptions, and Features (for example, those features of the physical environment that constrain the seed sequence). The representational trade-off is between dealing either with the comprehensive view provided by the above models or with the localized view of those various aspects of the models relevant to the use case under study.

3.1   Episode Structuring and Task Ontology

The main problem of the above heuristics is the apparently discretional nature of how narration can be structured into stories and episodes. Stories that take place in a business organization can be described according to a task ontology that addresses the episodes structuring issue. Task ontology (Mizogushi, 1995) is a system of vocabulary for describing the problem solving structure (in terms of objects and processes/procedures) of all the existing task domain-independently, to favor cross-domain reuse. In this framework task knowledge specifies domain knowledge by assigning roles to each object and to the relation between objects. A task structure typically requires only some specific domain knowledge. By resorting to the idea of task ontology and structuring we can assume the existence of a set of actions, episodes and stories that derive their ontological meaning ("objectivity") from the type of task they refer to. This assumption is shared by other approaches to task analysis, such as Task Knowledge Structure (TKS) (Johnson & Johnson, 1991). In TKS knowledge about the task is systematically represented by a graphical notation for the task goals and sub-goals structure, and a detailed structured textual description of the procedures and of the objects and their properties in the task. On the contrary, in STT goal structure and related procedures are embedded in a single formal representation in which the structuring of the seed sequence (How) implies a task ontology (social framing) and the overall representation, including Assumptions and What-Can-Go-Wrong is suitable for framing scenarios to support the "situated" actions to recover from difficulties either in perceiveing or applying the framing of the seed sequence. This latter aspect is demonstrated in the case study of sect. 3.4.

However, the ontology of a given task and its domain-related structuring is not easy to find. In the following example we illustrate a methodology for deriving it, in the case of the story of purchasing an item in a furniture store.

The methodology we propose starts by interviewing the client according to the story telling theory. We obtain the client's story as the sequence of the following episodes: *Visiting the exhibit; Selecting the item* (actions: Consulting the catalog - if not available take the old catalog-, Consulting the salesman); *Ordering the item to the salesman* (actions: Checking item availability, Reserving the item); *Paying the item to the cashier* (actions: Showing the reservation ticket, Paying the price); *Getting the item from the depot* (actions: Showing the payment receipt, Getting the item).

After verifying that the above actions can be assumed to be indivisible occurrences belonging to the task vocabulary, we are faced with the problem of the granularity of the identified episodes. With respect to the above story this problem can be formulated as follows: why i) *Visiting the expo*, ii) *Selecting the item* and iii) *Ordering the item to the salesman* are three different episodes rather than only one or two? An answer to this question is widely discussed in (Faro & Giordano,

1997), where it is demonstrated that an action is the last action of an episode if: i) it causes an effective modification in the information system of the business organization, and ii) its effect still holds when the actor resumes the story after an interruption.

Also, a sequence of actions should be grouped into a narrative unit if activity can be suspended and resumed without requiring memory of all the past actions but only knowledge that the sequence has been executed.

With these rules in mind we analyze one by one the actions involved in the three episodes:

- *Visiting the exhibit* is not an episode if the furniture store does not register the clients neither these clients pay a ticket to enter.
- *Consulting the catalog* and *Consulting the salesman* are the last actions of an episode if the catalog information changes daily.
- *Checking availability* cannot be, by definition, the last action of an episode.
- *Reserving the item* is by definition the last action of an episode.

According to this analysis, the story ontology of purchasing an item has to be rewritten as the set of two stories: one relevant to situations in which the catalog tends to remain unchanged, the other (shown in Figure 1) for situations characterized by frequent changes.

Story: Purchasing an item from a retail store (client)
Episodes:
  Selecting and ordering the item
                            Assumptions: item is discounted
                            Actions: Visiting the exhibit
                                                      Consulting the catalog
                                                            WCGW: catalog not
available

Take old catalog
                                                      Consulting the salesman
                                                      Ordering the item to the salesman
                                                      Checking item availability
                                                                Reserving the item
                      Paying the item to the cashier
                            Actions: Showing the reservation ticket
                                                      Paying the price
                      Getting the item from the depot
                            Actions: Showing the payment receipt
                                                Getting the item from the depot

---

Figure 1: Task ontology of purchasing item from a furniture store with frequent variations in the catalog.

3.2   *Story Progression*

After completing an episode, an actor has typically the possibility of enacting more than one episode. For the next episode to be executed, its assumptions have to be satisfied. By default, the episode's assumptions are satisfied by the successful completion of the previous episode of the story. Whenever the post-condition of the previous episode is not sufficient as a pre-condition for action, this has to be formulated in a specific section of the task ontology called *Assumptions*. In Figure 1, for example, the story will be enacted only if some special discount is offered, which is the post condition of some other story. In addition, the fact that episodes can be unfolded, i.e., the temporal ordering of some set of episodes can be arbitrary or multi-threaded is also expressed in the section Assumptions, by indicating the specific episodes that are preconditions. Thus, although for convenience the seed sequence expresses only one of the possible instances of the episodes interleaving, these instances can be computed by the analysis of the assumptions.

However, story progression cannot be modelled only from a single perspective because it needs collaboration. To illustrate the implications of this concept, let us consider the episode "Selecting and ordering the item" in Figure 1, and let us assume that the store management needs to count the number of catalogs given to the clients. Under this hypothesis it is easy to understand that the client's episode has to be subdivided into two episodes: i) Visiting the exhibit and ii) the rest of the other actions. In fact, although the first episode is meaningless for the client unless it is followed by the second one, if the client can't perform some action in the second episode, the first episode can't be aborted or "forgotten" because it corresponds to a goal achieved by another actor, i.e., the salesman counting the catalogs given to the clients. Thus in general in a story we have two types of episode: i) those associated with the goals of the episode's main character, and ii) the episodes associated with the goals of other participating actors.

The above analysis points out that all the stories have to be "orchestrated' so that the system behaves like a play, where all the actors interact following their scripts to form a whole action. Applying the metaphor of theater representation, motivated in detail in (Faro & Giordano, 1997), we call *scene* an aggregate representation of all the episodes enacted by an actor (the scene character) and by the collaborators who intervene to make the scene character achieve his/her goal. The exchange of information due to the impact of the goals of participating actors in the story of a main character results in the redefinition of the character scene in smaller ones.

If no part of the episode enacted by each actor in the scene can be associated with the goal of some other participating actor, then the scene is called *minimal scene*. As an example, the scene of the client selecting and ordering an item is not minimal, whereas the scene of the client visiting the expo and consulting the catalog handed by the salesman is minimal, the scene main character being the salesman.

The notion of minimal scene allows us to be more precise about the definition of scene and to introduce the concept of *context* as follows: i) a *scene* is a set of minimal scenes that are time-contiguous, i.e., that develop sequentially and/or concurrently, whereas ii) a *context* is a set of minimal scenes that are not necessarily time-contiguous, i.e., other scenes not highlighted might have occurred in between.

3.3 The Situated Action Calculus

The story telling theory would remain a sort of collection of guidelines unless it is provided with a formal basis to prove correctness and completeness of the specifications derived from the use stories. Thus we associate to the story telling framework a calculus of situated actions (CSA), inspired to the Extended Calculus of Communicating Systems (ECCS) (Carchiolo et al, 1989).

By CSA, each story is formalized by the temporal ordering of episodes pertaining to the seed sequence of the story and to the recovery branching sequences originating from aborted episodes. Branching sequences represent recovery strategies. Analogously, an episode is formalized by the temporal ordering of actions pertaining to the seed sequence of the episode and to the recovery branching sequences originating from "what can go wrong" events arising inside the episodes. Different stories, as well as different episodes, that have common root sequences can be grouped into trees.

In the calculus we use the notation $\{x?,context\}$ or $\{x!,context\}$ according to whether x is an input or output action from the viewpoint of the actor, whereas "context" is used by the interacting actors to give unique meaning to action x. The actions without ! or ? can be considered either internal actions or actions performed in cooperation with an external agent whose behavior is not relevant for the story (or episode) progression. By default x? and x! are used instead of $\{x?,scene\}$ and $\{x!,scene\}$ if the context that gives meaning to the actions coincides with the scene in which these actions arise. For example, the notation c? could be used to indicate compactly that the client is waiting for receiving the catalog from the salesman. The same action from the salesman point of view is denoted by c!. The story progression is given by a play consisting of sequential or "concurrent" scenes that can be implemented in parallel or by an arbitrary interleaving of them. A scene consists of sequential or concurrent joint actions (interactions) such as $[\{c?,context1\} \mid \{c!,context2\}]$, where the operator "|" is called parallel composition. Whenever context1 and context2 are overlapping, the likelihood of misinterpretation and future action breakdown is decreased.

After an interaction the actors can enact the next interaction of the scene. Two subsequent actions of the episode (as well as two subsequent interactions of the scene) are linked by the operator ";" also called sequential composition. From the point of view of an actor, story progression may not need that a rigid sequence of episodes must be followed, thus actors can flexibly schedule how their episodes will unfold. For example, story S= e1 ; (e2 | e3) means that after concluding episode e1 the story actor can perform either e2 ; e3 or e3 ; e2. In other words, both the assumptions of e2 and e3 contain only e1 as the enabling condition of these episodes.

The operator "+" allows the designer to model an actor who can enact his/her future behavior by choosing among different episodes or actions; it also affords a more compact representation of the set of use stories and related episodes.

There are main differences between ECCS and our calculus. The first one is that in ECCS there is no formal rule for partitioning a script into narrative units, therefore the cooperation among actors can be represented only by one all encompassing equation. On the contrary, by introducing the notion of goal, narration can be structured into meaningful contexts such as stories and episodes, and cooperation among actors is given by the parallel composition of stories, and, inside each story, by the parallel composition of episodes. Thus safety and liveness of narration can be proven by applying the ECCS equivalence relation to the narration units and the related scenes rather than to the entire narration and the related global scenario.

Whereas ECCS is a non deterministic calculus, because there is no means to indicate the context in which an action is unambiguously interpreted, the task ontology, on which the situated action calculus is based, affords eliminating the ambiguity by associating to every action the context that gives meaning to it. A source of non determinism common to ECCS and to our calculus stems from allowing internal actions to occur while an actor evolves, because these actions generally produce faults. In our calculus such non deterministic behavior is managed based on the *WCGW* sequences.

3.4   A Case Study

This illustrative case study concerns the definition of a suitable procedure to arrange meetings. This problem is considered a test case for methodologies aiming at handling ill-structured requirements (Potts, 1995).

The identified actors are: i) the meeting chair C, ii) the secretary S, and iii) the other participants P.

The chair's actions are:

- dp = Define participant list, agenda, and dates,
- sm! = Ask secretary to verify the meeting feasibility,
- rr? = Receiving response from the secretary,
- ck = Positive check on dates,
- fc! = Final convocation passed to the secretary.

The secretary's actions are the ones complementing the chair's actions plus:

- sp! = Send list, agenda, and dates to participants,
- rp? =   Receiving response from the participants,
- bta = Analysis of best time available for the meeting
- cc! = Send final convocations to participants.

The participants actions are the ones complementing the secretary's actions. The seed stories as told by these actors are as follows:

Story: meeting convocation   (Chair point of view)
>   *Episodes:*
>   Preliminary call for the meeting: dp ; **sm!**
>   Final call for the meeting: rr? ; ck ; **fc!**

Story: meeting convocation (Secretary point of view)
>   *Episodes:*
>   Preliminary call for the meeting: sm? ; **sp!**
>   Collecting participants preferences : rp?   ; bta ; **rr!**
>   Final call for the meeting: fc? ; **cc!**

Story: meeting convocation (Participant point of view)
>   *Episodes:*
>   Preliminary call for the meeting : sp? ; **rp!**
>   Final call for the meeting: **cc?**

Actions fc!, rp! and cc! (in bold) are clearly the main goals of the above stories. However, also sm! (or sp!) has to be treated as a goal since after its execution the job can be suspended and when resuming it the chair (the secretary) only needs to know that the necessary information was given to the secretary (delivered to the participants).

The algorithm to pass from the actors stories to the actors play is given in (Faro & Giordano, 1997). It generates a play consisting of sequential or concurrent scenes, and proves that each scene is safe and live. It is easy to understand that the most economic solution in terms of information exchanged at the actors interface can be obtained by a play consisting of the sequence of the minimal scenes:

Play: Meeting convocation (simplest solution)
Scenes: S1 = df ; [**sm!** | sm?] ;
>   S2 = [**sp!** | sp?] ;
>   S3 = [**rp!** | rp?] ;
>   S4 = bta ; [**rf!** | rf?] ;
>   S5 = ck ; [**fc!** | fc?] ;
>   S6 = [**cc!** | cc?]

It is interesting to note that this sequence of scenes coincides with that defined a priori in (Potts, 1995) to solve an analogous problem. However, there are other solutions, in which scenes are partitioned by linking more closely the actors' behaviors. In the most tightly coupled solution, each scene is characterized by having only one actor achieving his or her final goal :

Play: Meeting convocation (Tightly coupled solution)
Scenes: S1' = df ; [sm! | sm?] ; [sp! | sp?] ; [**rp!** | rp?]
>   S2' = bta ; [rf! | rf?] ; ck ; [**fc!** | fc?]
>   S3' = [**cc!** | cc?]

In this solution the actors have a better possibility of recovering wrong situations, at the cost of remembering all the actions executed to achieve their goals and being aware of what other actors in the same scene are doing. On the contrary, the simplest solution only requires that the actors remember some achieved goals.

Generally, the more powerful the interface among the actors (i.e., the wider the scene) the better the effectiveness in interpreting actions and recovering from obstacles. To decide on future actions each actor has to know only the action patterns that the other actors have performed in the same scene. The scene is therefore the basic context we have envisaged in section 2 to give meaning to the actors actions, i.e., to identify the actors acts.

4   Context Analysis and actors interface

So far we have shown how to identify the actors' acts and the related material implication by anchoring the actors' actions to a reference system consisting of scenes. However, sometimes knowledge of the current action and scene is not enough to interpret the actors acts and it is necessary to define an interface more powerful than the one given by the pair (action, scene). In these cases, the design problem is to find what information is needed and when it is needed by the users to support their situated action. Typically, the information mostly needed assists in avoiding execution of faulty actions and in overcoming obstacles.

Another facet of this design problem is to consider how the contexts of the actors in the system (i.e., users, staff and artificial agents) can be modified (by enhancing the actors interface) to avoid activity deadlocks or livelocks due to possible different perspectives or points of view of the interacting actors.

4.1   Contingencies

To illustrate the nature of the information that must be made available for deciding the right action, we take into account the simpler solution of the play illustrated in the previous section. If while performing action *bta* in the scene S4 the secretary finds that the participants' availability dates do not overlap, then S4 has to be aborted and the play restarted from S2. But if the secretary takes into account an extended context such as S1, S3 and S4 together then he/she might discover that the critical participants defined in the action *df* of scene S1 have expressed overlapping availability dates and propose the meeting to the chair anyway.

It is important to note that if the scenes S1 and S3 are not considered by the secretary as the context driving his/her current action, then the secretary remembers only the goals of these scenes, i.e., that all the participants were contacted and that they responded, but he/she does not know what the critical participants are and neither if their dates overlap. To provide the secretary with the information needed to effectively execute action *bta*, the designer has to modify the related episode as follows: *Episode:* Collecting participants preferences: rp? ; {bta, [S1, S3, S4]}; **rr!**. The context associated to each action represents either what must be remembered or exchanged during an interaction. A secretary executing {bta, S4} does not share the same context of a secretary executing {bta,

[S1,S3,S4]⟩, and consequently approaches the same situation differently. We say that these secretaries have *different points of view.*

4.2   *What Can Go Wrong*

The combination of minimal scenes that appears within the brackets is derived from a cross analysis of the *WCGWs* of each actor. In fact, although not explicitly noted so far, a meeting without the critical participants would be a *WCGW* for the chair, then he/she must give this information to the secretary. In this case we say that the chair shares his/her *perspective* (i.e., discloses some of his/her future goals) to prevent the secretary from causing an involuntary *WCGW*. However, if the dates proposed by the critical participants do not overlap, the secretary is not able to solve the problem to arrange the meeting. To overcome this obstacle the secretary can re-send a request to the critical participants (i.e. sp'!) and waiting for their answer (i.e. rp'?). Thus the secretary's episode dealing with collecting participants preferences should be modified by introducing a recovery episode R as follows:

Episode:

Collecting participants preferences:

rp? ; (bta ; **rr!** + not bta ; R)

where R = sp'! ; rp'? ; bta ; **rr!**

The same action *bta* is present in both the seed sequence and in the recovery episode. However, the secretary distinguishes these actions because they belong to different scenes, i.e. S4 and R.

5   Conclusions

A main lesson of the paper is that the scenes of the play derived from the actors scripts collected by the story telling approach are the building blocks for analyzing and designing information systems. Scenes are fundamental first because scene decomposition makes manageable the complexity inherent in designing how actors in distributed systems should interact to achieve their goals. This is possible because of the underlying formal apparatus of the situated action calculus. Also, scenes provide the actors with a sort of reference system that facilitate actions interpretation, thus preventing activity breakdown due to the different points of view (type of information known or available) and the different perspectives (goal to be reached) that cooperating actors bring to the task they perform. Since actors in the same scene share to a certain degree the representation of the task, the play's safety increases, and the actors need only to manage unexpected events originating from the outside. In a wider scene a greater amount of information is circulating, and liveness is increased; in this case the specification of the boundaries of the scene must ensue consideration of the cognitive load placed on each actor in the scene. Problems currently under study are how the notion of scene can be used for a step by step system verification and how such verification can be performed either by simulation or analytically, for example by extending, respectively, the Action Simulator illustrated in Monk & Curry (1994) or the analytical method proposed in Carchiolo et al. (1989).

References

Carchiolo, V., Di Stefano A., Faro, A. and Pappalardo G. (1989). ECCS and LIPS two languages for OSI systems specification and verification. *ACM Transactions On Programming Languages and Systems,* 11 (2), 284-329.

Carroll, J. M. (Ed.), (1995) *Scenario-based Design: Envisioning work and technology in system development.* John Wiley, New York.

Faconti, G. P., Fornari, A. and Zani, N. (1994). Visual representation of formal specification: an application to hierarchical logical input devices. In F. Paterno' (Ed.), *Interactive Systems Design and Specification, 1ˢᵗ Eurographics Workshop,* Bocca di Magra, Italy, June 1994. Springer-Verlag.

Faro, A. and Giordano, D. (1995). From information systems specification to user's mental models and viceversa by extended visual notation. In *Proc. IPCC'95, IEEE International Professional Communication Conference,* Savannah, Georgia.

Faro, A. and Giordano, D. (1996). Story telling reasoning to learn Information Systems design. In *Proc. Euro AIED96, European Conference on Artificial Intelligence in Education,* Lisbon, Portugal.

Faro, A. and Giordano, D. (1997). Between narration and drama : information systems modelling revisited. *In Proc. ECIS 97 European Conference on Information Systems,* Cork, Ireland.

Goffman, E. (1974). *Frame Analysis.* Harvard University Press, Cambridge.

Hayes P.J. (1971). A logic of actions, *Machine Intelligence,* 6, 495-520.

Harrè, R., Clarke D. and De Carlo N. (1985) *Motives and Mechanisms: an introduction to the psychology of action.* Methuen, London

Holtzblatt, K. and Beyer, H. R. (1993). Making customer-centered design work for teams. *Communications of the ACM,* 36 (10).

Johnson, H. and Johnson, P. (1991). Task Knowledge Structures : Psychological basis and integration into system design, *Acta Psychologica*, 78, 3-26.

Jordan, B. and Henderson, A. (1995). Interaction analysis: foundations and practice. *The journal of the learning sciences*, 4 (1), 39-103.

Kyng, M. (1995). Making representations work. *Communications of the ACM*, 38 (9), 46-55.

McCarthy J. and Hayes P.J. (1969). Some philosophical problems from the standpoint of artificial intelligence, *Machine Intelligence*, 4, 463-502.

Mizogushi, R.,Tijerino Y., and Ikeda M. (1995). Task analysis interview based on task ontology . *Journal of Expert Systems with Applications*, 9 (1), 15-25.

Monk, A. F. and Curry, M. B. (1994). Discount dialogue modelling with Action Simulator. In Cockton, G., Draper, S. W. And Weir, G. R. S. (Eds.), *People and Computers 9-* Proceedings HCI'94, Cambridge University Press.

Potts, C. (1995). Using schematic scenarios to understand user needs. *ACM Proc. DIS'95- Designing Interactive systems*. Ann Arbor, Michigan.

Suchman, L.A. (1987). *Plans and-situated actions: The problem of human-machine communication*. Cambridge University Press. New York.

Suchman, L.A. (1993) Response to Vera and Simon's situated action: a symbolic interpretation. *Cognitive Science*, 17, 71-75.

Turner, J. H. (1988). *A theory of social interaction*. Stanford University Press, Stanford.

Explorations in Sonic Browsing

M. Fernström & L. Bannon

Interaction Design Centre, Foundation Building, University of Limerick, Ireland,
Email: mikael.fernstrom@ul.ie, liam.bannon@ul.ie

This paper describes a novel browser prototype that has been designed and implemented on PC's and soundcards. Our focus has been on the development of a usable and engaging interface which exploits both visual and aural features of the data space. The project involves state-of-the-art work in human-computer interaction and multimedia development. We are working on a data set of musical compositions, and are designing and testing the prototype with a group of musicians. This paper provides some detail on the development process, the current architecture of the system, and describes some of the problems encountered.

Keywords: browsing, multimedia, visualisation, sonification, spatial audio.

1   Introduction

The BROWSE project is a 2-year research project focused on the development of *Novel Multimedia Browsing Mechanisms*. We are particularly interested in investigating how sound can be used more fully in order to assist users in comprehending complex data sets. Initially, a survey of browsing methods and techniques currently available in various software applications was conducted. This was followed by a number of exploratory interviews and observations on everyday browsing behaviours and strategies of specific user groups. We then decided to focus our attention on browsing in particular domains, in order to focus our activities in prototype development. We have focused our work to date on a musical data set, which is the well-known Fleischmann collection of Irish traditional music [Ó Súilleabháin 1997]. Our work with this data set has been assisted by our close collaboration with musicians - our user community - in the Irish World Music Centre at the University of Limerick. We have developed a prototype system running on a standard multimedia PC with Windows software where we are investigating a star-field type display [Shneiderman 1994] of data utilising a number of user-controllable parameters in the display — shape, colour, size, and location of objects. As already mentioned, we have been particularly interested in developing the audio output in the prototype, as this is a seriously neglected area in current systems. We have thus had to re-design a number of device drivers so that we now can support multiple stream audio. From the user's perspective, they are now browsing a soundscape as well as a screenscape, and as they move the cursor in the star-field display representation, they receive audio streams of the nearest neighbouring objects. We are currently conducting user trials on the prototype in order to determine the most optimal cues for browsing in this domain. We believe that the software environment that we have created can be used for a wider field of application especially within the field of sonification. The low-level drivers and application program interface can be applied in a multitude of ways and we intend to further develop these functions. In what follows, we provide a more detailed account of the issues that we have investigated, the data set we have been working with, and the development process that we have conducted in order to construct the prototype. We provide a snapshot of its current status, and finally discuss our plans for further work in the coming final year of the project.

1.1   Remarks on current systems

Browsing is an iterative and interactive activity, often with an opportunistic or serendipitous attitude. Initially facing an unknown space with unknown symbols, the users investigates items - noting similarities and differences in the properties of objects and drawing conclusions about links between the objects, thus becoming familiar with the information-space. They can then either be "lucky" or skilled enough to find an object worth a more detailed inspection, or to be in a position to apply more formal search methods [Jerke 1990, Marchionini 1995 pp 100-138]. In this context it is important to note that information objects have both external and internal properties. When people browse, they start by taking the external properties into account. When they have located objects of interest, they start to peruse the internal properties of the objects. Sometimes this exercise will force them to re-evaluate their understanding of the external properties and a new browsing session is initiated, studying the external properties again but now with a revised understanding of the mapping between external and internal properties of the objects.

The problem we are addressing in this project is how to make it easier for users to find items in complex data sets and to develop appropriate *domain metaphors* and *representational mappings*. These should help the user to get an understanding of the information-space available in specific domains and with a high level of' virtuality insofar as it enables users to understand and manipulate information in new ways, that are not possible on paper or with other media [Erickson 1990, Hutchins 1987, Marchionini 1995 p.45, Nelson 1990]. The development of multimedia has started to provide a richer user interface, with sound, images, video, graphics and text on a single platform — a computer, thus multimedia in itself is not a product or solution, it is merely a method with the potential to create a more effective communication with the user [Bannon 1993]. The common WIMP-ideas and the use of poor domain metaphors have become restrictive in allowing access to information [Nelson 1990] and new models and methods are required. It is also important to note that the user's requirements and abilities change; in time, with different tasks and with different individuals [Bannon 1991]. Most existing browsing systems only deal with visual representation, but some systems also provide audio representation. Systems like Albers' Audiable Web [Albers 1995B], and Blattner's digital interactive map [Blattner 1994] and LoPresti and Harris' loudSPIRE [LoPresti & Harris 1996] show how sound can be added and closely integrated with the interaction, with emphasis on ease of use and the sound cues applied discretely to provide a richer user experience. Brewster has demonstrated that sounds are easier to differentiate if more complex waveforms are used (as in MIDI controlled synthesisers with instrumental timbres), as well as enhancing the users' performance [Brewster 1994]. This is not surprising as timbre is a strong cue for perceptual grouping of sounds and stream segregation [Bregman 1990 pp 478-490].

As a starting point for the visual aspects of browsing, we investigated Shneiderman and Ahlberg's work with a *star-field representation* and *dynamic queries* [Shneiderman 1994]. The main features of their system is that it forms a domain metaphor of high virtuality by creating a graphic mapping of many different kinds of domains such as Filmfinder. With Ahlberg's latest implementation, *Spotfire* [IVEE 1996] the user only gets visual browsing-support, at least until an object is clicked on and an information-box opens up. In later realisations they have demonstrated browsing of, for example, demographic, financial and environmental information. In *Spotfire,* the information objects are represented as coloured dots displayed in a two-dimensional diagram and in the case of demographic and environmental data, this 2-D space can be mapped onto an image of geographical map. By means of sliders within the display area the user can build dynamic queries, which means that the coloured dots will be visible/invisible (or highlighted/greyed-out) depending on the query formed by the setting of the sliders. When information objects of interest have been located, the user can click an object (a coloured dot) for further inspection of the information contained in the object, i.e. the internal properties of the object.

1.2   *Browsing sound objects*

Most people that have worked with, for example, multimedia production have eventually faced the challenge of having hundreds or thousands of sound files (or other media files), having to navigate, browse and chose between them to fit into the production. With the traditional WIMPS interfaces, files or objects have to be clicked or double-clicked[1]. Alternatively some sort of media player that involves pull-down menus and clicking can be used for activation of sound playback.

A metaphor that came to mind while working on the early phases of this project was the old longwave radio, where the user could move a "cursor" along a dial, often with several radio stations heard at the same time, trying to turn the dial in such a way that a desired station would become stronger or clearer.

1.3   The selected data set

From a complexity point of view an ideal domain and data set would contain all the elements of multimedia: text, images, sound and video. Another important point is that due the fact that our design philosophy involves close links with user communities and utilising rapid prototyping methodology, we required close contact and direct access to suitable domains, data sets and individuals with domain knowledge expertise [Bannon 1991B, Marchionini 1995B].

We found a suitable domain and data set in the Irish World Music Centre at UL — the so called *Fleischmann collection*, or *"Sources of Irish Traditional Music c. 1600-1855"*. This data set contains 11,734 records of high complexity, including musical score notation and a number of different classifications and keys (Figure 1). As music is a very complex art-form in itself, the data set also contains cross-references between records for tunes that are similar, a feature that can be explored in terms of hyperlinks. The musical score in itself contains a very rich annotation, unfortunately mainly accessible to musicians with classical training. One important feature that can be considered is to make the data-set accessible to a larger population (including many traditional musicians) with notation in for example tin-flute tablature, numerical tablature, alphabetic notation, etc. With the score data available in electronic form, it is fully possible to let the user select among a number of different score representations as well.

Figure 1: An excerpt from the Fleischmann Collection.

---

[1] It seems that the developers of the PC never thought of the possibility that a user would like to, or would be able to, listen to more than one sound at a time.

1.4   Using Sound

We set out to investigate how to get a tighter coupling of the interaction with the data set and to provide users with richer support from the system. The application of sound in the user interface have been neglected for a long time and some of the important and early work by Blattner et al. and Gaver [Blattner 1989, Gaver 1989] is still not available on everybody's PC's, although attempts and trials have been running for several years.

In evolutionary terms, sound provides both an "early warning system" that eventually might guide our vision and attention to locations important for our survival, as well as having a strong influence on our mood and how we interpret what we see. Here, it is also interesting to note systems like the ARKola simulation [Gaver 1991] which improved the users performance by making them aware of surrounding activities by means of sound.

In the visual interface, we began to explore how to add and combine more dimensions. Relative to the *Spotfire* system, we added geometrical shape to the range of visual representation of information objects. In the sonic interface, we investigated multiple stream spatial audio representations. For the integration of multimedia in the browser interface we attempted to combine the visual and sonic representations, to provide consistent interaction and to increase the user's feeling of direct engagement [Gaver 1997].

What makes our browsing prototype different is also the fact that our data set containins music, and music is best perceived by listening. In our secondary data set, containing environmental data with no natural or direct representation or meaning from an auditory point of view, other strategies will have to be applied such as auralisation to represent multivariate data [Bly 1982, Albers 1995, Slaney et al 1996].

1.5   Mapping and meaning

With a musical data set such as the Fleischmann, it is quite easy and natural for the users to learn the mapping between visual and aural representations. When using the system it becomes clear that if, for example, the user has selected to map the type of tune (jig, reel, hornpipe, polka, etc.) to shape, and then moving around in the screen and soundscape, the musical meaning associated with the visual representation will be learnt as the user hears each respective type of tune played when the cursor is in the neighbourhood of, or on, the different visual representations.

Another aspect of browsing a musical data set in this manner is that the musical content itself has its own semantics and syntax such as tonality, rhythm, timbre, etc., which will assist the user to form streams and to keep each stream together in the general cacophony[1] when moving around the soundscape between and among

---

[1] Some may think that with this particular data set, it might sound like an Irish *Fleadh Cheoil* (Traditional music festival and competition) gone mad....

tunes. The kind of sounds used also seems to be quite important for the user's ability to discriminate between tunes, i.e. the timbres of the different tunes.

When the user moves the cursor in the screenscape, the soundscape is also active and changes. Up to eight of the objects closest to the cursor will be playing. Each tune is represented by its own sound source that is placed in 3-D audio space. The mapping of the of screenscape and soundscape is done so that an object above the cursor on the screen will be heard in front of the user, an object below the cursor will be heard behind the user, and vice versa. From initial user testing, we have observed that users seem to be able to navigate the soundscape quite well. Some researchers have reported problems with spatial sound representation and small movements of the head that seem to enhance the ability to localise sound [Kobayashi and Schmandt 1997]. In our system, this seems to be compensated by the fact that the user can move the cursor and the soundscape will the change. This tight coupling could be similar to small head movements, that are emulated by small movements of the cursor which in turn is controlled by the mouse. This would, of course, not fulfil exactly the same function for the user because a normal cursor cannot be turned around in a single location, but the dynamics in the interaction can make it easier for the users to localise the sound sources. The current version of the spatialization library that we are using does not support turning around in one point, but this function can be emulated by moving all sound sources around the listener, with which we are experimenting.

2   Implementing the Prototype

Based on a traditional WIMP approach, as much as possible of the active screen area is made available to display a visual representations of the data-set. In addition to this, a number of function areas are needed: menus for general control of the browser, tool bar for widgets and controls, and a status area to provide working memory support for the user for the visual representations in the main viewing area. (Figure 2).

Objects in the data set are displayed as different geometrical shapes in colours, sizes and horizontal and vertical locations. This level of symbolic representation would primarily reflect the external properties of the objects.

When the cursor enters the main window area, the objects closest to the cursor reveal something about their internal properties, and this level of representation is of course highly dependant on what kind of objects we are dealing with. The status area has icons that can be selected by the user to control aspects of the representation of the objects in the main window. When an association has been made by the user, a descriptive text is displayed above each respective icon. If the user clicks a specific icon, a dialogue-box opens up that allows the user to modify the mapping of the particular property.

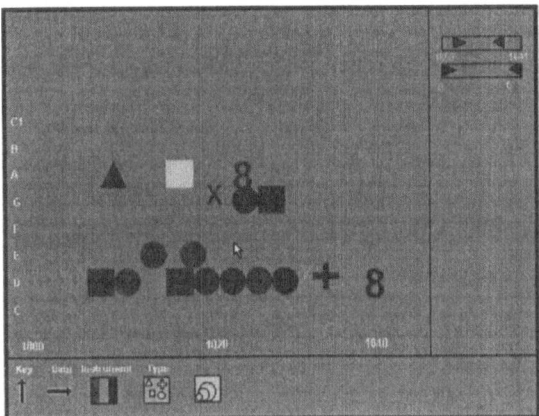

Figure 2: Screenshot of the prototype browser.

Initial default values for the mapping are provided and the user can arbitrarily modify the settings. Mapping to colour present problems because it does not naturally define an ordered continuum and since colour ordering does not have a strong population stereotype. It is also important to note that in a browsing task our ability to differentiate between colours is around five different colours [Marcus 1995, p.430, Wickens 1992, p.102]. Assuming that the user can set the general default order of colours (for example red, yellow, green, blue and violet in 16 steps), the hue will then be mapped accordingly. By selecting the property/colour icon the user can modify the mapping to fit the individual and the task.

Similar problems applies to the mapping of shape as there is no universal understanding of the meaning of different geometrical abstract shapes. For the geometrically minded it might make sense to regard a circle as 1, a line as 2, a triangle as 3, square as 4, etc., but it only makes sense to the individual that makes the choices and defines the mapping. Our ability to differentiate between different shapes is also limited and in general it is in the same range as the ability to differentiate between colours. In the prototype work on the browser we tried a number of algorithms to generate shapes, but because we wanted to make it possible for the user to override all defaults and create a mapping that suits the individual user and the task at hand we decided to use Windows TrueType fonts for a set of shapes as most basic geometric shapes are available in the *Wingdings* character set. This worked quite well, because the fonts is scaleable which made the mapping of size easy to implement and still all mappings can be modified by the user. It is important that the mapping makes sense to the user within a specific task, and the more complex the data-set is the greater the need for good mapping[1].

---

[1] In some cases it could be useful to map two or more representations to a single property, as this would then "amplify" the importance of that property. It is fully possible for most users to "switch" at will if they are looking for objects in terms of for example shape or colour [Wickens 1992, pp.179-193].

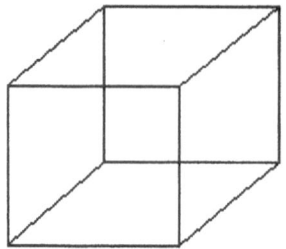

Figure 3: Necker cube

With multimedia PC's the potential to represent properties of objects with sound is great. The best way to describe this is to make an analogy with the visual representation. Sounds can be produced and controlled in a number of ways: pitch (fundamental frequency), timbre (relative spectral content, filtering) and envelope (change in amplitude by time). Everyday sounds or music and also be processed, modified and used. Sound can also have spatial properties, although the possibilities are more complex depending on what kind of equipment that is used. With normal loudspeakers in a stereo set-up, a sonic display with a maximum field of 180° azimuth can be created. If headphones are used instead of loudspeakers, the sonic browser software can emulate a head-related transfer function, and a full 360° surround projection is possible, as well as elevation in the vertical plane (3-D sound). It is important to note that with 3-D sound, there is sometimes a mirroring of sounds between front and rear projection ["reversal" Begault 1994, pp.39-73, "cone of confusion" Gaver 1997], making it difficult for the user to decide if a sound source is in front or behind. A visual analogy to illustrate this might be the *Necker*-cube (Figure 3) that sometimes seem to stands out, sometimes seem to fall into the display surface.

In a normal multimedia PC the resources available for sonification can first of all be divided into two main categories: synthetic or sampled waveforms. There is no fundamental difference from a general use point of view if synthesized or sampled sound is used and there are pros and cons with both. Synthesized sound often takes less space in disk storage, but is normally not as rich as sampled sounds (almost like in the visual domain, the difference between vector and bitmapped graphics). Both can have their fundamental frequency transformed, envelope and filters applied, and they can be assigned a spatial projection. To draw upon the analogy with visual representations, waveforms (or if sampled, the sound itself) could work out similar to shape, frequency similar to hue (colour), filter similar to (colour) brightness, envelope similar to size, azimuth and elevation similar to horizontal/vertical location. In sonification, there are even more uncertainties regarding what will work as generalisations, hence it is very important that the user can configure all aspects of the sonic representation [Anupindi 1990, Gaver 1992].

With sound objects we can provide the user with "sonic thumbnails" by playing the actual sound-files, and using the spatial dimensions to cross-correlate the visual and aural experience. In the first prototype we tried to demonstrate this by playing multiple soundfiles simultaneously and projecting each sound-source in a stereo field corresponding to their visual location on screen in relation the cursor. When the cursor is placed on a single visual representation, only that specific sound-file will play.

In everyday listening one is often exposed to perhaps hundreds of different sounds simultaneously and is still able to pick out important parts of the auditory scene. With musical sounds, or tunes, many different factors affect our ability to differentiate and select between the sources. Using instrumental sounds, the timbre, envelope, tonal range and spatial cues support the formation of streams. The tunes themselves also assist the formation of streams, as music has its own inherent syntactic and semantic properties [Bregman 1990 pp 455-528, Serafine 1988]. It is also interesting to note that sonic browsing in this manner is a practical demonstration of the "cocktailparty" effect. It is possible to switch one's focus at will between sound or tunes [Wickens 1992, p.103]. The actual number of musical tunes that can be differentiated by the user seems to be highly dependant on the user's ability and training as well as the characteristics of the tunes. A professional musician might be able to deal with anything from 5 to 15 different sources at a time[1]. Some tunes tend to form new patterns that users combine into one[2].

2.1   The experimental platform

For the development of domain metaphors, the "look and feel" of the system and for user testing, we have used the multimedia authoring tool Authorware from Macromedia. This tool allowed us to design and create the visual and sonic aspects of the browser. Due to the fact that we wished to achieve a tight coupling of the interaction with the data set and to provide users with a richer and more active support from the system, we added extra functionality to the interface by writing dynamic linked libraries containing the added functionality that could be called from inside the Authorware environment. Other experiments and software developments were primarily concerned with low-level interfacing of the data set and how to normalise the properties of the information objects versus the user interface. A minimalist approach was chosen with as little as possible hardcoded.

When the user selects options for mapping from the available properties, the information is filtered to a *Normalisation and Algorithmic Layer* (NAL, Figure 4). This layer is designed to accept the user selections and to compile a list from the

---

[1] Personal comment by Dr. Mícheál Ó Súilleabháin, Professor of music at UL, musician, composer and conductor. When exposing other musicologists in the IWMC at UL to 3 - 8 concurrent tunes, all had difficulties to differentiate the tunes when five or more tunes were played (informal tests).
[2] An effect often used by J.S.Bach, but also by later composers such as Irving Berlin (1914) in "Play a simple melody".

data set, normalise the properties of each element of this list and to compile a list of normalised values (nodes) and finally to assign representations to each node of the normalised list. For each node from the data set list, a corresponding node is inserted into the NAL list. When the user interface is ready to display (or to produce sound), it retrieves each node from the NAL list. Alternatively, a specific node can be accessed to allow the user to manipulate the mapping in detail. Each node of the NAL list contains a data element which is defined as a structure. If an element of the structure is to be for instance a colour representation, an index to the current set of colours is returned. The power of this architecture lies within the methods of the class in the way that it is designed in object oriented style by incorporating as much as possible into the methods of the class. This potentially allows for porting between data sets and systems and most of the methods are generic.

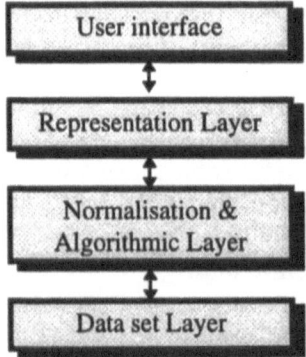

Figure 4: System architecture.

Most multimedia PC's with the Windows operating system cannot play multiple soundfiles concurrently due to that most drivers handle the sound device directly, a fact that more or less proves how neglected the sonic aspects are. To work around this problem we initiated coding of new drivers for the sound devices, which in turn brought us into collaboration with Creative Labs Inc., working with their *Audio Spatialization Library* routines (ASL). We also tried Microsoft's DirectX libraries with DirectSound that, amongst other things, is intended to cater for spatialization, but it only supports (at the time of writing) playing multiple files concurrently, panned out in a normal stereo field based on loudness cues. The DirectX functions have the advantage of playing wave-files (.WAV) directly, whilst files with the ASL have to be converted into *Vienna Soundfonts* (.SF2) so that they can be loaded into Soundblaster's MIDI banks. The actual sounds of the tunes are sampled real musical instruments such as flute, violin, accordion and uillean pipes. Using the ASL in this manner also implies that the maximum number of tunes that can be played and spatially processed simultaneously is eight on a SB 32 AWE board. In both cases, the tunes are played and positioned simultaneously when the user is moving the cursor amongst object representations on screen, the locations are updated approximately every 20 milliseconds. When the user moves to a new sonic neighbourhood (outside the currently loaded and playing sounds), it takes up to a second to load the new sounds into memory or sound banks. This delay will hopefully shrink with the arrival of new soundcard architectures in a not too distant future.

Sound sources can be positioned to correspond to the visual location of symbols on the screen versus the location of the cursor. To make a real world analogy, it is like walking into a record store and the tapes, CD's etc. in front of you are playing on low volume and when you touch a cover of a tape or CD, that particular piece can be heard exclusively. The resulting metaphor shows a high degree of virtuality insofar as it cannot be experienced in the real world, but still - in the browser - it enables the user to use his or her natural ability to listen to multiple concurrent sound sources and to navigate by sound.

The series of prototypes that we have developed and tested with users have provided important feedback for future implementations. Based on informal user testing, we have indications that the new ideas work, and that they are different to *Spotfire* and other browsers. The concept of representing information objects with geometrical shapes of different sizes and colours have been successful with the only exception that when several objects happen to coincide in the same horizontal and vertical location, the underlying objects become invisible to the user. This problem can very likely be resolved in future prototypes by using different kinds of highlighting or jittering of the location of visual representations to make otherwise hidden objects visible. Some users have requested the implementation of various forms of grids to support visual spatial read-out. We have also noted that it is important to enable the user to do continuous work with the browser and to avoid breakdowns in the interaction, e.g. that intermediate dialogues do not interrupt the browsing process for example when the user have clicked an object and an information-box pops up, the user should not have to close the information box - it should close automatically when the user moves the cursor outside the current object. Sometimes it is desirable to have multiple information-boxes open, to allow for comparison of the more detailed properties between different objects. This can possibly be implemented by, for instance, a shift-click operation.

The experimental platform is currently built of several different components:
One major implementation in Authorware that covers the general implementation of the Browser, with focus on the visual user interface and the Fleischmann data set.
Several smaller implementations in Authorware that we have used to test details of the user interface, for instance structure, sliders, highlighting and hotspots.
Applications and DLL's written in C/C++ to interface the Data set layer, NAL, Representation layer and to provide sonification.

3   Conclusion

The tight coupling between visual and sound dimensions allows the user to move the cursor around in the main window to get an idea of the sonic neighbourhood. It seems that users quickly pick up the domain metaphor and the mapping, although we will have to conduct further formal tests to quantify this. It seems to make better use of both our human abilities to localise sound and to listen to multiple concurrent sound sources. With the ability to place the objects along two dimensions based on arbitrarily selected properties of the objects, it becomes possible for the user to move within the space and explore the sonic assets in the data set. Such a browsing mechanism can also be of use for visually impaired users because the differentiation for navigation is based on spatial sound properties. The sound-files in the prototype are looped, i.e. when an active file reaches end-of-file the playback starts again from the beginning of the file. With a musical data set, it might be relevant to have a user configurable loop-length as most people tend to recognise a particular tune from the first few the first few seconds of sound. It is also important to note that apart from the spatial representation of sound, other aspects of the sounds help the user to differentiate the sound-sources, i.e. spectral characteristics and envelope. For data sets with musical content, the musical properties can also support differentiation. Our experience with the prototype indicate that there are many new avenues to be investigated using sound in the user interface and that by creating systems with tight coupling, new interface metaphors and ways of interaction can be developed. With our second data set, an environmental database, the issue of mapping is different. In this case there is no apparent natural mappings, which means that the system must provide the user with a set of functions and good default mapping templates that the user can explore, modify, assign and learn. We intend to provide a high degree of user configurability also for this function, and systems similar to Scalletti's Kyma [Scalletti 1994] are likely to serve as our inspiration.

The browser prototype that we have created and started to test allows the user to move around freely in a multimedia information space, using both vision and hearing to experience the scope of the data set, and to explore the properties of the information objects. When the user wants to examine an object in further detail, this is possible with a minimum effort. With a rich representation and flexibility for the user to modify the mapping of properties to suit the individual and the task at hand, it becomes easier to navigate the information space and to locate objects of interest.

Acknowledgment

Funding for this research has been provided by the Forbairt Strategic Research Programme.

References

Albers M.C., (1995) *Varese - Non-speech Auditory Interfaces*, http://www.isye.gatech.edu/chmsr/Mike_Albers/projects/Varese/AudInt.html

Albers, M. C., Bergman, E., (1995) *The audible web: Auditory enhancements for Mosaic. CHI'95 conference companion*, ACM Conference on Human Factors in Computing Systems, pp 318-319

Anupindi S., (1990) *A browser for Dynamic Multimedia Documents*, pp.747-751 in INTERACT '90, Elsevier Science Publications B.V., Amsterdam, Netherlands

Bannon L., Bødker S., (1991) *Beyond the Interface: Encountering Artefacts in Use*, in Designing Interaction: Psychology at the Human-Computer Interface, Ed. Carroll J., Cambridge University Press Cambridge, England

Bannon L., (1991b) *From Human Factors to Human Actors: the Role of Psychology and Human-Computer Interaction studies in systems design*, in Design at Work, Erlbaum

Bannon L., (1993) *Problems and Pitfalls in Multimedia or Multimedia What's the Fuss?*, Lecture Notes PMTC Course on Multimedia, University of Limerick Limerick, Ireland

Begault D.R., (1994) *3-D Sound for Virtual Reality and Multimedia*, Academic Press Inc., Cambridge, MA, USA

Bly, S. (1994) *Presenting information in sound*, in *Proceedings of CHI '82 Conference on Human Factors in Computer Systems*, ACM ,New York, pp 371-375.

Blattner M, Sumikawa D.A, Greenberg R.M., (1989) *Earcons and Icons: Their Structure and Common Design Principles*, pp. 5.48-5.74 in The Use of Non-Speech Audio at the Interface, ACM Press, CHI '89 Austin, Texas, USA

Blattner, M. M., Papp, A. L., Glinert, E. P., (1994) *Sonic enhancement of two-dimensional graphic displays.* In Kramer, G. (ed.), *Auditory Display*, Addison-Wesley, New York, pp 447 - 470.

Bregman, A.S., (1990) *Auditory Scene Analysis: the perceptual organization of sound*, MIT Press, Massachusetts, USA.

Brewster, S.A., Wright, P. C, Edwards, A. D. N. (1994) *A detailed investigation into the effectiveness of earcons*, In Kramer, G. (ed.), *Auditory Display*. Addison-Wesley, New York pp 471 - 498.

Erickson T., (1990) *Working with Interface Metaphors*, pp. 65-73 in The Art of Human-Computer Interface Design, Ed. Laurel B., Addison-Wesley Publishing Reading, Massachusest, USA 1990-93 5th ed.

Gaver W.W., (1989) *The Sonic Finder: An Interface that Uses Auditory Icons*, pp. 5.85-5.106 in The Use of Non-Speech Audio at the Interface, ACM Press, CHI '89 Austin, Texas, USA

Gaver, W. W. (1991) *Sound support for collaboration.* In *Proceedings of ECSCW'91*, Kluwer, Dordrecht.

Gaver W.W., (1992) *Synthesizing Auditory Icons*, Cambridge EuroPARC.

Gaver W.W., (1997) *Auditory Interfaces*, in Helander M.G., Landauer, T.K., Pabhu, P. (Eds.) Handbook of Human-Computer Interaction, 2nd edition. Elsevier Science Publishers, Amsterdam, The Netherlands.

Hutchins E., (1987) *Metaphors for Interface Design*, ICS Report 9703, Institute for Cognitive Science, University of California, San Diego, USA.

IVEE Development AB, (1996) *Seminar on World Wide Web design, User Interface Design and Interactive Information Visualization*, IVEE Development, Gothenburg, Sweden.

Jerke K.-H., Szabo P., Lesch A., Rößler H., (1990) *Combining Hypermedia browsing with Formal Queries*, pp. 593-598 in INTERACT '90, Elsevier Science Publications B.V., Amsterdam, Netherlands

Kobayashi, M., Schmandt, C., (1997) *Dynamic Soundscape: mapping time to space for audio browsing*, in *Proceedings of CHI '97*, ACM Press, Atlanta Georgia pp.194-209

LoPresti, E., Harris, W.M., (1996) *loudSPIRE, an Auditory Display Schema for the SPIRE System*, Proceedings of ICAD '96, Palo Alto, California, USA

Marchionini G., (1995) *Information Seeking in Electronic Environments*, The Press Syndicate of the Univeristy of Cambridge New York, USA

Marchionini G., (1995b) *User-centered methods for library interface design*, 37th Allerton Institute 1995,Graduate School of Library and Information Science, University of Illinois at Urbana-Champaign, http://edfu.lis.uiuc.edu/allerton/95/s4/marchio.html

Marcus A., (1995) *Principles of Effective Visual Communication for graphical User Interface Design*, pp. 425-441 in Readings in Human-Computer Interaction: Toward the Year 2000, Ed. Baecker R.M. el al, Morgan Kaufman Publishers Inc. San Francisco, USA

Nelson T.H., (1990) *The Right Way to Think About Software Design*, in The Art of Human-Computer Interface Design, Ed. Laurel B.

Ó Súilleabháin, M., McGettrick, P., Fleischmann, A. (1997) Sources of Traditional Irish Music (in press). Garland Publishing Inc., NY, USA.

Scalletti, C., (1994) Sound synthesis algorithms for auditory data representations. In Kramer, G. (ed.), *Auditory Display*. Addison-Wesley, New York, pp. 79 - 94.

Serafine, L.S., (1988) Music as Cognition: the Development of Thought in Sound, Columbia University Press, New York

Shneiderman B., Ahlberg C., (1994) *Visual Information Seeking using the FilmFinder*, ACM SIGGRAPH on Computer Graphics

Slaney, M., Covell, M., Lassiter, B., (1996) *Automatic Audio Morphing*, in Proceedings of the 1996 International Conference on Acoustics, Speech and Signal Processing, IEEE, Atlanta, Georgia.

Wickens C.D., (1992) *Engineering Psychology and Human Performance*, Harper-Collins Publ. Inc., NY, USA 1992. 2nd ed.

Remote homeplace communication: what is it like and how might we support it?

David M. Frohlich[+], Kathy Chilton[*] & Paul Drew[*]

[+]*Hewlett Packard Laboratories, Filton Road, Stoke Gifford, Bristol BS12 6QZ*
Email: dmf@hplb.hpl.hp.com

[*]*Department of Sociology, University of York, Heslington, York YO1 5DD*
Emails: ksc102@york.ac.uk, wpd1@york.ac.uk

We introduce the study of homeplace communication as being relevant to the design of new communication technology for the home market. After reviewing current approaches to the field, we go on to describe the nature of *remote* homeplace communication over the telephone, based on a quantitative and qualitative analysis of 315 household telephone calls. The findings are contrasted with aspects of workplace communication and used to identify 7 user requirements for support. We conclude with recommendations for future basic and applied research in the area.

Keywords: Home, homeplace, communication, interaction, telephone, call, relationship, user needs, requirements, technology.

1   The homeplace communication challenge

In the future, a majority of homes in Europe and the US will be connected by broadband communication networks capable of carrying many times the amount of data which is currently transported over traditional telephone lines. This infrastructure will allow people to interactively exchange multimedia information on a personal, community and global scale using new kinds of computers, phones and appliances. The key question which hangs over such developments is a social rather than a technical one. In what ways would people find it useful to enhance and extend their everyday communication using the new technology?

Somewhat surprisingly there has been very little direct research into this question. Most effort in the technological community has been directed towards understanding user needs in *workplace communication*, since the primary market for computer and communications technology has been the workplace. Indeed, the field in which most of this research has taken place is called 'Computer Supported Cooperative Work' (CSCW); a name which indicates that the key problem situation of study is cooperative or group work (Bannon & Schmidt 1991). By default, many of the technologies developed out of this tradition are making their ways into personal and domestic contexts, through the use of small portable appliances such as mobile phones, pagers and organisers, and through the rise of home computers for telework and internet access. However it is unlikely that these tools and technologies will be ideally suited to the support of what might be called *homeplace communication*, where the problem situation may have more to do with the maintenance of relationships between family, friends and others, communicating within, to or from a household unit. What is really needed here is the equivalent of a CSCW-like research effort in homeplace communication, to identify the relevant behaviours and needs and so address the question outlined above. We might call this effort *Computer Supported Social Interaction* (CSSI).

In this paper we begin to characterize aspects of homeplace communication **as it is carried out today**, as a first step in identifying broad classes of user needs and technological requirements for further study in CSSI. The approach is similar to that taken in a previous publication characterizing informal workplace communication, and this paper can be read both as an extension and companion to that one (Whittaker, Frohlich & Daly-Jones 1994). For further information on the workplace study see also Frohlich (1995), Isaacs, Whittaker, Frohlich & O'Conaill (1997), O'Conaill & Frohlich (1995).

An alternative approach to the area is to examine the **uptake and use of new communication technologies** in a domestic context. Work on the home use of internet communication services is probably the most advanced of this kind, and should be seen as complementing the picture we are about to present (e.g. Kraut, Scherlis, Mukhopadhyay, Manning & Kiesler 1996, Rhiengold 1995, Turkle 1995).

2   Building on previous work in homeplace communication

A detailed understanding of how people organize their domestic communication activities is not available from the scientific literature. Several fields of research intersect the topic without providing the necessary level of insight to reason about requirements for technological support. Family Studies have examined the changing pattern of family composition and relationships in different societies, without going into the details of everyday communication patterns (e.g. Burguiere,

Klapisch - Zuber, Segalen & Zonabend 1996). Time Use studies describe the allocation of personal time to several communication-related activities, but fail to specify what happens within those periods (e.g. Robinson 1988). Conversation Analysis (CA) utilizes complete recordings of naturally occurring conversations to examine micro-conversational practices, but has generally overlooked the ways in which conversations between the same partners are themselves are strung together over time (c.f. Frohlich 1994). Finally, the Social and Personal Relationships literature recognizes the importance of routine interactions in relationship maintenance, but has so far failed to examine them directly (c.f. Duck & Pittman 1994).

Research in this latter area is probably the most revealing of potential problems in homeplace communication. One big problem is that all relationships appear to require maintenance through contact, but that this becomes increasingly difficult over the years as local friends and family move away from each other (Dickens & Perlman 1981). People tend to protect family ties at the expense of friendships which don't carry the same sense of obligation; resulting in the common experience of always 'being there' but 'growing apart' (Rawlins 1994). Social trends towards higher divorce and separation rates exacerbate the problem for shared friendships, and have serious consequences for the relationships between children and their absent fathers and paternal grandparents (Bengtson & Robertson 1985).

In order to address the lack of observational data on homeplace communication, we decided to examine use of the domestic telephone through analysis of an existing corpus of calls. By examining the content as well as the pattern of telephone calls in the corpus we go beyond existing studies of telephone use (e.g. de Sola Pool 1977) and extend CA methods to the study of social and personal relationships. In this way we have chosen to characterize *remote* homeplace communication as it is done today over the phone, and so investigate the problem of remote relationship maintenance in its practical context.

3   Methods

We had available a particularly suitable corpus of telephone calls recorded by one family over a three year period. The family live in the south of England, and consist of a husband (Skip) and wife (Lesley), and their two children (Kath and Gordon). Note that all parties in the calls are identified throughout by pseudonyms to preserve their anonymity, and all other identifying details have been changed on transcripts of calls. They can be classified as professional middle class; Skip working in the financial management of a machinery company, and Lesley being a supply teacher. Kath is at university in the north of England, and Gordon is finishing A' levels (in the latter part of the 3-year period over which recordings were made, he also has left to go to university). They have not always lived at their current address, and so have family and friends in other quite distant parts of the country. For instance, the wife's mother lives approximately 150 miles away;

although the husband's mother lives close by, in the same town. The family, and in particular Lesley, is affiliated to a number of church and other local organizations.

Recordings were not continuous over the 3 year period: instead they were made at intervals - in the weeks before Christmas in the first year, for short periods during most months in the second year, and in May and then September/October in the third year. So that the corpus is a sample of the calls made by and to this family over 3 years; but in the periods sampled, all outgoing calls made by members of the family and incoming calls were recorded by a remote recording device. This resulted in a sample of 315 calls, totaling 22 hours of telephone conversations.

The conventional CA approach to these recordings would be to transcribe a sample of the calls so as to gain a better understanding of the kinds of social phenomena they contain, and then to collect multiple instances of some target phenomenon as a preliminary to looking at how it works. Indeed about a third of calls in this corpus have been transcribed in detail using conventional CA notation (c.f. Atkinson & Heritage 1984). In this analysis we supplemented this approach with an encoding of various properties of each interaction in the corpus such as who was calling who, about what and for how long. This allowed us to explore certain macro patterns in the data relating to the whole household's use of the telephone, and to pinpoint important phenomena at this level for more detailed collection and analysis.

The following characteristics were coded for each call: caller identity; identities of answerer, the intended recipient of the call, and others who may have participated in the conversation; relationships between caller/receiver etc.; duration; reason for call; principal topic(s) discussed; whether messages were taken during the call; local or long distance; whether the call was connected to some prior contact between participants, including whether it was pre-arranged; whether the call was one in a series (eg. `phoning around a group of people about some event); whether explicit reference was made to some physical materials, or environment; and the approximate time of day, and whether weekday or weekend.

In what follows, we try to illustrate some of the macro quantitative patterns which emerged from the data, with brief excerpts from the transcripts. Our aim is to give some flavour of the nature of remote homeplace communication as embodied in the corpus, through a mix of quantitative and qualitative analyses.

4   Understanding remote homeplace communication

4.1   The nature of calls

We found that calls in the corpus were essentially of two broad types. Of the 315 calls made, 166 (53%) were **single-topic calls** made with the express purpose of discussing the original reason for calling. Another 146 calls (46%) were **multiple topic calls** in which the reason for calling formed only one of a number of topics discussed. (A further 3 calls could not be classified as single or multiple topic because their recording was cut off before the end of the first topic). Extracts 1 and 2 below illustrate each type, and serve to give a flavour of the kinds of calls recorded.

Extract 1. A content-oriented single topic call (C258)

GORDON HAS JUST FORGOTTEN TO ATTEND A HAIRDRESSERS APPOINTMENT EARLIER IN THE EVENING.

1. Gordon:Hello:,

2.   (0.3)

3. Desk: Hello is Gordon the[:re

4. Gordon: [.mptch e-speaking,

5. Desk: Um (0.4) it's the hai:r dresser's. And eh you had'n

6.   appointment for: (0.5) tonight at at six thirty:

7.   (.)

8. Gordon:Ah yes I di-:d that's right.h · hh (.)

10. Gordon:I forgot completely about it

11.   (1.1)

12. Desk: Oka:y,

Extract 1 shows the opening of a brief call to Gordon by his hairdresser to remind him that he just forgotten his appointment (to Line 6). In the remainder of the call (not shown) Gordon responds by apologizing and then arranging a new appointment, and the call is closed after a total of 50 seconds without any talk on other matters. Note that the focus here is on the content of the talk.

In contrast, Extract 2 shows the opening of a regular weekly call that Lesley has with her mum. Each of them take it in turns to call the other on alternate weeks and this call begins with mum explaining why she is ringing on Saturday evening when it was Lesley's turn to call the following day (Lines 5, 7 & 8). Lesley doesn't wait for her mum to provide any further reason for calling than this, and goes on to broach a new topic in Line 9 by remarking on the snowy weather. This then becomes the second of 10 topics discussed over the next 4 minutes 41 seconds before the recording ends prematurely. The usual duration of these calls is 10 minutes 16 seconds. The fact that Lesley's mum has no particular reason for calling other than to chat to her daughter, captures the spirit of a number of calls in the corpus which seem to have as their function, just talking to the other party. In contrast to the content-focussed nature of single topic calls, the focus here is on the relationship between the talkers; where the talk is used to maintain and extend the relationship itself.

Extract 2.   A relationship-oriented multi-topic call (C30)

LESLEY AND HER MOTHER TAKE IT IN TURNS TO RING EACH OTHER ON SUNDAY EVENINGS.   IT IS LESLEY'S TURN TO RING ON THE SUNDAY BUT HER MOTHER OPTS TO RING ON THE SATURDAY EVENING INSTEAD. THE FIRST FEW TURNS ARE NOT SHOWN.

1.   Lesley: How are y<u>ou</u>:?

2.   Mum: <u>Oh</u> <u>fi</u>ne thanks l<u>o</u>ve,

3.   Lesley: .hh [I w'z go]ing tuh ring you t'morrow ni:ght.=

4.   Mum: [And you?]

5.   Mum: =<u>Oh</u>:. Well I-: I'm (.) g<u>o</u> <u>to</u> ch<u>ur</u>ch t'morrow even<u>ing</u>,

6.   Lesley: Ye[s,

7.   Mum: [So I thought I ring you th<u>is</u> <u>e</u>vening. I haven'been: going in the evening b't

8.   I'm going t'st<u>a</u>rt t'morrow

9.   Lesley: O<u>h</u>:- <u>You</u> know we had sn<u>o</u>w this evening,

10.   Mum: <u>So</u> did <u>we</u>::.

In actuality, Extract 2 seems to lie at the extreme end of a continuum within the multi-topic calls, which vary in their content versus relationship focus. A more content-oriented call which contains two topics is shown in Extract 3. Here Lesley calls the father (Arthur) of a friend of Kath's, Clive. She asks him to tell Clive that Kath is coming home on Sunday and would like to see Clive on Monday. After Arthur agrees to pass on the message he takes the opportunity of asking about the recent burglary at Lesley's home (Line 9). In this way a purely content-oriented call that might have taken 36 seconds, turns into a relationship-oriented one lasting 1 minute 26 seconds.

Extract 3. An extended content-oriented call (C212)

LESLEY PHONES ARTHUR, THE FATHER OF A FRIEND OF KATH TO ASK HIM TO PASS ON A MESSAGE TO HIS SON CLIVE. ARTHUR AGREES AND GOES ON TO ASK ABOUT LESLEY'S' RECENT BURGLARY

1. Lesley: [We're going t'this Fest'val'v Nine Lessons 'n Carols (0.2) Sundee evening ·hh but she said

2.   i-uh:-(0.2) tih (0.2) tell Clive to wander rou:nd or she'll wander round,h (.) an' meet him

3.   (0.3)

4. Arthur: iYes[okay

5.   [uh:m: (0.3) Mondee sometime

6. Arthur: Right that's fi:ne.

7.   (.)

8. Lesley: i[Yes

9. Arthur: [o-Okay I'll do that. .hhh (0.2) How how've you settled in now after the: (p) visitor.

10.   (0.2)

11. Lesley: ·hhh Oh: (.) eh hheh he hh Well- (0.2) h (.) I mus' say this finger print stuff makes a me:ss but

12. Arthur: Oh:.

13. Lesley: An' I can' get the mud off the cushion: but apart f'm that we're alri:gh[t?

14. Arthur:
[What a nuisance.

These three examples also illustrate a broader trend in the relationship between partners holding single-topic and multiple-topic conversations. Multiple-topic calls like Extracts 2 and 3 are largely between the family and friends of the household, whereas single-topic calls like Extract 1 are largely between friends or those we have classified as 'others'; including work colleagues, domestic business contacts (e.g. hairdresser), neighbourhood contacts and strangers. In this respect, the quantitative data reinforces the ambivalent nature of calls between friends, since these are the calls where the number of topics are most unpredictable (see again Extract 3). This pattern is shown in Table 1 and is significant at the .0001 level (X^2=74.01, df=2).

CALL PROPERTY	FAMILY	FRIEND	OTHER	TOTAL
Single-topic calls	29.00	65.00	72.00	166.00
Multiple-topic calls	69.00	72.00	5.00	146.00
TOTAL	98.00	137.00	77.00	312.00

Table 1:   The number of single and multiple-topic calls made by family, friends and others.

Other attributes of the calls between family, friends and others are shown in Table 2 and reveal further comparative differences in communication. It should be noted that these statistics apply to individual interactions rather than calls, since early in the coding process we discovered that the corpus contains 61 *multi-interaction calls* in which several two party conversations take place.   Since the attributes of these calls cannot clearly be coded at the call level, we switched to coding individual interactions in the corpus as a more meaningful unit of analysis; and Table 2 reports some of the key details of what we found.   It is based on a total of 384 interactions made within the 315 calls.   The phenomenon of multi-interaction calls is an important finding in its own right and is explored in further detail later.

INTERACTION PROPERTY	FAMILY	FRIEND	OTHER	TOTAL
Mean duration of completed interactions (min:sec)	4:43	4:01	1:67	–
Total number of Interactions	116	169	99	384.00
...of which: Scheduled	36	22	4	62.00
...of which: Incoming	70	73	27	170.00
...of which: Local	32	143	86	261.00
Total number of messages	33.00	54.00	13	100.00
References to local documents	59	46	29	134.00
References to local objects/scenes	354.00	237.00	79	670.00

Table 2:   A summary of some key properties of household telephone interactions by relationship.

Taken together, the findings of Table 2 suggests that remote homeplace communication has some quite different properties to informal workplace communication as revealed in our earlier study (Whittaker et al 1994).   In general, interactions with 'others' have the most business-like quality in the sense that they are more likely to be single-topic, they last about 2 minutes, and they tend *not* to be scheduled in advance. However, even these have some new features. For example many of them are one-off outgoing calls to shops or service organizations, most of them are local, and they involve about half the number of references to documents you might expect in a work context. In contrast they involve a large number of references to local physical objects and scenery. While this latter feature wasn't something we examined formally in the workplace, our sense is that references to the local physical surroundings are more pervasive and important in the home context.

The greatest differences between home and work interactions are revealed in our household's interactions with family and friends. These interactions are twice as long (4 minutes instead of 2), more likely to be scheduled in advance, involve even more references to 'domestic scenery', and contain a large number of messages for third parties. Furthermore, family and friend interactions themselves differ along some of these dimensions. Interactions with family tend to be longer, involving more references to documents *and* objects, to more long distance destinations, but with fewer messages.

In the following sub-sections we explore the most distinctive features of the corpus revealed by this analysis; including the scheduling of calls, the occurrence of multi-interaction calls, the exchange of messages, and the mentioning of domestic scenery.

4.2   Scheduling and initiation

In our earlier workplace study we found that only 5 out of 108 business phone calls (i.e. about 5%) were time or date scheduled in advance (unpublished data). In the current study we see the same low level of scheduling reflected in the interactions with 'others' (4%) but much higher levels of scheduling in interactions with friends (13%) and family (31%).

A major motivation for the higher incidence of scheduling in calls to family and friends is that there is simply less time when these contacts are likely to be mutually available to each other *without* scheduling. Interactions in the corpus took place most often on weekday evenings (38%) or at weekends (37%) - based on 266 interactions whose time and day could be identified. Given that family members share the phone and pursue a range of activities outside the home, the chances of getting through to an intended party spontaneously are slim. With scheduling however, callers in this corpus were able to achieve a successful connection up to 89% of the time - not counting engaged or unanswered calls which were unrecorded. This compares with a hit rate of 38% in the workplace context - where calls usually get answered by someone (Whittaker et al 1994).

A related finding was that pairs of family members often fell into a routine of regularly calling at certain times of the week. The best examples of this were the conversations between Lesley and her mum every Sunday evening. These calls were so regular that any deviation from the normal time of calling was accountable by the violating party (see again Extract 2). Other examples of regular family calls were Skip calling Lesley from work during the day and Kath ringing at the end of University terms to make arrangements for coming home.

In contrast, contact between friends was rarely scheduled and usually prompted by a specific reason for calling. Local calls between friends often arose out of prior face-to-face contact or were concerned with arrangements to meet. Although there was evidence of regular contact between local friends, such as Gordon and his girlfriend, the only regular long distance friendship calls were those prompted by events such as Christmas and birthdays. These events seemed to be used as an excuse to get back in touch.

We see this pattern as being dangerous for the maintenance of long distance friendships over the phone, which lack the kind of ongoing local encounters which trigger calls. In these cases it seems to take some sort of shareable experience, event or concrete object to invoke the relationship again and trigger the call. A good example of this is shown in Extract 4. In this case Lesley receives a holiday postcard from Anna, an old friend of hers now living on the South coast. Lesley responds to the postcard by ringing Anna that same day to thank her and re-establish contact. Note the measured tone of the opening questions by Lesley to check that the postcard was indeed from Anna (Line 8), and her reinforcement of shared experience with Anna by bringing in the connection with Kath's interest in the holiday destination (Line 14).

Extract 4.   Getting back in touch with a friend (C289)

A HOLIDAY POSTCARD FROM AN OLD FRIEND OF LESLEY'S TRIGGERS A FOLLOW-UP TELEPHONE CALL

1. Lesley: Oh hello (0.3) is that <u>Anna</u>?

2. Anna: Yes speaking

3. Lesley: Oh hello Anna (0.4) er- this is Lesley Field here

4.   (0.9)

5. Anna: ↑OH LESLEY!

6. Lesley: Yes hello

7. Anna: He↓<u>llo:</u>

8. Lesley: ↑<u>Did</u> we get a post↓card from you today from the Isle of Ar<u>ran</u>

9. Anna: Yeah you did

10. Lesley: OH! (0.2) HOW <u>LOVE</u>LY!

11. Anna: ha ha ha ha ha

12. Lesley: Were you havin holi<u>da</u>y the::re

13. Anna: Ye::ah!

14. Lesley: OH GREAT! (0.3) only Kath- its Kath's favourite stamping ground

15. Anna: Its <u>not</u>

4.3   Multi-interaction calls

The occurrence of multi-interaction calls in the corpus is related to the fact that the household telephone is a *shared resource*, and that it is often used to communicate with *common contacts*.

An example of a multi-interaction call stemming from the first factor is one in which the caller gets through to someone who is not the intended recipient of the call, and they in turn pass the phone over to the intended party. Fifty of the 61 multi-interaction calls (i.e. 82%) were of this type. Many such calls resulted from the fact that in this household, father, mother and son effectively compete to answer the phone. The equivalent format in the workplace is a call to a receptionist or colleague who subsequently passes the caller to the 'appropriate person'. Indeed we encounter a small number of these calls themselves in the household corpus as Lesley, Skip, Gordon and Kath phone *out* on domestic business calls, or contact friends and family at work. An interesting difference between the two formats is that when family members answer the phone on behalf of other members, they often strike up their own conversation with the calling party. This happened once in every three calls of this type. It was particularly common in Lesley's interactions with friends of her children calling in. She uses the opportunity of taking a 'missed connection' to Gordon or Kath to consolidate her relationship with them!

The remaining 11 multi-interaction calls are instances of the phone being passed around members of a household opportunistically. In these cases there has usually been a successful connection between the original calling and called parties, who then go on to engineer other connections with common contacts at either end. For example in one call, Lesley speaks to her mum for 2 minutes 33 seconds before passing her onto Gordon for 36 seconds. The transition is shown in Extract 5 below. In the rest of the call (not shown), Lesley resumes conversation with her mum for a further 1 minute 24 seconds. Her mum then hands over to 'Auntie Vanna' at the other end (for 2 minutes 12 seconds) who happens to be visiting her at the time. The phone finally returns to Lesley's mum who closes the call after a further 1 minute 19 seconds.

Extract 5.   Passing the phone around (C266)

MUM HAS CALLED LESLEY FOR THEIR ROUTINE WEEKLY CHAT AND DURING
THE COURSE OF THE PRECEDING CONVERSATION LESLEY REPORTS THAT
GORDON HAS JUST ARRIVED HOME FROM AN ALL NIGHT PARTY. GORDON'S
SUBSEQUENT INTERACTION WITH HIS GRANDMOTHER IS SEEMINGLY
OCCASIONED BY HIS OPPORTUNE AND NOISY ENTRANCE.

1.   Mum: M[m:.

2.   Lesley: [.hhhh N<u>o.</u> We- uh[<u>we</u> feel that when we come t'you we'd=

3.   [((noise))

4.   Lesley: =like (.) just have a r<u>e</u>st u- Oh say hello to .hhh Granny Anders.

5.   (0.3)

6.   Gordon: <u>He</u>llo:,hmhhh

7.   Mum: Hello:: ((mimicking his greeting))

8.   (.)

9.   Mum: Have yih hadda n<u>i</u>ce t<u>i</u>:me,

A variation on actually passing the phone around is to have a third party listening
into one half of the conversation and chipping in comments. Extract 6 shows an
example of this in which Skip's niece shouts out a question to him (in Line 4) while
he is talking to her dad. Again, this occurs because members of the household at
one end share some friendship or family relationship with someone at the other
end, and become involved in the call largely by virtue of their proximity to the
phone.

Extract 6.   A third party trying to get in (C233)

SKIP HAS TRIED TO CALL HIS SISTER. SHE IS OUT SO THE ANSWERER, HIS
NIECE DIERDRE, PASSES HIM ON TO HER DAD, DWAYNE. DWAYNE'S FAMILY
ARE JUST FINISHING THEIR TEA AND ARE ASSEMBLED IN CLOSE PROXIMITY
TO THE PHONE.

1.   Dwayne: <u>O</u>h: lovely. F<u>u</u>nny e[nough Deena[wz only (.) talking=

2.   Skip: [.hhh   [whh.

3.   Dwayne: =a[bout you the other d<u>ay</u>]

4.   Dierdre: [You coming to my w]eddi<u>::</u>n?

5.   Skip: .hhhh

6.   (0.6)

7.   Dwayne: dihyuh <u>hear</u> that,

8.   Skip: gihYeah I h<u>e</u>ard that th<u>a</u>t's why I r<u>a</u>ng <u>up</u> real<u>ly</u>

A final point to note is that we found some evidence of a tension between the shared and the private use of the phone in these circumstances. This is exemplified in Extract 6 in which Kath's ex-boyfriend Miles calls to speak to Kath who is out. He subsequently refuses to leave a message for Kath with Lesley (Line 5), suggesting that there are aspects to his relationship with Kath that he would rather keep private. Actually doing this turns out to be a perennial problem with the family phone which is often used in a very public context, and via people who will naturally want to take a personal interest in each other's relationships.

Extract 7. Evidence of a private relationship (C26)

KATH'S EX-BOYFRIEND MILES RINGS TO SPEAK TO KATH BUT GETS HER MUM INSTEAD. LESLEY OFFERS TO TAKE A MESSAGE BUT MILES DECLINES.

1. Lesley: O[o d'you wan't'give me a m e s s A] G E,

2. Miles: [D'y'know w't time s h e 'll be in.]

3. Miles: Pardon?

4. Lesley: D'you want t'give me a messAGE.

5. Miles: Oh no I better ring'er back myse:lf,

4.4 Exchanging messages

The passing of messages to third parties occurred in one out of every four interactions in the corpus. It occurred even more frequently as a proportion of interactions to family and friends; with one in three calls to friends containing a message (see again Table 2).

Exchanging messages was common in the workplace context also, although there it was usually done following a 'missed connection' event to pass on a message to the missing party (Frohlich 1995). Here we found that this kind of message accounted for only 28% of the total number of messages exchanged. The other 72% of messages involved the passage of information to some mutual contact of two people who had successfully established contact with each other.

An example of this second type of message exchange is shown in Extract 8. Kath is expecting to come home from University soon and calls Lesley to make arrangements. In the course of their conversation Lesley relays a message from a local friend of Kath's, Harriet, who has apparently asked for her to come home as soon as possible (see Line 1). As often happens in these situations, the message recipient, Kath, is able to construct her reply as a further message which Lesley is asked to pass back to Harriet (Line 6). This example also shows that some of these 'messages' may actually be rhetorical devices for the speaker to indicate the feelings or intentions of mutual contacts whether or not they have been voiced as such. Here Lesley may not be reporting words which Harriet has uttered, so much as her belief that Harriet misses Kath and would benefit from her contact.

Extract 8. Multiple message relay between successfully connected speakers (C196)

A MESSAGE FROM HARRIET IS RELAYED FROM LESLEY TO KATH AT THE END OF A CALL TO ARRANGE WHEN KATH IS COMING HOME FROM UNIVERSITY. KATH IMMEDIATELY ASKS LESLEY TO PASS ON HER REPLY.

1. Lesley: .hh Oh Harriet says pl<u>ease</u> come home as soon as possible and she looks <u>really::</u> w<u>a</u>shed <u>out</u>

2. Kath: Does she oh::

3. Lesley: I expect really its a bit traumatic at home at the moment   ['cos

4. Kath: [(   )

5. Lesley: I know erhm (.) <u>Norman</u>'s a bit cut up and I think <u>Jean</u> is t<u>oo</u>

6. Kath: Erh ye::ah tell her I'll be home soon anyway.

The practical effect of these messages is to extend the range of one's social network and to create some sense of a 'community' of mutual contacts. Both points are illustrated in Extract 9 taken from the same call as Extract 8. Lesley passes on advice to a friend of Kath's that she doesn't really know, following a stretch of talk discussing her back condition (Lines 1 and 8).

Extract 9. Advice to a friend of the family (C196)

LESLEY AND KATH ARE DISCUSSING THE BACK CONDITION OF FRIEND OF KATH'S. LESLEY INSTRUCTS KATH TO PASS ON SOME ADVICE.

1. Lesley: <u>Tell</u> her to lie on the fl<u>oor</u> as much as p<u>o</u>ssible.
2.   (1.1)
3. Kath: Yes I wonder if her bed['s
4. Lesley: [Sorry?
5. Kath: I wonder if her <u>bed</u>'s is: (.) uhm (0.3) h<u>a</u>rd en<u>ough</u>
6. Lesley: No her bed may not be may it
7. Kath: No
8. Lesley: ↑Tell her to put a be- erhm a <u>board</u> of some kind or an old <u>door</u> (.) under [the
9. Kath:
[Yeah

10. Lesley: Under the <u>bed</u>

4.5 References to domestic scenery

A final distinctive feature of the corpus was the large number of references to local physical materials. On average, such references were made twice in each interaction. This compares with one document reference in every two own-office conversations in our workplace corpus (Whittaker et al 1994). Document references were also important in the homeplace context; occurring in 35% of interactions. However, by far the most common type of reference was to parts of a local domestic scene.

Extract 10 shows how such references are used. Lesley has phoned Joan who is a friend of hers, to thank her for buying her a table decoration at her request. When Lesley tries to arrange payment Joan refuses and offers the decoration as a gift, whereupon Lesley thanks her effusively (Line 1). She illustrates how pleased she is with it by describing where it is placed in the house; essentially at the focal centre of the dining room (Line 5). Joan is clearly pleased with this description and reciprocates by telling Lesley something of what is going on in *her* house at that moment (Lines 10, 13 and 15).

Extract 10. References to domestic scenery (C202)

JOAN IS A FRIEND OF LESLEY'S WHO HAS BOUGHT LESLEY A TABLE DECORATION AT LESLEY'S REQUEST. LESLEY RINGS UP TO THANK HER AND ARRANGE PAYMENT BUT JOAN WANTS TO GIVE IT AS A PRESENT.

1. Lesley: <u>We</u>:ll. it's ever so k<u>i</u>nd of you I'm <u>really</u> thr<u>i:</u>lled

2.   with it.[ut's b<u>eau:</u>tiful i[sn't it.

3. Joan: [G<u>oo</u>d.   [Y<u>e</u>::s. Yes (   ),

4.   (0.2)

5. Lesley: (She's   it's) in the middle of my t<u>a</u>ble now in the dining ro[om.

6. Joan:
[L<u>o</u>vely.

7.   (0.2)

8. Joan: eh heh h<u>e</u>h

9.   (0.6)

10. Joan: [My c<u>a</u>t is]

11. Lesley: [Oh w<u>O</u>h: w<u>e</u>]:ll. (.)

12. Lesley: I'll[acce-

13. Joan: [cla:wing up all my ca:rpet he:re horrible thing?

14. Lesley: Sorry?

15. Joan: My cat's js clawing up all the ca:rpet he:re,

In other examples, callers refer to things they are cooking, recent shopping, clothes, books, running TV programmes, music playing, interior and exterior changes made to the house, plants and flowers in their gardens and the weather. We believe all these references can be seen as a form of self-disclosure in which people are metaphorically invited into each other's homes and gardens as an act of intimacy in their relationship. This may explain why so many of these references come in reciprocal pairs.

5   Supporting remote homeplace communication

Given these insights into what remote homeplace communication is like, we can now consider the implications for its support. There appear to be three sets of implications stemming from the properties of single topic calls, multiple-topic calls and calls of both types. We express these implications as user requirements in each category, and give examples of technologies which could satisfy those requirements. Because of the preliminary nature of this analysis and the immaturity of the field, these examples should not be read as product recommendations but as technology areas for further research and development.

Single-topic calls between friends and others actually made up the majority of calls in the corpus. These kinds of short business-like interactions are not what we might ordinarily think homeplace conversations are like, nor are they likely to be the kind of calls that people themselves will attach much significance to in interviews about their communication and relationships.   Nevertheless we should not forget them in our haste to support the more 'important' aspects of home communication, as happened in the workplace context until relatively recently (Kraut, Fish, Root & Chalfonte 1990). Since the single-topic homeplace calls have much in common with informal workplace communications, they may benefit from the same kinds of support applicable to that area (Isaacs et al 1997). In particular, we feel that the use of convenient lightweight messaging facilities such as voicemail, two-way paging, and handwritten (scribble) email would allow household members to make many of their practical arrangements with each other more quickly and efficiently, without having to ring round, ring back or tie up the phone from others. The rapid uptake of paging technology in the US seems to confirm this view, as does the growing use of text-based email for social contact. The same technology might also be used to pass messages directly to third parties, which would normally go through intermediaries.

A further user requirement for single-topic calls arises from the special problem of sharing a household telephone. Very brief and purposeful calls are often thwarted by the caller getting through to the wrong person and then falling into conversation with the answerer. This situation might be changed by routing incoming calls to the right person. This might be done by using caller id. information in conjunction with an on-line household phone book or 'called id.' information elicited from the caller, to route calls to individually addressable handsets. Alternatively, the same information might be used to change the ringing tone of a single phone. This technology can be seen as satisfying part of a more general need for increasing the privacy of certain calls to friends and others. In short, single-topic interactions would benefit from:

- *Lightweight messaging*
- *Incoming call routing*
- *Increased call privacy*

Multi-topic calls between family and friends, were the other major class of calls. These seem to have somewhat different sets of requirements to the business-like calls as can be seen from the findings on scheduling, calling distant friends and passing round the phone. Making prior arrangements to call was relatively common and might be supported by some kind of phone-based diary facilities. These could take the form of a phone booking system showing who is planning to call in and out from a given phone at any time, a household diary system to allow plans to be made in the context of other household members, or a personal diary system showing the social plans of individual household members. Obviously some of these options have broader benefits than the support of call scheduling, such as supporting the making of arrangements of all kinds and synchronizing joint household activities. Further care should be taken to integrate this support with existing practices and tools for personal time management.

Regarding the contact between distant friends, we believe that messaging technology might again be used to increase the frequency of mundane contact and provide triggers for replies and follow-up calls. The concept of an audiopostcard comprising a recent photograph with a voice message attached is a good example of what we mean by this, since it is a vehicle for friends to exchange details of recent life events which can then become something they can talk about. Another example is a magazine cutting or cartoon which might be sent to a friend electronically using the fax or its component technologies, as an item of interest showing that one party was thinking of the other.

Finally, the practices of passing the phone around and chipping into someone else's call suggest the need to open up the two party phone-call at one or both ends. Note that this is the exact opposite of increasing call privacy, since its aim is to make the call more public and sharable by several people at the same location. Current speaker-phone technology goes some way towards this, but might be extended to include some visual context for the call, provided through a video or live photo link (see below). In short, multi-topic calls would benefit from:

- *Phone-based diary facilities*
- *Message triggers for talk*
- *Increased call 'sharability'*

A user requirement which has emerged as important to **both single and multi-topic calls** is the sharing of a local speaker's viewpoint with the other party. This relates to the large number of references to domestic scenery and objects which might be enhanced by the speaker being able to introduce his or her current viewpoint into the conversation for both parties to talk about. This might be done by adapting current videoconferencing technology to support viewpoint capture with a portable camera, handset or headset, coupled to a display at the other end of the telephone line. We believe this arrangement would overcome many popular reservations with the videophone revealing too much about themselves or their surroundings, by giving people fine control of exactly what details they share, when and with whom. The same technology might also be used asynchronously to record, send and review audio and videopostcards. To reiterate then, all remote homeplace communications might benefit from:

- *Viewpoint transmission*

6   Future research

All the above requirements constitute areas for future research in CSSI. Care should be taken to evaluate the subjective as well as the objective effects of these technologies on each member of the household, since we have found evidence of conflicting user needs and preferences which do not necessarily correspond to communication 'efficiencies'. For example, we are concerned about the side effect of increasing call privacy by routing incoming calls directly to their intended recipients, even though this appears to have obvious benefits to the calling and called parties. This solution reduces the opportunity for members of the household to get to know each others' friends and aquaintances, and therefore play a mediating role in these relationships - an effect which is likely to be most unpopular with parents. The dilemma is reminiscent of one faced by some teleworkers who become more productive for working 'off-site', at the expense of being connected to the day-to-day activities of their on-site colleagues through monitoring, helping and mediating behaviours (O'Conaill & Loughran 1997).

Further basic research into homeplace communication could proceed in a number of directions from the current study. First, we hope to deepen the current analysis by looking at how some of the more significant phenomena work in detail across the corpus. Second, our initial findings need to be validated and extended using the same methods with other families, or by using larger scale research methods. Third, a more complete picture of remote homeplace communications could be provided by recording all forms of household communication at a distance, including correspondence as well as telephone calls. From here it would be a short step to researching homeplace communication in general, by recording the course of face-to-face interactions with visitors to the home, and with other household members. All these approaches might benefit from the mix of quantitative and qualitative analysis we have employed in this study, and from the ability to compare accounts of communication behaviour with actual practices.

7   Summary & conclusions

We have found that remote homeplace communication assumes two basic forms: single-topic calls to friends and others, and multi-topic calls to friends and family. Single-topic calls have a business-like quality and might benefit from the same kinds of support targetted at informal workplace communications, such as lightweight messaging. The added complication of making such calls over a shared household telephone line also suggests a need for incoming call routing and greater call privacy. Multi-topic calls, although often triggered by specific reasons for calling, have more of a recreational character, in which conversation is entered into for its own sake as part and parcel of maintaining the relationship between speakers. These calls would benefit from integrated diary facilities for call scheduling, asynchronous triggers for talk, and greater call sharability. The transmission of current speaker viewpoint would benefit both types of calls which involve extensive references to local domestic scenery. Future research should attempt to validate and extend these findings, and to develop technology satisfying each requirement.

Acknowledgements

We are grateful to the University of York for a priming fund grant to support this work (Code No. 60 890 910 U787), to Gail Jefferson for transcripts of calls, and to Brid O'Connail for her help and insights on the project. Thanks also to Alison Kidd and Phil Stenton for their comments on an earlier draft of the paper.

References

Atkinson J.M. & Heritage J.C. (1984). *Structures of social action studies in conversation analysis.* Cambridge: Cambridge University Press.

Bannon L.J. & Schmidt K. (1991) CSCW: Four characters in search of a context. In J.M. Bowers & S.D. Berford (Eds) *Studies in Computer supported cooperative work.* Amsterdam: Elscvier Science Publishers.

Bengtson V.L. & Robertson J.F. Eds (1985) *Grandparenthood.* Beverly Hills: Sage Publications.

Burguiere A., Klapisch - Zuber C., Segalen M. & Zonabend F. (Eds) (1996) *A history of the family: Volume II.* Cambridge: Polity Press.

De Sola Pool I (Ed.) (1977) *The social impact of the telephone.*Cambridge, MA: MIT Press.

Dickens W.J. & Perlman D. (1981) Friendship over the life-cycle. Chapter 4 in S. Duck & R. Gilmour (Eds). *Personal relationships 2: Developing personal relationships.* London: Academic Press.

Duck S. & Pittman G. (1994) Social and personal relationships. Chapter 17 in M.L.Knapp & G.R. Miller (Eds). *Handbook of interpersonal communication.* Second Edition. Thousand Oaks: Sage Publications.

Frohlich D. (1995) Requirements for interpersonal information management. In P.J. Thomas (Ed.) *Personal information systems: Business applications.* (pg 133-153). Cheltenham: Stanley Thornes in association with Unicorn Seminars.

Frohlich D.M. (1994) Interactions as turns: some observations from the shadowing of individuals across workplaces. Paper presented at the World Congress of Sociology, Bielefeld Germany. 18-23rd July 1994. *Sociological Abstracts 173*: 94528115/8376.

Isaacs E.A., Whittaker S., Frohlich D.M. & O'Conaill B. (1997) Informal communication reexammined: New functions for video in supporting opportunistic encounters. Chapter 22 in K. Finn, A. Sellen & S. Wilbur (Eds.) *Video mediated communication.* Hillsdale N.J.: Lawrence Erlbaum Associates.

Kraut R.E., Fish R.S., Root R.W. & Chalfonte B.L. (1990) Informal communication in organisations: Form, functions and technology. In S. Oskamp & S. Spacapan (Eds.) *Peoples reactions to technology in factories, offices and aerospace* (pp 145-199). Sage Publications.

Kraut R.E., Scherlis W., Mukhopadhyay T., Manning J. & Kiesler S. (1996) Homenet: field trial of residential internet services. *Proceedings of CHI '96*: 284-291. NY: ACM SIG-CHI

O'Conaill B. & Frohlich D.M. (1995) Timespace in the workplace: Dealing with interruptions. *Companion Proceedings of CHI '95*: 262-3. NY: ACM SIG-CHI

O'Conaill B. & Loughran S. (1997) Personal communications to business networks. Chapter 2.2 in J. Worthington & S. Taylor (Eds.) *Re-inventing the workplace: managing space, time and technology.* Oxford: Butterworth Architecture.

Rawlins W.K. (1994) Being there and growing apart: Sustaining friendships during adulthood. Chapter 13 in D.J. Canary & L. Stafford (Eds.) *Communication and relational maintenance.* London: Academic Press.

Rheingold H. (1995) *The virtual community: surfing the internet.* Minerva.

Robinson J.P. (1988) Time-diary avidence about the social psychology of everyday life. Chapter 7 in J.E. McGrath (Ed.) *The social psychology of time: New Perspectives.* Newbury Park: Sage Publications.

Turkle S. (1995) *Life on the screen: Identity in the age of the internet.* Simon & Schuster.

Whittaker S., Frohlich D. & Daly-Jones (1994) Informal workplace communications: What is it like and how might we support it? *Proceedings of CHI 94*: 131-137. NY: ACM SIG-CHI.

A Making-Movies Metaphor for Structuring Software Components in Highly Interactive Application

Michelle Jacomi[1,2], Stéphane Chatty[1] & Philippe Palanque[1,3]

[1]Centre d'Etudes de la Navigation Aérienne
7 avenue Edouard Belin, 31055 Toulouse Cedex, FRANCE
E-mail:{jacomi, chatty, palanque}@cena.dgac.fr

[2]CISI 13 rue Villet, 31029 Toulouse Cedex, FRANCE

[3]LIS-FROGIS, University of Toulouse 1,
1 pl. Anatole France, 31042 Toulouse Cedex, FRANCE

Structuring full scale, highly interactive applications still involve complex design choices for programmers. This is because current techniques do not cover the issue of structuring applications at all scales. Programmers thus have to make choices without a good understanding of their consequences. We consider that this is similar to the problem encountered by a user who explores a user-driven application and has little guidance on actions that can be performed. In the same way as metaphors have been used to help users anticipate the consequences of their actions, we propose to use metaphors to help programmers make their choices. This article describes a making-movies metaphor that provides guidance for organising the interface of an application, but also its links with the objects of the functional core. We show how this approach can be merged with current software engineering techniques to specify and build full scale applications. This is exemplified with a graphical editor acting as an interface to optimisation algorithms, and used for splitting air space into air traffic control sectors.

Keywords: Software architecture, user interface design, metaphors.

1   Introduction

Structuring interactive applications is still by many aspects an open issue for software engineers and programmers. General architecture models explain how the large blocks of an application should be organised, with little help on how to implement them. At the other end of the spectrum, object oriented toolkits help programmers to structure and build the interactive parts of their applications, but provide little guidance on how to organise the functional core and weave all the resulting classes together. Even though novel approaches such as design patterns try to bridge the gap between those methods, today's programmers are still on their own for many design choices. This is especially painful for highly interactive applications, because the links between interaction objects and functional core objects are many, tight and complex. This explains why programmers often have trouble to scale up techniques presented in academic papers to full scale applications.

In addition to current research on software engineering techniques that would solve those issues, this paper proposes to use a metaphor as a way of guiding programmers. Metaphors have been successfully used for many years for structuring user interfaces. They have been proposed to prevent users from getting lost when the complexity of these systems increases. Indeed, with the advent of user-driven style of interaction, users are driving the interaction and thus no guidance (or as less as possible) is provided to them. In order to fill in this gap metaphors have appeared as one possible way to help users in understanding the use and the meaning of interactive objects. This help is given for example by "providing paths through the jungle of functionality" (Tscheligi & Vanaanen 1995).

We believe that the same help that is offered by metaphors to end users can be offered to software engineers and programmers, in addition to classical software structuring techniques. The next section of this paper is devoted to the presentation of those structuring techniques. It shows that merging some of them can solve most of the problems encountered while designing large scale applications. Section 3 introduces a metaphor we have defined and used for the building of interactive systems. It explains how this metaphor relates to software architectures and shows how formal specification techniques can be used to define both the inner behaviour of objects and their communication protocols. A large scale case study is presented in section 4. This application is related to the Air Traffic Control (ATC) domain and is mainly characterised by the large amount of information that has to be displayed at the same time. In order to address this problem the application features a new "shelves-based" user interface with highly interactive interaction techniques such as movable filters in order to cope with information visualisation and handling.

2   Structuring techniques for interactive software

Structuring interactive systems has been recognised for a long time as a challenging problem (Coutaz 96). The main problem to solve is to define and organise the various components and to state clearly their relationships. The solutions proposed in order to address this problem usually come from software engineering techniques customised for interactive systems. This research work can be subdivided in four categories according to the kind of approach they promote: abstraction first, implementation first, reuse first and global first.

2.1   Abstraction First: Models

The kind of research proposes general models more dedicated to the understanding of interactive systems than to their actual building. Among them are the Seeheim model (Pfaff 1985), the Arch/Slinky model (Arch 1992). The main point of these models is to cope with complexity by splitting the interactive application into abstract entities. They are helpful for high level management of applications but they do not go easily towards implementation. For example the Seeheim model must not be followed too closely if implementation is to be object oriented, as the organisation in layers would be against object oriented principles that promote highly coherent and weakly coupled objects. For this reason more refined models such as the one presented in (Hudson 1987) refine the Seeheim model in order be closer to the implementation.

Another kind of approach that promotes abstraction first is the agent approach that organise the application into collection of cooperating agents. Such models can be used recursively to define the application at different levels of abstraction. The communicative aspect of interactive systems provide a basis for further structuring the system as a network of interactors, each dealing with different subsets of the human computer dialogue. The most used of those models are MVC and PAC (Coutaz 1987), that is now extended to the PAC-Amodeus model (Nigay & Coutaz 93) which is a merging of the Arch/Slinky model and the agent model PAC.

The main drawbacks of these approaches are the lack of methodology supporting the top-down process they promote and the fact that the number of elements in the model is too small to provide efficient classification and structuring of components in real size applications.

2.2   Implementation First: Toolkits

Toolkits provide functions and primitives for building interactive systems. Compared to models they address the problem of structuring interactive systems in the opposite way. Toolkits are usually based on conceptual models that impose a predefined way for organising the code of the applications. For example event-based environments such as Sassafras (Hill 1987) or more recently Visual Basic™ organise the code according to event-handlers. Some development environments are associated with other kind of architectural frameworks (InterViews, MacApp). They need a long time for designers to know how to use them and are heavily linked to the underlying toolkit used. Hence, they do not really provide reusable components and composition rules. The other problem is that they do not relate to abstract models and thus it is really hard for designers to have a global understanding of the application.

2.3 Reuse First: Design Patterns

A new tendency proposes design patterns as models to construct applications (Buschmann et al. 1996, Gamma et al. 1995). They provide useful information about both the structuring of a system and its actual implementation. These patterns can be seen as a "glue" between the abstract models and the implementation ones but they address more "low-level" aspects of the life-cycle of an application and are more suitable at implementation step than at conception level. In (Buschmann et al. 1996) two patterns (MVC and PAC) are addressing the problem of interactive systems, but they are only refinements of models used for a long time in the domain of interactive systems.

2.4 Insight First: Metaphors

A metaphor provides a method by which people can quickly learn and understand how to use a system. Through metaphors, users infer the meaning, the behaviour and the manipulation of objects by mapping their aspects in the system onto the associated one in the metaphor. For instance, with the desktop metaphor, users might infer that a trash can-like object is a container for objects that are to be discarded, and may infer that objects can be dropped into the trash without having to learn explicit instructions on how to throw away files: the knowledge for throwing away objects is contained in user's knowledge about trash cans in the real world (Lundell & Anderson 1995).

Metaphors have not only been used for organising the presentation of interactive systems. Several toolkits or development environments have been designed according to metaphors. A metaphor-based programming environment helps designers in organising software components. The need for a metaphor is even more important for interactive applications including advanced interaction tools since they are made up of a huge set of objects dedicated to the interface and interacting together. Several metaphors have already been proposed and used for structuring libraries see for example X_{TV} (Beaudouin-Lafon et al. 1990) and Whizz which is a library for building animated interactive applications based on a musical metaphor (Chatty 1992).

2.5 Discussion

Even though the different models presented before have proven their usefulness for designing interactive systems, they do not provide enough information for structuring the software components needed in a complex interactive application. Splitting such a system into agents means creating hundreds of user interface components. Those components, their roles and their relationships are difficult to identify for designers, and this can be even more difficult when it comes to maintain the system. The main problem with these approaches is that they only provide information at a generic level i.e. for all the interactive applications and no information for a given application that has to be built, and this particular point is addressed in the next section.

3 The Making-Movies Metaphor

We had to design an interactive application integrating new interaction techniques. To integrate such mechanisms, we had to face the problem of the architectural choice in order to ensure the flexibility and the modularity of the global structure of the application. To address these issues, we used a metaphorical architecture framework for interactive application based on PAC model for the internal description of the interactive objects. This section is devoted to present the metaphor that is based on making-movies domain. Of course, as stated by (Lakoff & Johnson 1980) "metaphors do not imply a complete mapping of every concrete detail of one object or situation onto another". Hence, in the design of interactive applications some aspects of the making-movies metaphor will be emphasised and other will be suppressed.

3.1 Context

As a starting point we used the X_{TV} -Whizz toolkit for the implementation of the application. The TV metaphor proposed in X_{TV} allows designers to structure most of the components of an application. However, this metaphor does not provide a basis for describing their behaviour and the relations between these components and those of the functional core. We thus extended the metaphor to address those problems. However, the resulting making-movies metaphor is not only dedicated to model components of the library but to describe precisely all the components that are to be part of the application.

3.2 The metaphor

All objects are articulated around the user and coordinated by a global object identified as the *Director*. Its role is to ensure the global coherence of the application according to its specification and its current state.

The director is helped in its tasks by assistants, that play as sub-directors for specific parts of the application. The hierarchical decomposition between the director and its assistants is directly linked to the functional decomposition of the application. Assistants are classified in three categories:

- Assistants linked to the Functional Core of the application, dealing with the communication and coherence between the Interface part and the Functional Core. These assistants correspond to the Adaptor to the Functional Core in Arch Model. The file manager in the desktop of the Macintosh™ could have been designed as an assistant linked to the functional core (the actual management of files).
- Assistants linked to the Interface, and dedicated to specialised interactions with users. They encapsulate a whole interactive functionality of the application. These assistants are located in the Dialog and the Presentation parts of the Arch Model. The help management in the desktop of the Macintosh™ could be designed as a assistant linked to the interface.
- Hybrid Assistants encapsulating the Arch Model from the Adaptor to the Functional Core to the Presentation part. Such an assistant includes a full interactive functionality of the application.

This distinction between assistants comes from the abstract models presented in section 2.1 and is really important as it preserves independence between the functional part and the presentation part of the application.

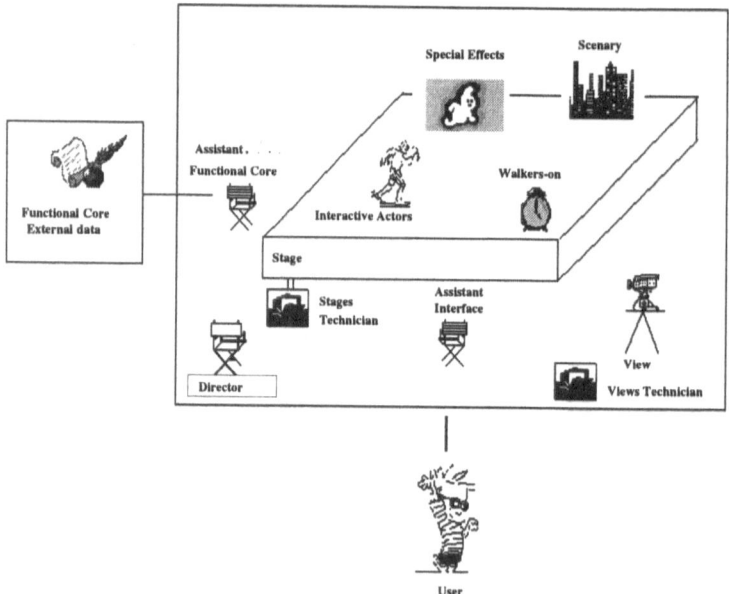

Figure 1: The components of the Making-Movies metaphor

The different objects of the making-movies metaphor can be seen in Figure 1. The objects of the interface, named *Actors*, have predefined characters (graphical dresses and audible abilities) and behaviours (scenarios), and may also react to user's actions or events emitted by other actors. Actors are organised on virtual surfaces named *Stages*, and can be viewed by users through objects named *Views* (i.e. windows).

Several stages may be displayed in a view. Their contents is organised consistently with the functional aspects of the application.

We identified two kind of views:

1. The *global* views, that permits to visualize stages managed by different assistants, corresponding in our metaphor to global shots directly controlled by the director.
2. The *local* views, specific to the assistants, corresponding to close shots (local interactions) but not necessarily 'retransmitted' to the director.

To ensure the global consistency of the application with the management of the global views and the stages two *technicians* are associated to the director: one responsible for all global views, and one having access to all stages.

In order to provide designers with more precise information on the actors featuring on stages, the metaphor distinguishes four kinds of actors:

1. *Interactive Actors* are entities that can be manipulated by the user and usually correspond to application domain concepts displayed on the interface.
2. *Walkers-on* are actors whose appearance and/or behaviour evolve according to the current state of the application, but cannot be manipulated by users. Walkers-on are only dependent on the application, and not directly linked to users' interactions.
3. *Special effects* are temporary actors created dynamically and used for providing feedback during interactions. The feedback is either visible or audible. For example, in the desktop metaphor, a temporary actor is created when the user drag a file on the screen.
4. *Scenery*, are non-interactive graphical objects defining the static appearance of the interface. Their appearance never changes during a session. They constitute the "background" of the display such as the pattern on the background of the desktop of the Macintosh™.

For each actor a *scenario* describes its behaviour according to its internal state and the current state of the application handled by the director.

However, neither the internal structure of the objects nor the communication mechanism among them are described by the Making-Movies Metaphor.

3.3   *Decomposition of Actors*

In order to describe the internal structure of the objects, we applied and refined the principles of the PAC model (Coutaz 1987). Figure 2 presents the graphical representation of this refinement.

- The Control describes the communication between objects. Two mechanisms are available. The first one, called distribution is used when the sender does not know the receiver (this corresponds to a kind of broadcast). The other one, called client-server, is used when the sender holds the reference of the receiver and directly invokes one of its services (or public functions). Those communication mechanisms have been formally defined using formal notations in (Palanque & Bastide 1994).

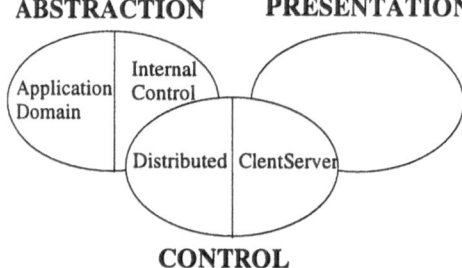

ABSTRACTION   **PRESENTATION**

CONTROL

Figure 2: Refinement of the PAC model

- The Abstraction is made up of two parts called Application and Internal. The first one contains attributes and functions linked to the application domain. The second one handles the internal state of the object, and contains attributes and functions ensuring the inner consistency of the object.
- The Presentation holds the graphical attributes of the actors. Those attributes can only be manipulated by functions according to the communication mechanisms described above.

4   A Full Scale Application

Osmose is a tool developed at CENA aimed at optimising airspace division into sectors and improving air flows affectation. Osmose represents more than 100,000 lines of code of which 90% are dedicated to the interface. To develop a software of such a size, we had to rigorously apply the structuring method presented above. This method provides answers to three questions:

- how to identify the interface objects?,
- how to establish the relationships between the objects?
- how to organise these objects?

The interface objects have to be defined univocally in order to ensure the everlastingness of the project, the global consistency of the application and the overall understanding of the software by any programmer stepping into its development.

The making-movies metaphor presented in this paper has been used both to structure the classes of objects defined in Osmose and design the global architecture of the application. All the software components built correspond to an entity of the metaphor.

4.1 Functional Decomposition

The functional analysis of Osmose permitted to determine different groups:

- The functions linked to the functional core, that permit to manage the relationships with:
    - the optimisation of the airspace division
    - the optimisation of the air flows assignment
    - the evaluation of the sector loads.
- The functions linked to the interactive aspect of the application:
    - the history of the interactions
    - the editing grid
    - the customisable filters
    - the printed outputs
    - the on-line help
    - the current state of the application
- The hybrid functions:
    - the editing of the sectors
    - the visualisation of information on airports, beacons, airways and flight plans.
    - the visualisation of geographical maps.

4.2 Description of the interface

Figure 3 shows the interface of the Osmose application. The graphical appearance of Osmose is based on shelves, closets and boards with 3D effects.

The Osmose interface consists in three areas: the editing board, the post-it boards (status data), and the set of closets and shelves.

- The editing board is aimed at presenting ATC information to the users and allowing them to interact with the objects presented. Data such as sectors, airports, or air-traffic flows can be modified by users using direct manipulation interaction style. In Figure 3, the black dots on the maps represent the airports, the polygons the sectors and the thick lines the flows between airports.

- The post-it boards (upper right corner of Figure 3) contain several indicators about the application status and displayed information: current activated function, scale used, mouse position in latitude/longitude coordinates, etc.
- The graphical objects that trigger Osmose functions are displayed as objects standing on shelves, enclosed in closets. A closet is devoted to objects from the same "semantic group": one for General Services such as print or save functions (the bottom left one), one for Sectors Tools (the middle right one), one for ATC tools (the bottom middle one), etc.

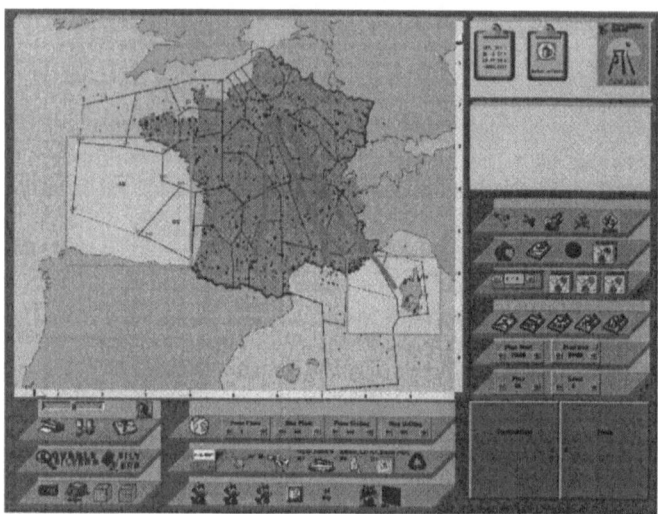

Figure 3: The user interface of the Osmose application

Movable filters for instance, provide the ability to focus on a selected area by visualising detailed information while simultaneously keeping the global context displayed. In Figure 3, two movable filters are instantiated:

- one located above Corsica displays only the map, airports and airports names,
- one on the Atlantic only displays the map, the sectors borders, the vertices identifiers, and the sectors names.

This user interface presents several characteristics that fit the requirements of the Osmose application:

- Modularity is easily supported: adding or removing a functionality to the application will correspond to removing one element on a shelf. Groups of functions can be handled as a whole by interacting directly with closets.
- Customisability is fully supported as users can dynamically change the appearance of the interface by moving the "graphical-objects" from one shelf to another one shelf according to their convenience (frequency of use, etc.). Using movable filters, this customisation is reinforced as not only the visualisation of functions but also data can be dynamically specified by the users.

5   Implementation

The Figure 4 presents the hierarchy of classes of our application. The making-movies metaphor presented above has been fully used for the structuring of the object classes used in Osmose. Thus any software component that has been built comes from the interpretation of the metaphor.

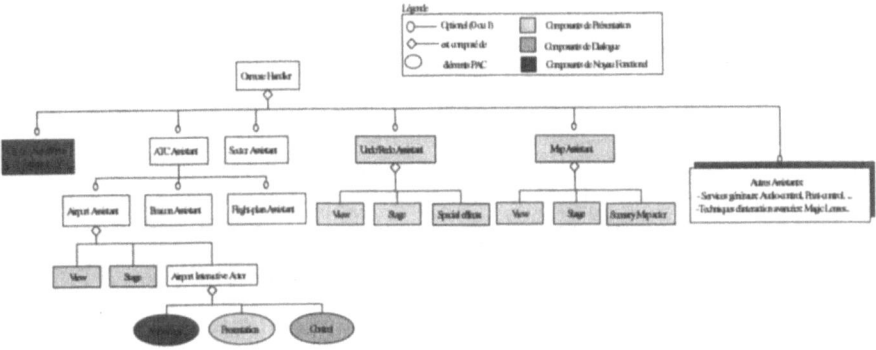

Figure 4: A subset of the class hierarchy in Osmose

5.1   Identification of the assistants

By applying our metaphor, we started by identifying the assistants responsible of each functional group. These assistants support the director *OsmoseHandler* that ensure the global consistency of the application. We identified the assistants according to the three categories distinguished in the metaphor:

- Assistants that are fully dependent from the functional core. Among them are the *Genetic Algorithms Assistant*, interfaces the results provided by the optimisation computation, and the *Sector Evaluation Assistant* undertakes the computation of the sectors loads according to air traffic flows.
- Purely interactive assistants, only depend from users' interactions. One of these is the *Magic Lenses Assistant* that manages the display of customisable movable filters according to user's requests.
- Hybrid assistants that have a dual role of communication with the functional core on one hand and with users on the other hand. The *ATC Assistant* and the *Sector Assistant* are hybrid assistants, since they manage interactive objects linked to the functional core (air space data). The *Map Assistant* is an hybrid assistant that ensures the display of the geographical borders of different countries.

5.2   Structure of the assistants

We then applied the metaphor in order to identify the roles inside an assistant. According to the metaphor, an Assistant is made of *views* that manage the display, *stages* that organise the displayed information, and *actors* that represent the interactive entities. We detail this composition in Figure 4 for the *Airport Assistant* that supports the *ATC* Assistant for the airports management. The *Airport Assistant* handles a view that permits the visualisation of interactive objects representing airports, organised on a specific stage. This composition being the same for all the assistants, we defined an abstract class *ATC Handler* from which *Airport Assistant, Beacon Assistant* and *Way Assistant* are derived. At this stage of the implementation, we scanned the existing software design patterns in order to check if one of them was adequate with our assistants. Among them, we selected the *Singleton* pattern (defined in (Gamma et &l. 95)) as a basis for the implementation of our assistants. Actually, this pattern ensures that a class has only one instance, and permits to have a global access point to it. This matches perfectly the unique aspect of each of the assistants of our metaphor. This is described in the following C++ code:

```
template <class ATCData> class ATCHandler: public DirectorAssistant {
protected:
  ATCHandler ();
public:
  ~ATCHandler ();
/* Interactive Objects */
  DictionnaryOf<ATCData> * ATCDataTable;
  ListHandler* TheDialogBox;
/* Stages */
  XtvStage DataStage;
  XtvStage DataLabelStage;
  virtual void ReadATCData (const char* filename);
  virtual void ResetData ();
  void ManageDisplay ();
};
class AirportAssistant: public ATCHandler <Airport> {
public:
  static AirportAssistant* GetInstance();
  void ReadATCData (const char* filename);
  void ResetData ();
protected:
  static AirportAssistant* AirportAssistantSingleton;
};
```

However, we can note that assistants are not only dedicated to the management of interactive objects. The *Map Assistant* for instance only deals with scenery actors that represent static borders of different countries. On the other hand the *Undo/Redo Assistant* deals with Special Effects that temporally materialise user's previous interactions.

5.3 The technicians

After having identified all the assistants of our application, we defined the technicians that help the director to centralise the global views and stages used by the assistants. We also used the *Singleton* pattern as a basis for those technicians. The technician that manages the stages is described by the following code:

```
class MemoStage: public Technician {
public:
    enum KindOfStages {MapBorders, SectorsShape,Ways...};
    enum {NbKindOfStages=20};
    static MemoStage* GetInstance();
    ArrayOf <XtvStage> ArrayOfStages;
    bool DefinedStages[NbKindOfStages];
private:
    MemoStage();
    ~MemoStage();
    static MemoStage* MemoStageSingleton;
};
```

To centralise the list of stages and views defined in the application is useful in many cases. We can consider stages as tracing papers that we can superpose or remove at will, thus controlling the visualisation of the data contained on each sheet. Hence, to handle the customisable movable filters the *Magic Lenses Assistant* invokes *MemoStage* to determine the stages available from the other assistants. Then, the *Magic Lenses Assistant* uses a specific view to visualise or not the content of the stages of the other assistants according to the user's choices. In the same way, to print data displayed on the screen, the *Print Assistant* will scan the list of stages provided by *Memo Stage* and will print the actors displayed on stages.

The technician that manages the views permits to visualise the contents of stages controlled by different assistants through a unique view directly handled by the director. This technician defines the set of the global views of the application, and the director dispatches the different stages of the assistants on those global views. We give here the code of the technician that handles views and then an example of the affectation of some stages on a view.

```
class OsmoseScenary: public Technician {
public:
    static XtvView* OsmoseView;
    static DraftView* EditorView;
    static XtvBltView* StatusView;
    static XtvBltView* BlackboardView;
    static XtvBltView* ServicesView;
    static XtvBltView* SectorsToolsView;
    static XtvBltView* ATCToolsView;
    static XtvBltView* OptimizationToolsView;
    static LimitedInterStage* OsmoseMainStage;
    static void InitOsmoseScenary ();
};
/* Example of stages affectation by OsmoseDirector at initialisation time
*/
OsmoseScenary::EditorView-
>AddStage(TheSectorHandler.TheSectorStage);
OsmoseScenary::EditorView->AddStage(TheMapHandler.MapStage);
OsmoseScenary::EditorView->AddStage
        (TheATCHandler.TheWayHandler.DataStage);

...
```

5.4   Description of actors

After defining the global structure of Osmose by identifying all the assistants and technicians, we applied our metaphor to describe the actors. Each interactive actor is built according to the PAC model in the way it is represented by the composition relationship at the bottom of Figure 4 for the *Airport* object. Indeed, *Airport* is an interactive actor, whose abstraction corresponds to the definition of an airport as an air space data, the presentation corresponds to a graphical object, and the interactive part handled a reaction to mouse clicks on the graphical part. The implementation of interactive objects is freely adapted from the PAC design pattern described in (Buschmann et al. 1996). We give here the code describing the *Airport* object, deriving from *ATCNode* class:

```
class ATCNode: public WhzPolymorph {
public:
    ATCNode ();
    ~ATCNode ();
/* Attributes linked to the Abstraction part (Application side) */
    ATCTrafficInfos ATCInfos;
/* Attributes linked to the Abstraction part (Internal subpart) */
    bool OwnsInfo;
/* Attributes linked to the Presentation Part */
```

```
GraphicInfosATCNode GraphicInfos;
/* Attributes linked to the Control Part */
  static XtvReflex* SelectNode;
  WhzReflexPlug FlowReflex;
/* Functions linked to the Presentation Part */
  void Appear (XtvStage& s);
  virtual void DisplayTimeSchedule ();
  virtual void DisplayFlowSchedule ();
/* Functions linked to the Abstraction part (Application side) */
  void AddDepartingPln (PLN& pln);
/* Functions linked to the Control Part (Client-Server) */
  const char* GetIndic();
  void ManageInfoSensors ();
/* Functions linked to the Control Part (distributed) */
  virtual void SelectAction (DnnEvent&);
  virtual void FlowAction (const WhzNote&);
};

class Airport: public ATCNode {
public:
  Airport ();
  ~Airport ();
/* Functions linked to the Control Part (Client-Server) */
const char* GetFullName();
/* Functions linked to the Presentation Part */
void DisplayTimeSchedule ();
protected:
/* Attributes linked to the Presentation Part */
static XtvIcon* AirportIcon;
};
```

5.5   Relations between the components of the metaphor

The metaphor models in an implicit way the objects' interactions, thanks to the relationships defined between assistants, views, stages and actors under the global control of the director. We identified different levels for the communications inside our application:

- High-level horizontal communications of, that imply the coordination between assistants. Those communications are directly handled by the director *OsmoseDirector* and its two technicians that manage the stages and views defined for the application. Those communications are performed by data transmission done through the invocation of client-server functions. We gave an example of this kind of communication when we described the *Magic Lenses Assistant* and the *Print Assistant* that need to know stages from other assistants. Another example of this kind of communication is the sectors load evaluation. This computation performed under the control of the *Sector Evaluation Assistant* involves current sectorisation data handled by the *Sector Assistant*, and traffic data managed by the *ATC Assistant*. Thus, the sector load evaluation is an example of a « global » functionality of the application, directly under the control of *OsmoseDirector* since it involves data managed by different assistants. We give here the code corresponding to the call of the sector load evaluation performed by the director:

TheSectorEval3D.EvalSectors
(TheSectorHandler.ThePresentationData.ListSectors,
                    TheATCHandler.TheWayHandler.WayParts);

- Low level horizontal communications, that concern the actors managed by an assistant. In this kind of communication, we fully use the distributed control facilities defined in the X_{TV}-Whizz library, the actors having no explicit knowledge of the global number of actors. The sector edition provides an example of such an horizontal communication. A sector is graphically represented by a polygon, composed by a series of vertices and borders. Each element corresponds to an interactive actor that can be moved directly by the user. Indeed, when a user clicks on a vertex to move it, all the adjacent borders and sectors will be moved too. The current position of the vertex is transmitted by distribution, using the propagation mechanism defined in Whizz and introduced in section 3.3. The connections between the different objects composing a sector are defined by the *Sector Assistant* at the sector initialisation step. The Figure 5 illustrates the data distribution in the case of sector's vertex movement.
- Vertical (or Hierarchical) communications of high and low levels, usually managed by the call of client-server functions in the top-bottom direction, and by distribution in the bottom-up direction. An example of top-bottom communication is the request of an assistant to display an actor on a stage. An example of bottom-up communication is the sending of a message indication the suppression of an actor performed by a direct user interaction.

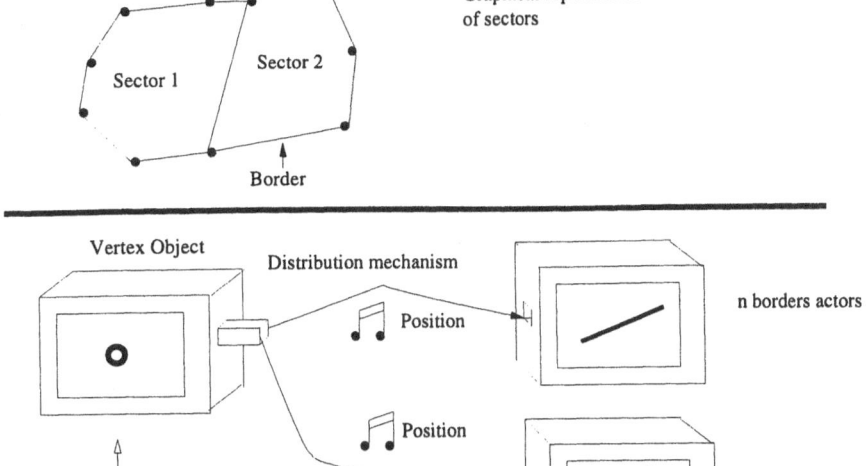

Figure 5: Graphical representation of sectors and links set when moving a vertex

6 Conclusion

In this paper, we have described the use of a metaphor to help programmers structure their highly interactive applications. We also have exemplified the use of that metaphor through the construction of a full scale application developed at CENA for air traffic experts.

Using a metaphor has shown to provide at least three kinds of help to programmers:

- as the metaphor is by definition object-oriented all the advantages of this approach such as reuse, reliability and encapsulation are fully supported by this approach.
- help in identifying presentation objects, functional core objects, and their relations. This is useful both at design time and at maintenance time, because it helps programmers navigate through the organisation of the application.
- help in distributing programming tasks in time or among programmers. Using the metaphor leads to easier integration.

However, though they have shown their usefulness in our developments, we are conscious that metaphors are only a help that cannot replace classical methods for structuring software. Our future research in that direction will focus at integrating such a metaphor with tools and methods for structuring interactive software, along several different lines. One of our approaches will consist in specifying more precisely the behaviour of objects (actors in our metaphor) with formal methods in order to perform static analysis of that behaviour (Palanque & Bastide 1995). Another approach will take the toolkit approach, and extend a graphical toolkit and its corresponding interactive editor (Esteban et al. 1995) to the description of the behaviour of objects and their relations.

References

(Arch 1992) A metamodel for the runtime architecture of an interactive system. The UIMS Tools Developers Workshop, SIGCHI Bulletin vol. 24, n°1, pp 32-37.

(Beaudouin-lafon et al. 1990) Beaudouin-Lafon M. Berteaud Y. Chatty S. Creating direct manipulation interfaces with X_{TV}. EX'90, European conference on X Window.

(Buschmann et al. 1996) A system of patterns. Wiley Publ.

(Chatty 1992) Chatty S. Defining the behaviour of animated interfaces. Engineering for Human Computer Interaction Conference pp. 95-109, North Holland.

(Coutaz 1987) Coutaz J. PAC an implementation model for dialogue design. Proceedings of the Interact'87 conference. North Holland. pp. 431-437.

(Coutaz et al. 1996) Coutaz J., Nigay L. Salber D. Agent Based architecture for modelling Interactive Systems. Critical Issues in User Interface System Engineering, pp. 191-209, Benyon & Palanque (Eds.), Springer Verlag..

(Esteban et al. 1995) Esteban O., Chatty S. Palanque P. Whizz'Ed: a visual environment for building highly interactive software. Proceeding of Interact'95 conference Chapman et Hall. pp. 121-126.

(Fekete 1996) Fekete J.D. Un modèle multicouche pour la construction d'applications graphiques interactives, PhD thesis, Université Paris Sud.

(Gamma et al. 1995) Gamma E., Helm R., Johnson R. Vlissides J. Design patterns. Addison Wesley.

(Hill 1987) Hill R. Supporting concurrency, communication and synchronisation in Human-Computer Interaction. The Sassafras UIMS. Proceedings of ACM CHI'87 pp. 241-248.

(Hudson 1987) Hudson S.E. UIMS support for direct manipulation interfaces. Computer Graphics vol.21 n°2. pp120-124.

(Hussey 1996) Hussey A. & Carrington D. Comparing two user-interface architectures: MVC and PAC. FAHCI'96, Springer Verlag.

(Lakoff & Johnson 1980) Lakoff G. & Johnson M. Metaphors we live by. The University of Chicago Press.

(Lundell & Anderson 1995) Lundell J. & Anderson S. Designing a "Front Panel" for Unix: The Evolution of a Metaphor CHI95 ACM p.573-579

(Nigay & Coutaz 1993) Nigay L. & Coutaz J. A design space for multimodal systems: Concurrent processing and Data fusion. Proceedings of INTERCHI'93, ACM Press, pp. 172-178.

(Palanque & Bastide 1994), Palanque P & Bastide R. Petri net based design of User-Driven Interfaces using the Interactive Cooperative Objects Formalism. Proceedings of Design, Specification and Verification of Interactive Systems, Springer Verlag, pp. 383-400.

(Palanque & Bastide 1995), Palanque P & Bastide R. Verification of an interactive software by analysis of its formal specification. Proceeding of Interact'95 conference Chapman et Hall. pp. 191-196.

(Pfaff 1985) Pfaff G.E. et al. User Interface Management Systems, G.E. Pfaff Ed., Eurographics Seminars, Springer Verlag.

(Tscheligi & Vanaanen 1995) Tscheligi M. & Väänänen-Vainio-Mattila. Metaphors in User Interface Development: Methods and Requirements for Effective Support. Critical Issues in User Interface System Engineering, pp. 249-263, Benyon & Palanque (Eds.), Springer Verlag.

The Impact of Time and Place on the Operation of Mobile Computing Devices

Chris Johnson

Glasgow Accident Analysis Group,
Department of Computing Science,
University of Glasgow,
Glasgow, G12 8QQ, UK.
Tel: +44 (0141) 330 6053
Fax: +44 (0141) 330 4913
http://www.dcs.gla.ac.uk/~johnson
EMail: johnson@dcs.glasgow.ac.uk

Recent improvements in the quality and reliability of wireless communications has led to the development of a range of mobile computing devices. Many portable computers now offer modem connections through cellular and satellite telephone networks. Taxi services, emergency vehicles, domestic repair teams all now rely upon mobile links to central computing systems. In spite of these advances, a number of technical problems still affect the quality of interaction with mobile applications. Electromagnetic interference blocks radio signals. Obstacles in the line of sight can interrupt microwave and infra-red transmissions. Tracking problems frustrate the use of low-level satellites. Transmission delays affect the service provided by higher, geostationary satellites. From the users' point of view, these problems manifest themselves as geographical constraints upon the usability of their 'mobile' device. This lead to delays in the transmission of critical information. These, in turn, lead to the frustration and error that often complicates the operation of mobile computer systems. In the short term, it seems unlikely that the technical limitations will be resolved. The following pages, therefore, argue that interface designers must consider means of reducing the impact of geographic allocation upon the operation of mobile computing devices.

Keywords: mobile computing, interface design, satellite communications, cellular networks.

1   Introduction

The Conference of European Telecommunication Authorities is currently working to 'harmonize' European networks for mobile communications. Similar initiatives have led to a digital mobile communications standard throughout North America. In Japan, there are plans for at least two different digital radio communications networks for mobile computing devices (Simon, 1996).   These initiatives have encouraged hardware and software developers to invest in a vast array of hand-held and lap-top devices.   Recent developments in the communications infrastructure, enables the users of these systems to access local and remote resources without being forced to connect to a physical telephone line.   These systems are, in turn, posing new challenges for human computer interaction (Dix, 1996).

1.1   The Impact of Geography on Mobile Interaction

In order to understand the nature of the problems that frustrate interaction with mobile computer systems, it is important to have some idea of the underlying technology.   Satellites offer a number of benefits for mobile interaction.   Unlike radio systems, they do not suffer from the problems of multipath transmission. This occurs when signals 'bounce' off objects in the environment.   This is a significant problem for interactive systems because mobile devices must then filter out any additional signals to recover the users' information. Unfortunately, satellites must filter and correct for atmospheric interference and for noise in space.   There are further limitations.   Geostationary satellites must maintain an orbit of approximately 36,000km in order to hold their position relative to the earth's surface.   This incurs a half-second delay on transmissions which, in turn, affects the usability of mobile devices.   For example, if an item of information is lost between the transmitter and the receiver then several seconds may go by before the missing item can be detected and corrected.   Low-earth orbiting satellites avoid this delay but the user's device must then track the satellite's movement across the sky.   Both forms of satellite communication currently suffer from a relatively low-bandwidth(8-20 Kbps).   This limits the range of tasks that users can perform over these links.

Figure 1 shows how cellular radio communications offer an alternative to satellite systems.   Each cell has its own transceiver.   As users move from one cell to another, their' calls' are passed between transceivers.   The idealized architecture shown in Figure 1 masks many of the problems that frustrate the development of mobile computer systems.   There is a trade-off between the volume of information that a radio signal can carry and the distance that the signal will travel.   High frequency signals carry more information but are susceptible to interference and dispersion.

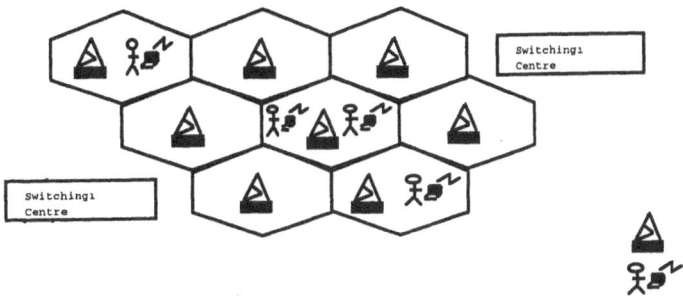

Figure 1: Cellular Communications Architecture.

Low frequency signals carry less information but will travel over longer distances. Radio-based communication also suffers from: signal fade due to adverse atmospheric conditions; unintentional electromagnetic interference; interference from other devices using the same channel and variable signal strength due to movement of the device. Until such problems are addressed, users will continue to suffer the delays, broken connections and interruptions that frustrate mobile, human-computer interaction.

1.2. Notations for Interface Design

The technological barriers to digital communication are gradually being eroded. For instance, the Iridium project plans to use low-earth orbiting satellites to provide mobile communications from any point on the earth's surface. Until such system shave been fully developed, interface designers must continue to work within the constraints imposed by existing technology. The complexity of these systems makes it important that designers have some means of reasoning about mobile interaction. For example, existing task analysis techniques can be extended to represent the transfer of information between mobile systems (Johnson, Diaper and Long, 1985). Figure 2 achieves this by introducing location columns into Hix and Hartson's (1993) User Action Notation (UAN). The user is currently within one radio-cell. Their request for information is sent through the underlying infrastructure to a transceiver. Before the request can be completed, the user moves out of the cell. The connection is temporarily lost until the system re-establishes communication through another transceiver.

	User		Computer (communications infrastructure)		
location	internal actions	user (articulatory) actions	perceivable computer actions	internal actions	location
Sector A	locate button	select button	button hilited	request sent	Sector A
				download begins	
Sector B			page displayed progressively		
				connection lost	
			"re-connecting" message		
				transfer request	
					Sector B

Figure 2: Extending UAN with Location Information

Unfortunately, a number of problems limit the utility of this notation. It provides no means of reasoning about temporal properties. This is important because the hand-over delay in Figure 2 might have a minimal effect if it lasted a few seconds. If it took several minutes then the "re-connecting" message might have to be reworded to provide more information about the cause of the delay. Temporal information can be represented using the extended XUAN notation(Gray and Johnson, 1995). There are, however, further problems. The column labelled' Computer (communications infrastructure)' represents a considerable simplification. This does not capture the distinction between the state of the user's local machine and the communications network that provides access to a remote site. This is significant because the 'reconnecting message' can only be generated if the local machine detects the cause of the problem and takes appropriate action tore-establish the signal. Additional columns might be introduced into the table to represent the behaviour of local and remote machines but this would further reduce the tractability of UAN's tabular form.

A range of mathematically based, notations have been developed to reason about the problems of communication over mobile, distributed systems (Johnson 1996). Temporal extensions to formal specification techniques are a now a standard feature in the development of digital telecommunications systems (Austin and Parkin. 1993).Unfortunately, these notations have not been used to support interface design for mobile computing devices. This paper, therefore, demonstrates that a formal logic can be used to reason about the problems that frustrate human-computer interaction over mobile networks.

2   Using Logic To Represent Mobile Interaction

First order logic offers a number of advantages for the design of mobile human-computer interfaces. For instance, the use of a mathematical notation provides a link between interface design and the use of formal methods in the systems engineering of distributed systems. Logic formalisms also support prototyping through the use of concurrent execution environments, such as Prelog (Johnson,

1995). The following clauses illustrate this approach through the application of a Horn-clause notation to represent interaction with a mobile device. A user's request is successful if it is handled by a local machine. Alternatively, it is successful if the request is dispatched to an appropriate transceiver. In clause (2) the *marshall* proposition is used to indicate the process by which the users' request is packaged into a form that the transceiver can process. This proposition might be refined to introduce additional detail if the user's task required particular error correction or security features. Similarly, the term *transceiver* might be refined to represent a satellite transmission system.

The previous clauses suffer from a number of limitations. In particular, they focus on high level architectural features of the communications protocols that support mobile interaction. They do not illustrate the ways in which logic might also be used to analyse interface requirements during human-computer interaction with remote resources.

$$initiate\_transaction(user, request, local\_machine) \Leftarrow$$

$$input(user, request), handled(local\_machine, request). \qquad (1)$$

$$initiate\_transaction(user, request, transceiver) \Leftarrow input(user, request) \wedge$$

$$nothandled(local\_machine, request) \wedge covered(local\_machine, location, transceiver) \wedge$$

$$marshall(request, message) \wedge dispatch(transceiver, message).$$
$$(2)$$

The first clause states that a user's request is initiated if they input a request and it can be handled locally. The second clause states that a user's request is initiated if they input a request and it cannot be handled locally and a transceiver cover's the users location and the local machine dispatches the request through that transceiver.

2.1   Supporting Display Design

The users of remote resources frequently become frustrated and may even abandon their requests if they cannot predict how long it will take to retrieve information (Johnson, 1995a). Such problems are particularly severe for the users of mobile systems which are dependent upon the underlying radio and satellite communications networks. The following clauses, therefore, builds upon(2) to specify that user confirmation is required if input cannot be handled locally. Even if a user cannot predict the amount of time that will be necessary for a particular request, they can at least determine whether or not a particular request is directed towards a remote machine.

confirmation_dialogue(user, request, local_machine) ⇐

    input(user, request)∧ *not handled(local_machine, request)*∧

    display(local_machine, transfer_dialogue_box)∧ *input(user, confirm)* ∧

    covered(local_machine, location, transceiver)∧ *marshall(request, message)* ∧

    dispatch(transceiver, message).   (3)

This states that a user's request is initiated if they input a request and it cannot be handled locally and the user issues input to confirm that they would like the request handled remotely and a transceiver covers the user's location and the local machine dispatches the request through that transceiver.

It is important to note that clause (3)does not specify the exact textual and graphical primitives that may be used to make up the *transfer_dialogue_box*. The following clauses illustrate the way in which such presentation information can be gradually introduced into high level specifications. Abstract images, such as the *transfer_dialogue_box*, can be described in terms of their component images.   These component images can, in turn, be described in terms of the primitive graphical objects that are finally presented to the user (Johnson, 1995).

    part(transfer_dialogue_box, left_arrow),   (4)

    line(left_arrow, 0.1,0.1,0.3,0.3).   (5)

    dimension(left_arrow, 0.3,0.3).   (6)

The first clause states that the left arrow is part of the initiate transfer icon.   The previous clauses also state that there is a line component of the left arrow and that the component has dimensions of (0.3, 0.3) relative to the entire display.

Previous clauses have shown that first order logic can be used to represent high-level interaction architectures for mobile systems.   They have also illustrated the way in which this notation can be used to represent particular interface requirements.   They have not, however, shown that logic can be used to analyse the systems behaviours which have a profound impact upon the usability of mobile computer systems.

2.2 Integrating Systems Engineering and User Requirements

A key requirement for the systems engineering of mobile computer systems is that the transceiver or satellite link should be able to unmarshall messages from remote users. This involves the use of error correction and encryption protocols. The transceiver must also determine whether the client and the destination are registered users of the service.

routing_service_request(transceiver, message) ⟸

    unmarshall(message,local_machine, destination, request) ∧

    registered(transceiver, local_machine) ∧registered(transceiver, destination) ∧

    marshall(request, message2) ∧ *dispatch(destination, message2).*

(7)

This states that a request is serviced by a transceiver if it can unmarshall, or unpack, a message to identify both the target server and the local machine and both the server and local machines are registered with the transceiver and the message is forwarded to the target server.

Such systems requirements have a profound impact upon the users of mobile computing systems. For example, the previous clause does not specify what should happen if the transceiver or satellite link could not immediately dispatch the user's request to its intended *destination*. This would happen if, for instance, the *destination* were another mobile user who was currently out of range of a transceiver. Under such circumstances, the user who initiated the request would be left waiting for a response. Systems engineers and interface designers can exploit a number of techniques to mitigate such problems. For instance, many distributed systems now make use of binding services. In this architecture, the user does not specify a particular destination for their request. Instead, their input is passed to any available machine that is registered and authorised to handle it. If a particular destination is not available, for example if it is out of range, then the binder may forward the user's request to another machine. Such a service might be implemented through the higher level protocols of the switching centres, shown on Figure 1. This approach is typical of high-integrity systems where users require a high degree of assurance that their input will eventually be handled by a server.

service_request(binder, message)⟸*unmarshall(message, local_machine, request)*∧

> *offers(server, request)*∧ *marshall(request, message2)*∧
>
> *dispatch(server, message2)*

.(8)

This states that a request is serviced by a transceiver if it can unmarshall, or unpack, a message to identify the local machine and the request and a server has registered an offer to fulfill such requests with the transceiver and the request is forwarded to the server.

This clause again illustrates the need to closely integrate interface design with the systems engineering of mobile systems. Many tasks can only be performed on particular machines. For example, if a person sent a message to another mobile user then that message must be directed towards a machine where that user has an account. Under such circumstances, it is important that interface designers provide users with mechanisms for directing binding services towards particular destinations.

3   What Happens When Things Go Wrong

This section builds upon the previous analysis and focuses more closely upon the impact that systems failures have upon human-computer interaction with mobile devices.

3.1   Transceiver Failure

Interaction with remote resources will be jeopardised if a user's local machine cannot access the gateway into the communications network. Tracking problems can prevent a mobile computer from locating low-orbit satellites. Atmospheric interference can disrupt communication with geostationary satellites. Adverse meteorological conditions and natural barriers can restrict access to the transceivers in cellular networks.

> *fail_transaction(user, request,transceiver)* ⟸ *input(user, request)*∧
>
> > *nothandled(local_machine, request)*∧ *not covered(local_machine, location,transceiver).*

(9)

This states that a transaction fails if a user inputs a request which cannot be handled locally and the user's location is not covered by a transceiver.

Such failures create a number of problems. For example, there may be no means for the user to know whether or not they are covered by a transceiver at any particular moment during interaction. One solution would be for the user to issue periodic requests to find out whether the mobile device was within range of the network. The success or failure of a request might then be reported using the display design techniques described in clauses (4,5,6). This approach is hardly transparent; the user must continually monitor the state of their connection in order to determine whether a request will be successful. Alternatively, store and forward techniques can be used. This approach relies upon the local machine storing the user's request until the remote network can be contacted again. As soon as a connection is re-established the user's message can be processed. Under this systems, users cannot assume that their requests will be immediately dispatched through the communications system. It is only possible to assume that their input will eventually be successful. Unfortunately, such delays cannot easily be captured using first order logic. The following clause, therefore, introduces the × (read as 'eventually') operator from interval temporal logic. The syntax and semantics of this notation are described in Johnson (1995). In contrast, the remainder of this paper focuses on the application of the approach to support the development of mobile, human-computer interfaces.

store_and_forward_transaction(user, request, transceiver) $\Leftarrow$

   fail_transaction(user, request,transceiver)$\wedge$

   not handled(local_machine, request)$\wedge$

   ◊covered(local_machine, location, transceiver) $\wedge$

   marshall(request, message) $\wedge$ *dispatch(transceiver, message).*

$$(10)$$

A user's request is stored and later forwarded to a transceiver if a requested transaction fails and eventually, the user's location is covered by a transceiver and the message is forwarded to that site.

Store and forward techniques offers substantial benefits because they shield the user from the underlying systems architecture. Unfortunately, these benefits carry a cost. Users may not recognize the reasons for the delays that occur when their requests are stored for later transmission. It is, therefore, possible for the user to issue multiple requests in the belief that their original input has been lost. Each of the requests would then be processed as contact is resumed with the communications system. This problem might be avoided if users were warned that a transfer was stalled until the message can be dispatched.

store_and_forward_display(user,request, transceiver) ⇐

    fail_transaction(user, request,transceiver)∧

    nothandled(local_machine, request) ∧

    display(local_machine,transfer_stalled) U

    (covered(local_machine, location, transceiver)∧

    marshall(request, message) ∧

    dispatch(transceiver,message)).   (11)

This states that a user's request is stored and that a warning is displayed if a requested transaction fails and an icon is displayed to show that the request is stalled until the user's location is covered by a transceiver and the message is forwarded to that site.

The previous clause used the *U* (read as 'until') operator. This describes the duration of the delay that might occur before the mobile machine moves within range of the nearest transceiver. This illustrates an important benefit of the logic notation; designers are not forced to specify the exact, real-time duration of the warning. Such details can gradually be introduced as empirical evidence indicates the probable time required for a user to note the warning in a given application (Kuhmann,1989).

3.2 Server Failure

Mobile human-computer interaction will also break-down if the communications infrastructure is in tact but the target resource is unavailable or unknown. The binding architecture, described in clause(8), is resilient to this form of failure because several machines may offer the same service. However, in a standard architecture the user may specify a particular destination *server* that cannot be recognized by the transceiver and itsassociated messaging system.

fail_server_request(transceiver, message) ⇐

    unmarshall(message, server,local_machine, request)∧

    not registered(server, local_machine).   (12)

This states that a server fails to fulfil a request if a request is unmarshalled by a transceiver but the local machine is not registered with the anticipated server.

This clause again illustrates the need to integrate human-factors and systems engineering during the development of mobile computer systems. For instance, systems engineers must implement the underlying protocols to determine whether a server is not responding through system failure or through unexpected delays in the communications system. Human factors engineers must design displays to alert the user that their request has failed. The exact content and format of such warnings must be heavily influenced by the underlying communications protocols. In a transparent architecture with asynchronous requests or a store and forward mechanism, users may be very surprised to learn that a request has failed several minutes after it was issued.

fail_server_request_2(transceiver, message)⇐

    unmarshall(message, server,local_machine, request) ∧]

    not registered(server,local_machine)∧

    O(marshall(registration_failure,message)∧

    dispatch(local_machine,message)).   (13)

display_server_failure(user, local_machine) ⇐

    unmarshall(message,local_machine, server, registration_failure)∧

    display(local_machine, registration_failure) U input(user,confirm),

                                        (14)

The first clause states that a server fails to fulfill a request if a request is unmarshalled by a transceiver but the local machine is not registered with the anticipated server and in the next interval a message is returned to the local machine to warn them that they are not registered for the server that they requested. The second clause states that a server failure is displayed to a user on a local machine if a message is unmarshalled on the local machine to provide notification of a registration failure and this warning is presented until the user confirms it.

Clause (13) exploits the O (read as 'next') temporal logic operator to specify that the user's local machine is alerted to the server failure as soon as possible after the failure is detected. This does not mean that the user's display will be instantly updated. If the transceiver or satellite loses contact with the local machine then the user may continue to interact with the local system as if the original command had been successful. Under a store and forward architecture, see clause (10), the local machine would then send these requests to the transceiver at the same time as the transceiver returned a warning about the server failure.

3.3   *Binder Failure*

As mentioned, binding architectures avoid the problems of server failure because more than one site may be able to service a user's request. Delays can be reduced if the underlying communications protocols route the user's input to the closest server or to a server with spare capacity. However, this does not avoid the problems that arise when no server can satisfy the user's request.

$binding\_service\_failure(transceiver, message) \Leftarrow$

   $unmarshall(message, local\_machine, request) \land$

   $notoffers(server, request).$ (15)

This states that a binding service fails if a local machine unmarshalls a request and no server has offered to satisfy that request.

The simplest solution to this problem would be to return a message that the input could not be handled. This is the approach described in (14).Alternatively, the local machine or the communications infrastructure could store the user's request in the hope that a server might eventually offer the service. This would cope with periodic systems failures where duplicate servers are not provided. The user could assume that their input would eventually be handled once the relevant resource became available. This approach characterizes the mobile control systems that are used to schedule repair teams, for instance in the domestic gas industry. Supervisors enter the day's duties into their local system. This is, typically, a PC with a modem connection to mobile receivers in each of the teams' vehicles. New jobs are allocated to a crew whenever they complete a previous *request*.

$binding\_service\_delay(binder, message) \Leftarrow$

   $unmarshall(message, local\_machine, request) \land$

   $notoffers(server, request) \land \Diamond offers(server, request) \land$

   $forward(server, request).$ (16)

This states that there is a delay in a binding service if a user's request is unmarshalled but in the present interval, no server offers to satisfy the request and eventually a server does become available and the request is forwarded.

Unfortunately, there are a number of problems with this approach. For instance, processing delays can lead to a backlog of requests. This problem can be avoided by specifying a time-out after which the user will be alerted that their request has blocked. An alternative approach relies on the fact that no single binding service will know of all of the possible destinations for a user's request. In some cases, input may be passed to other cells or areas in order to find a suitable server. This is analogous to additional repair vehicles being called in from outside of a controller's area. This approach has many benefits for the users of mobile computer systems. In particular, it can be used to perform load balancing in distributed applications. Tasks may migrate throughout the communications 'network'.

$$binding\_service\_forward\_request(binder, message) \Leftarrow$$

$$unmarshall(message, local\_machine, request) \wedge$$

$$not\ offers(server, request)\ \wedge$$

$$covered(binder, location, binder2)\ \wedge$$

$$marshall(request, message)\ \wedge$$

$$dispatch(binder2, message). \tag{17}$$

This states that a binder forwards a request if a message is unmarshalled and no server is registered to satisfy the enclosed request and the binder is covered by another binder and the first site marshalls the request and passed it on to the second site.

However, a request may pass through many intermediate sites before it finds a host that is willing to perform any associated computation. This is similar to the way in which agents may migrate through conventional networks. Such approaches depend upon users finding sites that are willing and able to satisfy their tasks. Further work intends to fully explore the parallel between agent based systems and the emerging architectures for mobile human-computer interaction. The delays that arise through communications problems in mobile systems can be thought of as the time taken for agents to access remote resources.

4   Conclusion

This paper has argued that mobile devices pose new challenges for human-computer interaction. The technological limitations of radio and satellite systems can delay to user requests. These disruptions frequently lead to frustration and error (Walters, 1995). A number of international initiatives are currently devising solutions to these problems. For instance, by building a global network of low-orbit satellites. In the short-term, however, it is important that interface designers can mitigate the problems of mobile interaction. We have, therefore, shown that temporal extensions to first order logic can be used to analyse a number of different interaction architectures for mobile systems. Store and forward approaches have been compared to binding services. Transparent approaches that hide the underlying communications infrastructure from the user have been contrasted with approaches in which the user specifically directs their requests to particular sites. A critical theme in all of this has been the need to integrate interface design and systems engineering. Unless systems engineers appreciate the consequences of transmission delays then it may not be possible to implement the protocols and architectures that mitigate the usability problems of mobile interaction. Unless interface designers understand the underlying properties of modern communications then there is a danger that users will continue tof ace unexplained delays and periodic system failures.

Acknowledgments

Thanks are due to the members of the Glasgow Accident Analysis Group and the Glasgow Interactive Systems Group (GIST) who provided valuable support and encouragement for the work reported in this paper. This research has been supported by the UK Engineering and Physical Sciences Research Council, grants GR/L27800 and GR/K55042.

Appendix A: Table of Propositions

The following table provides informal descriptions of the propositions that are introduced in the paper and that are not given an informal description as part of the running text.

Proposition	Informal meaning
input(user, request)	This is true if a user inputs a service request.
display(machine, display_element)	This is true if a machine displays a graphical image denoted by display_element.
part(display_elem1, display_elem2)	True if display_element2 is part of display_element1.
line(display_element, X,Y, X1, Y1).	This is true if there is a line from Cartesian Co-ordinates (X, Y) to (X1, Y1) in a graphical image denoted by display_element.
dimension(display_element, X, Y).	This is true if display_element occupies the X and Y dimensions of the screen where X and Y are in the

	range from 0.0 to 1.0.
handled(machine,request).	True if a machine can handle or service a request.
covered(machine, location, transceiver)	This is true if a machine falls within a transceiver's location.
marshall(request, message)	This is true if a request is translated into a common message format that can be understood by the potential recipient.
unmarshall(message, local_machine, destination_machine, request)	This is true if a message from a local_machine is translated into a request for a service on a destination_machine.
dispatch(machine,message)	This is true if a message is dispatched to a destination machine.
registered(transceiver,machine)	This is true if a machine is registered to access or be accessed by a transceiver.
offers(server,request)	This is true if a server offers to service a particular quest.
O(w)	This is true if a proposition w is true in the next state,
×(w)	This is true if a proposition *is* eventually true in some future state.
[w_1 U w_2]	This is true if a proposition w_1 is true until proposition w_2 is true.

References

S. Austin and G.I. Parkin,(1993) *Formal Methods: A Survey*, Division Of Information Technology And Computing, The National Physical Laboratory, Sponsored by the United Kingdom Department of Trade and Industry

A. Dix, (ed) 1997*CSCW Issues for Mobile and Teleworkers.* Springer Verlag, Berlin,

P. Gray and C.W. Johnson, (1995) Requirements for Interface Design Notations. In P. Palanque and R. Bastide (eds.), *The Design, Specification and Verification of Interactive Systems*, 113-133. Springer Verlag, Berlin.

D. Hix and H.R. Hartson, (1993) *Developing User Interfaces*, John Wiley and Sons, London.

C.W. Johnson. (1995) Integrating Human Factors And Systems Engineering To Reduce The Risk Of Operator 'Error', *Safety Science*, 22(1-3):195-214.

C.W. Johnson, (1995a) Time And The Web: Representing Temporal Properties Of Interaction With Distributed Systems. In M.A.R. Kirby and A.J. Dix and J.E. Finlay (eds.) *People And Computers X: Proceedings of HCI'95*, Cambridge University Press, Cambridge, United Kingdom, 39-50.

C.W. Johnson (1996) The Impact of Working Environments on Human-Machine Interaction, *Ergonomics*, (39)3:512-530, 1996

P. Johnson, D. Diaper and J. Long, (1985(Task Analysis in Interactive Systems Design and Evaluation. In G. Johansen, G. Mancini and L. Martensson (eds.)*Analysis, Design and Evaluation in Man-Machine Systems*. Oxford University Press.

W. Kuhmann, (1989) Stress Inducing Properties Of System Response Times, *Ergonomics*, (32)3:271-280.

E. Simon (1996) *Distributed Information Systems*. McGraw Hill, London.

R. Walters (1995) *Computer-Mediated Communications*. Artech House, Boston.

The Impact of Marginal Utility and Time on Distributed Information Retrieval

Chris Johnson

Glasgow Interactive Systems Group,
Department of Computing Science,
University of Glasgow,
Glasgow, G12 8QQ, UK.
Tel: +44 (0141) 330 6053
Fax: +44 (0141) 330 4913
http://www.dcs.gla.ac.uk/~johnson
EMail: johnson@dcs.glasgow.ac.uk

This paper argues that marginal utility can be extended from the domain of Micro-economics to explain some of the problems that frustrate interaction with distributed systems. In particular, it is argued that concave utility curves can be used to analyse the electronic gridlock that occurs when remote systems cannot satisfy the number of demands which users make upon their services. Convex utility curves represent the information saturation that occurs when users cannot extract important documents from a mass of irrelevant information. The paper goes on to argue that marginal utility can also be used to identify a range of interface techniques that reduce the problems associated with electronic gridlock and information saturation.

Keywords: electronic gridlock; information saturation; marginal utility.

1   Introduction

Recent estimates place the number of Internet users at almost seventy million (Johnson and Kavanagh, 1996). The very success of distributed computing has, however, exacerbated a range of existing usability problems. For example, retrieval delays have reached a stage where it can take thirty or forty minutes to download relatively small files from busy sites (Johnson, 1995)..

1.1   Electronic Gridlock

The term 'electronic gridlock' is used to refer to situations in which networks and servers cannot cope with the amount of information that is being requested from them.   Recent innovations in caching, including the widespread use of mirror sites, have done much to increase the efficiency of network communications (van Rijsbergen, 1979).   However, the majority of Internet users still suffer from the 'bottlenecks' created by modem and ethernet connections.   These bottlenecks increase the costs, in terms of retrieval delays, that are associated with information retrieval.   As more and more people access a greater and greater volume of data, there has been an increase in the amount of time that is required to download information (Johnson, 1995).   Kuhmann (1989) argues that these retrieval delays have a profound impact upon the quality of interaction with distributed systems.

1.2   Information Saturation

In contrast to electronic gridlock, the term 'information saturation' refers to situations in which users simply cannot cope with the volume of information that is offered by remote sites.   Hiltz and Turoff (1985)argue that this problem stems from 'information entropy'; distributed resources are insufficiently well structured for users to select the items that they need.   This again increases the costs associated with information retrieval because users must invest considerable time and energy in locating necessary information. The introduction of free-text retrieval systems has reduced these problems.   However, the rapid duplication and reproduction of electronic documents more than offsets the benefits that many of these systems can offer.

1.3   What is Utility?

Unfortunately, interface designers have relatively few techniques that can be used to represent and reason about electronic gridlock and information saturation (Johnson, 1995).   These problem stem from users' attitudes to the value of information and the time required to retrieve it.   For example, electronic gridlock occurs because users are forced to invest large amounts of time in order to retrieve each item of remote information.   As retrieval delays increase, the value of information decreases.   Users move to other tasks.   They may also develop coping strategies that avoid accessing remote information.   Information saturation occurs because users must invest large amounts of time in identifying relevant information from a mass of irrelevant data.   Again, these costs may outweigh any benefits to be derived from the information as users invest increasing amounts of time in locating necessary resources.   It is, therefore, important to consider the relationship between the value that users associate with information and the cost of retrieving that information in terms of the retrieval delay.   In order to do this there must be some means of representing and reasoning about the costs and benefits of interaction with distributed systems.

Micro-economists have developed the notion of marginal utility to analyse the relationship between cost and value (Puppe, 1991).   Marginal utility is defined to be the additional benefit that can be obtained through the consumption of an extra unit of some good or service. Marginal utility can be thought of in terms of the additional value that may be obtained through each additional unit of time that is invested in acquiring a remote resource. Utility, in turn, can be thought of as a measure of 'desire' or the capacity of a good or service to satisfy a need. The exact nature of this desire will vary from task to task, however, the underlying notion of value will not (March and Simon, 1958). A number of different approaches can be exploited to represent the utility that users associate with items of information. For instance, satisficing identifies the subjective 'desire' for a good or service by iteratively refining the constraining equations that characterise preferences between tasks and services. Unfortunately, the difficulty of accurately identifying an individual's preferences has been a common theme of recent research in economics and decision theory (Puppe, 1991). One means of avoiding this problem is to construct high level models that characterise common attitudes towards utility. This approach suffers from a lack of empirical evidence. It does, however, provide a starting point for more detailed discussions about the costs and benefits of information retrieval.

1.4   Outline of the Paper

Section 2 argues that electronic gridlock is characterised by concave utility curves. The perceived benefits to be obtained from spending time on a request will quickly fall as the retrieval delays increase. In order to reduce this effect, users must be able to assess the quality of a remote resource before they download it. This flattens the subjective utility curve; the anticipated value of information will maintained because users can determine whether or not it will be worth waiting for before they issue a request. Section 3 goes on to demonstrate that the problems of information saturation are characterised by convex utility curves. Here, the volume of information provided to the user initially results in relatively high levels of utility. However, diminishing marginal returns quickly set in as the user has to sift through the mass of data to find the information that they are actually interested in. Section 3 goes on to describe an information retrieval system that exploits user-defined measures of relevance to match natural language queries with large numbers of documents. This has the effect of delaying the point of diminishing marginal returns because users can filter the mass of detail that is presented by the system. Section 4 presents the conclusions that can be drawn from this work. Directions for further research are also identified. It is argued that more work is required if explicit or inferred measures of relevance and value are to effectively combat the problems imposed by information saturation and electronic gridlock.

2   Electronic Gridlock

Electronic gridlock stems from the bottlenecks and system failures that exacerbate information retrieval over distributed networks. These problems increase the costs, in terms of the users' time, that must be met in order to retrieve a remote resource.

2.1   Analysing the Problem: Convex utility curves

Figure 1 presents a cost curve that characterises the problems associated with electronic gridlock.   Initially, the user has some anticipated or predicted minimum for the amount of time that it will take to complete any transfer. Up to this point, the utility of any information retrieved will be relatively high. Documents received before the minimum predicted period can be seen as a bonus from the user's perspective.

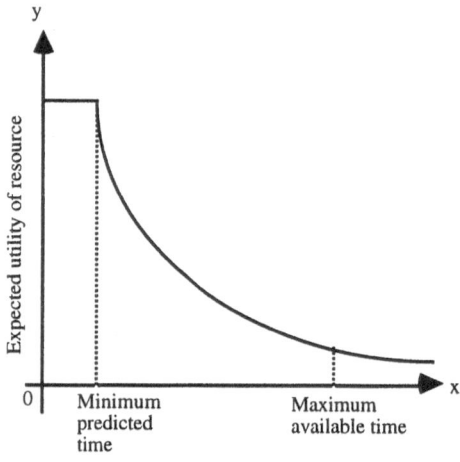

Figure 1: Expected Utility under Electronic Gridlock

After the minimum predicted time, the anticipated value of the information will decline.   There are many reasons for this.   The time taken to retrieve a document may exceed the total time that is available to for any associated tasks. Eventually, there will come a point when users simply 'run out of time'.   At this stage, the marginal utility of any remote information will be very low because the user simply cannot afford to wait for the data to be retrieved.   O'Donnel and Draper (1995) have shown that users will also begin to exploit coping strategies that reduce their reliance on remote information that carries high time penalties.

2.2   Solving the Problem: Indications of Cost and Quality

Figure 1 provides a high-level model of the costs and benefits of information retrieval under electronic gridlock.   It does not, however, provide interface designers with concrete means of combating the frustration and error that result from retrieval delays. Figure 2 illustrates a web page that does exploit' concrete" techniques to reduce electronic gridlock. Users are provided with an indication of the size of a remote resource before they access them. This, together with some contextual knowledge of network conditions, can help users to make better predictions about the minimum time to retrieve a remote resource (Johnson and Kavanagh, 1996). In this example, the size of a video was indicated in terms of clip length. This was chosen rather than file size because it had more meaning to the school children who were intended to access this resource.

Figure 2: Indicating the Cost of Remote Information

The interface shown in Figure 2 combats the problems of electronic gridlock by extending the period of high relative utility that is associated with the interval before the minimum expected retrieval period. This is illustrated in Figure 3. It is important to stress that the delay which is predicted by the user can be very different from the actual delay. This will be effected by transient conditions, such as the time of day and the loading of any intermediate networks. Figure 3 also shows how indications of resource size can help users to synchronise their retrieval tasks with their wider activities. For instance, if the anticipated delay extended any further in this graph than it might begin to exceed the maximum anticipated time available for the task. Users might then not decide to embark upon the retrieval until more time was available. Figure 4 illustrates an alternative means of combating electronic gridlock. Instead of representing the size of a remote resource, this interface provides users with information about the quality of a document. For example, the video material provided via the interface in Figure 2 was produced by a professional crew working for a national broadcaster. It was processed using 'state of the art' compression techniques. Usability studies were conducted into optimal file lengths for web-based retrieval. Unfortunately, simple hypertext links, such as those shown in Figure 2, provide users with little or no indication of these production values (Johnson and Kavanagh, 1996). Figure 4, therefore presents an alternative approach which uses still images from the compressed video to indicate the quality of the remote resource.

The revised interface shown in Figure 4 had a profound impact upon users' attitudes towards retrieval delays. Significantly more requests were abandoned

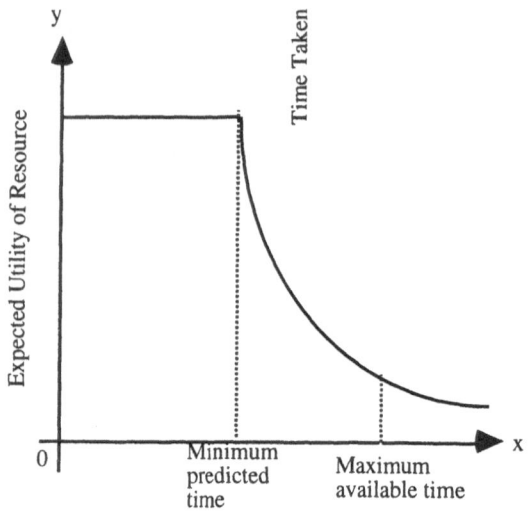

Figure 3: Indications of Cost Extend Minimum Predictions

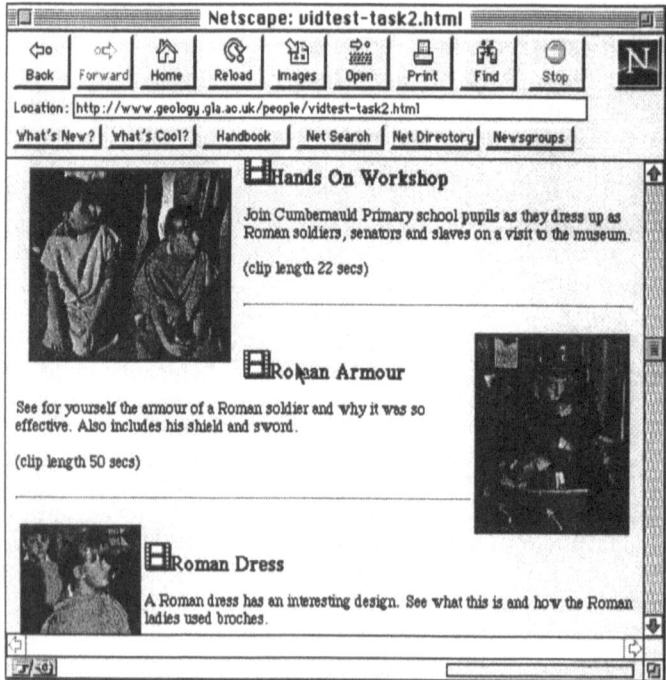

Figure 4: Indicating the Quality of Remote Information

using the simple hypertext tags of Figure 2 when compared to the thumb-nail images in Figure 4.   This was true even for relatively long clips of over 70 seconds (Johnson and Kavanagh, 1996).

Figure 5 presents a cost curve that explains the observed reduction in abandoned requests between the interfaces shown in Figures 2 and 4.   This curve shows the impact that indications of resource quality have upon expected utility.   The previous cost curve, shown as a dotted line in Figure 5, is transformed along the Y-axis. This indicates the rise in expectations that can be produced through effective interface design.

There is strong initial evidence to suggest that such techniques also encourage users to increase the time devoted to retrieval tasks (Johnson and Kavanagh, 1996).   This could be indicated in Figure 5 by moving the maximum available time along the X axis.   Conversely, an interface which indicated relatively low production values would have the opposite effect of reducing the absolute level of the anticipated utility.   This can be shown by a transformation of the cost curve down the Y axis.

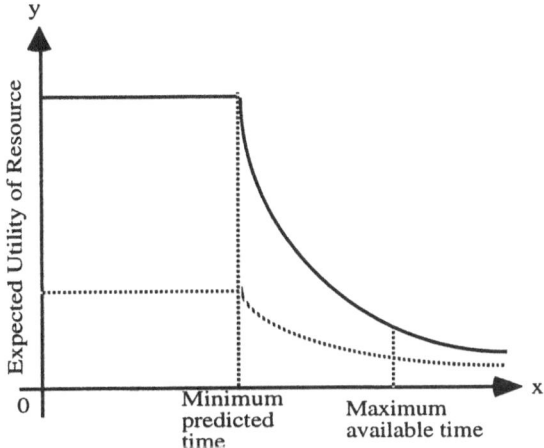

Time Taken to Complete Request

Figure 5: Indications of Quality Raise Expected Utility

Figures 6 a) and b) provide initial qualitative evidence to back up the assertions made in the previous paragraph.   These diagrams present the results of an evaluation using twenty school children to access the two competing interfaces illustrated in Figures 2 and 4.   The graph on the left shows a strong negative reaction to the simple textual labels.   The absence of any results for the longer videos over 50 seconds indicates that all attempts to retrieve these clips were abandoned.   The graph on the right presents the same results for the web page shown in Figure 4. In this instance, the school children were very satisfied even for the longer clips.   Further details about this empirical work and a justification for the relatively small sample size can be found in Johnson (1997).   The important point here is that the retrieval delays and video material were held constant between the two conditions. The indications of production quality resulted in an observable increase in qualitative satisfaction or utility.

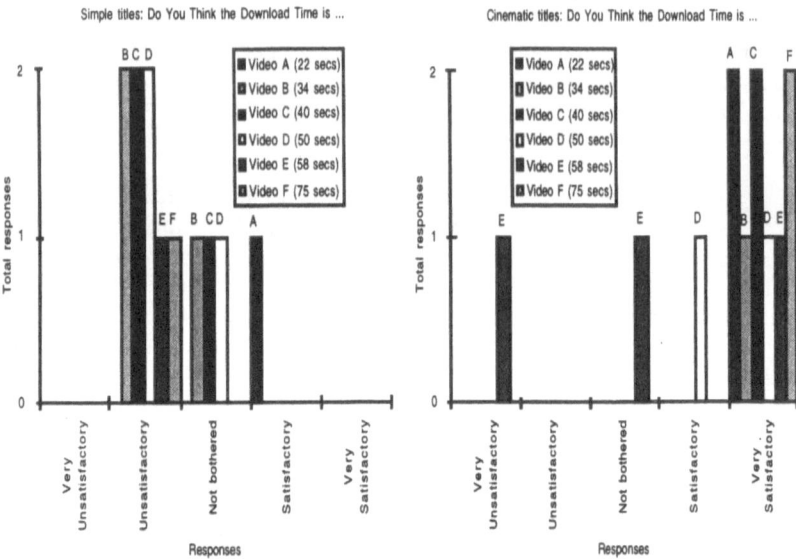

Figure 6: Qualitative responses to indications of quality

Figure 6 raises further questions about the validation of our utility curves. In particular, it illustrates some of the problems that arise when trying to map subjective concepts, such as utility, onto empirical results. This is a well known problem in the field of economics. The key result is that it is impossible to define a unit of utility without reference to the users information retrieval task. Terms such as 'cost/benefit', 'value', 'need', 'desire' or 'preference' cannot really be measured except in terms of particular domain or problem characteristics. It, therefore, follows that figures such as Figure 6 cannot fully capture the utility of Figures 2 and 4 for all information retrieval tasks. Here we are testing school children performing a browsing task. Elsewhere we contrast these results with other groups of users pursuing more goal directed tasks(Johnson, 1997).

3   Information Saturation

Information saturation occurs when users simply cannot find relevant documents amongst the mass of information that is provided by remote sites. Cost curves can be used to analyse the underlying reasons for this problem in terms of the relationship between the utility of information and the time taken to access it over remote networks.

3.1   Analysing the Problem: Diminishing Marginal Utility

Figure 7 characterises the marginal utilities that are associated with information saturation. Initially, the value of remote information will be high. This represents the situation in which users quickly find the information that they were looking for. As time goes on, the value associated with an item of information will decline. In particular, the marginal utility will fall more rapidly as users approach the maximum amount of time that is available for their task. Beyond this point, users will not be able to use the information even if they can find it. In contrast to the previous cost curves, Figure 7 is convex because users increase their chances of finding exactly the item that they are looking for by increasing the amount of time that they invest in the search process. This is represented by the relatively high marginal utilities shown immediately after the minimum predicted search time.

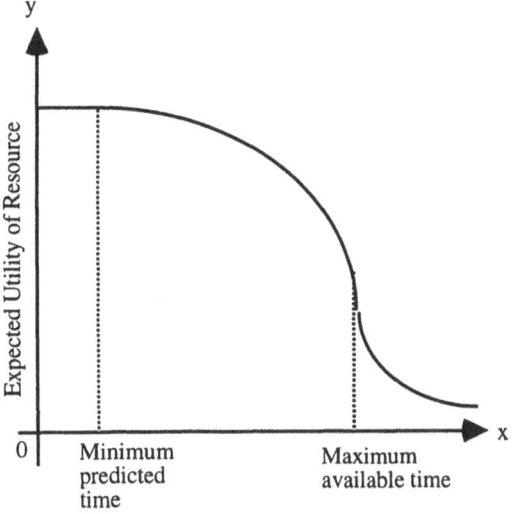

Time Taken to Locate Resource

Figure 7: Expected Utility under Information Saturation

3.2   Reducing the Impact of Information Saturation

Information saturation occurs when users are over-whelmed by the volume of data that is provided by remote sites. This is not a novel problem. There are a large number of search engines that can help users extract relevant information from a mass of background 'noise' (van Rijsbergen, 1979). For instance, we have recently extended the In query tool to support free-text retrieval for multimedia information. Figure 8 shows the results of a query about wooden artefacts in an ethnographic collection. The hypertext links can be selected to retrieve photographs, videos or text about the objects in question. Alternatively, users can build their own pages by selecting any of the check boxes under the assemble page, AP, column. The rankings are automatically calculated from the relevance of the document to the query. In order to do this, the system exploits a thesaurus of pre-defined synonyms. Associated with each synonym is a degree of belief. If for example, a user entered a query about a canoe then the system might retrieve any document which contained the word kayak. Associated with that document might be a 70% belief that any query relating to canoes would be satisfied by a document referring to kayaks. In Figure 8, this is illustrated by a belief of 0.501 (50%) that a query about wood will be satisfied by a document on a 'Hand Adze or Chisel'. This systems, therefore, automates the filtering process that would otherwise have to be performed by the manual inspection of distributed resources.

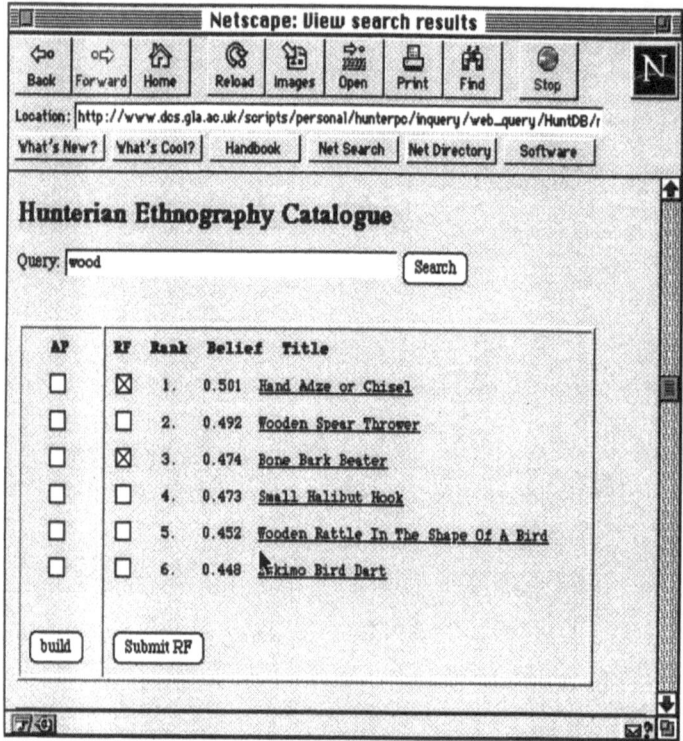

Figure 8: Degrees of Belief Ranking A Query

Figure 9 illustrates the impact that such systems have upon the expected utility of remote resources. Retrieval engines offer relatively high levels of utility for a minimal investment of time. A range of documents may be returned for an initial query. These can then be searched by subsequent queries to find the exact document that the user is looking for. This iterative search process ensures that the marginal utility of time spent on a search task can remain relatively high. The more time that a user invests in a query, the better the results may be.

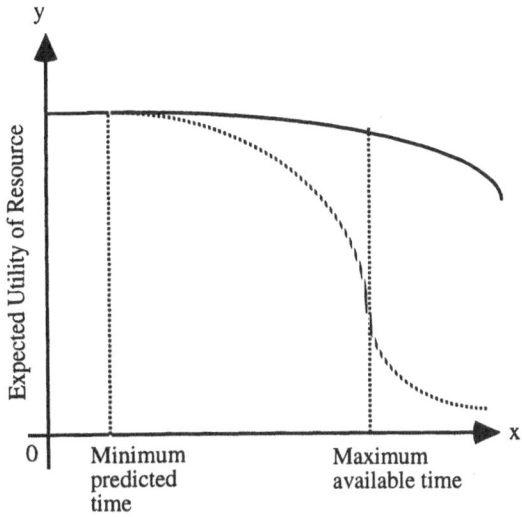

Time Taken to Locate Resource

Figure 9: The Effects of Retrieval Engines on Expected Utility

Figure 9 presents an almost constant rate of marginal utility. This is an ideal. In reality, the cost curves associated with retrieval engines are liable to exhibit a number of peaks and troughs. If there were a rapid rise in marginal utility then any query which terminated before that rise would be unlikely to contain a relevant document. Conversely, if there were a rapid fall in the marginal utility then many users would abandon their requests before that point. These peaks and troughs are caused by the precision and recall characteristics of the system. Precision indicates the extent to which a tool retrieves only those documents that are relevant to a user's task. Recall indicates the extent to which a tool retrieves all of those documents that might be relevant to a user's task. Figures 10 a) and 10 b) illustrate what can happen as the precision and recall of an information retrieval tool moves away from the ideal shown in Figure 9.

In Figure 10 a) the low recall of an information retrieval system initially results in a lower marginal utility than that of Figure 7, the previous cost curve is shown as a dotted line in Figure 10. This lower utility occurs because users cannot be sure that the system will retrieve all of the documents that may be relevant to their task. The peak to the right of the minimum predicted recall time occurs because users will have to issue further queries to ensure that they have actually seen all of the documents that may be relevant to a particular query. Figure 10 b) illustrates the effects of low precision. The retrieval of many irrelevant documents alters the shape of the cost curve so that it begins to resemble the characteristic shape of that associated with information saturation, shown in Figure 7. In a pathological case, successive queries may not refine the selection to find the necessary documents, as shown in Figure 9, but may actually reduce the value of the results by introducing new documents that are not relevant to the users' task.

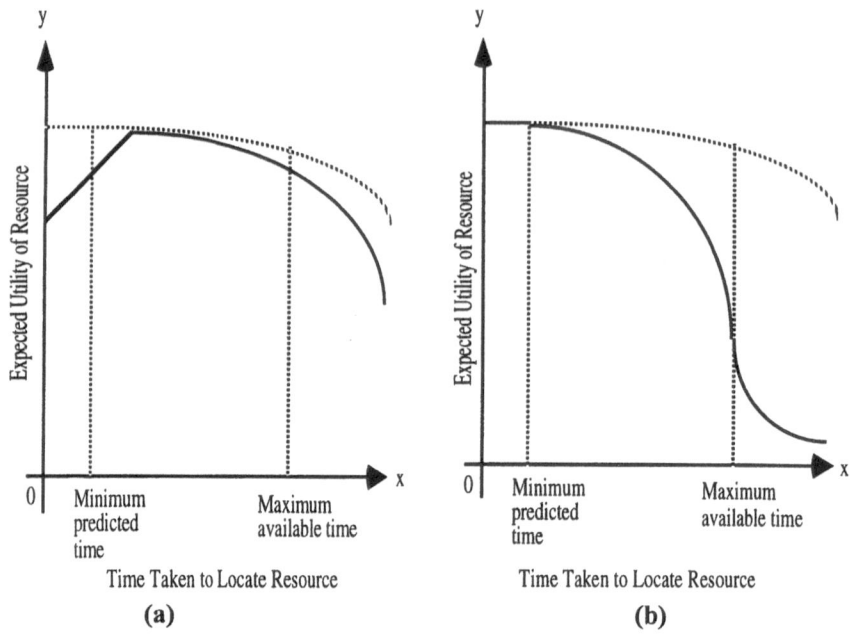

Figure 10: The Effects of Retrieval Engines on Expected Utility; (a), low recall;
(b), low precision

4   Conclusion

This paper has argued that marginal utility can be used to explain some of the
usability problems that frustrate interaction with distributed systems. The
limitations of network technology and server capacity have introduced significant
delays when sending or receiving information over the Internet.   This problem
has be entermed 'electronic gridlock'.   We have shown that such conditions are
characterised by concave utility curves.   The returns associated with investing
more and more time into a request rapidly fall to a point where most users will
simply abandon their requests.

   We have also used the concept of marginal utility to analyse the problem of
information saturation.   This arises because many sites provide so much
information that users are forced to invest large amounts of their time looking for
necessary information.   Such problems are characterised by convex utility
curves.   Initially, users can increase the rewards associated with their retrieval
task by investing more time in their search.   They will, however, reach a point
where diminishing marginal returns set in.   At this point, the search task may
actually eat into the time reserved from any associated tasks that depend upon the
remote information.

   We have also described how a range of interface design techniques can be used
to alter the utility curves associated with electronic gridlock and information

saturation. For example it its possible to raise subjective assessments of utility by providing users with clear indications about the production value of remote resources. Similarly, information retrieval engines can be used to reduce the impact of diminishing marginal returns for search tasks; users can increase the value of their queries over time by successively refining their initial selection.

As mentioned in the introduction to this paper, it is important to provide empirical confirmation of the subjective observations that are reported in the paper. Elsewhere we describe initial work that has determined the tolerance thresholds for retrieval delays over the world wide web(Johnson and Kavanagh, 1996). However, this evidence was obtained using conventional experimental techniques. There is growing evidence in the field of economics to indicate that these techniques are insufficient. In particular, Puppe (1991) argues that attitudes towards utility cannot be correctly understood without considering individual attitudes towards risk. In other words, the utility curves presented in this paper must be further refined to show the attitudes of risk preferring and risk adverse people when faced with retrieval delays and complex search tasks. Further work intends to explore the consequences of such an analysis, For example, a risk preferring user may choose to issue and abandon many requests in the hope that they will 'strike lucky' when looking for a remote resource, A risk adverse user might choose a more 'rigorous' strategy which completes more transactions but issues less requests.

Acknowledgements

Thanks go to the members of the Glasgow Interactive Systems Group (GIST)and Glasgow Accident Analysis Group. Particular thanks go to Paul Hunterand Jim Kavanagh who drove the implementation work behind the video pages and the catalogue retrieval application. Chris Johnson's work is supported by the UK Engineering and Physical Sciences Research Council, grants GR/JO7686, GR/K69148 andGR/K55040.

References

S.R. Hiltz and M. Turoff (1985). Structuring Computer-MediatedCommunication Systems to Avoid Information Overload. Communications ofthe ACM, 28: 680-689.

C.W. Johnson (1995), Time and the Web: Representing and Reasoning aboutTemporal Properties of Interaction with Distributed Systems. In M. Kirby,A. Dix and J. Finlay (eds.), People and Computers X, 39-50, CambridgeUniversity Press, Cambridge, United Kingdom.

C.W. Johnson (1997) The Ten Golden Rules for Providing Video over the Web.In. C. Forsythe (editor), Human Factors and the Web, Lawrence Erlbaum,New York, United States of America. In press.

C.W. Johnson and J. Kavanagh (1996), Electronic Gridlock. In H. Thimblebyand A. Blandford (eds.) Adjunct Proceedings of HCI'96. British ComputerSociety, London, United Kingdom.

W. Kuhmann (1989). Stress Inducing Properties of System Response Times.Ergonomics, 32(3):271-280.

J.G. March and H.A. Simon (1958), Organisations, Wiley, New York, UnitedStates of America.

P. O'Donnel and S. Draper (1995), How Machine Delays Change UserStrategies, Adjunct Proceedings to HCI'95, British Computer Society,London.

C. Puppe (1991) Distorted Probabilities And Choice Under Risk, SpringerVerlag, Lecture Notes In Economics And Mathematical Systems, No 363, Berlin,Germany.

C.J. van Rijsbergen (1979) Information Retrieval. Butterworths, London,United Kingdom, 2nd edition.

Computer-Assisted Remote Control for the User with Motor Impairment

Peter E. Jones

Electrical and Electronic Engineering, The University of Western Australia, NEDLANDS WA 6907, Western Australia
EMail: peterj@ee.uwa.edu.au

Two projects are described for children with Cerebral Palsy. The first one is a computer controlled radio car, *CAR*. This provided the inspiration for the solution needed in the second project — a remote control for a user with motor impairment. This resulted in a prototype controller box that we named *Rico*. It is a low cost device attached via the parallel port to any PC. It is capable of adapting to the infrared signals of most remote controls for domestic devices such as CD players, TVs and VCRs. Users with severe motor impairment can interact with a computer and through *Rico* have it mimic the action of the domestic remote controls. In first learning to use both *CAR* and *Rico*, we found it necessary to allow simultaneous interaction by the user and the teacher or occupational therapist. Therefore we have two humans in the HCI! The user who is motor impaired interacts via any one of a number of simple selection devices whilst the teacher uses the keyboard. In our case the users were teenagers severely disabled by Cerebral Palsy, who are confined to wheelchairs and are at the stage of just learning to read. The adaptability of the hardware and software would allow the use of *Rico* for a wide range of users suffering motor impairment through other causes.

Keywords: assistive technology, motor impaired, cerebral palsy, remote control, novel input-output.

1   Introduction

In 1994 we began working with a group of teenagers at a special school for children with Cerebral Palsy. They are all severely disabled by Cerebral Palsy, are in their early teens, are confined to electric wheelchairs, are unable to speak and have little voluntary control over anything. Educationally they are at the pre-school stage and are just learning to read. They had some limited experience of interacting with computers, mainly playing simple games.

Cerebral Palsy is a non-progressive disorder of movement resulting from damage to the brain before the age of three years [CPA WA 1994, Cogher et al 1992]. The term *Cerebral* refers to the brain and *Palsy* means weakness, paralysis or lack of muscle control. Cerebral Palsy is a disorder of muscle control which results from brain damage or lack of development in the motor cortex. The problems faced can range from a mild affliction through to total incapacity of the body. It is neither contagious nor progressive, but its effects on the body and development of the mind can worsen their state of health. The causes have been attributed to a range of agents, from viruses to more physical constraints on development of the brain. In Australia there are 20,000 known people with it, and more than 2,000 in Western Australia. World wide the figures are guessed to be more than 15 million.

We had some initial meetings with the teachers, the therapists and the teenagers. For several weeks we considered the problems the school faced in using computers. Other groups of children at the school were not as disabled and were able to make use of the more usual assistive technologies such as speech boards, constrained joy-sticks and keyboards with special overlaid guards. However, our group of users were generally limited to being able to press their head against switches mounted in the head restraints on their wheelchairs and also to using their hand to literally hit a single large mushroom shaped "banger" switch. This severely limits the type and speed of interaction.

The school has several other options besides head switches and the large mushroom shaped "banger" switch. We have investigated alternatives, as have others [Borden et al 1993, McInnes 1995, Goossens & Crain 1992, Galvin & Scherer 1996, Mann & Lane 1995]. However, for the moment, we continue with what is simple, cheap and currently used for other activities. For the first project we used either or both head-mounted switches because the user would be interacting for some time. This meant unplugging the switches from their wheelchair controller. The second project worked mainly with the "banger" switch as it was envisioned that the user would interact only momentarily and then need to control their wheelchair.

We also noted other problems. Often the teachers and therapists would be thwarted in their use of the computers through failure to accurately diagnose and cure errors in the system. None of the existing software allowed simultaneous interaction of both the child and the teacher or therapist. Both of our projects make good use of allowing the two simultaneous users of the system, seen as especially important during the learning phase. Afterwards, we realised that this is very similar to the use of dual-control motor vehicles when first taking a learner driver out on busy roads. It is also important to not only give feedback to the user but also to the teacher or therapist so that they know when to give their own feedback or to intervene as unobtrusively as possible. This intervention can be both to aid the learner and to avoid situations where the user is going to get into difficulty.

2 Related work and resources

Around the world there are societies concerned with cerebral palsy. In Western Australia there is the Cerebral Palsy Association and they have a web site [CPA WA 1994]. Similar associations exist in the UK [SCOPE 1997] to support people with cerebral palsy and their parents and carers (it is also the publisher of "Disability Now") and another in the USA [United Cerebral Palsy 1997].
In terms of printed resources — there are several texts [Alliance for Technology Access 1996] discusses both the technology tools, the current laws, through to listing of resources. The problems of dealing with the physical and emotional aspects of adjusting to using assistive technology is discussed in [Scherer 1996]. In [Flippo 1995] the US legal initiatives are discussed along with various assistive technologies for use in schools and the workplace through to training. However, it again does not directly address some of the issues faced at our school. A paper [Muller et al 1997] addressed the concerns about the need to improve access to computer systems for people with disabling conditions. It still failed to consider the needs of children in this area. In [Roy et al 1994] a gesture based method is described for students with Cerebral Palsy. A Neural Net was used to distinguish gestures using both EMG electrodes and a 3D tracker. This could well be far better than trying to hit the large target of a banger switch.

The textbook material is somewhat limited. Several of the HCI texts used in undergraduate courses in HCI barely mention the disabled, except maybe for very obvious comments on input-output devices. In the Readings in HCI [Lazzaro 1995] the section on Computers for the Disabled does not address the issues of children and those with severe motor impairment. Other sections in the compendium of papers do discuss the special needs for those who are disabled, but again do not discuss the even more special needs of children. Even in texts addressing human performance [Bailey 1996] little is made of what to do when it is the performance of the disabled user that is of interest. Few of the mainstream IT journals recognise the area of assistive technology. An issue in February [ACM 1997] missed this out virtually entirely in looking forward to the next 50 years of computing. Though there are exceptions [Friedlander 1997], in that same journal in the following month is an inspirational account and at the same time it offers some hope that more attention will be paid to assistive technology.
The professional computing organisations have groups concerned with the issues of disability. In the USA, the ACM has a special interest group on computers and the physically handicapped [SIGCAPH 1997] which is aimed at promoting the professional interests of computing personnel with physical disabilities and the application of computing and the information technology in solving relevant

disability problems. It produces a newsletter three times a year for its members. In the UK, the British Computer Society's Specialist Group [BCS Disability Group 1997] is a voluntary organisation which aims to identify and promote ways in which computer technology can improve the quality of life of disabled people. It publishes a journal quarterly.

Since we began the project, the World Wide Web has developed many resources for information relevant to the area of people with impairments. The Consortium [World Wide Web 1997] itself has its own site for resources for the disabled. In the USA [EASI 1997, West Virginia 1997] there are several sites with resources. In the UK and the USA there is a site [Disability Net 1997] that aims to be an information and news service for all disabled people and people with an interest in disability issues. There is another site funded by the UK National Lottery Charities Board [Disabled Living Foundation 1997] with a helpline for the disabled. In the USA there is the national information and referral centre [NICHCY 1997] that provides information on disabilities and disability-related issues for families, educators, and other professionals. Their special focus is children and youth (birth to age 22). Ability, an Australian research centre [Ability Research Centre 1997] undertakes research and assessments to assist people with disabilities to obtain the maximum benefit from computer and related technology. It is located within Australia's largest rehabilitation complex, the Royal Rehabilitation Centre at Ryde, near Sydney, Australia. Another Australian association the Australian Rehabilitation & Assistive Technology Association [ARATA 1997] has as its purpose to serve as a forum for issues in rehabilitation & assistive technology. In Canada [Indie 1997] and the USA [EASI 1997] are other resources for the individual with disabilities. In addition there are newsgroups [USENET 1997] for the support of the disabled.

Computer companies are now following the lead of Apple Computer [Apple 1997, IBM 1997, Microsoft 1997 and Sun Microsystems 1997] in developing more assistance for their disabled users. There are also companies specialising in this area too. In Australia [Technical Solutions 1997] have systems that would directly benefit from our *Rico* project. In the USA there are associations [Assistive Technology Resource Alliance 1997] and companies [LAB Resources 1997] that provide product demonstrations and training courses for this field of Assistive Technology.

3   Project #1

We first met the people at the school when our department was asked for help with donating redundant computers. From there we saw the potential for applying assistive technology — specifically to increase motivation (some of the applications were rather boring), to provide group work (most of the applications were aimed at the solo user), to provide for expression of individuality (to allow personal growth) and to increase their sense of autonomy and to grow cognitively. For our users their principal handicap was one of motor impairment. That is, they were restricted in their interaction with their environment, often being passive observers.

At the beginning we concentrated more on how the children's interaction with a computer could be improved — either to make it less tiring, to speed it up or to be less error prone. We examined a range of possibilities, most requiring physical contact; but we also looked at operating input devices without touch. We also analysed their usage of the existing computer systems and the capabilities, requirements of the children themselves. For the original group of the five teenagers, and following several consultations with the staff, we found that all were confined to a wheelchair throughout the day, they could operate both head-switches and the "banger" switch for operating their wheelchairs and interacting with a computer. The problems with the existing computer systems were that often the whole system would fail and it was difficult to track down the source of the problem. For example, the interface to the computer was via a flimsy plastic switch interface which often had contact problems. The software was unhelpful in many ways with little feedback or on-line help. Most of the software was failing to hold the users' attention and their was little motivation to continue.

Therefore, our intention moved away from the input selection to instead seek a system that could be matched to specific user's needs, to avoid the technical problems, to avoid the need for continual supervision, to provide for group working, to avoid just "on-screen" activities and most of all it had to be fun. It was emphasised to us that tangible rewards should be provided for the least effort by a child in the correct direction.

In using donated computer equipment we could only rely on a base system that was the power of an IBM PC-XT, the MS-DOS operating system with simple graphic capabilities and sound generation. The school budget does not allow for the purchase of high cost systems. Whatever we produced would have to make use of low cost computers, probably those that were redundant from the office environment. Also, we wanted to avoid costly adaptations of equipment — it would be best if we could use standard off-the-shelf domestic electronic equipment.

We decided on a radio-controlled car. This would be highly interactive, be fun, provide rapid rewards and allow for group activities. We knew of the work of Seymour Papert [Abelson & diSessa 1980] on the computer language LOGO for children, developed at MIT around 1969 — this used a mechanical turtle which held a pen that could be raised and lowered. By writing a program to drive the turtle around the floor the behaviour of a program could be seen as a graphic. This visibility in the classroom itself instead of on the sterile display surface was where the fun came in!

The first project was then this radio-controlled electric car. The user would be in their electric wheelchair (see the photograph in Figure 1) with up to two leads from their head-switches plugged into the car-controller box. They then watched both the display from the PC and the effect on the electric car — no mean feat for anyone and extremely difficult for them. The display was of a simple analogue of the car together with a stepping compass-points directional cursor around a simple graphic of the car. The user could then press the switch when the desired selection was presented. The PC used the controller box to then send the appropriate command to the car via a radio signal and the car would execute the operation.

Much of the software in use at the school was problematical to start and difficult to adapt to different children. One of our design aims was to avoid these problems and have the system readily changed. For this we had a simple textual-based state-transition network (STD). The computer, when started would run this software presenting an initial menu of several available STDs. These can be readily changed, although the initial offerings provided enough range of choice to cope with the variability of our five users and to allow them to progress to more challenging versions. For example the simplest one was for teaching simple cause and effect. It would allow the user to send the car forward, it would then stop and could be sent backward. The top of the range allowed full control of the car — although there were in-built checks to avoid some problems. Even so, the car could still get into difficulty requiring intervention by a carer.

Following the initial trials of the system we had to make some changes. The car had been slowed down so as to give more time for reacting to its behaviour. This caused some difficulty when steering on carpet, and so a compromise on speed versus turning ability had to be made to allow both motion and steering. The therapist suggested that learning would improve if more than one sense is used and so sound was added to accompany the commands sent to the car. A long sound for motion and a short one for turning. And the staff could also add in their own feedback. Time-outs of various kinds were added so that the car would not undergo continuous turning, or if the user was slow to respond the car would be automatically stopped. For some users, tracking the car on the ground from a wheelchair and paying attention to the display was difficult. We have considered operating the car on a constrained table top, but this was difficult to arrange. For a follow on project we have considered using either a small robot on a table or a train set to overcome these problems. Another problem would occur if the car hit an object and overturned itself, the system would be unaware of this.

The current system uses open-loop control. We wondered if we should provide some feedback from the car to provide a closed-loop control. It could indicate problems from the car such as low battery, the car is stuck (i.e. the wheels are driven and no motion is taking place). And finally, by tracking the car the display could be updated to reflect reality. However, we felt that any possible gains were outweighed by the increase in complexity and costs.

Figure 1: A user in a wheelchair with the head-operated switches

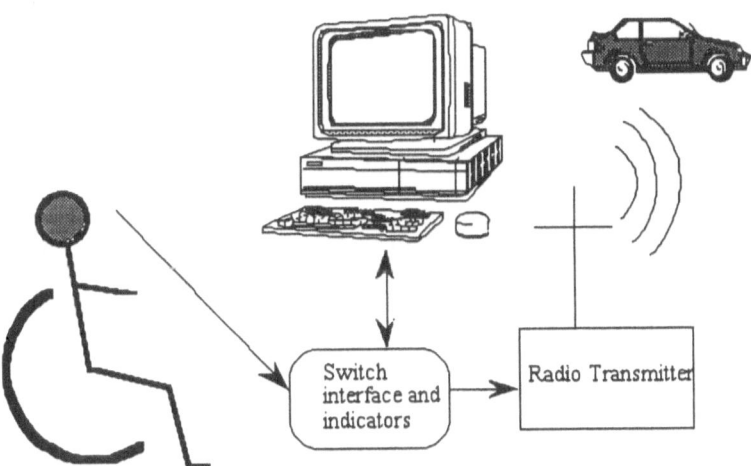

Figure 2: Layout for using *CAR* — the radio controlled car

The schematic in Figure 2 shows a of a user in the wheelchair connected to an interface box that provides connection to a parallel port of a PC together with visible indicators. Attached to this was the modified radio transmitter.

A group of teenagers in their chairs together with the project engineer can be seen in Figure 3 below. The toy car is in the foreground, with the computer just to the rear. So although only one teenager is actually controlling the car, the rest of the group are actively collaborating and enjoying the fruits of the labour. For our evaluation five of the teenagers took part.

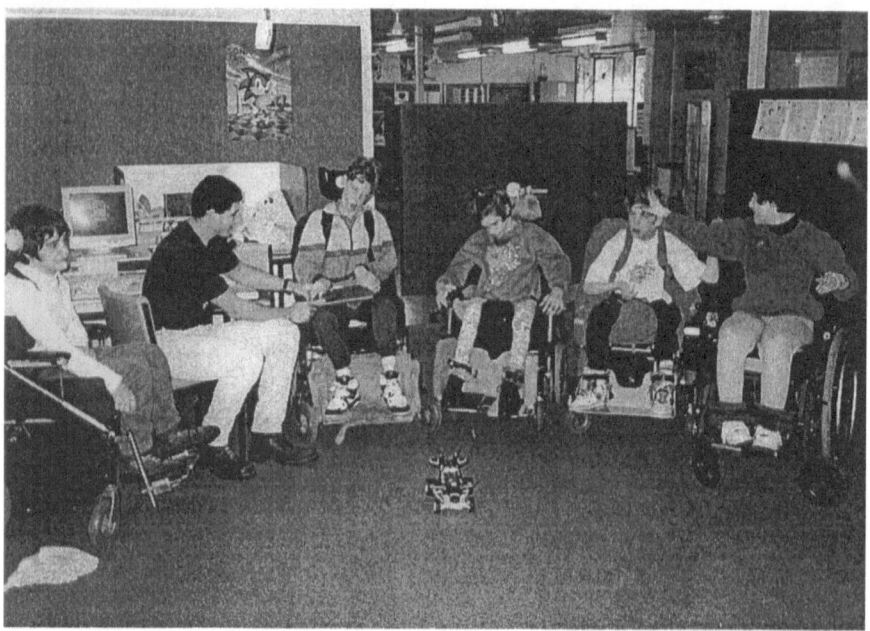

Figure 3: Group using the radio controlled toy — *CAR*

Our observation of the use of computers in the school had highlighted several problems. Often the equipment used with the computers would not work because of some simple yet hard to trace fault. For instance, if the connection from the user's switch was not fully home in its socket then the symptom would often point at some other area. None of the teachers or therapists were computer trained, they would prefer that the computer was so transparent in operation that they could concentrate on their primary goals.

This observation lead to our first design aim— our controller box had to visibly and obviously indicate that all its connections were operational. That is, we had LED indicators to show that power was there, that the user's switch was correctly plugged in and that the connection to the controlling computer was active. If any of the lights was out it was a simple diagnosis and fix. The software too was easy to load and start and the steps in its control visible and straightforward to use.

At the end of the trials the occupational therapist commented "it enabled the children to learn cause-effect responses, it provided some measure of control of the environment, it would form a useful pre-requisite for driving the electric wheelchairs and for sheer recreation it was above all fun!"

CAR would benefit by a greater range of sound, including speech, to augment the interaction and we need a more visual programming model instead of the STDs to enable the teachers themselves to develop new versions for the system.

4   Project #2

This project, which we developed during 1996, was sparked off out of our discussions with the children following the success of the earlier project with the car. One of them wanted to control his CD player, rather than being dependent on a teacher or carer realising he wanted to do something with the CD. Our first thoughts concentrated on the buttons etc. that would need to be pressed to achieve this and so we had visions of the computer controlling a robot that would push the buttons on the player!
Instead, at some stage it dawned on us that we could use a similar technique to the radio controlled car. That is, use a stepping cursor over a menu operation to have the computer emit the appropriate infrared signals to mimic the action of the now familiar household item — the remote control.

The system we ended up with is named *Rico* — Remote Infrared Computer Operator — and it is a low cost peripheral device that connects to the parallel port found on most Personal Computers. The schematic layout for *Rico*, Figure 4, is very similar to the *CAR* project, with the peripheral device connected to both the computer and the child's switch and some domestic equipment controllable by infrared emitted under computer control. In this case we used the "banger" switch operated by hitting with a hand.

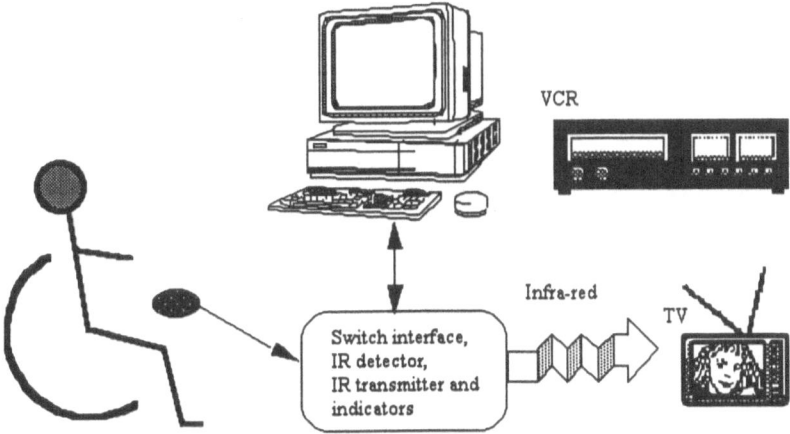

Figure 4: The layout for using *Rico* — the infrared remote control

The general population use computer technology for a range of activities from entertainment through to work and additionally benefits from the use of hidden computers embedded in other systems. For those users with disabilities, computers have the potential to improve the quality of life. They can enable users to communicate and control their environment.

Input devices are also important, our users cannot use any of the standard ones such as the keyboard or mouse. For *Rico* we settled on using either of two familiar input devices already in use at the school. These are simple switches operated either by moving your head in the wheelchair headrest or hitting a large mushroom shaped switch with your hand. In the latter case the size and robustness of the switch coped with the error prone attempts by the user to press it. Further discussion [Edwards 1995] on a range of input devices and other HCI issues for users with disabilities shows that much work can be done in this area too.

We had several design aims for *Rico*. The hardware had to be low cost. The device would need to clearly indicate that it was securely connected with both the user's switch and to the computer. The device would be capable of learning the infrared codes for the functions from any remote control. This would avoid the need for any intervention by us to adapt *Rico* as new equipment is purchased. In use the software would be simple to start and also be straightforward to adapt to different situations. For instance, the same equipment would be used by children with quite different abilities and at different stages in their development.

4.1   Infrared remote control

In the modern home we have all grown used to the convenience of remote controls for our hi-fi systems, televisions, video recorders, air conditioners, etc. For the motor impaired user the remote control offers an opportunity to be independent. We realised that we did not need a computer controlled robot at all if we could use the idea of a remote control. But, how are they to operate the remote control?

The early remote controls used ultrasonic techniques but with the advent of low cost optoelectronic devices most manufacturers now use infrared. This allows quite sophisticated and reliable communication [Nunley and Bechtel 1987]. Here then is the answer — we could use a computer to emit the infrared signals, and our previous project had shown how we can get our users to interact with the computer.

There are only *de facto* standards for remote controls, although there now exists a more formal approach for the use of infrared in data communications [Infrared Data Association 1996]. It was found that one transmission scheme was followed by most manufacturers. This is a simple modulation of a carrier using pulse code modulation. Using a filter at the receiver reduces interference from other sources of infrared in the environment. The coding system employed does vary and there are at least two widely used encodings, REC-80 and RC-5. Finally, there is also variation in the sequencing of these codes.

Faced with this variety of schemes we decided that the simplest method was to record the demodulated signal and then it is ready for replaying as an exact copy.

4.2   The hardware

Rico's hardware is based on the use of a Sharp optical integrated circuit sensor (IS1U60) for ease of decoding the infrared signal. This takes in the incoming infrared and filters it, demodulates it and produces a signal compatible with digital logic. This kept the hardware simple and the cost as low as possible.

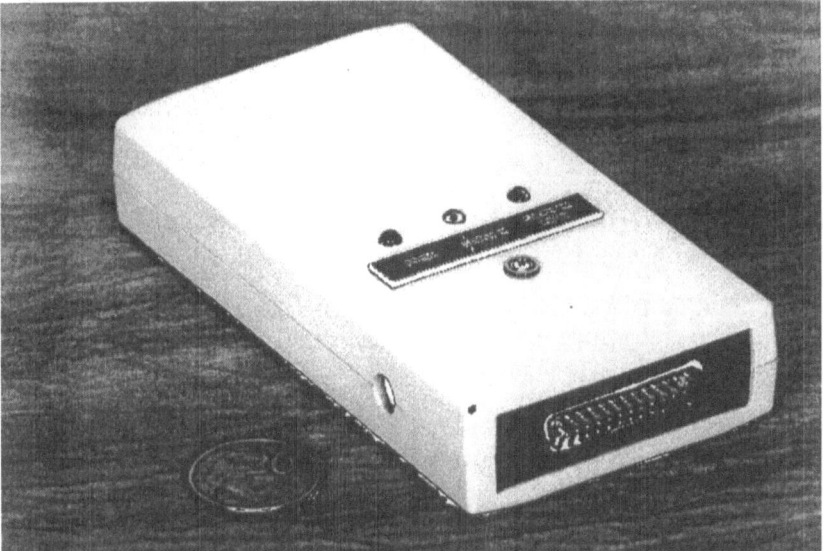

Figure 5: *Rico's* prototype

During the learning phase the digital output of this chip is presented to the computer on one of the inputs on the parallel port together with a sampling clock. The latter simplifies the decoding because it is independent of the speed of any particular computer.

To playback the signal, the recorded data is retrieved and using the same external sampling clock the coded data is sent to one of the output lines of the parallel port. This signal is then used to modulate the usual carrier frequency and this drives a pair of infrared emitting diodes. This has proven capable of an adequate range and allows for a reasonable misalignment.

The packaging encloses the printed circuit board allowing a window for the receipt and transmission of infrared. A low voltage power supply is used instead of batteries that can go flat. A parallel cable connects *Rico* to the computer, and a socket is used to accept the input from the user's switch device. Finally, there are three indicators that light up to indicate the correct connection of power, computer and user's switch.

From the figure you can see that the $0.20 coin (similar to a £0.10 coin) gives a scale for it. There is the parallel port connection facing out, to the left is the entry for the low voltage power, the top of the case has the socket for the user's switch and the three LEDs with their labels just behind that. At the far end is a transparent window for both the transmission of the infrared signal (which has a range up to about 10m) and for receiving the signals from the handset during the learning phase. The total cost of the parts is around $80 (or about £40) — and of course you need a second-hand PC, in our case a 386 based one. The speed of the PC is not critical as the hardware takes care of the time critical aspects of modulating and de-modulating the signals.

4.3 The software

The software for the learning phase is based on a question-answer dialogue with the user and then the recording of the signals from each of the remote control's buttons is carried out. That is, the teacher or occupational therapist aims the new remote control at *Rico* and presses each of its buttons in turn.

In normal use it is then a matter of loading up the already learned signals to playback and the presentation of a block graphic menu representing the functions from the remote control to be mimicked.

The initial design was that the user would watch the stepping cursor on the display and as it highlighted the desired operation the switch would be pressed by head or the mushroom switch hit by an arm. The software would then playback the signal for that function and the infrared beam would be transmitted to the TV or other device. The software was designed to run on a Windows 3.11 PC and so used simple button graphics. The labels for each button were entered as the system learns the remote control. For instance, to make one version of the system you could enter a label of "on", then press the corresponding real button on the remote, then enter a label of "play" and again press the appropriate real button and finally the same for "stop". Then when this version is loaded the user would be presented with three buttons, each highlighted in turn.

For the teenager who had suggested the project this seemed to be quite successful. Within minutes of being shown how to use the system he was operating his CD player to the delight of himself and the audience of other children.

However, for many of the other teenagers there was too much to grasp. We then found that the system worked better in the early stage of a new user learning the system if the teacher or occupational therapist could simultaneously interact with the system. As there was already a keyboard with the PC, the software was modified to cope with two users interacting with the system at the same time. With this new version, the teacher and the teenagers were both able to interact with *Rico* and this proved to be more effective. The teacher could intervene unobtrusively and the child learnt more rapidly with less frustration through constant failure.

Another change was to have multiple versions for each remote control and so have a variety of levels for selecting from. In other words a beginner would be faced with a simpler version and as they grew more capable could be exposed to more functionality. For instance, the simplest one for the CD player is "On" (and play automatically) and "Off" (and of course no sound). Later on they could be introduced to further features of the controller.

The initial trials showed that all eight users, who had never seen the system before were able, with only a small amount of unobtrusive intervention by the teacher, to control the CD player. Some changes had to be rapidly made, for instance it was too easy to eject the CD and then they would need to wait for someone to pop it back in again. The CD player itself took time to spin up and produce the music, this was disconcerting for the users who would think that they had not made the correct selection. It was easy to create several versions for the CD player, starting with the simplest one of just having two buttons on the screen — play and stop. For the more adept users there were more complex interactions to allow changing of the full range of functions. Another trial with a TV was equally successful. Again all users were able to switch the TV on and off and change the channel up and down. More functionality is possible of course, especially with a VCR and cable input.

5   Conclusion and further work

Making computers accessible and useful to children with a handicap is beneficial to them in additional ways besides the primary use of *Rico* for controlling domestic equipment. For instance it stimulates autonomy and encourages independent decision making. It is a form of communication which is often lacking because of inadequacies in the other forms such as oral or written communication. So as well as attending to the functional needs of the users we see it aiding their non-functional needs leading to higher motivation and giving them a sense of achievement and control over their destiny.

Following the success in this particular context we are eager to evaluate its use with other users. Will the two user interaction still be as beneficial with motor impaired users who are further along educationally? For example, will an adult meeting *Rico* for the first time need a helping hand? We see this as no different to dual control cars used when learning to drive. Additionally, the graphics and feedback to the users does need improving and the system should be made automatically adaptive to grow with the user and also to be more supportive in offering predictive selections to speed up what is still a very tedious way of interacting with a computer.

In addition to a version supplied to the school we plan on placing one system in the library of equipment at the nearby community service centre [Independent

Living Centre 1997]. Earlier this year the department hosted a technical meeting of the group "Technical Aids for the Disabled (WA)" and demonstrated the system to them. Finally the principal newspaper for Western Australia is about to publish an article on the project at the school. With these efforts at publishing the work we are hopeful of adapting the system to a wider range of users

In a recent book by a suddenly disabled journalist [Bauby 1997] (he wrote the 25,000 words using 200,000 blinks of his left eye to select from frequency ordered letters Sadly, he died shortly after the book was published) he describes the frustration of watching half of a soccer final only to have the TV set turned off by an inconsiderate nurse. *Rico* would surely have saved him that sort of loss.

We are also exploring the use of *Rico* with off the shelf systems for controlling other household appliances. For example, at the Rehabilitation Engineering Research Center [Trace Center 1997] (located at the Waisman Center and the Department of Industrial Engineering at the University of Wisconsin-Madison), they are proposing a standard named "Strawman Protocol for the Infrared Communications Link" which may be of interest for these other uses for *Rico*.

Finally, for our particular students, it is hoped that they will be able to move on to overcome any learning disabilities [Gardner 1997] — to quote "To be able to function as independent individuals and to take full advantage of their potential and capabilities, they need a way to compensate for their weaknesses."

Acknowldegments

It is a pleasure to acknowledge the work of Leon Wende and Andrew Umney in contributing to the design and implementation of these ideas, and to the support of the staff and the inspiration of the children of the Sir David Brand School.

Also, we thank the referees for very constructive comments on this paper.

References

Abelson, H. and A.A. diSessa, Turtle Geometry, Cambridge Mass. MIT Press.

ACM (1997) The Next 50 years, Communications of the ACM Special Issue, February 1997-Volume 40, Number 2.

Ability Research Centre (1997), Australia,
     URL: http://www.abilitycorp.com.au/index.html

Alliance for Technology Access (1996) — Computer Resources for People with Disabilities: a guide to exploring today's assistive technology, 2nd edition, Alameda, CA: Hunter House. Also see URL: http://www.ataccess.org/

Apple Computer, Inc. (1997) — Disability Solutions Group —
    URL: http://www.apple.com/disability/welcome.html

ARATA (1997), Australia — URL: http://www.iinet.net.au/~sharono/arata/
Assistive Technology Resource Alliance (1997), USA —
    URL: http://www.atra.com/

Bailey, R.W. (1996) Human Performance Engineering: Designing High Quality
    Professional User Interfaces for Computer Products, Applications and Systems,
    3/e. Prentice Hall ISBN 0-13-149634-4.

Bauby, Jean-Dominique (1997) Diving Bell and the Butterfly. Translated by
    Jeremy Leggatt, Allen & Unwin.

BCS Disability Group (1997) — The UK British Computer Society's Specialist
    Group — URL: http://www.bcs.org.uk/siggroup/sg16.htm

Borden, Peter A., et al (1993) Trace Resource Book: Assistive Technologies for
    Communication, Control and Computer Access, Trace Research and
    Development Center.

Cogher, L., E. Savage and M.F. Smith eds. (1992) Cerebral palsy : the child and
    young person, London: Chapman & Hall Medical ISBN 0-41230900-9.

CPA WA (1994) Cerebral Palsy Association of Western Australia, See the Person
    not the Problem. — URL: http://www.iinet.net.au/~cpawa/cpawa.html Also
    see Web site URL: http://www.iinet.com.au/~scarffam/cpa.html

Disability Net (1997)— In the UK — URL: http://www.disabilitynet.co.uk/
    In the USA — URL: http://www.disability.com/

Disabled Living Foundation (1997) — The UK helpline for the disabled —
    URL: http://www.atlas.co.uk/dlf/

EASI (1997) Equal Access to Software and Information, USA,
    URL: http://www.rit.edu/~easi/

Edwards, Alistair D.N. (1995) Extra-ordinary Human-Computer Interaction —
    Interfaces for Users with Disabilities, Cambridge University Press.

Flippo K. F., K. J. Inge, and J. M. Barcus (1995) Assistive technology : A
    Resource for School, Work, and Community, Baltimore. P.H. Brookes Pub.
    Co. ISBN 1-55766189-8

Friedlander, C. (1997) "Speech Facilities for the reading Disabled",
    Communications of the ACM, March 1997-Volume 40, Number 3 pp24-25.

Galvin, J.C and M. J. Scherer, eds. (1996) — Evaluating, selecting, and using appropriate assistive technology, Gaithersburg, Md.: Aspen Publishers, ISBN 0-83420664-1.

Gardner, C. (1996) "Assistive Technology And Learning Disabilities", Journal of Information Technologies and Disabilities Volume 3, Number 2, June 1996 at URL: http://www.rit.edu/~easi/itd/itdv03n2/article6.html

Goossens, C, and S.S. Crain (1992) Utilizing Switch Interfaces With Children Who Are Severely Physically Challenged : An Emphasis On Communication Strategies, Pro-ed.

IBM (1997) Special Needs Solutions —
    URL: http://www.austin.ibm.com/sns/index.html
Independent Living Centre (1997) — In Western Australia
    URL: http://www.iinet.net.au/~ilcwa/ilc.html

Indie (1997) — Canadian Resources for Disability and Education,
    URL: http://www.indie.ca/eg/main.html

Infrared Data Association (1996) URL: http://www.irda.org/

LAB Resources (1997), located in Brookfield, Wisconsin, USA —
    URL: http://www.execpc.com:80/~labres/

Lazzaro, J. J, (1995) "Computers for the Disabled" in Readings in Human Computer Interaction 2nd ed. (Baecker, Grudin, Buxton and Greenberg), Morgan Kaufmann, San Francisco, ISBN 1-55860-246-1, pp724-727.

McInnes, Peter, David Hailer and Delma Cowley (1995) Assistive Devices for People with Disabilities, Australian Institute of Health and Welfare, Commonwealth of Australia, ISBN 0-64443356-6.

Mann, W.C. and J.P Lane (1995) Assistive technology for persons with disabilities, 2nd ed. Bethesda, Md. : American Occupational Therapy Association.

Microsoft Corporation (1997) — Accessibility and Disabilities —
    URL: http://www.microsoft.com/enable/

Muller, M.J., C. Wharton, W.J. McIver and L. Laux (1997) Toward an HCI Research and Practice Agenda Based on Human Needs and Social Responsibility, CHI 97 Human Factors in Computing Systems, 22-27 March 1997, ACM, Atlanta pp155-161.

NICHCY (1997)— The National Information Center for Children and Youth with Disabilities, USA — URL: http://www.nichcy.org/index.html

Nunley, William and Scott Bechtel (1987) Infrared Optoelectronics — Devices and Applications, Marcel Dekker Inc., 197-201.

Roy, D.M., M. Panayi, R. Erenshteyn, R. Foulds and R. Fawcus (1994) "Gestural Human-Machine Interaction for People with Sever Speech and Motor Impairment due to Cerebral Palsy", CHI 94 Conference Companion, ACM, Boston, Massachusetts April 24-28, pp 313-314.

Scherer, M.J. (1996) Living in the State of Stuck: How Technology Impacts the Lives of Persons with Disabilities, 2nd ed. Cambridge, Mass.: Brookline Books.

SCOPE (1997), United Kingdom's Cerebral Palsy Site — URL: http://www.scope.org.uk/
SIGCAPH (1997)— The Special Interest Group on Computers and the Physically Handicapped (ACM) —URL: http://www.acm.org/sigcaph/

Sun Microsystems (1997) — Enabling Technologies Program, URL: http://www.sun.com/tech/access/

Technical Solutions (1997), Australia — URL: http://melbourne.dialix.oz.au/~tecsol/

Trace Center (1997) — Rehabilitation Engineering Research Center, University of Wisconsin-Madison, USA, URL: http://www.trace.wisc.edu/

United Cerebral Palsy (1997) — USA's National Organization — URL: http://www.ucpa.org/

USENET (1997) — Newsgroup for Cerebral Palsy — URL: news:alt.support.cerebral-palsy — and URL: news:alt.education.disabled

West Virginia (1997), Rehabilitation Research & Training Center, USA — List of web sites, URL: http://www.icdi.wvu.edu/Others.htm

World Wide Web (1997) W3C Disabilities Developments, URL: http://www.w3.org/pub/WWW/Disabilities/

Research and the Design of Human-Computer Interactions or 'What Happened to Validation?'

John Long

Ergonomics and HCI Unit
University College London
26 Bedford Way, London WC1H 0AP, UK
j.long@ucl.ac.uk

This paper argues the need for more effective: human-computer interactions; design of such interactions; and research to support such design. More effective research would result in more effective interactions. One contribution to more effective research would be the specification of relations between research and the design of human-computer interactions in support of the validation of new knowledge. The aim of this paper is to propose such a specification both for HCI and Cognitive Science research and the relations between them. Meeting the HCI specification renders HCI knowledge coherent, complete and 'fit-for-design-purpose'. The paper concludes that specification of relations is required for more effective research support for the design of human-computer interactions.

Keywords: research; design; human-computer interactions; effectiveness

1 Introduction

1.1 Human-Computer Interactions

Computing technology continues its inexorable advance. Computer applications pervade the home, the factory and the office. Public services, such as health and education, cannot operate without computers. No more can commercial and industrial organisations, such as banks and vehicle manufacturers. Computer developments continue to extend the limits of the technology - from novel hardware, such as speech recognisers and touchscreens, to novel software, such as graphical user interfaces and spreadsheets. Novel complete technologies have been developed for work and entertainment, such as integrated broadband communication and virtual reality (Long, 1991).

Once the requirement was the computer and 'getting it to work at all', that is more effective computers. Now the main requirement might be said to be human-computer interaction, and 'getting the computer to work for us effectively', that is more effective human-computer interactions (Long and Dowell, in press). There are many needs which could be met by more effective interactions with current computing technology.

1.2   Design of Human-Computer Interactions

Design of human-computer interactions has also continued to advance. Design here is understood broadly. It includes both the specification of interactions and their subsequent evaluation. It also includes the selection and training of users. Initially, and still to a large extent, the design of such interactions was a craft, which resided in the practices of programmers, designers, and user managers (Long and Dowell, 1989). Subsequently, attempts have been made to influence and change these design processes by the behavioural sciences, such as Psychology and Sociology (also Cognitive Science - see Section 3), and the computing sciences, such as Software Engineering (Long, 1987). More recently, Human-Computer Interaction (HCI) research has also attempted to contribute to these design practices (Long and Whitefield, 1989).

Taken together, such design practices have achieved some notable successes by recruiting novel computer developments to new computer applications. However, the success of such design practices can also be viewed as limited. Notable failures have also been associated with such practices (Three Mile Island nuclear meltdown; French Airbus and Kegworth aircraft crashes; SNCF 'Socrates' booking service; London Stock Exchange 'Taurus' transaction system; London ambulance scheduling system; UK MoD battlefield communication system; etc).

This view of current interaction design as being limited is reinforced, if the design practices are considered in terms of the 'capability maturity' model (Paulk, Curtis, Chrissis and Weber, 1993). The model characterises differences in process maturity, that is, the guarantee offered by a process with respect to the resulting product. The model has five levels of maturity. Although without formal assessment, it would be difficult to classify current design practices of human-computer interaction as higher than Level 3, that is 'defined'. Without the specification of such practices (and their relationship to research), their process cannot rise to the maturer levels of 4 'managed' and 5 'optimised'. Indeed, many design practices, currently, would be unlikely to achieve even Level 2, that is 'repeatable', that is, from project to project.

Taken together, the association of failures of human-computer interactions with current design practices, and their modest level of process capability maturity, suggest the need for more effective design (Dowell and Long, 1989).

1.3   Research

Research has also continued to advance. Research here is understood to be the acquisition and validation of new knowledge to support design. The advance has been both technical and institutional. Technically, the behavioural sciences have acquired new knowledge concerning the phenomena of interactions. Technically, HCI research has acquired new knowledge concerning techniques, methods, and tools to support design (Long and Whitefield, 1989). Institutionally, a number of initiatives have funded research to support design. Such initiatives have indeed led to the acquisition of new knowledge to support more effective design.

Although much useful research was conducted under various initiatives, little is known about the effectiveness of such knowledge, to support design. What has been established is often negative (Bellotti, 1989). In addition, little of the research has been validated and verified. (Here, validation will be assumed to include verification). As a result, little of the knowledge acquired has been incremented. Failure to increment constitutes a failure in progress. As a consequence, the potential for applying such knowledge has been limited (Long and Dowell, in press). In terms of the maturity model cited earlier, many of the design practices are neither 'defined', 'repeatable', 'managed' nor 'optimised'. Taken together, the failure to validate what new knowledge was acquired, and to increment general knowledge (theory and underlying principles), which supports more effective design, suggest the need for more effective research.

1.4   Specifying Relations between Research and the Design of Human-Computer Interactions

More effective research for design would result in more effective human-computer interactions. Such research would require the validation of new knowledge. Thus would knowledge be incremented, and so progress made. However, such incrementation would only be effective, if the new knowledge were 'fit-for-design-purpose', that is to support design practices. The criterion here is relevance. If research is not relevant to design, its incrementation will not provide better support. The application of such knowledge could only be by trial and error.

A pre-requisite for more effective research, and one logically prior to, but in support of, the validation of new knowledge, is the specification of relations between research and design. Specification of these relations would constitute one contribution to more effective research. Only if such relations are specified, and subsequently implemented, will new research knowledge be incrementable with respect to its effectiveness. Only then will validation of knowledge result in more effective human-computer interactions. The specification of such relations is the aim of this paper. A schematic representation is shown in Figure 1.

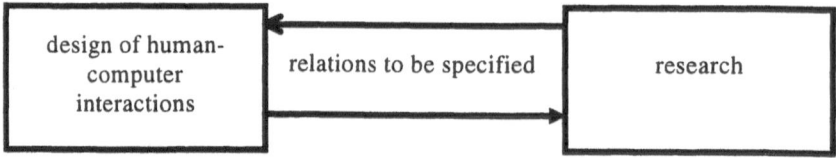

Figure 1: Relations to be specified between research and the design of human-computer interactions.

In summary, it is proposed to specify the relations between research and the design of human-computer interactions. Such specification is intended to support validation of knowledge, and so to contribute to more effective research. In turn, more effective research is expected to support the design of more effective human-computer interactions.

2 Specifying Relations between Research and the Design of Human-Computer Interactions

2.1 Pre-requisites for Specifying Relations

Initially, specifying the relations between research and the design of human-computer interactions appears simple. Informally, research should support design. Relations, then, might be identified and enumerated, providing details to the schematic representation of Figure 1 earlier. Such a scheme, however, is inadequate. First, 'research' is a more general expression than 'designing human-computer interactions'. There is a requirement, then, to express 'research' at a lower, commensurate level of description. Second, 'designing human-computer interactions' is too rudimentary an expression to provide support for research. An expression is required, which is more coherent, complete and 'fit-for-research-purpose'. Third, neither 'research' nor 'design of human-computer interactions' specifies its relation to validation. These requirements indicate the following pre-requisites.

The first pre-requisite is a framework for disciplines. Such a framework should generalise design of human-computer interactions, so that it can be expressed at the same high level as that of research. Such a framework could then be used to model, and so to specify, relations between HCI research (as well as other' research) and the design of human-computer interactions.

The second pre-requisite is a framework for the HCI general design problem. The framework must be more coherent, complete and 'fit-for-research-purpose' than 'design of human-computer interactions'. However, it must also be expressed at a high enough level to support the modelling of alternative lower level descriptions of design of human-computer interactions. The model would specify the relations within the scope of the design of human-computer interactions to support research.

The third pre-requisite is a framework for validation. The framework should be expressed at a high enough level to model both research (as characterised by the disciplines framework), and design of human-computer interactions (as characterised by the HCI general design problem framework). Together, resulting models would, thus, embody, and so specify, the relations between research and design of human-computer interactions to support validation. A schematic representation of the frameworks is shown in Figure 2.

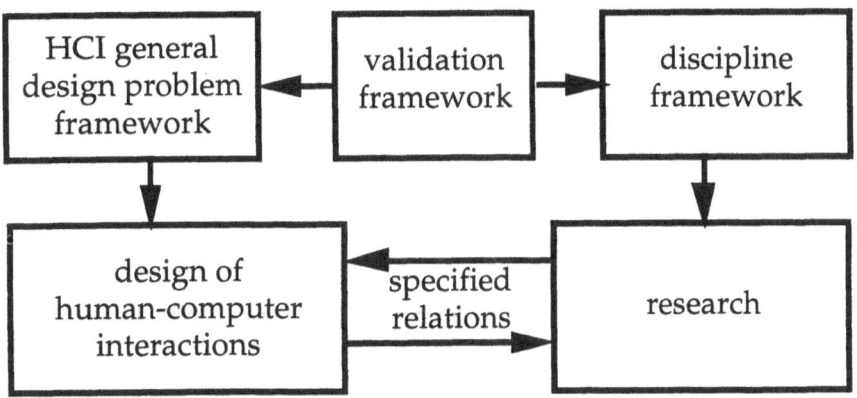

Figure 2: Frameworks to specify the relations between research and design of human-computer interactions to support the validation of knowledge.

Meeting these pre-requisites would support the specification of relations between research and design of human-computer interactions, to support validation of knowledge, and so more effective design.

2.1.1 Discipline Framework

The discipline framework proposed here to model relations between HCI research (as well as other research) and design of human-computer interactions is taken from Long and Dowell (1989).

Following Long and Dowell, a **discipline** (concepts are highlighted on first introduction) is assumed to possess three characteristics: **knowledge**; **practices**; and a **general problem**. **Research**, by its **research practices**, acquires knowledge. Knowledge supports practices solving the general discipline problem.

Disciplines are, thus, distinguished by the general problem which they address. General discipline problems, however, also have a scope. Decomposition of a general problem, with respect to its scope, exposes general problems of **particular scope**. This decomposition allows the further division of disciplines into sub-disciplines. A discipline can thus be defined as: 'the acquisition by research practices, and use of knowledge to support practices, seeking solutions to a general problem having a particular scope'. A schematic representation is shown in Figure 3. For additional information, see Long and Dowell (1989).

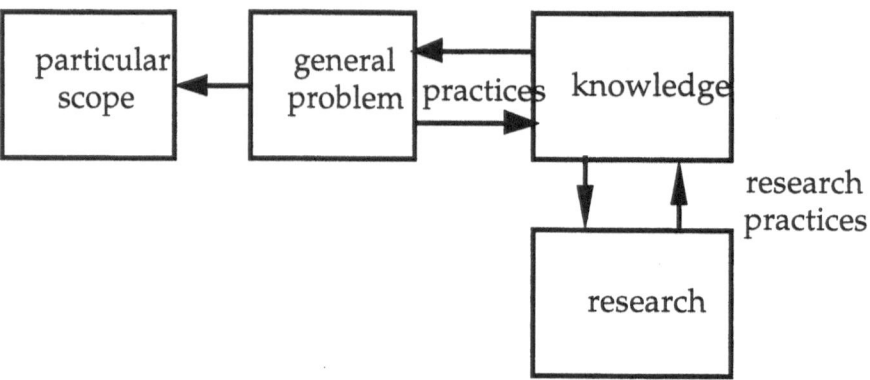

Figure 3: Framework for disciplines (following Long and Dowell, 1989)

2.1.2   General Design Problem of HCI Framework

The HCI general design problem framework, proposed here to model alternative descriptions of design of human-computer interactions, is taken from Dowell and Long (1989). Following Dowell and Long, a **domain of application** (concepts are highlighted on their first introduction) of an HCI **worksystem** is where **work** originates, is performed, and has its consequences. **Goals** express a requirement for work. Goals are allocated to worksystems by organisations. A domain is distinct from, and delimits, a worksystem. A worksystem comprises at least two separate, but interacting, sub-systems - namely **human(s)** and **computer(s)**. Humans interact with computers to perform effective work. **Effectiveness** expresses how well the worksystem performs the work. The HCI general design problem, thus, can be expressed as: 'design humans interacting with computers to perform effective work'. A schematic representation of this framework is shown in Figure 4.

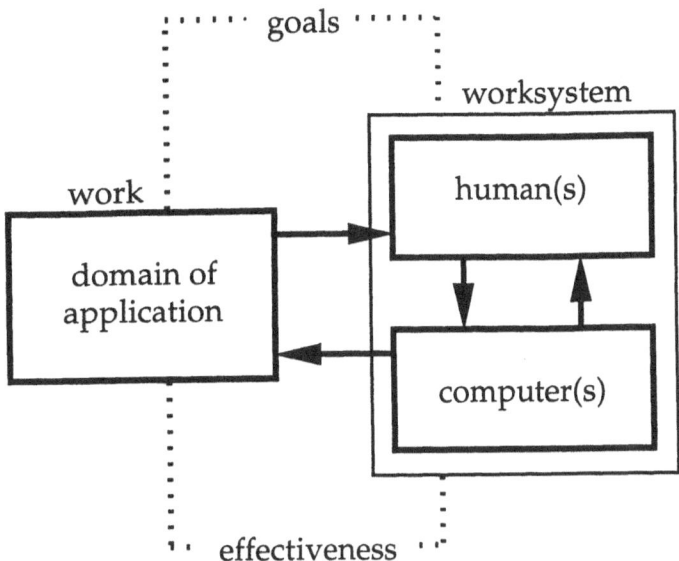

Figure 4: Framework for the HCI General Design Problem (following Dowell and Long, 1989)

2.1.3 Validation Framework

The validation framework proposed here was used by Dowell and Long (1989) and Long and Dowell (1989). However, it is quite standard and can be found in most engineering and science textbooks. Validation involves four processes: conceptualisation; operationalisation; test; and generalisation, and so four changes in the resulting products (concepts are highlighted in their subsequent description). **Conceptualisation** involves specified, and so explicit, representation. **Operationalisation** involves the mapping of concepts onto observables and eventually metrics. **Test** involves the evaluation of the assertions implicated in the concepts, which have been operationalised. Lastly, **generalisation** involves the abstraction and generification of the outcomes of the tests. The framework can be applied generally to knowledge, problems, etc. which are validated, if conceptualised; operationalised; tested; and generalised. They can also be partially 'validated', for example, if conceptualised, but not operationalised, etc. Validation is required to ensure knowledge, problems, etc. are 'fit-for-purpose'. A schematic representation is shown in Figure 5. The framework is represented only with respect to the logic of the process (hence, no feedback loops, etc).

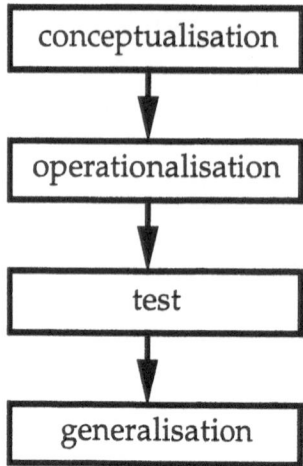

Figure 5: Framework for Validation.

The pre-requisites for specifying the relations between research and the design of human-computer interactions to support validation of knowledge, and so more effective design, have now been met. It remains to apply the frameworks to specify those relations.

2.2   Specified Relations

To specify the relations between research and the design of human-computer interactions, it is necessary to specify: the relations between HCI research and the HCI general design problem; and the relations within the particular scope of HCI to support HCI research, both with respect to the validation of knowledge, and so more effective design.

2.2.1   Specified Relations between HCI Research and the HCI general design problem

The discipline framework and validation framework proposed earlier are now used to model the relations between HCI research and the HCI general design problem. Following Long and Dowell (1989), as reflected in Figure 3, it is necessary to specify its particular scope (that is, its ontology). They suggest the specification of the particular scope of HCI as: 'humans interacting with computers to perform effective work'.

Given this particular scope of HCI, its general problem can now be specified as: 'the design of humans interacting with computers to perform effective work'. Given this HCI general problem, its practices can now be specified as: 'diagnosis (of work (in)effectiveness) and prescription (of humans interacting with computers)'. Such practices solve the general design problem of humans interacting with computers to perform effective work. HCI knowledge supports HCI practices to solve this general design problem. Research, as supported by its practices, can now be specified as: 'the acquisition and validation of HCI knowledge'. Given HCI research, the validation of its knowledge can be specified as: 'the conceptualisation; operationalisation; test; and generalisation of its HCI knowledge'. Hence, a coherent and complete model of the discipline of HCI can be specified as: 'research supporting the acquisition and validation by research practices, as: conceptualisation; operationalisation; test; and generalisation, of HCI knowledge to support HCI practices of diagnosis and prescription, to solve the general HCI design problem of humans interacting with computers to perform effective work.' A schematic representation is shown in Figure 6. This specification relates research to design of human-computer interactions.

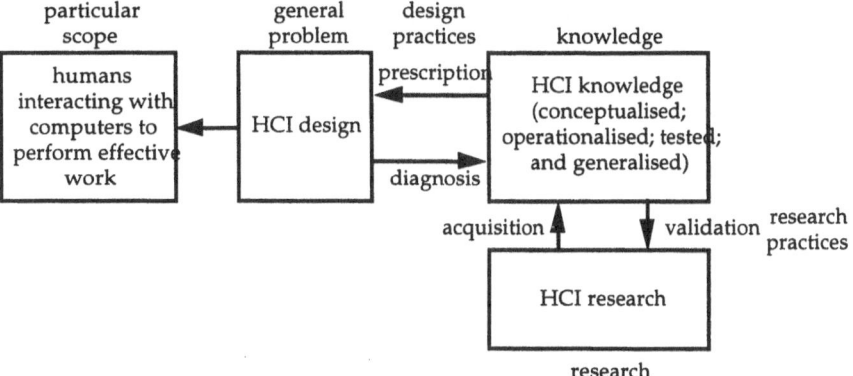

Figure 6: Model of the HCI discipline (Long and Dowell 1989) specifying the difference between HCI research and the HCI general problem.

2.2.2 Specified Relations within the particular scope of HCI, to support HCI research.

The HCI general design problem framework and the validation framework are now used to model the relations within the particular scope of HCI, to support HCI research. It might, of course, be thought that such specification exists - 'the design of humans interacting with computers to perform effective work'. However, this expression is not adequate to support an expression of the HCI general problem for the acquisition and validation of HCI knowledge, that is research. Concerning the validation of HCI knowledge, the expression is insufficiently conceptualised to support: operationalisation, test and generalisation. Concerning the application of HCI knowledge, that is HCI practices, the expression is insufficiently conceptualised to support design, as diagnosis and prescription. A more completely conceptualised definition is thus required. This more complete definition, however, must be coherent and complete with respect to the expression used earlier for the HCI discipline. It is precisely this coherence and completeness which supports the specification of relations between HCI research, as it relates to the HCI discipline, and the design of human-computer interactions, as the particular scope of the HCI general design problem.

Following Dowell and Long (1989), as reflected in Figure 4, to model the general design problem of HCI, it is necessary to specify: work; the worksystem, which performs the work; the goals of the worksystem; and the effectiveness with which the worksystem achieves its goals. The particular scope of the HCI general design problem is: 'humans interacting with computers to perform effective work'.

Dowell and Long (1989) have proposed a conceptually more complete specification of HCI design as a general problem. The specification (or conception as they describe it) is also coherent with the definition of the general HCI problem of 'the design of humans interacting with computers to perform work effectively'. A description of the conception follows. The description is selective, but adequate. Concepts are highlighted on their first introduction.

In the conception, a **domain of application** (of an HCI **worksystem**) is where **work** originates, is performed, and has its consequences. It comprises one or more **objects,** constituted of **attributes,** which have **values.** **Goals** express a requirement for change in the value of these attributes, and goals are allocated to worksystems by organisations. A domain is distinct from, and delimits, a worksystem. A worksystem comprises at least two separate, but interacting, sub-systems - of **human behaviours** interacting with **computer behaviours.** These behaviours are supported by mutually exclusive **human structures** and **computer structures**, and are executed to perform work effectively. Effectiveness is expressed by the concept of **performance**, that is, how well a worksystem achieves its goals - that is, **task quality**, and the **system costs** that are incurred in so doing. Costs are incurred by both the human and the computer and are **structural** and **behavioural**.

Given this conception of the particular scope of HCI, the validation of its general design problem (and solution) can now be specified as: 'the conceptualisation; operationalisation; test; and generalisation of the HCI general design problem (and solution)'. A schematic representation is shown in Figure 7. For a complete description of this conception for an engineering HCI discipline of design, see Dowell and Long (1989).

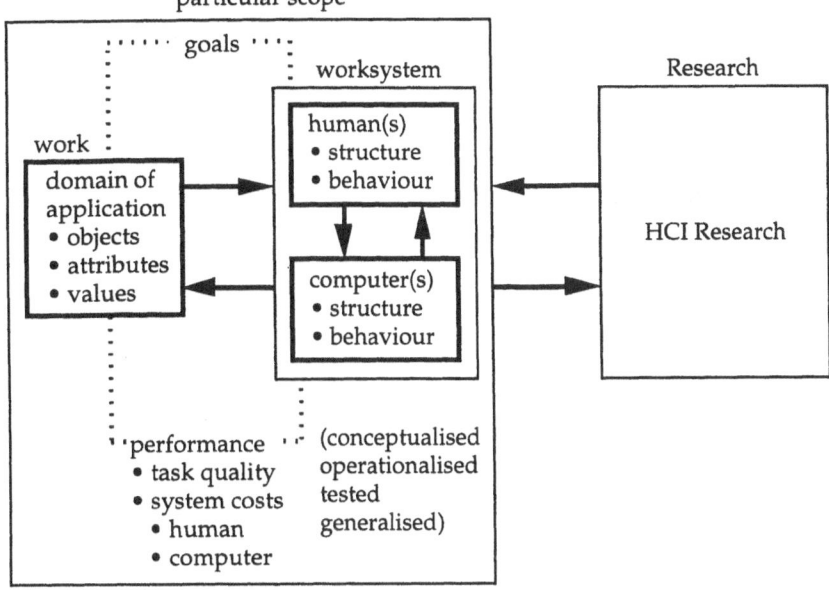

Figure 7: Model of the HCI General Design Problem (following Dowell and Long 1989) sepcifying the relations within the particular scope of HCI to support HCI.

The particular scope of the HCI discipline is the design of 'humans interacting with computers to perform effective work'. More completely, its particular scope would be the design of behaviours constituting a worksystem {S}, whose actual performance (P_A) conformed with some desired performance (P_D). The design of {S} would require the design of human behaviours {H} interacting with computer behaviours {C}. Hence, conception of the general HCI design problem would be:

> design {H} and {C},
> such that {H} interacting with {C} = {S}$_{P_A = P_D}$
>
> where $PD = fn\{Q_D, K_D\}$.
>
> Q_D expresses the desired quality of work for the domain of application.
>
> K_D expresses acceptable costs incurred by the worksystem (both human and computer).

Design here should be understood to include both the specification of interactive worksystem behaviours and the evaluation of actual and desired performance. Design also includes: the physical and organisational environment; and selection and training of humans, to the extent that these factors determine interactive worksystem behaviours, and so actual and desired performance.

This model of the HCI general design problem specifies the relations within the particular scope of HCI to support research. Thus, according to this general design problem model, research is only 'fit-for-design-purpose' if it meets these specifications, that is, acquires and validates knowledge which supports the solution of HCI general design problems, so expressed.

The specification of relations within the particular scope of HCI, to support HCI research is now complete. The specification thus relates design of human computer interactions to research, adequately to support the acquisition and validation of HCI knowledge.

2.2.3   Specified Relations between HCI research and the HCI general design problem, and within the particular scope of HCI, to support HCI research

Specified relations between HCI research and the HCI general design problem were modelled in Figure 6. Specified relations within the particular scope of HCI to support research were modelled in Figure 7. To specify the relations together, it suffices to integrate the two earlier sets of specified relations into a single model. A schematic representation of that model is shown in Figure 8.

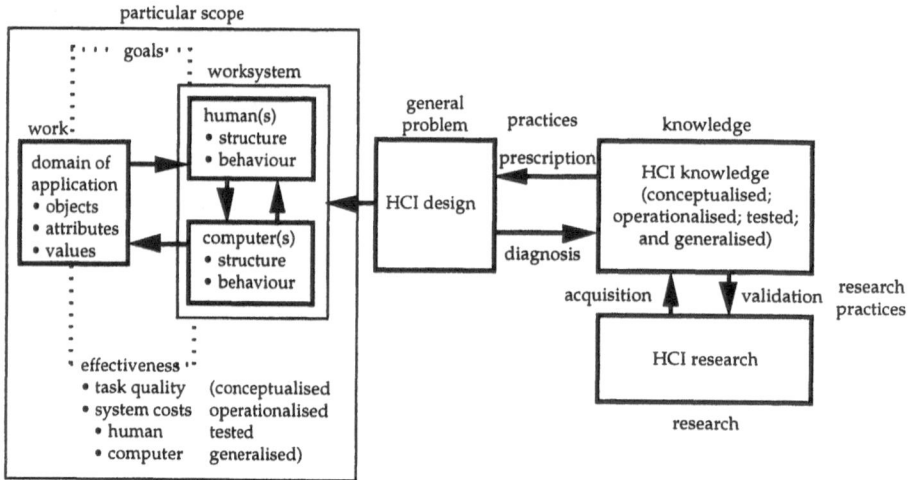

Figure 8: Model of the HCI discipline (following Figure 6) and model of the HCI general problem (following Figure 7) specifying the relations between HCI research and the HCI design problem, and within the particular scope of HCI, to support HCI research.

Thus, according to these models of the HCI discipline and the HCI general design problem, research is only 'fit-for-design-purpose', if it meets these specifications, that is acquires and validates knowledge which supports the solution of the HCI general design problem, so expressed.

The specification of relations is now considered to be complete: between HCI research and the HCI general design problem; and within the particular scope of HCI, to support HCI research, both with respect to the validation of knowledge, and so more effective design. Taken together, these relations constitute one possible specification of the relations between research and design of human-computer interactions.

3 Relations between other research, HCI research and the design of human-computer interactions

3.1 Other research and HCI research

It has been proposed how relations can be specified between research, defined here as related to the HCI discipline, and the design of human-computer interactions, expressed as the HCI general design problem. The question can now be posed, as to what relations obtain between other research, HCI research and the design of human-computer interactions. In particular, the concern is with research not conducted to support the design of human-computer interactions. The example selected here is Cognitive Science. Note that Cognitive Science is not unique, concerning its relations with HCI. Similar relations, proposed later, could similarly be suggested for: Sociology; Ethnomethodology; Ethnography etc. The same frameworks and models used earlier will also be used here.

3.2 Specified relations between Cognitive Science research and understanding natural and artificial forms of intelligence

Cognitive Science generally seeks to understand knowledge-based behaviours. Such behaviours include: perceiving; categorising; thinking; reasoning; communicating; problem-solving, etc. Cognitive Science might be defined non-controversially as: 'understanding the general principles underlying natural and artificial forms of intelligence'. Such a definition is adequate for present purposes.

3.2.1 Specified relations between Cognitive Science Research and the Cognitive Science general understanding problem.

To specify the relations between Cognitive Science research and understanding natural and artificial forms of intelligence, it is necessary to model the Cognitive Science discipline (see Figure 3). Given the particular scope of Cognitive Science, as natural and artificial forms of intelligence, its general problem can be specified as: 'the understanding of natural and artificial forms of intelligence' (understanding being the general problem of science as a discipline). Given this general problem, the understanding practices can be specified as: 'explanation and prediction'.

Cognitive Science knowledge supports such practices. Cognitive Science research practices acquire and validate such knowledge as: conceptualised; operationalised; tested; and generalised. The model of the Cognitive Science discipline, specifying the relations between research and the general understanding problem is shown in Figure 9. (Compare with the HCI model in Figure 6.)

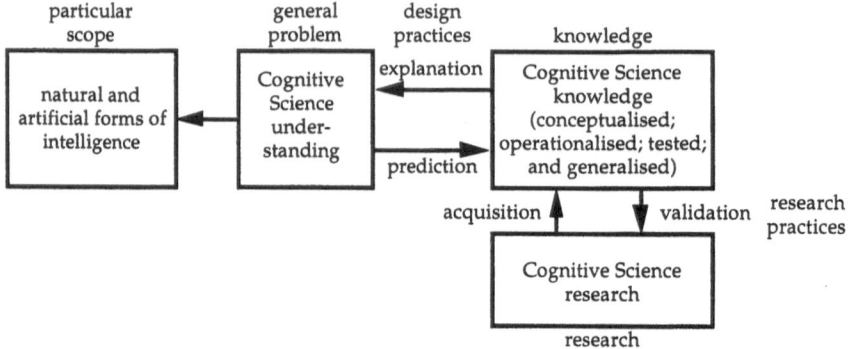

Figure 9: Model of the Cognitive Science specifying the relations between Cognitive Science Research and the Cognitive Science General Understanding Problem.

3.2.2   Specified relations within the particular scope of Cognitive Science, to support Cognitive Science Research

For present purposes, the particular scope of Cognitive Science, as natural and artificial forms of intelligence, is assumed to include at least: natural, that is human, intelligence and behaviour; artificial, that is, artefact intelligence and behaviour; and natural and artificial worlds. Humans and artefacts are assumed to interact with one another, and with the world. Cognitive Science seeks to understand the: intelligence; behaviour; and interactions. A model of the Cognitive Science general understanding problem specifying relations within its particular scope, to support research is shown in Figure 10. (Compare with the HCI model in Figure 7.)

3.2.3   Specified relations between the Cognitive Science discipline and the Cognitive Science general understanding problem

Specified relations between Cognitive Science research and the Cognitive Science general understanding problem are modelled in Figure 9. Specified relations within the particular scope of Cognitive Science, to support Cognitive Science research are modelled in Figure 10. To specify the relations between the Cognitive Science discipline and the Cognitive Science general understanding problem, it suffices to integrate the two earlier sets of specified relations into a single model. A schematic representation is shown in Figure 11.

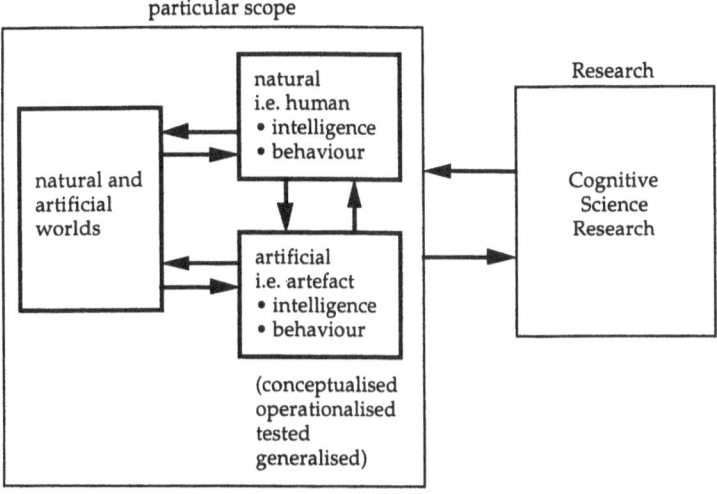

Figure 10: Model of the Cognitive Science general understanding problem specifying relations within the particular scope of Cognitive Science to support Cognitive Science Research.

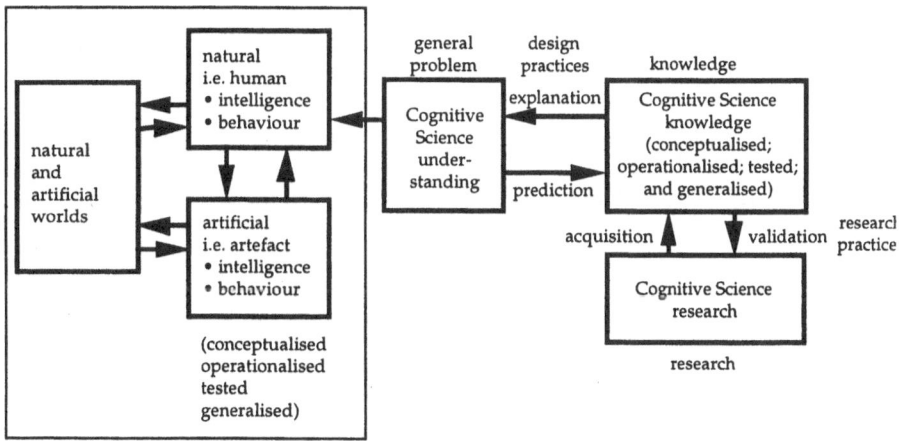

Figure 11: Model of the Cognitive Science discipline (following Figure 9) and Model of the Cognitive Science general understanding problem (following Figure 10) specifying the relations between Cognitive Science research and the Cognitive Science general understanding problem, and within the particular scope of Cognitive Science, tosupport Cognitive Science Research.

Thus, according to these models of the Cognitive Science discipline and the general understanding problem, research is only coherent, complete and 'fit-for-understanding-purpose', if it meets these requirements. That is, it acquires and validates knowledge, which supports the solution of the Cognitive Science general problem, so expressed. The claim is the same as made earlier for HCI. Knowledge produced by Cognitive Science research, and intended to support understanding, which embodies these relations, is more effective, than knowledge not embodying such relations.

3.3   Relations between Cognitive Science Research and Design of Human-Computer Interactions

The question posed earlier can now be addressed. What relations obtain between other research, in this case Cognitive Science, and the design of human-computer interactions? An assessment of possible relations can be made by comparing the relations within the particular scope of Cognitive Science, to support Cognitive Science research, as specified by the model of the Cognitive Science discipline and the Model of the Cognitive Science general understanding problem (shown in Figure 11), with the relations within the particular scope of HCI, to support HCI research as specified by the model of the HCI discipline and the model of the HCI general design problem (shown in Figure 8). Inspection of these figures shows there to be no specified relations between Cognitive Science research and the design of human-computer interactions. For example, as concerns discipline relations, Cognitive Science understanding practices have no specified relations with the diagnosis of general design problems and the prescription of general design solutions. As concerns relations within its particular scope, the Cognitive Science general understanding problem has no specified relations with the performance (of worksystems).

It can, thus, be concluded that there are no specified relations between Cognitive Science research and the design of human-computer interactions. Cognitive Science research is, therefore, not coherent, complete, nor 'fit-for-design-purpose'.

Note that a comparable conclusion must necessarily be drawn concerning the relations between HCI research and understanding natural and artificial forms of intelligence. Inspection of Figures 8 and 11 shows there to be no specified relations between HCI research and the understanding of natural and artificial forms of intelligence. For example, as concerns discipline relations, HCI design practices have no specified relations with the explanation of general understanding problems and the prediction of general understanding solutions. As concerns relations within its particular scope, the HCI general design problem has no specified relations with (natural) intelligence, as expressed by humans.

It is, thus, concluded that research, not exhibiting the relations specified here with the design of human-computer interactions, such as that undertaken by Cognitive Science, is not coherent, complete or 'fit-for-design-purpose', that is for designing human-computer interactions. Its resulting knowledge does not support practices of diagnosis and prescription and its practices of explanation and prediction do not solve the general HCI design problem of designing humans interacting with computers to perform effective work.

3.5 Unspecified Relations between Cognitive Science Research and Design of Human-Computer Interactions.

It has been concluded that Cognitive Science research is not coherent, complete nor 'fit-for-design-purpose'. However, some researchers claim such a relationship. How might such a claim be understood with respect to the specified relations for Cognitive Science and HCI proposed here?

This question can be addressed, if some relationship can be established between the HCI discipline and its general design problem (Figure 8) and the Cognitive Science discipline (Figure 11). The relevant models are shown in Figure 12. A comparison of the models suggests two ways in which Cognitive Science might contribute to the design of human-computer interactions. First, Cognitive Science knowledge might contribute to HCI research practices of the acquisition and validation of HCI knowledge, such practices having specified relations with the design of human-computer interactions. Second, Cognitive Science knowledge might contribute to HCI practices of diagnosis and prescription, and so of design, such practices having specified relations with design.

However, in both cases, the relations between Cognitive Science knowledge and HCI research, and HCI practices are unspecified, as established earlier. Hence, any relations could only be implicit. Such implicit relations could only be realised via the explicit relations specified between HCI research and the design of human-computer interactions. Without such specified HCI relations, implicit Cognitive Science relations could not be achieved. Further, the realisation of such implicit relations could only have the status of a 'craft'. That is, any 'knowledge' of transforming the Cognitive Science knowledge base to support either HCI research or HCI practices, is likely to reside only in the experience and skill of the individual researcher or design practitioner. There is unlikely to be a 'discipline', whose general transformation problem is the transformation of the Cognitive Science knowledge base to support HCI. Thus, there would be no validation of the transformation with respect to its support for the design of human-computer interactions. Without validation, knowledge concerning the transformation could not be explicitly incremented. Without incrementation, Cognitive Science research could not support design more effectively.

Cognitive Science knowledge, thus, is able to contribute to HCI design and research practices. However, such contributions can only be implicit, since unspecified. They cannot as such be known. Specified relations would be required to support more effective research contributions to design.

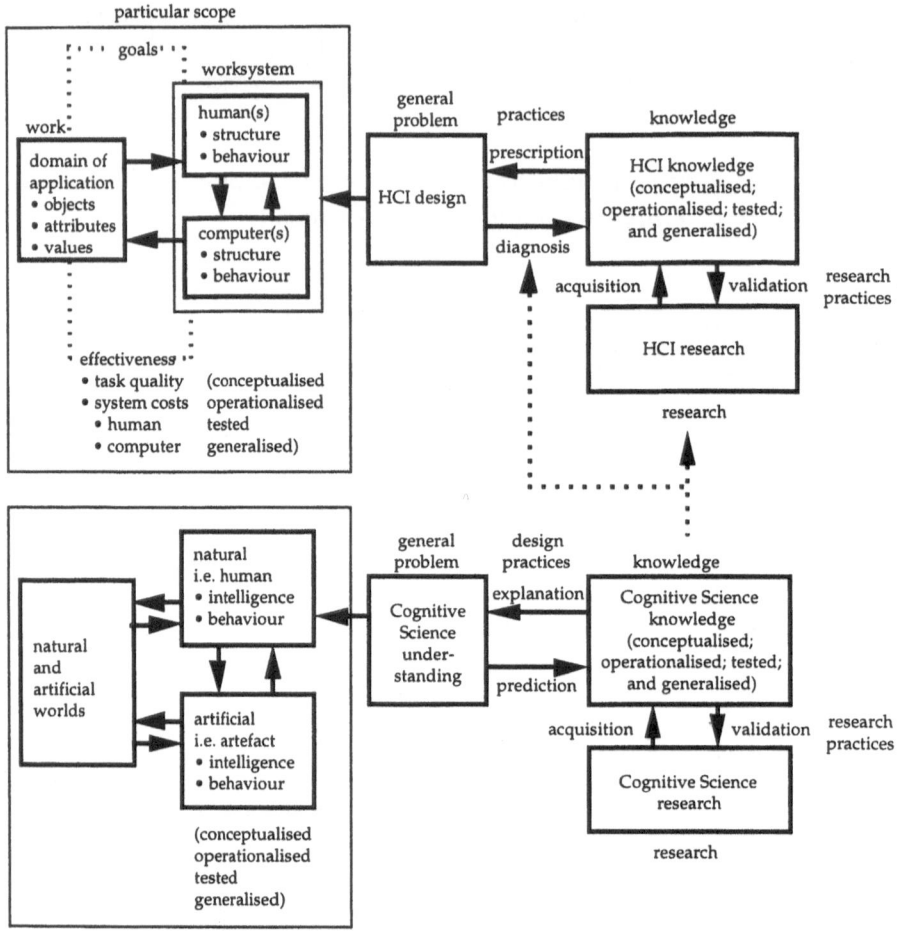

Figure 12: A Model showing the specified relations (as dotted lines between the HCI discipline and the general design problem (Figure 8) and the Cognitive Science general understanding problem (Figure 11).

3.6   Assessing Relations between Other Research, HCI Research and the Design of Human-Computer Interactions

Readers might be interested to assess the relations between their own research (and that of others) and the design of human-computer interactions, in terms of the relations specified here. The assessment of research can be conducted in a number of ways. First, research can be assessed against the model of the HCI discipline and the model of the HCI general design problem (Figure 6). The research can be further assessed against the relations within the particular scope of HCI, to support HCI research (Figure 7). Second, research can be assessed against the model of the Cognitive Science discipline and the model of the Cognitive Science general understanding problem (Figure 9). The research can be further assessed against the relations within the particular scope of Cognitive Science, to support Cognitive Science research (Figure 10). Third, research can be assessed for unspecified relations between Cognitive Science research and the design of human-computer interactions (Figure 12).

However, if research is neither HCI nor Cognitive Science (for example, Ethnomethodology, etc), then, the frameworks proposed for disciplines (Figure 3), the HCI general design problem (Figure 4) and for validation (Figure 5), must be used to construct models of the kind appearing in Figures 8 and 11. Relations can then be specified. Assessment of the research can then be made against the models of specified relations. Such construction of models of specified relations will also be required, if the frameworks are accepted, but not their model instantiations. Researchers would have to instantiate their own models and specified relations, using the frameworks.

Lastly, assessment of research could be made at the level of the frameworks themselves (Figures 3, 4 and 5). Researchers are encouraged to assess their own research, and that of others, in these different ways. Such assessment would be expected to lead to more implementation of specified relations between research and the design of human-computer interactions. In turn, more implementations would be expected to improve the effectiveness of HCI research support for design.

4   Summary and Conclusion

This paper began by summarising current and past technical and institutional developments, as they concern the design of human-computer interactions and research. The paper argues the requirement for more effective: human-computer interactions; design of such interactions; and research support for such design. Greater effectiveness of interactions, practices and research will derive from the validation of new HCI knowledge, and the specification of relations between HCI research and the design of human-computer interactions, such that research is 'fit-for-design-purpose'. This paper attempts to specify such relations. It is suggested how research with unspecified relations to the design of human-computer interactions, such as Cognitive Science, can only contribute implicitly to the design of human-computer interactions. Such implicit contributions can only be realised via the specified relations of HCI.

In conclusion, if a serious attempt is to be made to improve the effectiveness of: human-computer interactions; the design of such interactions; and the research support for such design, there is a need to ensure coherence, completeness and the 'fitness-for-design-purpose of research to support the design of humans interacting with computers to perform work effectively, including validation for that purpose.

All disciplines, which conduct research claiming to contribute to the design of human-computer interactions for effective work, need to specify the relations between their research and the design of human-computer interactions. Specifying relations between HCI research, and the HCI discipline, and within the design of human-computer interactions, expressed as the general HCI design problem, to support HCI research, as proposed in this paper, is one means of so doing.

Acknowledgments

I would like to acknowledge my debt to colleagues at the Ergonomics & HCI Unit, UCL, and especially to John Dowell by whom or with whom all the important ideas in this paper have been developed.   Any remaining infelicities of specification or implementation are of course my own.

References

Bellotti, V.M.E. (1989). Implications of the current design practice for the use of HCI techniques. In A.Sutcliffe and L.Macaulay (eds), *People and Computers IV, Proceedings of the Fifth Conference of the BCS HCI SIG*. Cambridge, UK: CUP.

Dowell, J. (1993). Cognitive Engineering and the Rationalisation of the Flight Strip. PhD Thesis.

Dowell, J. and Long, J. (1989). Towards a Conception for an Engineering Discipline of Human Factors. *Ergonomics*, **32** (11), 1513-1535.

Long, J. (1987). Cognitive Ergonomics and Human Computer Interaction. In *Psychology at Work*, P. Warr (ed). Harmondsworth, UK: Penguin.

Long, J.B. (1991). Human-Computer Interaction and the Information Technology Revolution, or Getting Computers to Work for Us Effectively. In British Gas White Paper series.

Long, J. (1994). Building Relations between Cognitive Science and Human-computer Interaction - the United Kingdom Experience. In *Proceedings of the Workshop for Cooperation between Japan and the United Kingdom on SOFT Science and Technology, Osaka, Japan.* Tokyo, Japan: STA.

Long, J. (1995). Integrating Human Factors with Software Engineering for Human-Computer Interaction. In *Proceedings of IHM'95, Toulouse, France.*

Long, J. and Dowell, J. (1989). Conceptions for the Discipline of HCI: Craft, Applied Science and Engineering. In A.Sutcliffe and L.Macaulay (eds), *People and Computers IV, Proceedings of the Fifth Conference of the BCS HCI SIG.* Cambridge, UK: CUP. 9-32.

Long, J. and Dowell, J. (in press). Cognitive Engineering or 'getting users and computers interacting to perform work effectively'. *The Psychologist.*

Long, J.B. and Whitefield, A.D. (eds) (1989). *Cognitive Ergonomics and Human-Computer Interaction.* Cambridge, UK: CUP.

Paulk, M.C., Curtis, B., Chrissis, M.B. and Weber, C.V. (1993). Capability Maturity Model, Version 1.1. *IEEE Software*, 18-27.

Using Diagrams to Support the Analysis of System 'Failure' and Operator 'Error'

Lorna Love and Chris Johnson

Glasgow Accident Analysis Group,
Department of Computing Science,
University of Glasgow,
Glasgow, G12 8QQ, UK.
Tel: +44 (0141) 330 6053
Fax: +44 (0141) 330 4913
http://www.dcs.gla.ac.uk/~{johnson,love}
EMail: {johnson,love}@dcs.glasgow.ac.uk

Computers are increasingly being embedded within safety systems. As a result, a number of accidents have been caused by complex interactions between operator 'error' and system 'failure'. Accident reports help to ensure that these' failures' do not threaten other applications. Unfortunately, a number of usability problems limit the effectiveness of these documents. Each section is, typically, drafted by a different expert; forensic scientists follow metallurgists, human factors experts follow meteorologists. In consequence, it can be difficult for readers to form a coherent account of an accident. This paper argues that fault trees can be used to present a clear and concise overview of major failures. Unfortunately, fault trees have a number of limitations. For instance, they do not represent time. This is significant because temporal properties have a profound impact upon the course of human-computer interaction. Similarly, they do not represent the criticality or severity of a failure. We have, therefore, extended the fault tree notation to represent traces of interaction during major failures. The resulting Accident Fault Tree (AFT) diagrams can be used in conjunction with an official accident report to better visualise the course of an accident. The Clapham Junction railway disaster is used to illustrate our argument.

Keywords: accident analysis; fault trees; operator' error'; system 'failure'.

1   Introduction

Accident reports are intended to ensure that human 'error' and systems' failures' do not threaten the safety of other applications. Unfortunately, these documents suffer from a range of usability problems (Johnson, McCarthy and Wright, 1995). Each section of the report is, typically, compiled by experts from different domains; systems engineering reports follow metallurgical analyses, software engineering reports follow the findings of structural engineers; human factors enquiries follow meteorological reports. This structure can prevent readers from gaining a coherent overview of the way that hardware and software 'failures' exacerbate operator 'errors' during major accidents (Norman, 1990). The following pages argue that graphical fault trees can be used to avoid these limitations. Readers can use these diagrams to gain an overview of an accident without becoming 'bogged down' in the mass of contextual detail that must be presented in the official report. These structures increase the accessibility and salience that Green (1991) and Gilmore (1991) identify as being important cognitive dimensions for notations which are intended to represent interactive systems.

2   The Case Study

The Clapham Junction railway accident report (Department of Transport, 1989) is used to illustrate our argument. On the morning of Monday the 12th of September, 1988, a wiring error led to a series of faults in the signalling system just south of Clapham Junction railway station in London. A crowded commuter train collided head-on into the rear of a stationary train. The impact of this collision forced the first train to veer to it's right and strike a third oncoming train. This resulted in five hundred people being injured, thirty-five of those fatally and sixty-nine seriously. This accident provides a suitable case study because it typifies the ways in which human interaction with the underlying safety applications can cause or exacerbate system 'failures' (Reason ,1990). In this accident, human 'error' and organisational 'failure' led to a wring error in the signalling system. This error, in turn, provided drivers with false indications about the state of the railway network.

3   Alternative approaches

A number of alternative techniques might be recruited to describe the interaction between human' error' and system 'failures' in accident reports.

3.1   *Petri Nets*

Figure 1 shows how a Petri net can represent the events leading up to the Clapham railway accident. The filled in circle represent tokens. These 'mark' places, the unfilled circles, which represent assertions about the state of the system. In this diagram, a place is marked to indicate that Mr Hemmingway introduced a hardware `fault' by leaving two wires connected at full on fuse R12-107. If all of the places leading to a transition, denoted by the rectangles, are marked then that transition can fire. In this example, the transition labelled 'The five drivers preceding the collision train do not realise that the irregularity of the signals they have passed was due to a signalling failure' can fire. All of the output places from this transition will then be marked. This would then mark the place denoting the fact that the five drivers preceding the collision train did not report a signalling failure..

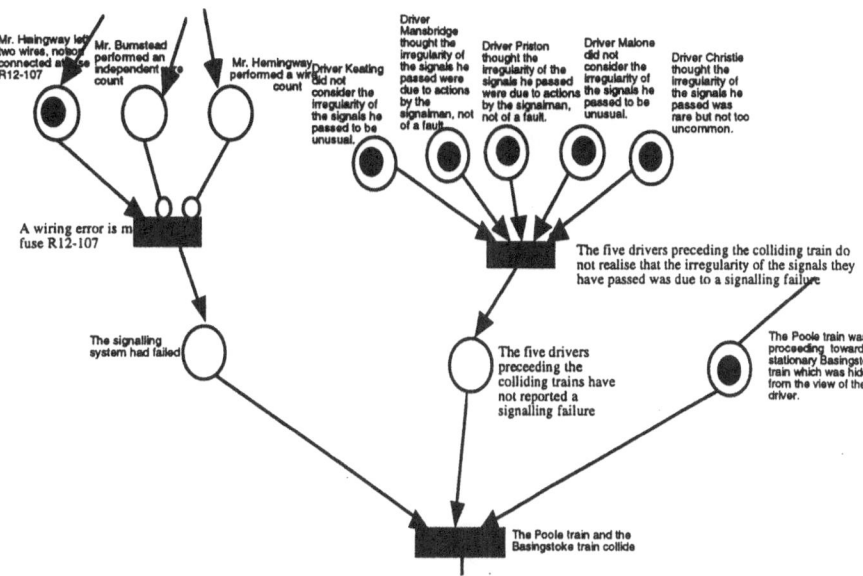

Figure 1: Petri net representing the events leading up to the Clapham accident

There are a number of limitations that complicate the application of Petri nets to analyse accidents that involve interactive systems. In particular they do not capture temporal information. Various modifications have been applied to the classic model. Levi and Agrawala (1990), use 'time augmented' Petri nets to introduce the concept of 'proving safety in the presence of time'. Unfortunately, even if someone can understand the complex firings of a 'time augmented' Petri net, they may not be able to comprehend the underlying mathematical formulae that must be used if

diagrams, such as Figure 1, are to be used to analyse human' error' and system
'failure' (Palanque and Bastide, 1995).

3.2   *Cause-Consequence Diagrams*

Cause-Consequence Analysis was developed by Neilson in the 1970s. The causes
of a critical event are determined using a top-down search strategy. The
consequences that could result from the critical event are then worked out using a
forward search technique. Gates describe the relations between causal events.
Figure 2 shows a Cause-Consequence diagram for the hardware problem that led
to the system failure in the Clapham accident.   Mr Hemmingway's concentration
was interrupted as he worked on fuse R12-107.   It can be argued that such
diagrams illustrate the consequences of such problems in amore tractable format
than the many pages of natural language description that are presented in most
accident reports.

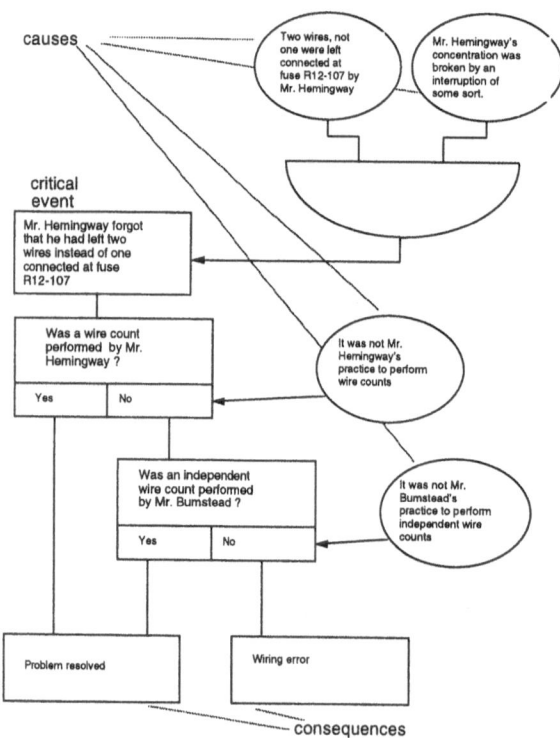

Figure 2: Cause consequence diagram of one aspect of the Clapham accident.

In cause-consequence analysis, separate diagrams are required for each critical event. Unfortunately, in an accident, there maybe dozens of contributory factors and so several diagrams will be required. For instance in the Clapham accident, other diagrams would be required to represent the causes and consequences of bad working practices, limits on safety budgets and the events on the day of the accident.   Such characteristics frustrate the application of these diagrams to represent and reason about the complex interaction between human and system failure during major accidents.

3.3 Fault Trees
Fault-trees provide a relatively simple graphical notation based around circuit diagrams. For example, Figure 3 presents the syntax recommended by the U.S. Nuclear Regularity Commission's, 'The Fault Tree Handbook' (Vesely, Goldberg, Roberts and Haasl, 1981).

Figure 3: Fault tree components

Fault trees are, typically, used pre hoc to analyse potential errors in a design. They have not been widely used to support post hoc accident analysis.   They do, however, offer considerable benefits for this purpose. The leaves of the tree can be used to represent the initial causes of the accident (Leplat, 1987).   The symbols in Figure 3 can be used to represent the ways in which those causes combine.   For example, the combination of operator mistakes and hardware/software failures might be represented using an AND gate.   Conversely, a lack of evidence about user behaviour or system performance might be represented using the OR/XOR gates. Basic events can be used to represent the underlying failures that lead to an accident (Hollnagel, 1993).   Intermediate events can represent the operator 'mistakes' that frequently exacerbate system failures. An undeveloped event is a fault event that is not developed further, either because it is of insufficient consequence or because information is unavailable. This provides a means of increasing the salience of information in the notation (Gilmore, 1991).   Less salient events need not be developed to greater levels of detail.

There are a range of important differences that distinguish the use of accident fault trees from their more conventional application. Fault trees are constructed from events and gates.   However, many accidents are caused because an event did not take place (Reason, 1990).   These errors of omission, rather than errors of commission typify a large number of operator 'failures'. Figure 5 illustrates the way in which fault-trees can be used to represent these errors of omission; Mr

Hemmingway failed to perform a wire count, Mr Hemmingway's boss failed to perform an independent wire count.

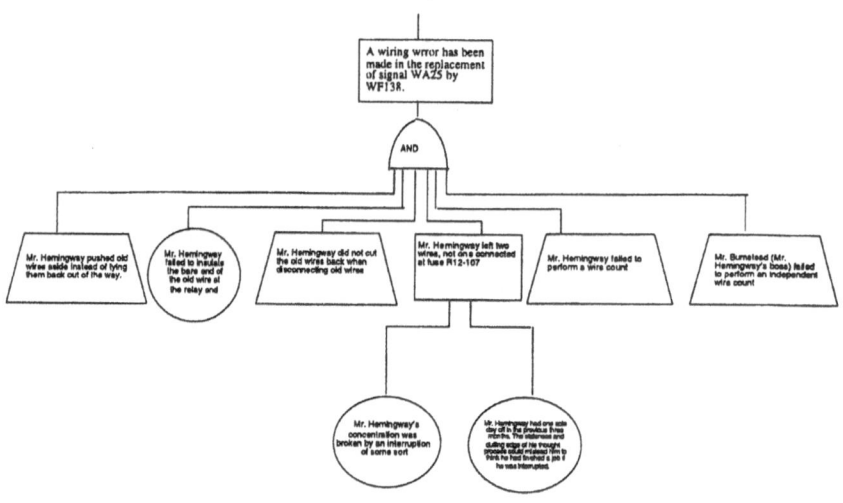

Figure 4: An example of a fault tree representing part of the Clapham accident

Further differences between conventional fault trees and accident fault trees arise from the semantics of the gates that are used to construct the diagrams. Conventionally, the output from an AND gate is true if and only if all of its inputs are true. Accidents cannot be analysed in this way. For example, Figure 4 shows that the hardware error was the result of six events. In a 'traditional' fault tree the error would have been prevented if interface designers or systems engineers had stopped any one of these events from happening. In accident analysis, however, there is no means of knowing if an accident would actually have been avoided in this way. Most accident reports do not distinguish between necessary and sufficient conditions. An accident may still have occurred even if only one or two of the initiating events occurred. In this context, therefore, an AND gate represents the fact that an accident report cites a number of initiating events as contributing to the output event. No inferences can be made about the outcome of an AND gate if any of the initiating events do not hold.

The output of an OR gate is true if and only if at least one of it's inputs is true. An OR gate can be used in an accident fault tree to represent a lack of evidence. Evidence can be removed accidentally or deliberately from an accident scene. Alternatively, evidence may be missing because the person holding the information died in the accident. For example, in the Clapham accident, we do not know if Driver Rolls actually noticed the irregularity of the signals he passed. The output of an XOR (exclusive OR)gate is true if and only if exactly one of the inputs are true. They are useful in accident fault trees when we know an intermediate event was caused by either of two events, but not both. This again raises an important semantic difference between our use of the Fault Tree notation and its more usual application to risk analysis. In particular, if both of the initial events are true in our interpretation then the intermediate event does not happen. This contrasts with the more conventional interpretation, of an XOR gate in which mutual exclusion is guaranteed. We retain our interpretation here because if it were found that both initial events were true then any subsequent analysis based on the XOR gate would have to be substantially revised. Figure 5 shows how an OR gate can be used to represent two reasons why Driver Rolls reduced his speed; either he was concerned about the behaviour of the signalling system or he saw the train ahead of him brake. It also illustrates the use of an XOR gate. There was no testing plan for the signalling system in this area because either a key official ignored his responsibilities or he was not aware that he was responsible for this task.

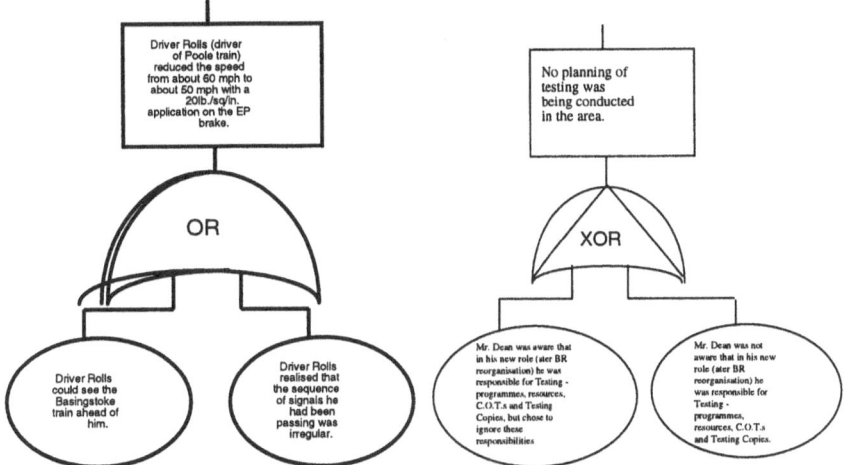

Figure 5: Illustration of the use of OR and XOR gates in the context of an accident

4   Accident Fault Trees (AFT diagrams)

The previous section identified some differences between the conventional application of fault trees to the design of safety-critical systems and their use in accident analysis for interactive systems. These differences could be supported by relatively simple changes to the interpretation of the notation. This section builds on the previous work by proposing a number of syntactic extensions.

4.1   Introducing Page References

Previous sections have argued that fault-trees provide a complementary notation which can be used in conjunction with conventional accident reports. The results of an initial usability test with accident analysts indicated that the standard notation did not support cross-referencing between the tree and the original document. Figure 6, therefore, shows how the events in a fault tree can be annotated to include paragraph number. This number refers to the paragraph number of the accident report that the information in the node is taken from. At first sight, this may appear to be a trivial change. However, it is important to emphasise that the fault tree represents an abstraction of the events that are recorded in an official report. As such, they emphasise some aspects of an accident, while choosing to abstract away from others. It is, therefore, vital that other members of investigation teams can challenge the sequences of events as they are recorded in any fault-tree. By requiring supporting references, analysts are forced to justify their interpretation of critical events from in the interaction between a system and its operator (Johnson, 1996).

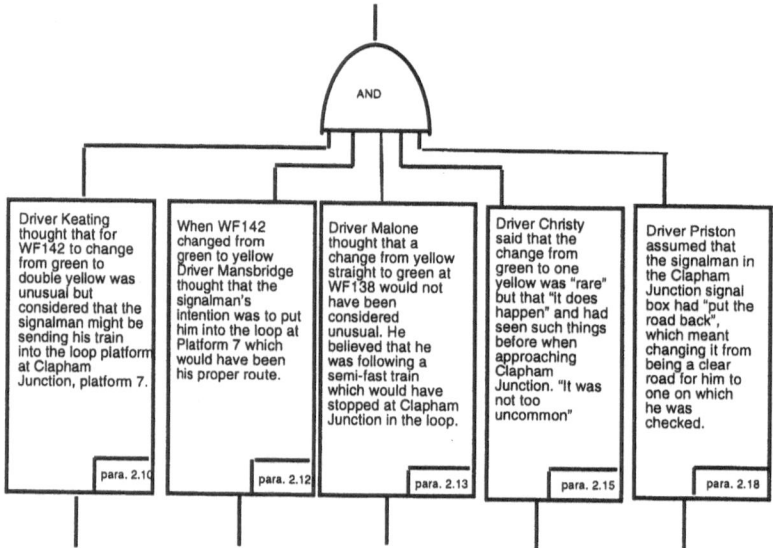

Figure 6: Grounding AFT Diagrams In A Report

4.2   *Representing Post-Accident Sequences*

Fault trees typically stop at the 'undesired event'. In accident reports, events after the accident are important too. These, typically, include the operator actions that are taken to mitigate the effects of system failure. For example, the Ambulance service played an important part in the Clapham accident. Although their actions did not cause the accident, they contributed to the saving of lives. They reduced the *consequences* of the accident. It is, therefore, important to extended fault trees to include post-accident events. Figure 7 illustrates this approach. The rooted AFT explicitly frames the accident. Branches spread out both above and below the accident. The accident is at the centre of the tree. The roots below the tree represent the factors influencing the accident. The leaves above the centre specify the actions taken and the subsequent events following the accident.

This diagram illustrates the way in which post-accident sequences stem from the collision. As can be seen, no gates are used after the central event. This reflects the certain, causal flow from the consequences of the collision. OR and XOR gates are not used because the accident investigators could accurately reconstruct the response to this failure. In other accidents, however, it will be necessary to extend the use of gates to reflect the lack of evidence about the aftermath of a major failure.

Figure 7 illustrates both the strengths and the weaknesses of AFTs. The lines between nodes represent causal, temporal and logical relationships amongst the events leading to and from an accident. This overloading provides considerable expressive power. It can also be misleading. It is, therefore, important to introduce explicit representations of the flow of time between the elements of AFT diagrams.

4.3   Introducing Time

Temporal properties can have a profound impact upon the course of human-computer interaction. Delays in system responses can lead to frustration and error. Conversely, rapid feedback from monitoring applications can stretch an operator's ability to filter information during critical tasks (Johnson, 1996). Figure 8 illustrates the PRIORITY-AND gate that has been proposed by the U.S. Nuclear Regulatory Commission's to capture temporal properties of interaction (Vesely, Goldberg, Roberts, Haasl, 1981). Sequential constraints are shown inside an ellipse drawn to the right of the gate. The gate event is not true unless the ordering is followed.

Unfortunately, there are a number of limitations with this approach. In particular, real-time is not supported. This is significant because precise timings can have a critical impact upon an operator's ability to respond to a critical incident. We have, therefore, extended the fault tree notation to include real-time. It is important to note, however, that is not always possible or desirable to associate an exact time with all of the events leading to an accident. For instance, Figure 9 only provides approximate timings. Given limited evidence in the aftermath of an accident it is unlikely that operators will be able to recall the exact second in which they did or did not respond to a system failure.

A limitation with the approach shown in Figure 9 is that it does not account for the inconsistencies that may arise in any accident reporting process. Experience in applying AFT diagrams has shown that witnesses may frequently report different timings for key operator 'errors' or system 'failures'. In order to address such uncertainty, Figure 10 illustrates an annotation technique that we have used to explain potential contradictions in a timing analysis. This technique has proved particularly useful as it provides a focus for the detailed investigation of the timing evidence that is presented in a conventional accident report.

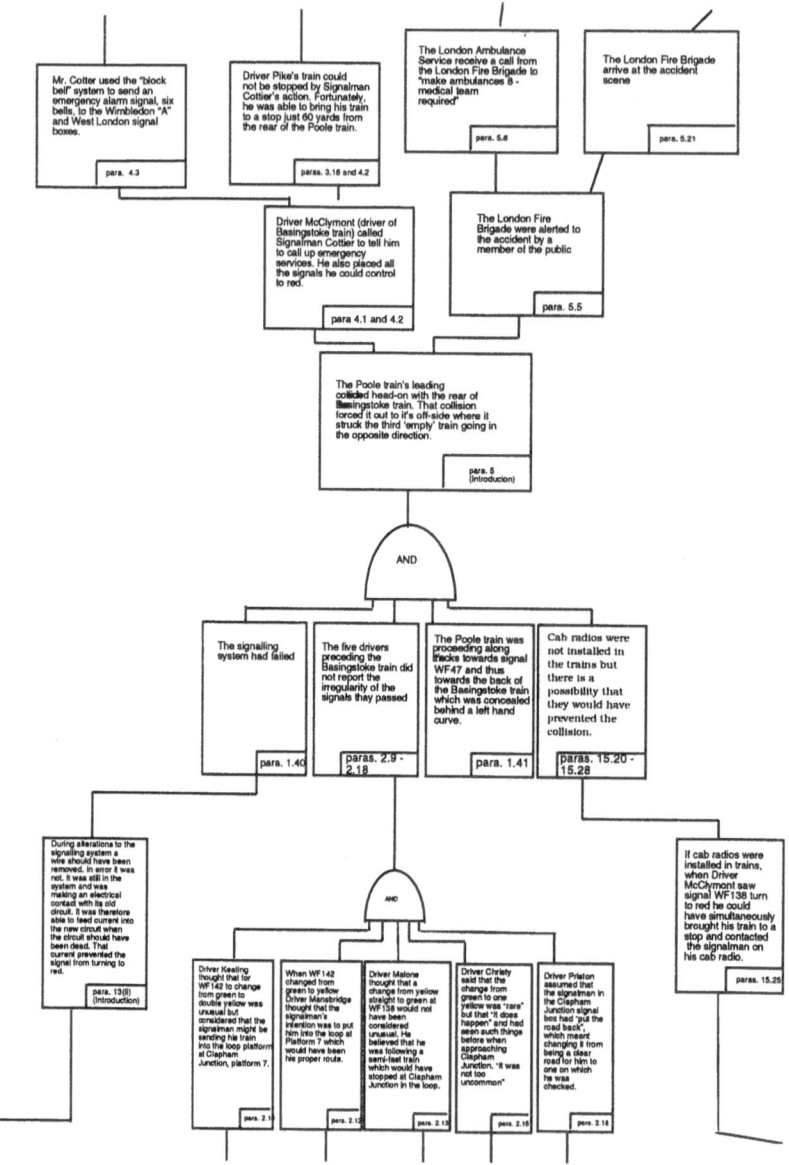

Figure 7: Extract from the Clapham fault tree showing after-accident events

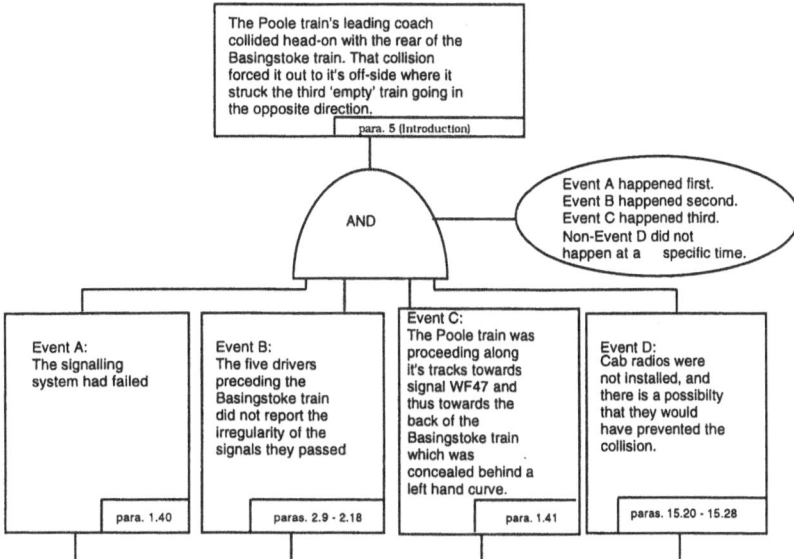

Figure 8: The PRIORITY-AND gate.

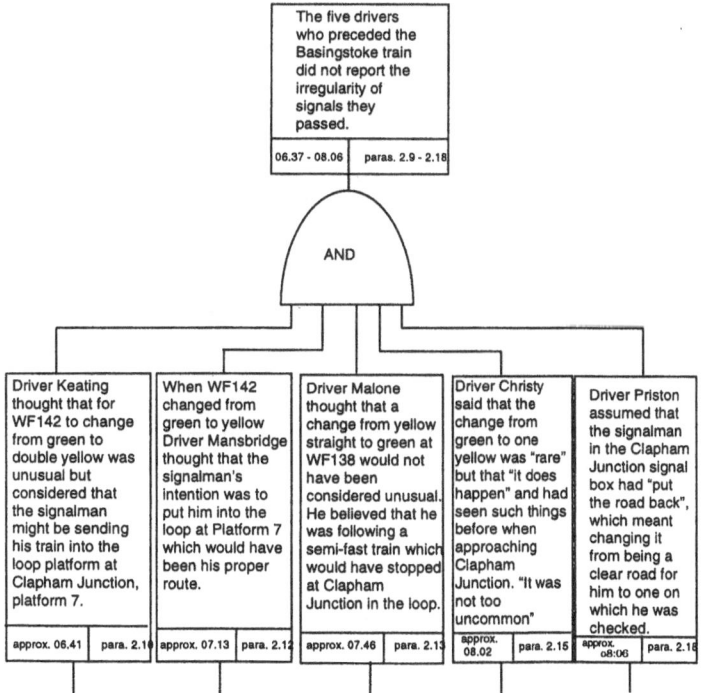

Figure 9: Extract from Clapham fault tree illustrating relative time orderings

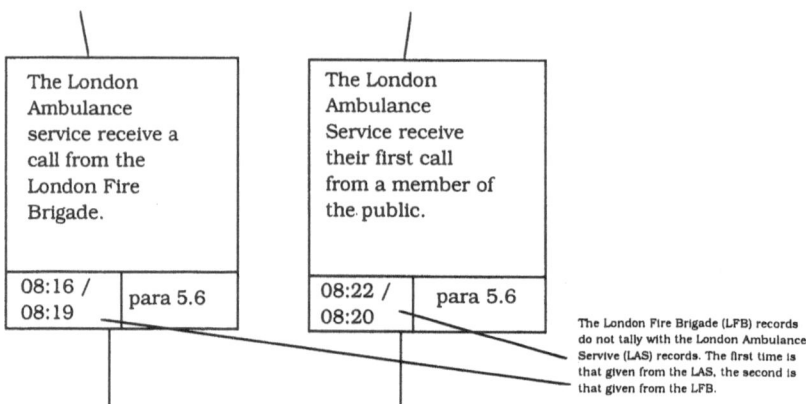

Figure 10: Extract from Clapham fault tree illustrating conflicting timings

4.4   *Introducing Criticality*

Many existing fault-trees fail to represent the criticality of an event.   This is
surprising because different faults will carry different consequences for the
continued operation of an interactive system.   For example, keystroke errors may
only have a marginal impact whilst more deep-seated mode confusion can have
catastrophic consequences.   Figure 11 illustrates a graphical extension to the fault-
tree notation that can be used to represent criticality. The exact definition of levels
of criticality depends upon the application domain (Leveson, 1995).   There are,
however, some widely accepted definitions.   For example, the United States
Department   of   Defence   (MIL-STD-882B: System   Safety   Program
Requirements)defines a negligible failure as one that will not result in injury,
occupational illness or system damage.   A marginal failure may cause minor
injury, minor occupational illness or minor system damage.   A critical failure
causes severe injury, severe occupational illness or major system damage .A
catastrophic fault may causes death or system loss. It should be noted that we are
currently evaluating a range of alternative presentation formats for these symbols.

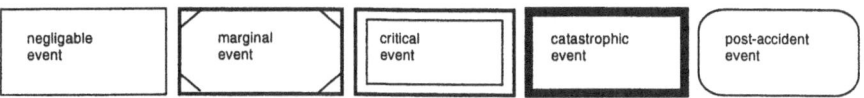

Figure 11: Weighted fault tree nodes

Figure 12 illustrates the application of this extension. The failure of the signalling system was a catastrophic event. The failure of the five preceding drivers to report the irregularity of the signals was a marginal 'error'. Such reports could not have prevented the accident if it had happened to the first train.

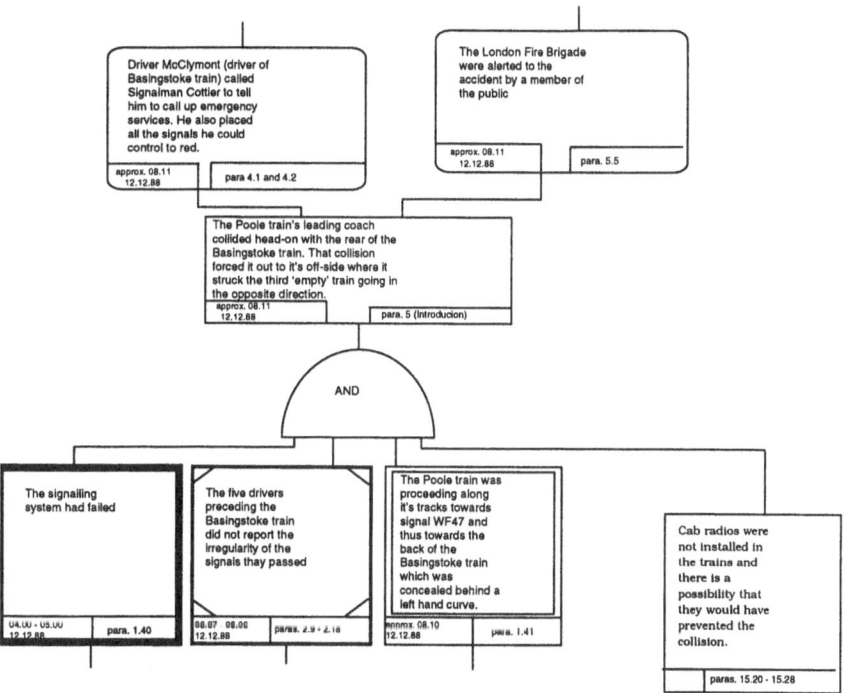

Figure 12: Extract from Clapham AFT illustrating weighting properties

In order to apply this technique, analysts must decide whether criticality assessments will be based upon a pre-accident risk analysis or whether they will reflect changes that are the result of experience gained during the accident. In our view, both approaches are beneficial. They emphasise the relationship between the predictive use of risk assessments to support future design and our more analytical, descriptive approach to accident analysis. It is also important to emphasise that the categorisation is a subjective assessment. What is important is not whether the reader agrees with our particular assessment, but that the diagram makes the categorisation explicit. Too often these assessments are left as implicit judgements within the natural language of an accident report.   As a result, accidents have occurred because companies and regulatory organisations have disagreed about the criticality of the events described in conventional documents (Johnson, 1996).

6   Further Work and Conclusions

An increasing reliance upon computer-controlled safety systems has led to a number of accidents which were caused by a complex interaction between operator 'error' and system 'failure'. Accident reports help to ensure that these 'failures' do not threaten other applications.   This paper has argued that fault trees can be used to support natural language accident reports. They provide an overview of the human factors 'errors' and system 'failures' that contribute to major accidents. Unfortunately, existing approaches do not capture the temporal information that can have a profound impact upon system operators. They do not capture the importance that particular failures have for the course of an accident. They only represent contributory causes and not post-accident events. We have, therefore, introduced an extended fault tree notation that avoids all of these limitations.

Much work remains to be done.   Brevity has prevented us from providing empirical evidence that AFTs improve the usability of existing accident reports. We have, however, conducted a range of evaluations (Love, 1997).   Initial results from these trials indicate that our extended notation can improve both the speed of access to specific material about an accident and can improve the overall comprehension of accident investigations.   It is important to emphasise that the evaluation of AFTs is a non-trivial task. Accident analysts have little time to spare for experimental investigations.   There are further methodological problems.   For instance, it is difficult to recreate the many diverse contexts of use that characterise the application of accident reports.   Finally, there are many reasons why evaluations should focus upon the long term effects of improved documentation rather than the short-term changes that are assessed using conventional evaluation procedures from the field of HCI. It may be many weeks after reading a report that engineers need to cross-reference a fact in it (Johnson, 1996).   Further work intends to build upon research into the psychology of programming to determine whether it is possible to test for these long term effects through the improvement of documentation.   For instance, Green has argued that structure maps can be used to analyse the cognitive dimensions of complementary notations (Green, 1991). This approach has not previously been applied to the graphical and textual notations that have been developed to represent human 'error' and system 'failure' during major accidents.

We have criticised a number of other techniques as being unsuited for accident analysis because they quickly become intractable.   In particular, we have argued that the multiple diagrams needed to represent different causes in Cause-Consequence Analysis would produce an unwieldy number of unconnected diagrams in the aftermath of an accident.   We have not, however, demonstrated that AFTs will be any better. It seems unlikely that our approach will have significantly fewer nodes than these competing techniques. The benefits of our approach rest on the argument that a unified representation of multiple causes will provide a better overview than that provided by multiple Cause-Consequence diagrams. Further work intends to provide empirical evidence to validate this claim.

Brevity has also prevented a detailed discussion of tool support for AFT diagrams. We are developing a number of browsers that use the graphical representations to index into the pages of conventional accident reports. Many questions remain to be answered. In particular, it is unclear whether such tools can support multiple views of an accident without hiding the overall flow of events leading to major failures. Human factors analysts typically focus upon different areas of a tree than systems engineers. It is difficult to support such alternative perspectives and at the same time clearly show the interaction between systems 'failure' and operator 'error'. One possible solution would be to exploit the pseudo-3D modelling techniques provided by VRML.

Acknowldgements

Thanks go to members of the Glasgow Accident Analysis Group and the Glasgow Interactive Systems Group. This work is supported by UK Engineering and Physical Sciences Research Council Grant No. GR/K55042.

References

Department of Transport. *Investigation into the Clapham Junction Railway Accident.* Her Majesty's Stationery Office. London, United Kingdom, 1989.

D.J. Gilmore, *Visibility: A Dimensional Analysis,* In D. Diaper and N. Hammond, People and Computers VI,Cambridge University Press, Cambridge, 317-329, 1991.

T.R.G. Green, *Describing Information Artefacts with Cognitive Dimensions and Structure Maps.* In D. Diaper and N.Hammond, People and Computers VI, Cambridge University Press, Cambridge,297-315, 1991.

E. Hollnagel, *The Phenotype Of Erroneous Actions,* International Journal Of Man-Machine Studies, 39:1-32,1993.

C.W. Johnson, *Documenting The Design Of Safety-Critical User Interfaces,* Interacting With Computers,(8)3:221-239, 1996.

C.W. Johnson, J. C. McCarthy and P.C. Wright. *Using a Formal Language to Support Natural Language in Accident Reports.* In Ergonomics(38):6, 1265 - 1283, 1995.

L. Love, Assessing the Usability of Accident Fault Trees. In C. Johnson and N. Leveson (eds) *Human Error and Systems Development,* in press.

J. Leplat. *Accidents and Incidents Production: Methods of Analysis.* In J. Rasmussen, K. Duncan and J. Leplat(eds.), New Technology and Human Error. John Wiley and Sons Ltd, 1987.

N. Leveson, *Safetware: System Safety and Computers.* Addison Wesley, Reading, Massachusetts, United States of America, 1995.

S. Levi and A. Agrawala. *Real Time System Design* . McGraw-Hill International Editions, 1990.

D.A. Norman, The 'Problem' With Automation :Inappropriate Feedback And Interaction Not 'Over-automation'. In D.E. Broadbent, J. Reason and A. Baddeley, Human Factors In Hazardous Situations, 137-145, Clarendon Press, Oxford, United Kingdom, 1990.

P. Palanque and R. Bastide. Formal Specification and Verification of CSCW Using The Interactive Co-operative Object Formalism. In M. A. R. Kirby, A.J.. Dix and J. E.. Finlay (eds.), People and Computers X, 213-232, Cambridge University Press, Cambridge, 1995.

J. Reason, *Human Error*, Cambridge University Press, Cambridge, United Kingdom, 1990.

W. E. Vesely, F. F. Goldberg, N. H. Roberts, D. F. Haasl. *Fault Tree Handbook.* U.S. Nuclear Regulatory Commission, 1981.

The Interactional Affordances of Technology: An Ethnography of Human-Computer Interaction in an Ambulance Control Centre

David Martin[1,2], John Bowers[1,3] and David Wastell[2]

Departments of Psychology[1] and Computer Science[2]
University of Manchester
UK

[3] *Centre for User-Oriented IT-Design (CiD)*
Department of Numerical Analysis and Computer Science (NADA)
Royal Institute of Technology (KTH)
Stockholm
Sweden

This paper reports an ethnography of ambulance dispatch work in a large UK metropolitan region. The interplay between control centre ecology, usage of a computerised dispatch system, and cooperative work of control personnel is analysed. The methods by which a 'working division of labour' is sustained to effectively manage dispatch in the face of high workload and manifold contingency are explicated, and contrasted with methods employed by workers in other control room settings known from the literature. The implications of the study for system improvement and for several emphases in HCI research (including discussions of 'affordances') are explored.

1   Introduction

Ethnographic research methods are becoming increasingly influential in research fields such as Computer Supported Cooperative Work (CSCW) and Human Computer Interaction (HCI). For many researchers, an ethnographic study involving prolonged participant-observation at a real-world work setting is an invaluable resource in technology design and development. In the CSCW literature, for example, there exist studies in settings as varied as Air Traffic Control (ATC), banks, management training centres, the print and fashion industries (Hughes, Randall and Shapiro, 1992; Randall, Rouncefield, and Hughes,

1995; Rouncefield, Hughes, Rodden and Viller, 1994; Bowers, Button and Sharrock, 1995; Pycock and Bowers, 1996)—studies which have been frequently coupled to system design projects.

The ethnographic work reported in this paper was conducted in the control room of the ambulance service of a large metropolitan region in the UK. It forms part of a long-term collaboration between university-based researchers and the ambulance service but it is only recently that concerted ethnographic research has been added to the mix of methods in this collaboration. Control rooms studies, however, are quite familiar territory for ethnographers. Previous work, for example, on London Underground control (Heath and Luff, 1992) and ATC (Hughes, Randall and Shapiro, 1992) point to a number of issues that seem to be important to cooperative work in control room settings: mutual monitoring and awareness, the affordances of artefacts (some of which are at first sight quite mundane) which support 'at-a-glance-perception' within an appropriately organised workplace ecology, the maintenance of flexible working divisions of labour which enable 'running repairs' and so forth.

However, those are studies of air traffic and London Underground controlling. We do not know from *them* the inflections in control work in our new setting— ambulance control—which to our knowledge has been little studied in the same ethnographic depth as those others[1]. This seems important to redress for a number of reasons. The ambulance control room we have studied differs from other settings in the CSCW/HCI literature in that, *first*, control work is driven by calls from the public, *secondly*, the control centre we have studied is quite advanced in its computerisation, and relatedly and *thirdly*, there have been some highly visible failures to automate ambulance dispatch (e.g. the London Ambulance Service controversy of 1991) though the setting we have studied mostly works well. Thus, we intend to learn from it to see what makes for workable computer systems in such settings as well as to reciprocally contribute to their improvement.

2   The Fieldsite: UK Ambulance Control Centre

The ambulance control room in this study serves the whole of a large region of around 2.5 million people and is situated centrally in the region's main city. The site also serves as one of the 35 ambulance stations for the region. The control room communicates with all ambulances (30 to 70 operational at any one time) and the stations from which they operate. Essentially, the centre takes calls from the public (999s), police, fire service, doctors and hospitals and provides ambulances for all incidents arising from these calls according to certain Government-stipulated rules, regulations and targets. The targets specify that for emergency calls 95% of ambulances should be mobile 3 minutes after receiving a call, 50% at the scene by 8 minutes and 95% by 14 minutes. Currently, the region consistently outperforms these figures. The major task for control room workers is

---

[1]Whalen's (e.g. 1995) work is a partial exception to this though he does not focus, as we do, on ambulance controlling as a species of cooperative work.

to meet the need for ambulances, according to target, while operating with limited resources. The control room is staffed by between one and six Call Operators depending on the time of day, four Dispatchers, two Supervisors and a Control Manager. The present paper will focus on the Dispatchers and Supervisors who organise the distribution of ambulances over the region and responses to incidents. Further work is planned to examine call operation in greater detail.

Central to the job of ambulance control is a computer system which supports control room staff and links to the ambulances themselves via radio. Telephones, a global positioning system (GPS) and other artefacts are also employed intermittently. The computer system principally comprises a relational database containing details of calls, incidents, vehicle availability and so forth, which a number of client applications make requests to. The most important of these applications for ambulance dispatch are discussed shortly. The database server is networked to over 20 terminals in the control room. The system is mainly DOS-based and has been developed by an independent software company to the regional service's own specifications.

Our most intensive contact with the centre took place in the period from April to October 1996, during which about 40 person-days were spent on-site. We ensured that the visits covered both 'quiet' and 'busy' times and sampled the daily and weekly rhythms of the work. The centre's IT Manager was an initial point of contact and informant who provided us with introductions to all centre staff, whereupon we were able to intensively observe control room work as it happened. Much of this study involved 'sitting in' with different staff members, observing their work and occasionally getting them to describe what they were doing. Informal interviews, where we were concerned to clarify our emerging understanding of control room activity, were undertaken opportunistically on the job or during breaktimes. Field notes, ambulance service documents, forms, training materials, system manuals and other related materials were collected. Our methods of ethnographic analysis broadly follow the programme of ethnomethodological ethnography as exemplified in CSCW and HCI by Hughes et al. (e.g. 1992) and discussed by Bowers (1996). Amongst other matters, this involves attending to the real-time details of work and how, in and through them, the orderliness of control room activity is produced as a recognisable social accomplishment.

2.1   Incoming Incidents

Ambulance control work commences on receipt of a call reporting an incident. Incoming incidents are logged by the Call Operators onto computer based forms containing fields for, for example 'name', 'address', 'incident type' and so forth. The minimum information the Call Operator requires from the caller to initiate response is an address and incident type. This is because, on making a 'fix' on the address, the computer system automatically assigns an A-Z (street atlas) grid reference and a zone number to that location, which are displayed on the Call Operator's screen. Once these details have been entered the form automatically passes over to a incident pending list ('Incident Stack') displayed for the Dispatchers and Supervisors, while the Call Operator attempts to gain the information to complete the rest of the form. This feature, whereby Dispatchers can start formulating their dispatch decisions while the call is still being taken, is considered by the service to be a time saving advantage of an electronically based system.

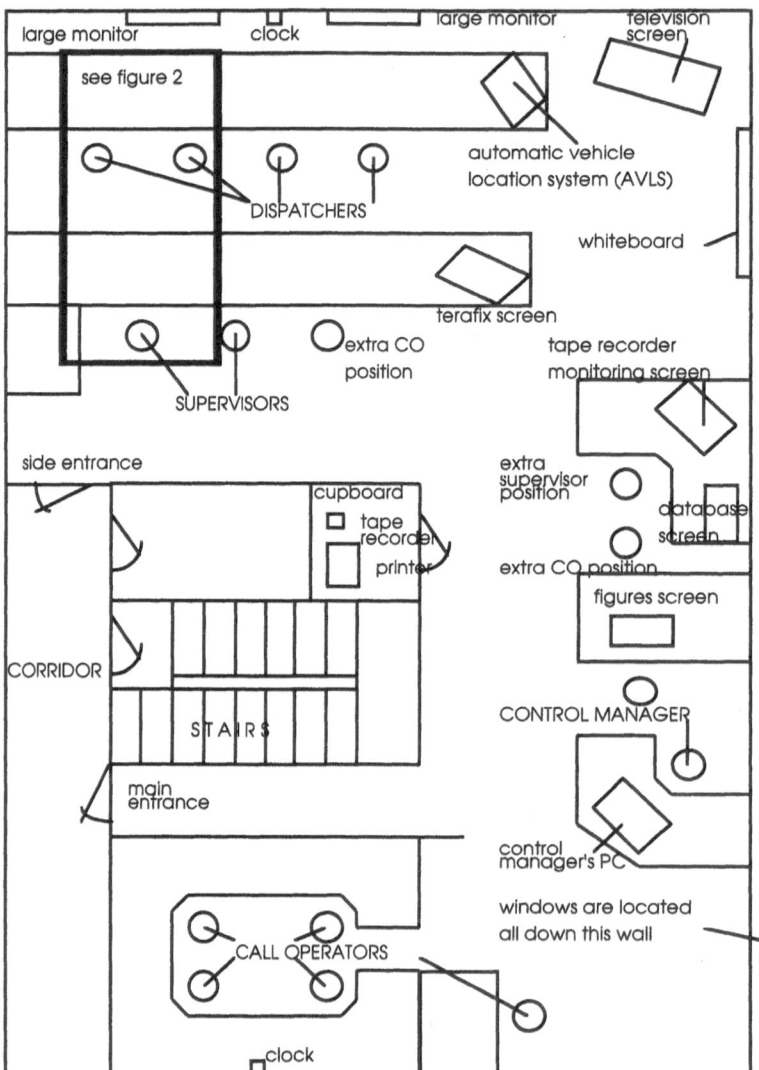

Figure 1: Plan view of the ambulance control room (most of the technologies noted in the figure are discussed in the main text).

The control room also deals with another type of call, 'urgent incidents', which are received from doctors, and cover cases where a patient requires transportation to hospital from either home or surgery. These cases are logged on similar forms, however they can be completed between one and four hours after receipt rather than immediately, and even this deadline can be extended occasionally. Urgent incidents can create problems in the management of dispatch and cover. For instance, a number of urgent cases may have been allocated due to the service being quiet, when suddenly there is a rush of emergency incidents.

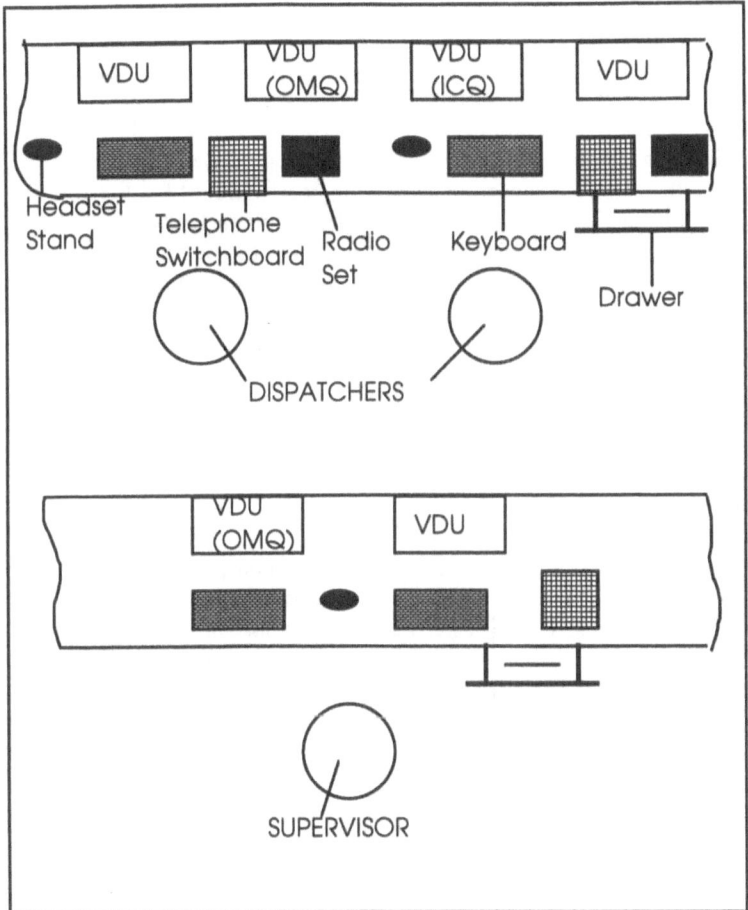

Figure 2: Plan of Dispatchers' and Supervisors' local environment within the control room. (In addition to the technologies discussed in the main text, the ICQ (Incoming Message Queue) and the OCQ (Outgoing Message Queue) screens display the flow of packets of information between the control room and ambulances.)

2.2   Dispatchers and Supervisors

Although there may be occasioned discussions with Call Operators (e.g. if the details of a form need clarification), for the most part the Dispatchers and Supervisors operate as a self contained group located at the other end of the control room (see Figure 1). The Dispatchers are primarily concerned with assigning incidents to ambulances and sending the details, as an abridged message, through to the ambulances where they are presented on a small panel containing an alphanumeric display and keypad.

Initially, it might seem to be a reasonable strategy for a Dispatcher to send the nearest available ambulance to the incident as soon as a geographical fix has been obtained. Often, this is what a Dispatcher will do. But this cannot be done without consideration of a decision's implications for the provision of *cover*. If the dispatch of a certain ambulance would lead to an area of the region being inaccessible within target times, then an ambulance other than the nearest might be dispatched. Indeed, with limited resources, it is *essential* for Dispatchers to be mindful of the implications for cover of their responses to incidents. In the face of these demands, and with a workload which can rise to several hundred calls a day, how is the complexity of dispatch and cover to be managed?

First, the region is separated into four main areas (or 'boards'—a term which reminds one of earlier non-computer-based systems). Each Dispatcher is assigned the duties of dispatch and cover management for a single board. However, while their board forms their focus, interaction and collaboration across boards is a required and indeed common feature of the work. The Supervisors' job is to ensure the management of dispatch and the adequacy of cover for the whole region. This entails overseeing activities with the Supervisor providing advice and making checks on the Dispatchers' work. Furthermore, it is common for a Supervisor to actually dispatch ambulances in order to lessen the workload for Dispatchers, or deal with emerging problems. In this way, the Supervisors and the Dispatchers maintain a 'working division of labour'. That is, each person has their own job to do but they routinely coordinate with each other and, when necessary, help each other out. We shall return to the question of exactly *how* they maintain their working division of labour later.

2.3   Computing Technology

Although Dispatchers and Supervisors deploy a number of non-computer-based artefacts (e.g. street atlases, manuals and personal notepads), the centre's computer system comprises the central technological resource for dispatch. In this section, we describe most important applications within this system. In the typical character of DOS-based systems, moving from one application to another is accomplished by a key sequence whereupon the entire screen changes to show the new application.

2.3.1 The Incident Stack

When an incident is passed over to a Dispatcher it appears at the top of the 'Incident Stack' screen, pushing earlier incidents down one row. Each Dispatcher has an Incident Stack for their own region displayed on the terminal in front of them. An incident's description will be routed to the terminal associated with the Dispatcher who has working responsibility for the board containing the incident's geographical fix. The screen is split into two with the upper half listing all the incidents that are 'WAITING' to be assigned to ambulances and the lower half those that are 'ACTIVE', that is, being attended to. Top of the list in the 'WAITING' half is the oldest unassigned emergency. A variety of information is displayed in each line including when the call was received, the number of ambulances attending and their IDs, and various items provided by the GPS including the 'as-the-crow-flies' distance the ambulance is from the incident. 'WAITING' incidents show similar details but, being unassigned, have no ambulance information. While each individual Dispatcher has an Incident Stack for their board, the stack for the whole of the region is permanently displayed on a large screen on the left hand side of the wall in front of the Dispatchers (see Figure 1).

2.3.2 The Dispatch Selection Screen

When an incident appears on a Dispatcher's stack and they select it by pressing the enter key, the top half of the incident form appears on screen along with a list of the nearest ambulances to the incident. This is defined in terms of the nearest stations to the zone the incident has occurred in. The list presents ambulances irrespective of whether they are active or free. However, the nearest free ambulance is flagged in blue as a guide to allocation. When the selection of ambulance is made the rest of the data which has been entered by the Call Operator appears on screen. The Dispatcher then checks and edits this before transmitting it to the crew, typically without any accompanying voice-radio contact. On receiving the details of incident, the crew must respond by pressing a designated button on the keypad in the ambulance cab. This updates the listing for the incident on the Incident Stack and the listing of the ambulance on the VAM screen.

2.3.3 The Vehicle Availability Map (VAM)

To ensure that cover is adequate or to manage the risk of leaving a station 'empty', Dispatchers must monitor the status of ambulances on the VAM. This is displayed on the wall in front of them on the large monitor shown at the top-centre of Figure 1 and in Figure 3, and can also be accessed from the Dispatchers' individual terminals. The VAM consists of a set of lists of ambulance IDs, each list depicting ambulances from 2 or 3 proximate stations. The lists are arranged on screen to give an approximate representation of the geographical relations between stations (e.g. stations in the same 'board' will be listed close to each other). Colour is used to signify the statuses which are most pertinent to dispatch decisions. If flagged in red the ambulance is active on an emergency, if in green active on an urgent call, and if unflagged the ambulance is available. If the number flashes this indicates that the ambulance is on standby, placed at a designated location between two or more stations to provide emergency cover for not only its home station but another nearby that is low or without cover. Thus, the Dispatchers and Supervisors can see at a glance what the general configuration for the region is and identify potential problems of cover. (The detail of the VAM is shown in Figure 3 with the colour highlighting given a greyscale approximation.)

WIG	ATH	BOL	HIG	BUR	ROC	ECC	ALT
7345	5578	5661	3346	4110	2120	9786	2336
7563	4242	5563	3217	4243	2115	9866	3114
7224	4455	6245	2354	3447	2332	9786	3122
6224	4411	6562	3737	3388	2112		2255
7797	4116	4113			2689		
8761							
7556							

BEL	CEN	SAL	OLD	DUR	STO	GLO
4466	5778	6536	6684	8843	4426	3557
4117	5331	6868	7553	8854	4473	3749
4119	5462	6565	7776	9982	4335	2561
4421	5567	6769	7787	8822	4333	2239
4434	5579	7652	8114			
5337	5882					
	6577					

Figure 3: The Vehicle Availability Map (VAM) which lists ambulances by regions. Ambulances active on emergencies are here shown with their IDs against a black background. Ambulances on urgent calls are shown against a grey background. Ambulances on standby are shown 'flashing'. Available ambulances are just depicted by their ID. See main text for further explanation.

2.4   Contingencies

Although often the ambulance suggested on the Dispatch Selection screen (the nearest available one) is chosen, there are multiple varying contingencies that must be considered in the on-going flow of work. Each dispatch decision is in the context of various previous decisions and in turn will influence others. In addition to proximity and availability and a consideration of implications for cover, the kinds of contingencies which must be reckoned with from time to time include:

- Are the crew due a meal-break?
- When does the crew's shift end? When will a new crew's shift begin?
- Have the crew just dealt with one or more harrowing incidents?
- Does the ambulance have the right equipment for the incident?
- Is the nearest (as the crow flies) ambulance on the fastest route?
- Are there road works, traffic problems etc. on a particular route?
- Which side of the motorway is a particular accident on?
- How serious is the incident?
- Are there urgent cases which must be allocated soon?
- And so forth.

Furthermore, ensuring cover is no simple algorithmic matter, as the demands on the service fluctuate dramatically at different times of year and on different days of the week. Public occasions may require special deployment and an emergency call-out at the region's major international airport (which can be actioned by, amongst others, an incoming pilot in difficulties) immediately commits 5 ambulances through a standing agreement with the airport authorities.

It should be clear that it would be negligent to simply select the system's suggestion for dispatch without attending to these many and varied matters. Accordingly, Dispatchers and Supervisors often need to examine whether, for instance, there is the possibility of allocating another ambulance in the vicinity to the job, or whether standby cover can be arranged, or whether another ambulance from the station will become available soon.

2.4.1 Workload and Contingency Management

Ironically, it is precisely when workload is at its highest, and there is the least time for Dispatchers to reason about contingencies, that they most urgently impact upon the work of ambulance dispatch. Consider, for example, a crew which has just attended a particularly harrowing accident. If there are few other incidents outstanding, there will usually be a suitable alternative to this crew for attending any new incident. But difficult problems occur when, for instance, any respite due to a crew has to be weighed up against the disquiet of several others who are overdue on their meal-beaks and there are still new incidents coming in! Plans may be made (e.g. greater cover on a Friday night) but these must be open to constant revision as the situation unfolds. Although proximity, availability and cover are always relevant, there is not a simple hierarchy in operation. Contingencies compete against one another and become more or less important according to the situation. For example, sending the closest available ambulance may leave no cover and mean that the crew must work longer than their allotted shift. However, if the incident is a serious road traffic accident (RTA), and there appears no other feasible option, this will be the case.

The management of contingencies, especially at times of high workload, is facilitated by occasioned cooperation between Dispatchers and between Dispatchers and Supervisors. Not only might Supervisors assist with dispatch itself, they will provide advice over vehicle allocation based on their overview of the region, an overview which is hard to obtain for individual Dispatchers especially if their workload is high. Additionally, a Dispatcher whose 'board' requires less attention may assist a Dispatcher who is having to make many dispatch decisions in short order. While knowledge and experience is routinely 'pooled' and exchanged both on the job and during coffee breaks, this becomes most perspicuous at times of high workload when the control room is a flurry of mutual assistance, cross-checking and shouted suggestions.

2.5   Dispatch in Action

In order for the group of two Supervisors and four Dispatchers to effectively cooperate and achieve the successful management of dispatch and cover, they have to maintain a *mutual awareness* of one another's work. To do this, the Dispatchers and Supervisors monitor each other peripherally in a continual manner while a certain person who is in difficulty or requires advice may be focused on more directly if the need arises. Let us examine in more depth how this mutual monitoring is achieved.

2.5.1   The Ecology of Dispatch and Supervision

Crucial to achieving mutual awareness between Dispatchers and Supervisors is the interplay between the ecology and technology of the control room and cooperative activity within it. Refer again to Figures 1 and 2. How does the physical layout of the room, the positioning and design of artefacts within it and the placement of workers effect the way workers act and interact?

The Dispatchers and Supervisors share the same computer based artefact allowing them, in principle, to view through their own terminals one another's work as it occurs. However, this facility tends to be only used by the Supervisors as most of the Dispatchers' time is taken up deploying ambulances. The large regional Incident Stack and VAM monitors, on the other hand, are routinely inspected by everyone in the control room, not just Supervisors and Dispatchers, and hence constitute the major shared artefacts in the work in that all personnel are always presented with the same data. Dispatchers visually monitor each other's work mainly through these artefacts and also through directly viewing the screens and actions of those beside them. Supervisors are afforded more opportunity for visual monitoring, as their seating position allows them a more direct view of all of the Dispatchers' screens and indeed, of any activity that the Dispatchers are involved in.

These physical and technical arrangements afford opportunities for becoming aware of critical factors which can inform a dispatch decision. However, they alone do not *guarantee* that information will be picked up by the appropriate recipient of it or attended to for the appropriate details. Consider, for example, the VAM containing its lists of ambulance IDs colour-flagged to indicate their current status. To the experienced worker, this shows at-a-glance how busy the service is. Swathes of red across the VAM screen (as is typical on a Friday night) reveals a service whose resources are stretched. If this is combined with a similar abundance of red on the WAITING portion of the Incident Stack, then we have a service which, for the moment, is finding it hard to cope. While such summary impressions are available at-a-glance, both the VAM and the Incident Stacks can be engaged with to a further degree to find out exactly which individual ambulances are deployed and exactly which incidents are being attended to. While the displays afford the pick-up of both sorts of information, what exactly a Dispatcher or a Supervisor will get from the screen depends upon the kind of attentiveness they show to it. Accordingly, we often see co-workers explicitly signalling to each other to point out details or to draw attention to anomalies. That is, in the control room the sharing and use of information must be worked at collaboratively in order for the successful management of dispatch and cover to take place.

In short, the ecology of the control room may afford opportunities for information pick-up but it is only through social interaction between personnel and the appropriate degree of engagement with artefacts that these opportunities are realised in actual situated dispatch decisions.

2.5.2   Mutual Monitoring and Occasioned Cooperation

As we have noted, it is common for control room personnel to monitor each other peripherally for opportunities to correct mistakes, offer advice or work collaboratively. For instance, Supervisors often suggest dispatch choices to Dispatchers for incidents they are not yet dealing with, that is, for incidents which are outside a Dispatcher's current 'focus of work'. The degree of shared understanding within the group is readily discernible from the terseness of talk between personnel, talk which is inextricably immersed in and indexically tied to its situation of utterance. For example on one occasion a Supervisor uttered to a Dispatcher (whose back was turned): "I've got that Moss-way job". The Dispatcher then acknowledged this with a small glance towards the Supervisor. The Supervisor had decided to allocate an incident on behalf of the Dispatcher and a mutual awareness of the action was gained simply through a brief statement which could be readily interpreted as a WAITING incident changes its display to ACTIVE.

Here, the monitoring activity of the Supervisor did not disrupt the Dispatcher's activity, and indeed the Dispatcher may have been unaware that it was even occurring. However, in the control room this is not always the case, and, for instance we have witnessed numerous occasions where personnel rendered their monitoring obvious by asking questions of those they are observing either for checking or clarification, and it is common for Supervisors to get out of their seats and stand directly behind the Dispatchers.

Intervention by those who are monitoring the work of a Dispatcher is not the only way in which cooperation within a working division of labour is achieved. We observed a case where a first Dispatcher gained the attention of a second beside her by giving her a small nudge. The first had been conducting a radio conversation with a crew who were having trouble finding a suitable route to an RTA. A discussion then ensued between the second Dispatcher and a third Dispatcher sitting further away (who voluntarily joined in) as to the location of the ambulance and how it should reach its required destination. An A-Z atlas was used as the focal point of their discussion, with the Supervisor positioned behind the first two Dispatchers also volunteering suggestions. The first Dispatcher then asked the second to take over the call, with the second then providing updated information for the ambulance crew.

This compactly demonstrates several of the points made so far. On this occasion, the first Dispatcher established interaction with the minimal effort of a nudge, however during the course of the incident workers other than the initial addressee negotiated their way into the discussion indicating that they were at least peripherally aware of what had been occurring. Furthermore this instance shows how the division of labour in the control room can proceed with great flexibility with different workers entering into direct collaboration when they have the opportunity, before relatively seamlessly returning to their own work.

2.5.3   Negotiating Interaction Opportunities

There are many ways in which Dispatchers or Supervisors will attempt to solicit assistance. We have numerous examples of Dispatchers or Supervisors looking, or gesturing to attract attention to themselves, or sighing, or muttering while they face the screen, or asking questions either generally or directedly in order to solicit assistance. Often these behaviours are used in combination or one after the other until a satisfactory contact has been made or solution offered. For example, if a Dispatcher asks a question about whether to put a certain crew on their meal-break out loud while looking at their screen and there is no response, they may turn and face the Supervisor behind them and ask the question more directly. The Supervisor may indicate with a wave of their hand that they are too busy, meanwhile the Dispatcher beside her may make a suggestion because she has been listening in. The original Dispatcher may act on this suggestion or try to solicit other opinions. While in a similar situation the Dispatcher may simply hear a "yes" from the Supervisor or the Supervisor may reply that they have independently put the crew on a meal-break.

When one control room worker tries to establish an interaction with another they will often first try and do this with minimal intrusion. However, due at least in part to the number of different personnel there are in the control room, their involvement in other duties and also occasional ambiguity as to whom (if anyone specifically) a question or statement is addressed, satisfactory interaction is often not immediately established. Both the addresser and the addressee(s) regularly need to negotiate their positions through qualifying remarks, questions, looks and gestures, in order to successfully engage. In short, a perspicuous feature of this control room is how *persons' availability for interaction has to be itself negotiated*, sometimes by progressively upgrading from (for example) glance to gesture to direct request for help and on occasion to an insistent plea-ful raising of the voice.

3 Discussion

Let us bring out some points of general interest grounded in our studies of this control room. In so doing, we will make comparisons with related studies, while also giving an impression of the prototype applications we are developing for consideration by ambulance personnel. Necessarily our treatment here will be brief but we hope to indicate how ethnographic work can not only motivate system design but also offer new perspectives on HCI research agendas. We order our remarks around 4 key observations.

3.1 (1) Contingencies are Interactionally Managed

We have noted that ambulance dispatch is a contingent affair with multiple considerations impinging upon dispatch selections. Commonly, Dispatchers can resolve these contingencies through interaction with the different resources available to them, juxtaposing, for example, the VAM's representation of the state of the service with their own Incident Stack and those of neighbours. However, oftentimes contingencies will be managed not merely through the interaction of individual Dispatchers with system resources but through *social* interaction amongst Dispatchers and Supervisors. Indeed, on occasion, the significance of a contingency may be resolved through interaction between control room personnel and others outside—a member of the public still on the line or an ambulance crew. For example, we noted earlier that the timing of meal breaks for crews has to be considered in making dispatch decisions. The *severity* of an overdue meal break— and hence its significance for the work of dispatch—is often argued out between Dispatchers and the crew themselves. Indeed, the use of voice-radio is predominantly occasioned by such discussions!
Observations like this make us sceptical about the feasibility of automatic decision making systems in the ambulance service—systems which might, say, dispatch ambulances on the basis of algorithms operating to satisfy multiple constraints. And this for two reasons. One, the list of contingencies which we have begun to document shows no obvious sign of terminating and, two, the practical weight to be attached to considerations is often socially interactively determined and negotiated. Accordingly, our development agenda is to investigate how systems can be designed for a socio-technical setting where *co*-operation is a normal feature of how work is done[2].

---

[2]This is not to say that we see no future for, say, the use of constraint-satisfaction algorithms and other pieces of formal machinery in supporting ambulance dispatch. While not highest on our own research agenda, we do intend to consider the applicability of such computational techniques. We imagine, though, that the recommendations deriving from such algorithms should be just that: recommendations, which are defeasible by personnel much like the results of the 'find the nearest available ambulance algorithm' currently are.

3.2   (2) Divisions of Labour are Working Ones

While there exist distinctions between control personnel in terms of what they do, these are defeasible in the light of the exigencies of work. In the terms of Hughes et al. (1992) and Sharrock and Anderson (1992), personnel simultaneously maintain an *egological* orientation to the division of labour (what is there for *me* to do? what's on *my* board?), and an *alteriological* orientation (what can I do to make the work of *others* easier? how can I help with *their* overdue dispatches?). In Hughes et al.'s studies of ATC, control room assistants are oriented (alteriologically) to create a "protective cocoon" around the controllers so that the controllers have all that they need to do their work ready-to-hand and do not have to search out for it themselves. In the ambulance service, however, there is no such cocoon and the intervention of personnel in each other's work is a much more perspicuous feature. In dispatch[3], the ambulance room's working division of labour is differently achieved, through extensive mutual monitoring, oftentimes peripherally (while personnel engage in their own work) and, when required, more focally (as others attract attention to their difficulties).

The kind of mutual awareness and extensive intervention (especially when the tempo of work is high) which is observable in our setting also marks out a difference with Heath and Luff's (1992) findings in London Underground control. While Heath and Luff did observe controllers engaging in exaggerated gestures and the like to gain attention, the abiding impression one has from their research is of two workers seamlessly coordinating their activities without interruption. As we have argued, in the ambulance control room, interaction opportunities sometimes require extensive and more perspicuous negotiation. This is not because personnel are refusing an altereological orientation and resisting giving help. Rather, in the hurly burly of dealing with very many emergencies at one time, others may happen to be engaged in some activity they cannot interrupt, or which they momentarily regard as more pressing, or the level of noise means that an imploring request has been missed. It is also important to note that the existence of *several* others in the ambulance control room means that an exaggerated gesture (or whatever) may not be automatically picked up as being for *a particular* other's benefit. Projecting one's activity so that it can be monitored by others or attempting to attract attention has an element of 'specific-other-selection' in the design of gesture and talk not necessary in settings (like Heath and Luff's) where essentially just two persons are working.

We would suggest that the maintenance of working divisions of labour is a more subtle and variable affair than some methods of 'task analysis' or 'process modelling' in HCI and computer science indicate. The ready defeasibility of the tasks associated with individual jobs (Dispatcher, Supervisor and, even, if required, Control Manager) are not experienced or negotiated as 'exceptions' to

---

[3]For there is, indeed, a sense in which a protective cocoon exists around the Call Operators so that they can attend to the business of interacting with an often extremely distressed public.

normal procedure or to a standard task or process model. Indeed, it would be exceptional (and reprimandable) *not* to show an orientation to others. 'Normal operation' *is* this essential flexibility in conduct. Accordingly, our development strategy is to consider the design of computing technologies with respect to how they can support a working division of labour, rather than, say, encoding a process model or assuming a differentiation between persons with respect to the tasks they perform.

In this regard, there is a lot to learn from our control room. There are artefacts devoted to 'individual views' (the Incident Stacks for each board) and to 'collective views' (the combined Incident Stack and the VAM). These different views are shared in their accessibility and can be juxtaposed the one to the other. Interestingly, part of what makes those views juxtaposable is that the system is *not* end-user configurable at the screen-interface. Indeed, the continued use of a mouseless, DOS-based, keyboard-driven, window-free system helps ensure that one Incident Stack has the same basic design as any other. Hence, visible differences between them will be work-related differences and not due to any idiosyncratic preference of the end-user. Supervisory functions could well be disrupted by seemingly more sophisticated interface techniques and ideologies of user-choice[4].

However, while current arrangements enable the region to exceed target performance, we feel there is scope for further supporting the awareness that co-workers have of each other through technology. Workers currently complain of the high levels of noise as people shout at each other at peak times. If some of what is achieved through that noise (an awareness of what others are doing) is removed from the medium of speech and supported with enhancements to, say, the individual Incident Stacks, the 'air would be clear' for managing the most difficult contingencies. Our prototype explorations in this area will be made the subject of another paper.

3.3 (3) Representations are Work-Oriented

It is possible to regard the VAM, the Incident Stacks and the computer forms completed by Call Operators as representations of (various aspects of) incidents and ambulance service. However, it is necessary to emphasise that these representations are oriented in their design to the effective support of *cooperative work in the control room*. While, naturally, they are intended to be easily perceivable and manipulable for the individuals before whose eyes they fall, their status as *work-oriented artefacts* within the cooperative assembly of the control room must not be missed. Again, *for the purposes of the cooperative work of ambulance controlling*, textual representations and displays, organised around

---

[4]Bentley, Hughes, Randall, Rodden, Sawyer, Shapiro and Sommerville (1992) make a similar point in connection with supervisory duties in air traffic control, even though, as we have argued, these are differently realised in that setting.

lists, with sparse and carefully selected embellishments and colour highlighting, are most effective.

Let us illustrate this point with an example. While several features of the centre's GPS are frequently used, the 'flagship feature' often promoted by the manufacturers—a map-like display of ambulance locations on a large computer screen—is rarely consulted. The Automatic Vehicle Location System (or AVLS as this display is known) is typically turned away from the sight of the Dispatchers even though it is on the work-surface alongside them, and only easily inspectable by Dispatchers or Supervisors if they come close (see Figure 1). To understand this, it is important to realise that obtaining geographical fixes on the ambulance fleet is only *one part* of judging which to dispatch and how to maintain adequate cover (remember the many other contingencies), and a swiftly visible presentation of the *relevant* aspects of ambulance-location can be given by the GPS's computation of as-the-crow-flies distances and highlighting proximal, available candidates. A literal visual representation of ambulance locations might require a worker to engage in further deliberation to *extract* these details from a cosmetically impressive display[5]. Furthermore, the AVLS screen only shows one part of the region at any one time. Horizontal and vertical scrolling to find visualisations of ambulance locations on a map mostly full of 'empty' streets and countryside is needlessly time-consuming when, in contrast, the VAM compactly shows ambulances with a geographical sensitivity that is *appropriately approximate* for dispatch decisions. Importantly, on the VAM, *all* the ambulances are represented *there* (along with relevant status information), they do not have to be *found* in a 2D map-space[6].

In short, for the purposes of dispatch and cover, seemingly crude lists may be the most appropriate form of representation, giving an easy impression of how many ambulances are available at every station. However, again, it is possible that more (and more detailed) cover-relevant information could be introduced to the Dispatchers' own resources for ambulance selection. In this regard, in our prototyping work, we are considering re-designs of the Dispatch Selection screen

---

[5]Indeed, it seems that (currently) one of the prime usages of the map-like visualisation is to impress visitors!

[6]Or a 3D space. While the so-called 'infinite interface' offered by immersive Virtual Reality systems may overcome the limitations of conventional visualisations which are bounded by the borders of the screen, it is hard to see the immediate utility of these forms of 3D computing technology to ambulance control settings (though applications of VR are commonly mooted for control purposes). In a sense, the 'dimensionally challenged' VAM (and other screens in the control room) 'filters out' details from view which would detract from effective ambulance controlling. Pycock and Bowers (1996) make a similar point in the context of fashion design work when they argue that it is 2D representations of garments which are found to be most appropriate for highlighting of significant detail for standard manufacture. This argument, of course, does not rule out the possibility that, for purposes *other* than manufacture (e.g. a customer viewing a garment draped over a representation of their own body through an advanced interactive shopping system), 3D visualisations may have uses.

to contain 'at-a-glance-what-if information': e.g. alongside the as-the-crow-flies distance, some representation of the number of ambulances remaining at local stations if the one represented by the row of the list were selected.

3.4 *(4) Human Computer Interaction is a Public Phenomenon*

As we have emphasised, the sharing of artefacts within a shared ecology facilitates mutual awareness and coordination between control room personnel. In this respect, human-computer interaction is itself a *public phenomenon* in that any act of engagement by a person with a computer system, screen or display is potentially available to *third parties* and a resource *for them* in noticing or repairing troubles or gaining an impression of generally how stretched the service is. This suggests the opportunity to, as we might put it, *design for third parties,* that is, to design interaction techniques, key sequences, screen changes and so forth so that they can be detected by others as appropriate occasions for, say, initiating interaction (cf. Greatbatch, Heath, Luff and Campion, 1993). Accordingly, in the ambulance control room, we are considering re-designs of the screens and interaction techniques used in dispatch to make it more noticeable by third parties when (and which) selections are made and when (and which) changes in view (Incident Stack or Dispatch Selection etc.) take place.

Gaver (e.g. 1991) has done much to popularise within HCI the emphases of J. J. Gibson (e.g. 1979) on the affordances of artefacts and show how everyday affordances can be exploited in system design. We speak of *interactional affordances* to particularly highlight that, in real work settings, *first* many artefacts (and not merely communications technologies) afford *occasions for social interaction* between co-workers, and *secondly* it is often only through *interaction and engagement* that affordances are revealed (cf. Coulter's, 1990, respecification of Gibson's account of ecological perception). We noted earlier that there is a sense in which the VAM affords several different kinds of 'seeing' depending on the engagement personnel have with it, e.g., an at-a-glance perception of the load on the service or a more detailed picture of the activities of individual ambulances with more careful scrutiny[7]. Our point now is that the ecology of the control room makes it available *to others* whether someone takes a swift glance or a more protracted stare. This often enables the act of visual inspection to be taken as an act of information pick-up: whether someone is picking up the details or the overall picture is available in the manner of their looking. That is, the status of human-computer interaction as a public phenomenon often links our two senses (above) of 'interactional affordance'. The fundamental challenge, we believe, arising for an ecologically-oriented HCI is to systematically support design, evaluation and implementation with these senses in mind. We have indicated some of our next tentative steps.

---

[7]Indeed, this further testifies to the subtlety of such list-based representational formats in this setting.

Acknowledgments

We would like to thank all ambulance service personnel who generously accommodated us throughout this research. The support of the European Communities' ESPRIT project *eSCAPE: Electronic Landscapes* is also acknowledged.

References

Bentley, R., Hughes, J., Randall, D., Rodden, T., Sawyer, P., Shapiro, D. and Sommerville, I. (1992). Ethnographically-informed systems design for air traffic control. In *Proceedings of CSCW '92*, the Fourth Conference on Computer Supported Cooperative Work. New York: ACM Press.

Bowers, J., Button, G. and Sharrock, W. (1995). Workflow from within and without. In *Proceedings of ECSCW'95*, the Fourth European Conference on Computer Supported Cooperative Work. Dordrecht: Kluwer.

Bowers, J. (1996). Hanging around and making something of it: Ethnography. In Haworth, J. (ed.) *Psychological Research: Innovative Methods and Strategies*. London: Routledge.

Coulter, J. (1990). The praxeology of visual perception. *Inquiry*, 33, 251-72.

Gaver, W. (1991). Technology affordances. In *Proceedings of CHI 1991* (New Orleans, Louisiana, April 28 - May 2, 1991). New York: ACM Press.

Gibson, J. J. (1979). *The Ecological Approach to Visual Perception*. New York: Houghton Mifflin.

Greatbatch, D., Luff, P., Heath, C. and Campion, P. (1993). Interpersonal communication and human computer interaction. *Interacting with Computers*, 5, 193-216.

Heath, C., and Luff, P. (1992). Collaboration and control : Crisis management and multi-media technology in London Underground Line Control Rooms. *Computer Supported Cooperative Work*, 1, 69-94.

Hughes, A., Randall, D., and Shapiro, D. (1992). Faltering from ethnography to design. In *Proceedings of CSCW '92*, the Fourth Conference on Computer Supported Cooperative Work. New York: ACM Press.

Pycock, J. and Bowers, J. (1996). Getting others to get it right: An ethnography of design work in the fashion industry. In *Proceedings of CSCW '96*, the Sixth Conference on Computer Supported Cooperative Work. New York: ACM Press.

Randall, D., Rouncefield, M. and Hughes, J. (1995). Chalk and cheese. In *Proceedings of ECSCW'95*, the Fourth European Conference on Computer Supported Cooperative Work. Dordrecht: Kluwer.

Rouncefield, M., Hughes, J., Rodden, T. and Viller, S. (1994). Working with "constant interruption". In *Proceedings of CSCW '94,* the Fifth Conference on Computer Supported Cooperative Work. New York: ACM Press.

Sharrock, W. and Anderson, R. (1992). Can organisations afford knowledge? *Computer Supported Cooperative Work*, 1, 143-162.

Whalen, J. (1995). Expert systems versus systems for experts: Computer aided dispatch as a support system in real world environments. In Ed. Thomas, P. *The Social and Interactional Dimensions of Human-Computer Interfaces.* Cambridge: CUP.

Why, What, Where, When: Architectures for Cooperative Work on the World Wide Web

Devina Ramduny and Alan Dix

School of Computing, Staffordshire University
PO Box 334, Beaconside,
Stafford, ST18 0DG
D.Ramduny@soc.staffs.ac.uk
Tel: 01785 353255

School of Computing, Staffordshire University
PO Box 334, Beaconside,
Stafford, ST18 0DG
A.J.Dix@soc.staffs.ac.uk
Tel: 01785 353428

The software architecture of a cooperative user interface determines *what* component is placed *where*. This paper examines some reasons determining *why* a particular placement should be chosen. Temporal interface behaviour is a key issue: *when* users receive feedback from their own actions and feedthrough about the actions of others. In a distributed system, data and code may be moved to achieve the desired behaviour — in particular, Java applets can be downloaded to give rapid local semantic feedback. Thus we must choose not only the physical location for each functional component but also when that component should reside in different places.

Keywords: software architecture, CSCW, Internet, caching, replication, applets, feedback, feedthrough, temporal problems, delays

1   Introduction

The world-wide web provides a ubiquitous infrastructure and platform independent interface for developing remote collaborative applications. Although such systems can be developed in an ad hoc fashion it is widely recognised that, for both single-user and multi-user interfaces, an appropriate software architecture is required as an aid for design, portability and maintenance [4,19,23]. In this paper we will investigate some architectural decisions for distributed collaborative applications focusing especially on collaboration over the web.

Software architecture is about dividing systems into components in order to perform certain functionalities — *what* the system can do. But in order to work as a complete system the components must be linked together in such a way that they can communicate effectively with each other. While all the components are running as part of the same program on the same machine these communications are easy. However, as soon as the system is distributed over a network, as is the case with many cooperative systems, components placed at different locations face higher communication costs and delays than those at the same location. Hence the choice of location—*where* the components are placed—has a significant effect on performance.

One of the principle effects of location decisions is on the pace of interaction. For many years temporal issues in interface design have been largely ignored with a few exceptions [10,11,13,17]. However, recently the importance of time and delays has become more widely recognised [18], due no doubt in part to experiences of Internet use. This *when* question is only of importance to the user when it becomes apparent to the user. Thus behavioural issues are the driving force that determine *why* one architectural solution is better than another.

In many systems data is moved about in order to improve interactive performance. Furthermore in the world-wide web Java applets allow code to move and execute on user's own machines. Thus placement decisions for the web are not just about what is placed where, but also about *when* the data and code is at a particular location.

In the next section we start by looking at mature architectures for single-user interfaces which will later be used as a pattern for looking at collaborative architectures. This is followed in section 3 by an analysis of important behavioural issues for collaborative work. We will then return to architectures, looking at what components are necessary in collaborative interfaces, modelled on those found in single-user interfaces and the requirements established in section 3. In section 5, we will look at different placement options, where to place different components in a distributed architecture. Section 6, examines the issue of mobility of data and code and we are able to plot different options in a when/where matrix for each. Finally, in section 7 we look at the way these two matrices interact focusing on the options available for world-wide web applications.

2 Background—single user architectures

Architectures for single-user interfaces such as Seeheim [23] and Arch/Slinky [29] support the partitioning of the application semantics and the user interface functionality. The dialogue component mediates the communication between them. Separation enhances portability, reusability, customisation and adaptability of an application [16]. However, a case against separability is the problem of rapid semantic feedback—modern direct-manipulation interfaces require information to be exchanged extensively between the user interface and the application.

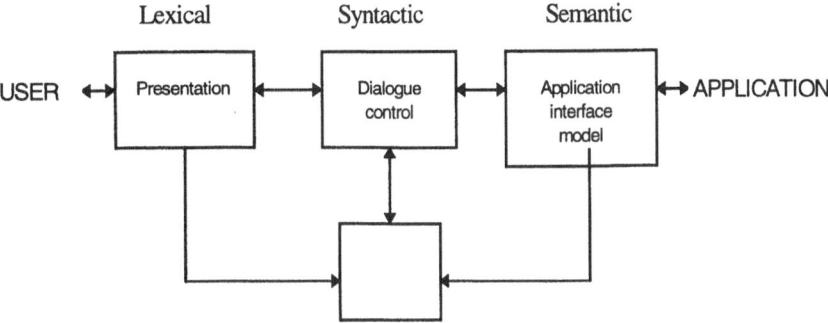

Figure 1: Seeheim model.

Figure 1 shows the logical components of the Seeheim model. The *presentation* component is responsible for the external appearance of the user interface while the *application interface model* holds the data and defines the semantics of the application. The *dialogue control* component mediates the interaction between the user and the application to provide semantic feedback. Whilst Seeheim has been developed in various ways, most notably in the Arch/Slinky framework, most user interface architectures preserve some notion of layering between the surface output and input devices and the deep application semantics.

The linear nature of communication between the components in the Seeheim model is often seen as a bottleneck for direct manipulation user interfaces. However the fast-switch represented by the lower box in Figure 1, allows the application to bypass the dialogue component when its state is not affected by output events. The application can then communicate directly with the presentation component and thus provide rapid feedback. But unlike the other functional components, the fast-switch is less well defined and correspondingly more difficult to implement as an architectural feature.

We can view the Seeheim model (and indeed other architectural models) in two ways: either as a conceptual (or logical) architecture, helping us to think about user interface development; or as a physical architecture demanding that there really are components of the system with the named roles and communicating along the paths specified in the architecture.

This is particularly obvious when all the components are placed on the same machine. As we have seen, the decoupling of the user interface functionality from the application functionality via the dialogue control is sometimes difficult to achieve, especially when rapid semantic feedback is required. Consequently aspects of the user interface may 'leak' into the application semantics component or vice versa. This is possible as there are typically no constraints to stop, for example, the application semantics from directly calling window toolkit functions. This fluidity of boundaries is recognised in the Arch/Slinky model [29] which still maintains the central role of layering and separability (in fact adding additional layers), but accepts that the precise placement of these layers into coded modules may vary between systems and even between parts of the same system.

When the software is no longer running on a single machine, as is the case in a distributed environment, the application and the user interface components are usually on different machines. One can no longer fudge the boundary and communications between these as they are enshrined in the physical location and network connectivity. As a result the issue of *where* the various components reside is decisive in order to achieve rapid feedback.

In addition to architectures which divide the entire system into a small number of large components, there are many agent-based or object-oriented user interface architectures. However, these either identify individual agents as belonging to one of the traditional layers or include a layering within each agent. For example, the PAC architecture [6] regards each agent as possessing a presentation, abstraction (roughly corresponding to application) and control component.

3   Why—behavioural issues

The reasons for determining *why* a particular placement should be chosen influence the behaviour of an application. The behavioural aspect affect the way users view the display on the screen (presentation). The behaviour of any application depends on its architecture. The most significant behavioural implication enforced by the architectural decisions is often the temporal impact. For instance, if one ignores the temporal issues then from the behavioural viewpoint, the location of the data is not important. However, for performance reasons, it is crucial that there is no perceived lag between any updates to the data and the subsequent changes being reflected on users' displays. Consequently, this may influence the selection of for example, a centralised or a replicated architecture [20]. The rest of this section describes the major behavioural issues which arise within web-based collaborative work.

3.1   Triggers and shared objects

A previous study [14,15] highlighted the importance and function of triggers, that is events which initiate activities. An important class of triggers are environmental cues [26], objects in the physical objects which by their presence remind users that activities need to be performed and help maintain the status of ongoing processes. Similarly, in an electronic cooperative setting, triggers can be associated with shared objects, reminding users that some actions have been carried out by others and/or some further actions need to be taken. Furthermore, the coordination of cooperative work can be mediated via shared objects. Although this form of coordination is less explicit than direct communication, it does play an important role. Indeed, in many cooperative processes there may be little direct communication. Instead coordination is mainly achieved by communicating implicitly through the artefact [8].

3.2   Feedback

Feedback manifests itself as a response from the display after a user's actions. It is a common feature of direct manipulation interfaces where objects change their behaviour when they are manipulated by the user. For instance, a button is highlighted when it is clicked onto by the mouse. Feedback may depend on the underlying application semantics. Within the web environment, the feedback loop involves transmission over a network. If the network traffic is high, the delays associated with the feedback will be significant. Consequently, it may be difficult to achieve rapid semantic feedback and acceptable response times.

3.3   Feedthrough

Collaborative participants not only interact individually with the system but also with other group members via the shared objects. As a result, it is important to see both the user's own updates (feedback) and the effects of other users' actions (feedthrough). Feedthrough is the reflection of a user's actions on other users' screens [9]. For example, gIBIS [5] allows participants to be aware of any updates through a notification mechanism.

The requirements for feedthrough are not so stringent as for feedback [9]. Feedthrough depends on two major factors: the granularity of the updates and the propagation of those updates. In tightly-coupled cooperative activities, such as group drawing, the granularity of updates is small and rapid feedthrough is vital. In other words, the updates have to be broadcast to all the users after each action. On the other hand, in loosely-coupled applications, the update rates can be reduced significantly. The user who initiated the action still requires rapid feedback but the feedthrough to other users may be less frequent. Because some objects are more significant for obtaining a sense of engagement, concepts of quality-of-service [24] can be applied giving different levels of feedthrough on shared objects within a groupware architecture.

The very nature of cooperative work introduces delays as users have to wait for feedback from their own actions and feedthrough of the actions of others. In addition, with the web, there are further delays and lags which are implicit in the network. Thus the provision of rapid feedback and feedthrough becomes more problematic. Current web-based collaborative applications often weakly support feedthrough even though it is essential in maintaining fluid collaboration.

3.4   Awareness

Traditionally, distributed systems have applied different types of transparency to hide information from the users. However, within the context of CSCW, users need precisely that information for effective cooperation. Awareness of individual and group activities is critical for establishing successful collaboration. Different kinds of awareness have been identified in the research literature.

The three major forms that enhance group work are:

(a) Awareness of the presence of group members and their availability for cooperative work,

(b) awareness of the effects of group members actions (i.e. what changes have occurred) and

(c) awareness of how changes happen.

Nevertheless, in remote cooperative work, users are often faced with unpredictable timing delays over the network due to remote site failures or network bottlenecks. This may lead to a complete breakdown in work. We therefore require an additional form of awareness:

(d) Awareness of the state of the communication channels.

An interesting observation which can be made is the fact that awareness of type (b) is basically conveying the notion of feedthrough [12]. Also the pace of feedthrough is directly proportional to the rate of providing awareness of type (c). In other words, we can infer the reasons changes happen by noticing the intermediate steps and the way changes happen. However, both awareness of type (b) and (c) will be negatively affected by network delays and lags.

Awareness of type (c) is not easy to manage especially when the web is used as an asynchronous environment. Some traditional groupware with shared workspaces record who has made the updates and when. Such temporal information is however hard to reconstruct at a distributed level. Even synchronous interaction will pose a similar problem in the event of delays over the communication channel.

3.5   Control

Due to the common focus on work, collaborative participants have to access the same data. Therefore some form of control is required to manage the shared data and the shared objects. This will determine the nature of the cooperation dealing with issues such as who can update what, where and when; who can see the changes and whether the changes can be noticed in a reasonable amount of time.

One of the most common control mechanisms is locking including explicit floor control policies [1,28] and implicit locking which is automatically applied when users attempt to access an object. In some systems additional protocols are built on top of the locking mechanisms, such as access rights or roles [21]. Users perform certain tasks depending on the roles they are assigned. Unlike access rights which normally impose a restriction on users functions, roles are more dynamic in nature.

Finally, certain applications do not provide any mechanism for locking, relying on participants using a social protocol to negotiate simultaneous access in a free-for-all situation. However such systems must usually include some form of mechanism to detect conflicts in order to automatically restore consistency or at least alert users.

4 What—architectural components of cooperative systems

The support for collaborative work has seen the development of architectures which present a number of interfaces for simultaneous interaction by multiple users. One of the main functions of cooperative architectures is the presentation and manipulation of shared information by a community of users. As we have discussed earlier in section 2, the separation between the application semantics and the user interface is acknowledged to be a desirable feature for a number of reasons.

Whereas in single-user applications, the logical separation is sometimes ignored to reduce the complexity and speed of development, in collaborative applications, logical separation is a necessity for supporting alternative views of the system for different participants. It is necessary to identify which elements of collaborative interfaces are shared between participants and which are different for each one. This logical separation is also essential when deciding where elements are placed in a networked environment. The web for instance, allows extensions or modifications at the server-end, client-end and the communication protocol, an issue we return to in section 6. Let us now consider how the Seeheim model can be mapped onto cooperative systems.

4.1 Presentation

The *presentation* component of collaborative applications must support alternative representations of the users' display. Shared information can be presented as a single view to all the participants (WYSIWIS systems) or it can be viewed differently by different users (multiple views). For instance, a user may view the data in tabular form while another may view it as a graph. Similarly, group members can have their own private view or they can also share views of the display. Some systems allow users to shift between a tightly coupled mode where they share the same presentation and a loosely coupled mode where users can view and scroll independently. In cases where the presentation or view is shared there must be some component of the systems to manage the shared information.

4.2 Shared data

The key element in any collaborative system is the shared application data. In the Seeheim model the *application interface* component manages the mapping between application data and the rest of the user interface. This is important as it emphasises the fact that the visualisation of information requires both the raw data and the semantics of the data — in a computational setting embedded in code. In the web setting this aspect is often embedded in CGI scripts which communicate with the user interface component (the web browser) using web pages and forms (dialogue level information). However, Java applets have opened up the possibility of including far more of the application semantics at the user interface itself.

4.3   Control

In section 3 we discussed why control mechanisms were necessary to avoid conflicts and maintain consistency. However, behavioural level control itself has be to driven by some lower level control that has to be maintained by the architecture, the most common mechanism for this being locking. In a single-user interface the *dialogue* component is responsible for determining the allowable order of user actions. The control component satisfies a similar role in that it controls the possible order of actions by different participants.

Traditional distributed systems view control as dealing with the problems of distribution and masking such problems from applications [25]. For instance, most distributed systems allow users to know who *can* access which objects but they do not allow users to know who *is* accessing a particular object at a particular moment. The control decisions are thus embedded into the system and hidden from the users. However, due to the dynamic requirements of CSCW applications, one of which is awareness, transparency is the wrong approach.

Because data is shared in collaborative applications, there is a clear distinction between the mechanisms for enabling distribution and sharing (e.g. ability to move an object) and the policies for managing those mechanisms (decisions about when and where the object should be moved to). Effective groupware systems therefore need separate low level control mechanisms to support those higher level control policies. Architectural level control may be either of a centralised or a peer-peer nature and can be supported by a separate server or be part of the shared data's infrastructure.

4.4   Notification

In collaborative work users operate simultaneously on the shared data — some users may view some part of the data while others may perform an update. MEAD [3] is an example groupware application which allows detailed level sharing of the scrollbars. Consequently, there is a need to maintain consistency between the users views and the underlying data. Without such consistency feedthrough is lost and users cease to have a common focus for collaborative activity.

In a single-user interface, similar issues arise whenever there are multiple views of the same underlying object. However, because there is ultimately a single locus of control (the user) this can be managed within the *dialogue* component. For example, the PAC architecture [6] has a hierarchy of PAC agents within the dialogue controller which manage consistency between views. In a distributed collaborative setting it is fundamentally more complex to maintain this consistency· because of the multiple loci of control.

Notification mechanisms address this problem by informing the presentation component of various updates so that the latter can replicate the changes on the users' display. A low level notification mechanism is therefore required to maintain feedthrough by informing the application of changes to the data and by keeping track of the activities of collaborative participants to support awareness.

5   Where—placement decisions

In the previous section we looked at some of the components of the Seeheim model and how they parallel components required of cooperative systems. However, we did not consider the fast-switch which allowed the application to communicate directly with the presentation component. This is because the fast-switch is not really part of the conceptual architecture (which is perhaps why it is so often omitted in descriptions of Seeheim), but instead is there as an optimisation. In principle all feedback could be routed through the dialogue component with more or less translation and interpretation on the way. The problem with this is that the dialogue component introduces a computational delay between application and presentation thus reducing the pace of feedback.

Arguably this is not a great problem today for single-user single-machine systems as it is often possible to perform several levels of processing and still achieve acceptable interactive response. However, for collaborative systems it is likely that shared data will be stored remotely from the user's workstation — instead of a computational delay we have a network delay. Whenever data is stored remotely from the interface feedback delays are bound to occur.

Unfortunately, we cannot simply add an extra component similar to the fast-switch as it too would have to sit remote from the data or remote from the interface. You can bypass computational components, but not space! The location of data and code (where) inevitably effects the pace of feedback (when).

One solution to this problem is to accept that semantic feedback will be delayed. Instead one can adopt a paradigm of mediated interaction with instant local feedback that the user's action has been recognised followed by subsequent semantic feedback when the effect has occurred remotely [7]. However, this will not be acceptable where user's demand direct manipulation interfaces similar to those for local single-user applications, in which case alternative solutions must be found.

5.1   Replication and Caching

Most solutions which aim at providing rapid feedback and increasing the availability of data involve some form of replication or caching (Figure 2). The objective is to bring the shared data closer to users.

Caches are merely temporary repositories and hold an ephemeral copy of the data at any instant. Each user's workstation therefore uses local copies of the shared data (Figure 2(*b*)). The actual shared data is held in a central repository. Because there is centralised control over the data, consistency can be easily maintained as each cache only needs to communicate with the central repository.

Replicas on the other hand, are equally valid full copies of the data which are stored locally. Replicas are more persistent than caches as they are the real data. However, it is more difficult to maintain data and interface consistency as replicas have to communicate between each other on a peer-to-peer basis. Replicas are synchronised by sending input from each workstation to each replica (Figure 2(*a*)). Consequently the multiple points of updates may lead to race conditions and potential data inconsistency. For example, if a user deletes a selected object in a WYSIWIS group drawing program while another user is changing the selection to a different object, inconsistent interfaces can result due to events arriving in a different order at each workstation.

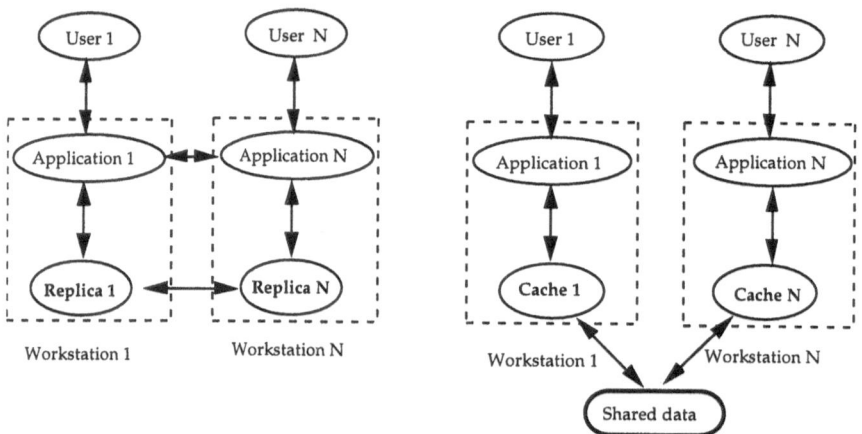

Figure 2: (a),   Replication; (b),   Caching..

In distributed systems, the traditional approach to replication has been transparency. The system avoids race condition by maintaining consistency among the different copies of the data via some complex synchronisation algorithms. In the event of inconsistencies, the solution is to *rollback* [27] the replica(s) and re-execute the events in temporal order. However, this policy is unacceptable in collaborative interfaces as display screens would already have been updated and alternatives based on transforming updates to prevent rollback have been developed [4].

5.2   Control

When rapid feedback is not the major concern, concurrency control mechanisms, such as locking or floor control can be applied to prevent race conditions altogether or tolerate race condition only in situations where users obtain locks or other large scale events [9]. However, real-time synchronous update may demand special-purpose algorithms.

All such mechanisms require meta-data, for example recording who has the lock on which object. This meta-data must itself be maintained and has similar issues as the real data. It can be maintained in a replicated fashion using complex distributed algorithms, or more commonly be maintained using a central server. When the data is stored centrally the same server may deal with both data and meta-data as is usually the case with traditional databases. However, it is also possible to use a separate locking server. For example, the UNIX file system has no in-built locking mechanism, instead applications request locks on remotely stored files from a special process, the lock daemon. Obviously where no off-the-shelf locking is available, or where the locking supplied is unsuitable, application developers are forced to use their own ad hoc locking mechanisms. This is usually the case with web-based cooperative applications.

5.3   Notification

Although feedback causes problems, feedthrough is even more difficult — no amount of careful placement of components can change the fact that the user making a change is a long way from other users who see the effects of the change. Happily, we have seen that feedthrough can usually be of a lower pace than feedback, hence ordinary network delays are usually acceptable. What is not acceptable is if changes made by one user are never reflected on other users' interfaces or only do so after a long delay — hence the need for notification mechanisms as discussed in the previous section.

Similar issues arise as for locking. If no notification service is provided then an ad hoc mechanism will be necessary, for example, individual clients may poll one another for changes. Alternatively, a notification service may be incorporated within the data-management infrastructure, for example, Lotus NSP [22] offers a generic data storage and notification server and ALV [19] supports distributed constraint maintenance between shared data and user views. Finally, a stand-alone notification server can be used.

Whichever notification alternative is used there will be meta-data concerning this: what objects are being managed, who wants to know about which object. This meta-data must again be stored in either a replicated or centralised fashion.

5.4   Different kinds of remoteness

In a single-user system, when accessing remote data using traditional client-server techniques, it is clear what we mean by local and remote. In a cooperative application we need to be more careful as for each user the definition is different as their own machine is local, but data stored or updated on another user's machine is just as remote. So, if semantic feedback relies on data held at another user's machine, the feedback delays will be as great as for centrally held data, perhaps greater as central servers may have better networks response.

This gets even more complicated when using the web as an infrastructure. Each user may be accessing several web servers as well as other central servers such as databases. To an extent the web makes the physical location of data unimportant, except insofar as the location affects response time. However, the physical location is very important when using Java applets. The security mechanisms of Java only allow the applet to access Internet services lodged on the same machine as the web server that supplied the applet.

In summary for the web we have four kinds of 'remote' application:

  (i) Another user's client,
  (ii) the web server for the current page,
  (iii) a different server on the same machine as the current web server,
  (iv) server on a different machine.

Thus for the web placement decisions do not stop at local vs. remote, or even client vs. server. The decision about where server software is placed is intimately related to the techniques used to implement client software.

6   When—moving information and code

In a networked environment it is common for data to be dynamically moved or copied in order to improve performance. Also some distributed infrastructures support the migration of objects or code between machines. We will now discuss the various mobility aspects of data and code individually in preparation for considering their interaction in the next section.

6.1   Moving data

Consider caching—the 'golden' copy of the data is stored remotely, but a copy is made locally to speed feedback. The fact that data can be copied over networks means that in distributed collaborative applications, the place where shared data is permanently stored is not necessarily the same place as it (or a copy of it) is used. Using the simple local/remote distinction we can classify both the permanent storage place and the place of use giving rise to the matrix in Figure 3.

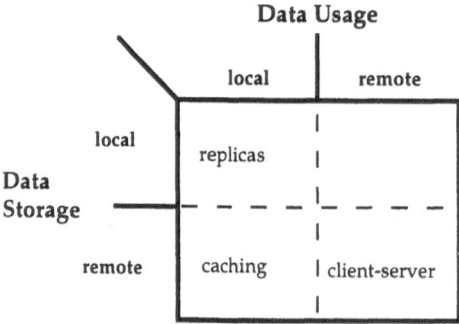

Figure 3: Data Usage v/s Data Storage.

This matrix clearly shows the distinction between caching, where the local copy of the data is ephemeral and the 'real' data is central, compared with replication, where the local data is a more persistent. Where data is held and used remotely we have traditional client-server interfaces. Only the information necessary to generate the interface presentation of the data is transmitted to the user's local machine. Notice the empty location. In a groupware context, it is highly unlikely to have a scenario where the data is held locally and yet is used or processed remotely. However, such a situation does exist for non-groupware solutions, for example super computers.

6.2   Moving code

In a collaborative distributed interface we must also decide where the code for different architectural components resides. In particular, for web-based systems application specific code may run at the server-end (CGI scripts or independently running servers) or at the client-end (applets and helpers or browser plug-ins [30]). Notice again that in some cases (e.g. CGI scripts) the code is stored remotely, in others (e.g. helpers) it is stored locally. In the case of both CGI scripts and helpers the code executes in the same place as it is stored. However, in the case of Java applets remotely stored code is executed locally. This is a form of migration as is found in many object-based distributed systems.

Code execution and code storage are key architectural options. It is essential to decide where the code gets executed for efficiency reasons in order to provide rapid feedback. Similarly, the rate at which changes to the code occur and the ease of distributing those changes (a form of feedthrough) are affected by where the code is stored.

Using these two axes the matrix in Figure 4 classifies code options using a similar matrix as that we had for data.

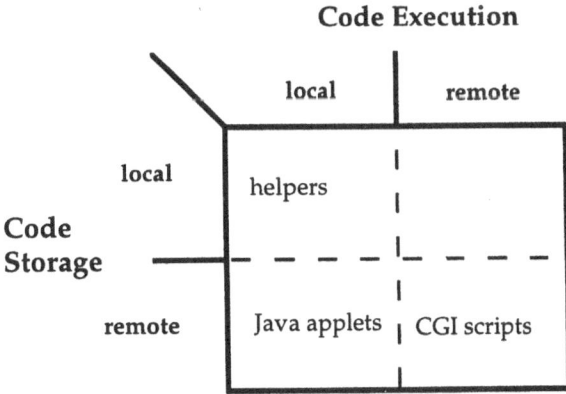

Figure 4:   Code Usage v/s Code Storage.

As with the data matrix we find a gap in Figure 4. The web does not cater for locally stored code to be executed at the server end and it seems an unlikely option for groupware systems in general. However, in some client-server database applications, quite complex SQL queries can be sent to the server and which may be regarded as a form of locally stored code with SQL queries being executed remotely.

7   World Wide Web—narrowing down the options

We saw that shared data can be stored and used either locally or remotely (Figure 3). Similarly, code can be stored at the client-end (locally) or at the server-end (remotely) and the same applies to code execution (Figure 4). So, for each component of a collaborative application we need to decide where in the respective matrices the code and data for that component resides.

At first this looks as though we have 16 different architectural options to consider for every component as there are 4 possibilities for both code and data. In fact it is not this bad! For general distributed collaborative applications and in particular for the web we can narrow down the potential architectural options.

From the matrices in Figures 3 and 4, we noted that in each there was a gap which appears an unreasonable option for any collaborative application. Thus there are only 3 real possibilities for code and data and at most 3×3=9 combinations.

If we also look at the combinations of code and data the possibilities further reduce. Although data and code can be <u>stored</u> in different places, the code must execute where the data is used. The data and code matrix must 'agree' in the location of execution and use (Figure 5). Therefore there is only one possibility for remote execution/use and 4 possibilities (2x2) for local execution/use. We'll look at the former and latter in turn.

7.1   Remote execution and use

The only possibility for remote execution and use in a collaborative application is where both code and data are stored, used and executed remotely (although each could conceivably be stored at different remote sites only coming together for execution/use). A component of this kind could be implemented in several ways.

It may be a traditional transaction-based client/server application using CGI scripts for central processing of transactions. In fact, many web-based repositories are of this form, for example BSCW [2]. Alternatively it may be achieved using a specialised central server as is the case with most chat-based web applications [30].

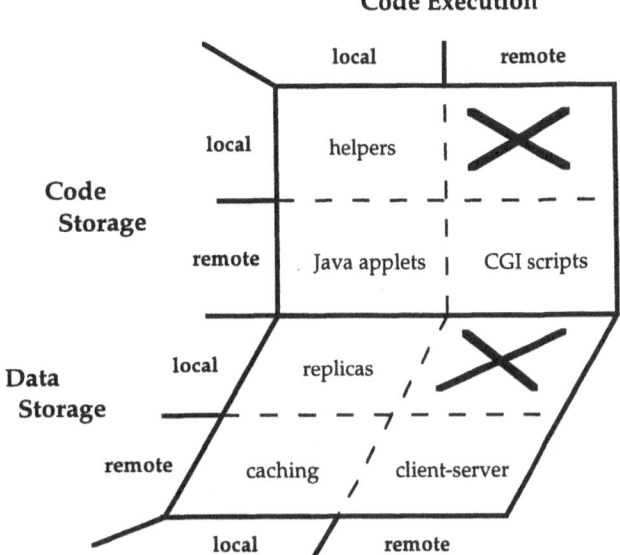

Figure 5: *Linked matrices*

Note that these two implementation options differ principally in the pace of cooperative interaction they enable.

Local execution and use – applet restrictions

We had 4 storage options for code and data which is locally executed:

    (a) code local–data local
    (b) code local–data remote
    (c) code remote–data local
    (d) code remote–data remote

In both (a) and (b) we have a helper or stand-alone application using caching or replication to handle shared data. Given the limited ability of most web servers to allow uploading of documents, it is likely that (b) will use a non-web based data base or bespoke server. In both cases the web may act as a way of locating shared resources and initiating a specialised collaborative application, but is not intrinsic to the running application.

For cases (c) and (d) we are principally considering code in the form of Java applets (although other forms of downloaded scripts are available). The security limitations of Java applets mean that they can not access files stored on the user's local machine. This means they cannot operate in mode (c) with permanently locally stored data. Furthermore as they can only connect to a server on the same machine as the web server they were downloaded from, they cannot enter into peer–peer communication (except by using a central switchboard server). Thus they cannot even operate using locally held replicas. <u>All</u> feedthrough must be through a central server at the same site as the web server.

This effectively leaves only case (d) as a truly web-based option and even then only when using a data repository situated at the same location as the applet is stored.

8   Summary

Architectures have been influential within single-user interface design for both construction and conceptualisation. An examination of significant behavioural issues for cooperative interfaces allowed us to identify key components which roughly correspond to those in traditional single-user models. However, the placement of these components within a distributed system leads to conflicts between feedback and consistency. This is commonly dealt with by using caching or replication, both of which bring the shared data 'closer' to the user.

It is now common for web applications to use Java applets to download code to users' own machines. That is code and data may each have a permanent location where they are stored and an ephemeral location where they are executed or used. The resulting storage/use matrix for data and storage/execution matrix for code can be used to examine the placement of each part of a cooperative system.

At first there appear to be many possible combinations of data and code placement within these matrices, but an examination of their interaction within distributed environments in general and the web in particular narrows this down considerably leaving only 2 'real' web-based placement options.

The behavioural and component analysis brought out the importance of various kinds of meta-data, for locking, consistency maintenance and feedthrough. Of particular importance are the notification mechanisms which enable an appropriate pace of feedthrough. The issues surrounding the design options for notification services are too complex to deal with in this paper and are the focus of on-going work.

References

[1] Begeman, M., Cook, P., Ellis, C., Graf, M., Rein, G. and Smith, T. (1986) Project Nick: meetings augmentation and analysis. In *Proceedings of CSCW'86* (Austin, Texas), ACM Press.

[2] Bentley, R., Horstmann, T., Sikkel, K. and Trevor, J. (1996) The BSCW Shared Workspace System. In *ERCIM workshop on CSCW and the Web* (Sankt Augustin, Germany), GMD/FIT.

[3] Bentley, R. (1994) Supporting Multi-User Interface Development for Cooperative Systems. *Ph.D. Thesis, University of Lancaster, UK.*

[4] Bentley, R., Rodden, T., Sawyer, P. and Sommerville, I. (1994) Architectural support for cooperative multi-user interfaces. In *IEEE COMPUTER special issue on CSCW*, **27**(5), pp 37-46.

[5] Conklin, J. and Bergman, L.M. (1989) gIBIS: A Tool for Exploratory Policy Discussion. In *Journal of American Society for Information Science* (May), pp 200-213.

[6] Coutaz, J. (1987) PAC, An Object Oriented Model For Dialog Design. In *Human-Computer Interaction - INTERACT '87*, Eds. H.J. Bullinger and B. Shackel, pp 431-436.

[7] Dix, A.J. (1995) Cooperation without (reliable) Communication: Interfaces for Mobile Applications. In *Distributed Systems Engineering*, **2**(3), pp 171–181.

[8] Dix, A.J. (1994) Computer-supported cooperative work — a framework. In *Design Issues in CSCW*, Eds. D. Rosenburg and C. Hutchison, Springer-Verlag, pp 9-26.

[9] Dix, A.J., Finlay, J., Abowd, G., Beale, R. (1993) *Human-Computer Interaction*, Prentice Hall.

[10] Dix, A.J. (1992) Pace and interaction. In *Proceedings of HCI'92: People and Computers VII*, (Sept. York) Cambridge University Press, pp 193-208.

[11] Dix, A.J. (1987) The Myth of the Infinitely Fast Machine. In *Proceedings of the Third Conference of the BCS HCI SIG: People and Computers III*, Cambridge University Press, pp 215-228.

[12] Dix, A. (1996) Challenges and Perspectives for Cooperative Work on the Web. In *ERCIM workshop on CSCW and the Web* (Sankt Augustin, Germany), GMD/FIT.

[13] Dix, A. (1994) Que sera sera — The problem of the future perfect in open and cooperative systems. In *Proceedings of HCI'94: People and Computers IX*, (Glasgow) Cambridge University Press, pp 397-408.

[14] Dix, A., Ramduny, D., & Wilkinson, J. (1996) Long-Term Interaction: Learning the 4Rs. In *CHI'96 Conference Companion Proceedings: Human Factors In computing Systems* (Apr. Vancouver, British Columbia), ACM Press, pp 169-170.

[15] Dix, A., Ramduny, D., & Wilkinson, J. (1995) Interruptions, Deadlines and Reminders: Investigations into the Flow of Cooperative Work. *RR9509, University of Huddersfield*, available as: <http://www.hud.ac.uk/schools/comp+maths/research/reports/RR9509.html>.

[16] Gram, C. and Cockton, G. editors (1996) Design Principles for Interactive Software, *Chapman & Hall, UK*.

[17] Gray, P., England, D. and McGowan, S. (1994) XUAN: Enhancing UAN to Capture Temporal Relationships among Actions. In *Proceedings of HCI'94: People and Computers IX,* (Glasgow) Cambridge University Press, pp 301-312.

[18] Johnson, C. and Gray, P. editors (1995) Workshop on Temporal Aspects of Usability. In *SIGCHI Bulletin*, **28**(2).

[19] Hill, R.D., Brinck, T., Rohall, S.L., Patterson, J.F. and Wilner, W. (1994) The Rendezvous architecture and language for constructing multi-user applications. In *ACM Transactions on Computer-Human Interaction*, **1**(2), pp 81-125.

[20] Lauwers, J.C. and Lantz, K.A. (1990) Collaboration Awareness in support of Collaboration Transparency: Requirements for the next generation of shared window systems. In *CHI'90 Conference Proceedings: Human Factors In computing Systems* (Apr. Seattle, Washington), ACM Press, pp 303-311.

[21] Leland, M.D.P., Fish, R.S. and Kraut, R.E. (1988) Collaborative document production using quilt. In *Proceedings of CSCW'88* (Sept. Portland, Oregon), ACM Press, New York, pp 206-215.

[22] Patterson, J.F. Day, M. and Kucan, J. (1996) Notification Servers for Synchronous Groupware. In *Proceedings of CSCW'96* (Nov. Boston, Massachusetts), ACM Press, pp 122-129.

[23] Pfaff, G. and Hagen P.J.W., editors (1985) Seeheim Workshop on User Interface Management Systems, *Springer-Verlag, Berlin*.

[24] Rada, R. (1995) Interactive Media, *Springer-Verlag, New York*.

[25] Rodden, T. and Blair, B. (1991) CSCW and Distributed Systems: The problem of Control. In *Proceedings of the second European Conference on CSCW,* (Bannon, L. Robinson, M. and Schmidt, K. eds).

[26] Rouncefield, M., Hughes, J.A., Rodden, T., & Viller S. (1994) Working with "Constant Interruption" CSCW and the Small Office. In *Proceedings of CSCW'94* (Oct. Chapel Hill, North Carolina), ACM Press, pp 275-287.

[27] Satyanarayanan, M., Kistler, J.J., Kumar, P., Okasaki, M.E., Siegel, E.H. and Steere, D.C. (1990) Coda: a highly available file system for a distributed workstation environment. In *IEEE Transactions Computers*, **39**(4), pp 447-459.

[28] Stefik, M., Bobrow, D.G., Foster, G., Lanning S. and Tatar, D. (1987) WYSIWIS revisited" early experiences with multiuser interfaces. In *ACM Transactions on Office Information Systems*, **5**(2), pp 147-167.

[29] UIMS (1992) The UIMS tool developers workshop: A metamodel for the runtime architecture of an interactive system. In *SIGCHI Bulletin*, **24**(1), pp 32-37.

[30] Welie, V.M. and Eliëns, A. (1996) Chatting on the Web. In ERCIM workshop on CSCW and the Web (Sankt Augustin, Germany), GMD/FIT.

BUILD-IT: a computer vision-based interaction technique for a planning tool

M. Rauterberg[1], M. Fjeld[1], H. Krueger[1], M. Bichsel[2], U. Leonhardt[2] & M. Meier[2]

[1]Institute for Hygiene and Applied Physiology (IHA)

[2]Institute of Construction and Design Methods (IKB)
Swiss Federal Institute of Technology (ETH)
Clausiusstrasse 25, CH-8092 Zurich, SWITZERLAND
http://www.ifap.bepr.ethz.ch/~rauter/science.html

In this article we wish to show a method that goes beyond the established approaches of human-computer interaction. We first bring a serious critique of traditional interface types, showing their major drawbacks and limitations. Promising alternatives are offered by Virtual (or: immersive) Reality (VR) and by Augmented Reality (AR). The AR design strategy enables humans to behave in a nearly natural way. Natural interaction means human actions in the real world with other humans and/or with real world objects. Guided by the basic constraints of natural interaction, we derive a set of recommendations for the next generation of user interfaces: the *Natural User Interface* (NUI). Our approach to NUIs is discussed in the form of a general framework followed by a prototype. The prototype tool builds on video-based interaction, and supports construction and plant layout. A first empirical evaluation is briefly presented.

Keywords: augmented reality, natural user interface, video based interaction, computer aided design

1   Introduction

The introduction of computers in the work place has had a tremendous impact on task solving methods in that area. Mouse based and graphical displays are everywhere, the desktop workstations define the frontier between digital (computer) and analogue ('real') worlds. We spend a lot of time and energy transferring information between such worlds. This effort could be reduced by better integrating the virtual world of the computer with the real world of the user and vice versa.

In the past, several dialogue techniques were developed and are now in use. The following dialogue techniques and objects can be distinguished: command language, function key, menu selection, iconic, and window [15]. These five essential terms can be cast into three different *interaction styles:*

- *Command language:* This interaction style (including action codes and softkeys) is one of the oldest way of interacting with a computer.

Pros: In the command mode the user has a maximum of direct access to all available functions and operations.

Cons: The user has no permanent feedback of all currently available function points.

- *Menu selection:* This includes rigid menu structures, pop-up and pull-down menus, fill-in forms etc. It is characterised by dual usage of the function keys. They support dialogue management as well as application functionality.

Pros: All available functions are represented by partly or fully visible interaction points.

Cons: Finding a function point deeper in the menu hierarchies is cumbersome.

- *Direct manipulation*: This type of interaction only took on weight as the bit mapped graphical displays were introduced. The development of this interaction style is based on the desktop metaphor, assuming that realistic depiction of the work environment (i.e. the desk with its files, waste-paper basket etc.) helps users adjust to the virtual world of electronic objects.

Pros: All functions are continuously represented by visible interaction points (e.g. mouse sensitive areas). The activation of intended functions can be achieved by directly pointing to their visible representations.

Cons: Direct manipulation interfaces have difficulty handling variables, or distinguishing the depiction of an individual element from a representation of a set or class of elements.

In all these traditional interaction styles the user cannot combine real world and virtual objects within the *same* interface space. Nor do they incorporate the human hands' enormous potential for interaction with real and virtual objects. This aspect was one of the basic incitements to develop data gloves and data suits. Users equipped with such artefacts can interact in an immersive, virtual reality (VR) system. Another reason to realise VR systems, was the emergence of the of head mounted displays with 3D output capabilities . However, VR systems are still subject to serious, inherent limitations, such as:

- the lack of tactile and touch information, leading to a mismatch with the proprioceptive feedback. Special techniques are proposed to overcome this problem [4].
- the lack of depth perception, due to visual displays only generating 2D output. Many informational concepts offer a remake of the 3D impression by superimposing 2D pictures [12].
- a consistent delay in the user-computer control loop, often yielding severe problems with reference to the perceptual stability of the ear vestibular apparatus [5].
- an influence from communication on social interaction. A shared sound space, as well as a shared real social world, stimulates humans to mutual interaction [11].

The advantage, but at the same time disadvantage of immersive VR, is the necessity to put the user into a fully modelled, virtual world. Bringing users into the computer world, ignores their on-going interaction with the real world, because mixing of real and virtual objects is not yet possible. Nevertheless, humans are most of the time part of a real world where they interact with real objects and humans.

To overcome the drawbacks of immersive VR, the concept of *Augmented Reality* (AR) [18] was introduced. This approach is promising because it incorporates fundamental human skills: interaction with real world subjects and objects. Hence, the AR design strategy enables humans to behave in a nearly natural way; we call this way natural interaction.

Guided by the AR approach *and* the basic constraints of natural interaction, we derive a set of recommendations for the next generation of user interfaces: the *Natural User Interface* (NUI). The NUI approach is discussed in form of a general framework and in the form of a prototype. The prototype tool builds on video-based interaction, and supports construction and plant layout. A first empirical evaluation will be briefly presented.

2 Behaviour in the Real World

Interaction with real world objects is constrained by the laws of physics (e.g. matter, energy, mechanics, heat, light, electricity and sound). In a more or less similar way, human interaction is based on social and cultural norms.

Task related activities has been a topic in various behavioural approaches. Mackenzie [8] introduced prehensile behaviour as "... the application of functionally effective forces by the hand to an object for a task, given numerous constraints." Sanders [14] proposed certain classes of motor movements: "(1) *Discrete movements* involve a single reaching movement to a stationary target, such as reaching for a control or pointing to a word on a computer screen. Discrete movements can be made with or without visual control. (2) *Repetitive movements* involve a repetition of a single movement to a stationary target or targets. Examples include hammering a nail or tapping a cursor on a computer keyboard. (3) *Sequential movements* involve discrete movements to a number of stationary targets regularly or irregularly spaced. Examples include typewriting or reaching for parts in various stock bins. (4) *Continuous movements* involve movements that require muscular control adjustments of some degree during the movement, as in operating the steering wheel of a car or guiding a piece of wood through a band saw. (5) *Static positioning* consists of maintaining a specific position of a body member for a period of time. Strictly speaking, this is not a movement, but rather the absence of movement. Examples include holding a part in one hand while soldering, or holding a needle to thread it".

In the context of this article we are primarily interested in purposeful motor activities. These activities are executed by a person to achieve some goal (in contrast to erroneous or exploratory behaviour). Actions (e.g. motor based movements) will be functionally, but not anatomically nor mechanically defined. The catching of a ball could be carried out by either the left or the right hand, the starting position of the approach and the catching position of the ball might change from one reach to the next, and no two reaching trajectories will look exactly alike. However, these movements are classified as the same action because they share the same function.

Following the argumentation of Fitzmaurice, Ishii and Buxton [7] a grasp-based user interface has the following advantages:

- it encourages two handed interactions
- shifts to more specialised, context sensitive input devices
- allows for more parallel input specification by the user
- leverages off of our well developed skills ... for physical object manipulations
- externalises traditionally internal computer representations
- facilitates interactions by making interface elements more 'direct' and more 'manipulable' by using physical artefacts
- affords multi-person, collaborative use.

Summarising the above discussion about real world behaviour, we come to the following design recommendation: To enhance human computer interaction, users must be able to behave in a *natural way*, bringing into action all of their body parts (e.g. hands, arms, face, head and voice). To interpret all of these expressions we need very powerful and intelligent pattern recognition techniques.

3   A Framework for Natural User Interfaces (NUI)

Augmented Reality (AR) recognises that people are used to the real world, which strictly cannot be reproduced by a computer. AR is based on the real world, augmented by computer characteristics. It is the general design strategy behind "Natural User Interfaces" (NUI) [13].

A NUI based system supports the fusion of real and virtual objects. It understands visual, acoustic and other human input forms. It also recognises physical objects and human actions like speech and hand writing in a natural way. Its output is based on pattern projection such as video, holography, speech synthesis and 3D audio strips. NUI necessarily implies inter-referential I/O [6], meaning that the same modality is used for input and output. Hence, a projected item can be referred directly by the user as part of his or her non-verbal input behaviour. Figure 1 gives an overview of what a NUI based system could look like.

The spatial position of the user is monitored by one or more cameras. This could also create a stereoscopic picture for potential video conference partners. Speech and sound is recorded by several microphones, enabling the system to maintain an internal 3D user model. From above, a close-up camera permanently records the state of the user activity taking place in the horizontal working area. In this very area, virtual and physical objects are fully integrated.

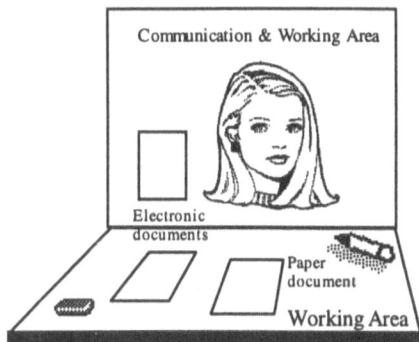

Figure 1: Architecture of a Natural User Interface.

The set-up of several parallel input channels makes it possible to communicate multiple views to remote partners, such as a 3D face view [17], and a view of shared work objects [20]. Multimedia output is provided by a) the vertical display, b) the projection device illuminating the working area, and c) a multichannel audio system. Free space in the communication area can be used for other work (see Figure 1). Of course, traditional I/O devices can be added on. As required by Tognazzini [16], NUIs are multimodal, so users are allowed to (re-)choose their personal and appropriate interaction style at any moment.

Since humans often and easily manipulate objects in the real world with their hands, they have a natural desire to bring in this faculty when interacting with computers. NUIs allow users to interact with real and virtual objects on the working area in a 'literally' direct manipulative way. Since the working area is basically horizontal, the user can place real objects onto its surface. So there is a direct mapping of the real, user manipulated object onto its corresponding virtual object. We can actually say that perception and action space coincide, which is a powerful design criterion, discovered and empirically validated by Rauterberg [10].

4   The prototype "Build-it"

In a first step, we designed a system primarily based on the concept of NUIs. However, we did not support the communication aspects of a computer based, co-operative work environment. As our task context, we chose that of planning activities for plant design. A prototype system, called "BUILD-IT", was realised. This is an application that supports engineers in designing assembly lines and building plants. The realised design room (see Figure 2) enables users, grouped around a table, to interact in a space of virtual and real world objects. The vertical working area in the background of Figure 2, gives a side view of the plant. In the horizontal working area there are several views where the users can select and manipulate objects.

Figure 2: The design room of BUILD-IT.

The hardware comprises seven components:
- A table with a white surface is used as horizontal working area.
- A white projection screen provides the vertical working area.
- An ASK 960 high resolution LCD projector projects the horizontal views vertically onto the table.
- An ASK 860 high resolution LCD projector projects the vertical view horizontally onto the projection screen.
- A CCD camera with a resolution of 752(H) by 582(V) pixels looks vertically down to the table.
- A brick, size 3cm x 2cm x 2cm, is the physical interaction device (the universal interaction handler).
- A low-cost Silicon Graphics Indy (IP22 R4600 133MHz processor and standard Audio-Video Board) provides the computing power for digitising the video signal coming from the camera, analysing the user interactions on the table, and rendering the interaction result in the two views.

The software consists of two independent processes communicating via socket connection:

- A real time process for analysis of the video images. This process extracts and interprets contours of moving objects [2, 3], and determines the position and orientation of the universal interaction handler (the brick).
- An application built upon the multi-media framework MET++ [1]. Based on the position and orientation of the interaction handler, it interprets user actions. It modifies a virtual scenario, and renders the above (and side) view of the new scenario via the vertical (and horizontal) projector (Figure 2).

The application is designed to support providers of assembly lines and plants in the early design processes. It can read and render arbitrary CAD models of machines in VRML format. The input of a 3D model of the virtual objects is realised by connecting BUILD-IT with the CAD-System CATIA. Thus, the original CAD-models were imported into BUILD-IT.

Geometry is not the single aspect of product data. There is a growing need to interact in other dimensions, like cost, configurations and variants. Therefore, it will be possible to send and receive additional metadata from BUILD-IT.

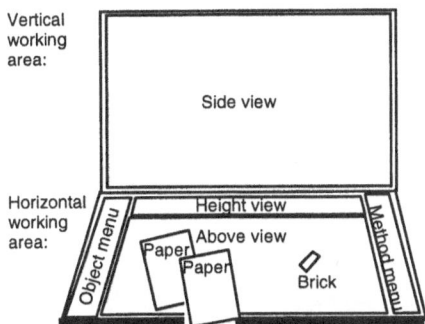

Figure 3:(a) The two working areas and their views. (b) The object menu (white), the above view (grey), and the user hand moving the interaction handler (the brick).

BUILD-IT currently features following user (inter-) actions (Figures 3, 4, 5):

- Selection of a virtual object (e.g. a specific machine) in a 'virtual machine store' by placing the interaction handler onto the projected image of the machine in the object menu.
- Positioning of a machine in the virtual plant by moving the interaction handler to the preferred position in the above view of the plant layout.
- Rotation of a machine is supported through a coupling of the machine and brick orientation.
- Fixing the machine by covering the surface of the interaction handler with the hand and removing it.

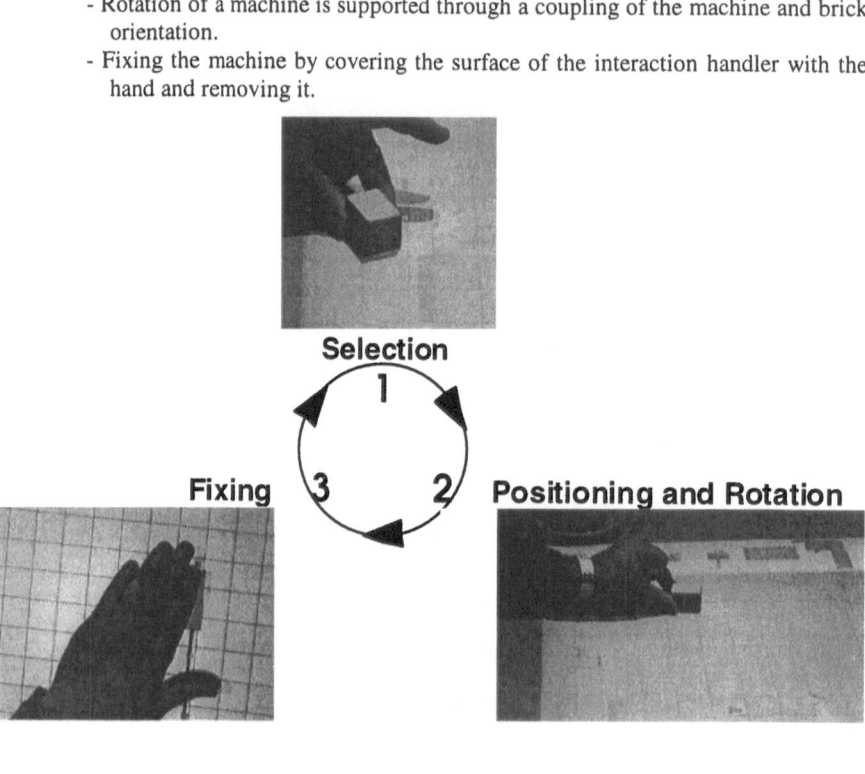

Figure 4: This cycle gives the three basic steps for user manipulations with the interaction handler (the brick).

- Re-selection of a machine by placing the interaction handler onto the specific machine in the above view.
- Deleting the machine by moving it back into the object menu (the virtual machine store).
- Printing of the views, offered by a method menu icon.
- Saving of the working area contents, also offered by a method menu icon.
- Modification of object size and height by operators in the method menu applied on objects in the above view.
- Direct modification of object altitude in the height view.
- Scrolling of above view and menus.

    - Automatic grouping of two or more objects along predefined contact lines within the above view.

In the above view (Figure 3b) the user is permanently given a look from far above, giving the impression of a 2D situation. The camera is picked up in the method menu and manipulated like any other virtual object (Figure 5a).

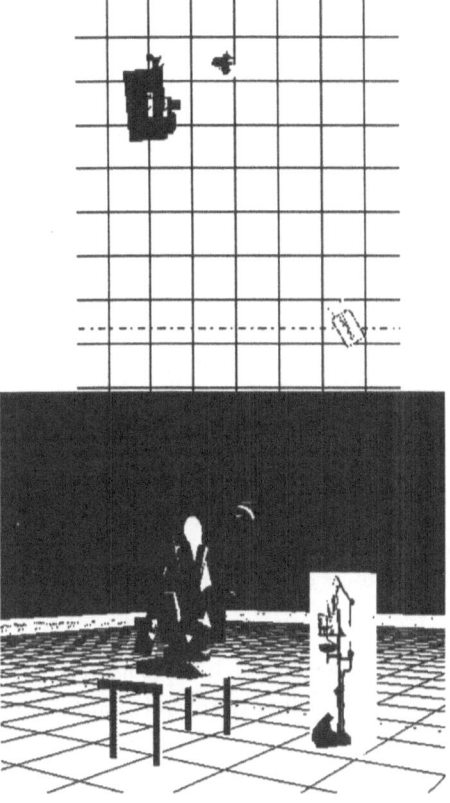

Figure 5: a) The above view showing the position of the camera and the robot etc. b) Side view perspective of the robot etc. as seen with the same camera setting.

In the side view (Figure 5b) a perspective is offered that gives the user an impression of a virtual human looking at a real situation. As the user moves the camera around, a real time update of the side view takes place.

5   First empirical evaluation

The system has been empirically tested with managers and engineers from companies producing assembly lines and plants. These tests showed that the system is intuitive and enjoyable to use as well as easy to learn. Most persons were able to assemble virtual plants after only 30 seconds of introduction to the system.

Some typical user comments were:
- The concept phase is especially important in plant design since the customer must be involved in a direct manner. Often, partners using different languages sit at the same table. This novel interaction technique will be a means for completing this phase efficiently and almost perfectly.
- This is a general improvement of the interface to the customer, in the offering phase as well as during the project, especially in simultaneous engineering projects.
- A usage of the novel interaction technique will lead to a simplification, acceleration, and reduction of the iterative steps in the start-up and concept phase of a plant construction project.

6   Conclusion

One of the most interesting benefits of a NUI-based interface is the possibility to combine real and virtual objects in the same interaction space [7, 16, 19]. Taking this advantage even further, we will implement two or three interaction handlers, allowing simultaneous interaction of several users grouped at one single table.

With this new interaction approach, customers whether CAD experts or not, can equally take part in discussions and management of complex 3D objects. Products and technical descriptions can easily be presented, and new requirements are realised and displayed within short time. The virtual camera allows a walk-through of the designed plant. Such inspection tours can give invaluable information about a complex system.

In the near future, one could imagine a direct, NUI-based information flow between customers and large product databases. It is conceivable that users wanting to change one detail of a machine, will have several configuration options presented on their table. As soon as one has been selected, the exact configuration cost will be calculated and displayed.

References

[1] Ackermann P: Developing Object-Oriented Multimedia Software Based on the MET++ Application Framework. Heidelberg: dpunkt Verlag für digitale Technologie, 1996.

[2] Bichsel M: Illumination Invariant Segmentation of Simply Connected Moving Objects. 5th British Machine Vision Conference, University of York, UK, September 13-16, 1994, pp. 459-468.

[3] Bichsel M: Segmenting Simply Connected Moving Objects in a Static Scene. Transactions on Pattern Recognition and Machine Intelligence (PAMI), Vol. 16, No. 11, Nov. 1994, pp. 1138-1142.

[4] CyberTouch, Virtual Technologies Inc., 2175 Park Boulevard, Palo Alto, CA.

[5] DIVE Laboratories Inc: Health and HMDs. On URL: http://www.divelabs.com /deeper.html

[6] Draper S: Display Managers as the Basis for User-Machine Communication. In Norman D, Draper S (eds.) User Centered System Design. Lawrence Erlbaum, 1986, pp. 339-352.

[7] Fitzmaurice G, Ishii H, Buxton W: Bricks: Laying the Foundations for Graspable User Interfaces. In Proc. of the CHI '95, 1995, pp. 442-449.

[8] MacKenzie C, Iberall T: The grasping hand. Elsevier, 1994.

[9] Newman W, Wellner P: A Desk Supporting Computer-base Interaction with Paper Documents. In Proc. of the CHI '92, 1992, pp. 587-592.

[10] Rauterberg M., Über die Quantifizierung software-ergonomischer Richtlinien. PhD Thesis, University of Zurich, 1995.

[11] Rauterberg M, Dätwyler M, Sperisen M: From Competition to Collaboration through a Shared Social Space. In: Proc. of East–West Intern. Conf. on Human–Computer Interaction (EWHCI '95), 1995, pp. 94-101.

[12] Rauterberg M, Szabo K: A Design Concept for N-dimensional User Interfaces. In Proc. of 4th Intern. Conf. INTERFACE to Real & Virtual Worlds, 1995, pp. 467-477.

[13] Rauterberg M, Steiger P: Pattern recognition as a key technology for the next generation of user interfaces. In Proc. of IEEE International Conference on Systems, Man and Cybernetics--SMC'96 (Vol. 4, IEEE Catalog Number: 96CH35929, pp. 2805-2810). Piscataway: IEEE.

[14] Sanders M, McCormick E: Human Factors in Engineering and Design. McGraw Hill, 1993.

[15] Shneiderman B: Designing the User Interface. Addison-Wesley, Reading MA, 1987.

[16] Tognazzini B: Tog on Software Design. Addison-Wesley, Reading MA, 1996.

[17] Watts L, Monk A: Remote assistance: a view of the work and a view of the face?. In Proc. of the CHI'96 Companion, 1996, pp. 101-102.

[18] Wellner P, Mackay W, Gold R: Computer-Augmented Environments: Back to the Real World. Communications of the ACM, 36(7), 1993, pp. 24-26.

[19] Wellner P: Interacting with Paper on the Digital Desk. Communications of the ACM, 36(7), 1993, pp. 87-96.

[20] Whittaker S: Rethinking video as a technology for interpersonal communications: theory and design implications. Intern. Journal of Human-Computer Studies, 42, 1995, pp. 501-529.

Formally Comparing and Informing Notation Design

C. R. Roast

Computing Research Centre,
Sheffield Hallam University
Sheffield, S11 8HD, UK.
Telephone: +44 (0)114 235 3768
Fax: +44 (0)114 235 3161
Email: C.R.Roast@shu.ac.uk

This paper uses the analytic framework of cognitive dimensions to provide formal interpretations of dimensions for appraising the suitability of interactive systems for particular tasks. The framework also provides an effective terminology to support a wide range of assessments including interface evaluation, and the resistance of notations to modification. We propose that interface design can benefit from interpreting cognitive dimensions as tools for assessing software characteristics such as usability and modifiability. Our interpretation of these dimensions has the benefits of being formal and at the same time yielding practical measures and guidelines for assessment.
In this paper our formalisation of cognitive dimensions examines and illustrates the dimensions of `viscosity' --- resistance to change. We demonstrate the appropriateness of the measures developed as a means of assessing notational resistance to change and the general results that their formalization enables.

Keywords: Cognitive Dimensions, Formal Methods, Notations, Programming

1   Introduction

The design of interactive system is complicated by the requirements for such systems being inadequately expressed. Numerous techniques have been developed to alleviate the complexities of effective interface design. Here we build upon a strand of this work which is concerned with characterising user interface requirements. Employing formal representations has a number of potential benefits: it provides a precise representation that can focus discussion and negotiation, tools and techniques can be employed to analyse a formal design priorto implementation and empirical evaluation,and design tools and techniques may directly feed off such representations.

In this paper we are concerned with the first two of these benefits, with the aim of bridging the gap between usability, as a poorly expressed requirement, and precise design representations, as necessitated by the eventual system. In some cases this has involved developing enhanced system models that reflect inherent usability requirements [3, 21, 24], while in others explicit models of the user (or task) have been formally combined with system representations [1, 10, 4]. Building upon the former of these we investigate the possible formalisation of the broad-brush cognitive perspective upon interaction, offered by cognitive dimensions [8], in terms of generic interactive system properties. An analytical framework incorporating formal interpretations of some of the cognitive dimensions has been developed and applied to systems ranging from individual dialogue boxes to programming environments [22, 23].

The effective use of a wide range of interactive systems is largely dependent upon the characteristics of the notations made available to users and the facilities provided to interrogate and manipulate them. The specific focus of this paper is the investigation of how easily alternative environments enable the manipulation of notations. In terms of cognitive dimensions, the resistance to change embodied by a system is termed *viscosity*. Two alternative notions of viscosity are formally characterised in terms of a common under-pinning design representation, each provides a comparative measure for ease of change. First, we illustrate the application of these two measures, demonstrating how they can inform the use of notations and tools used to manipulate them. Second, the formal treatment of these measures enables their application a generic level independent of specific design details. We illustrate this generic use of the measures in assessing hybrid tools.

The remainder of this paper is organised as follows: section two describes the psychologically rich informal notation of cognitive dimensions.
Section three outlines and illustrates our system oriented interpretation for cognitive dimensions. Section four details the application of our the framework by means of a case study based on a program development environment.Section five considers the same measures applied to a generic class of systems, term hybrid tools.

2   Cognitive Dimensions & Viscosity

Cognitive dimensions [8] have been developed as psychologically motivated metrics for a wide range of interactive devices that focus upon factors central to successful use.

It is proposed that the dimensions provide effective (and efficient) support for interface evaluation within a variety of contexts [9].
However the existing treatments of cognitive dimensions have largely been informal and anecdotal [7, 12, 27].

The main focus of this paper is one type of cognitive dimension known as ``viscosity'' which, as the metaphor suggests, concerns the ease with which change can be achieved while using a particular interactive system or medium.
Intuitively, high viscosity means that a high degree of effort is required in order to achieve change because the medium is highly resistant to change, and by contrast low viscosity means that some changes can be achieved with low resistance from the system, and hence little effort.

Green [8] distinguishes two types of viscosity: repetitive and knock-on.

Repetitive viscosity refers to the 'resistance' to change encountered where a modification involves the user in effort intensive, and often repetitive, inputs.

Hence, a conceptually simple modification becomes a complex activity. For example, when preparing a document a user may wish to expand an abbreviation used throughout the document, without appropriate tools such a change may require considerable, though almost mechanic, work.

Knock-on viscosity refers to the situations in which a developer, having made a change, finds that a number of additional 'corrections' are necessary in order to preserve the desired state.

Knock-on viscosity concerns the manner in which a system environment can often limit or restrict how a goal is reached. For instance, if a word processor does not support automatic section numbering, and a section needs to be demoted or moved, then there is a knock-on effect for subsequent section and subsection numbering. Hence, a conceptually simple modification can result in a chain of alterations, which can be difficult to for the user to manage.

Repetitive and knock-on viscosity are cognitive phenomena which are intended to reflect the cognitive overhead of alternative uses of particular notations and tools. Repetitive viscosity tends to focus upon the extent of the work required to complete a change, where as knock-on viscosity focuses upon the complexity of managing changes. The role of tools and notations can be seen as a relevant since, the mechanisms they provide have strong influence upon how efficiently changes can be achieved and managed.

3   Modelling Viscosity

Adopting the familiar concept of `dimension' suggests that it should be possible to locate individual artifacts within a cognitive space so that their (relative) locations inform us about their (relative) merits. In the absence of appropriate dimension definitions, we propose a basic vocabulary of concepts intrinsic to their description and characterise the vocabulary in terms of a generic interactive model involving:

- the goals (and sub-goals) which users may achieve,
- the inputs which have to be performed to achieve goals,
- goal objects central to achieving user goals.

The concepts can be directly related to a generic interactive system model.
Drawing on our work [20] and others (see [20]) on developing formal accounts of interaction, a user goal corresponds to a system configuration which coincides with the satisfaction of the goal. This notion is analogous to the representation of post-conditions to `user objectives' as proposed in [10, 5].

To support our illustrations, which follow, we can envisage the alternative goals that may be entertained by users when authoring tabular information and when developing programs. In the first case, users may be concerned with correctness of the content and format of rows, columns and cells, in addition goals could also identify the visual distinctiveness of regions within a table. In the second case, users (as programmers) may employ a number of goals focusing upon the flow of control and information and the manipulation of data. For either case, we do not wish to propose that one specific goal perspective predominates, but that alternative perspectives are not ignored in any complete analysis. (In fact if one view did predominate interface design may not be so problematic.)

3.1   *Notation*

To formalise the concepts introduced we employ an action logic notation which provides a relatively concise language for characterising dimensions and supports formal reasoning. From our system perspective goal properties correspond to system state configurations. Hence, given a goal properties p and q, we can develop logical expressions such as their conjunction $(p \wedge q)$ and disjunction $(p \vee q)$ correspond to more specific and more general goals respectively. In addition, we use of the following ACTL constructs [13]. For any proposition p:

- $[op]\, p$ is true iff following the input op , p is true.

Hence, op leads to a state in which p is true.

- **EF** is true iff there is some sequence of operations that may make *p* true.

Alternatively read as: `it is possible that *p* will be true'.

- **AG** is true iff following any sequence of operations *p* is true.

Alternatively read as `in all future states *p* is true'.

Although the entire repertoire of the action logic is not exploited here, the logic seems to provide a suitably rich framework for the current and future examination of cognitive dimensions.

3.2 Repetitive Viscosity

Repetitive viscosity is characterised by the complexity/repetitiveness of inputs necessary to achieve some goal. This attribute can be assessed by examining the `language' of input sequences that are capable of achieving a goal (from a state in which the goal does not hold). Thus, for a given change we can identify a language of user inputs which can implement that change, where the change is characterised by a pre-condition goal and a post-condition goal.

pre-condition	T	?	?	?
post-condition	F	....	F	T

as input proceeds→

Initially, the pre-condition is true and the post condition false, following an appropriate input sequence the change is achieved once the post condition is true. In general, we write *pre* REP *post* to denote the language of input sequences:

Definition *The input sequence* $i_1, \ldots, i_n$ *is in pre* REP *post provided*:

$$\text{EF} \; pre \wedge \neg \, post \wedge [i_1] \, (\neg post \wedge [i_2] \, (\ldots \neg \, post \wedge [i_{n-1}] \, (\neg \, post \wedge [i_n] \, post)\ldots))$$

In words: From a state in which *pre* is true, the input sequence is able to achieve *post*.

Repetitive viscosity can be assessed in terms of the complexity of this input language, *pre* REP *post*. A variety of `measurements' of language complexity may be considered ranging from simple measures such as length of language elements to those that assess cognitive complexity [19, 17].

Of course in general, these languages will include limitless sequences of inputs which eventually achieve the post condition. For our treatment of viscosity in this study, the shorter the elements within the language, the easier it would be to achieve the change characterised by the pre- and post- conditions and, hence, the lower the viscosity.

3.3   Knock-on Viscosity

Knock-on viscosity concerns the manner in which a system can often limit or restrict how a goal is reached. With examples of knock-on viscosity, the user achieves a primary goal and the system negates some other property which was generally required by the user.

Assuming the user wishes to reach the conjunctive goal $p \wedge q$, then knock-on viscosity can arise from the system hindering the achievement of both conjuncts. We characterise knock-on viscosity in terms of how a system makes the satisfaction of some goals unnecessarily interfere with others. The manner in which a goal p can interfere with another q is characterised by a relation disrupts— p DIS q as achieving p negates q. The disruption of q by p complicates achieving their conjunction. In general viscosity of this sort is particular to the means of achieving p, hence it is defined with respect to the input operation which achieves p.

Definition   *The formal definition of disrupts relates two goals, and an input—* p DIS q *for the input in iff*

$$\textbf{AG} \ (\neg p \wedge [in] \ (p) \Rightarrow [in] \neg q)$$

To ensure that this behaviour is not necessitated by the domain model, we also require that p and q are not mutually exclusive: $\textbf{AG} \ \textbf{EF} \ (p \wedge q)$.

In words: For all future states whenever the input *in* achieves p it negates q.

One view of *disrupts* is that it can indicate an inappropriate order for achieving particular goals.
Thus, if q holds and the user wishes to ensure $p \wedge q$, then achieving p would have the knock-on effect of negating q, hence, it may be more appropriate to achieve p first, then q.
However, since DIS can be symmetric (and dependent upon particular inputs) the relation cannot provide an optimal order in which to achieve to goals.

3.4   Interpretations of Dimensions

The above characterisation of repetitive and knock-on viscosity represents an interpretation of an informal cognitive view of interaction.

The specific purpose of this interpretation is to relate the informal concepts to a formal system orientated framework. The system framework is clearly not cognitive in nature and hence our interpretations are best viewed as comprises between the cognitive view and the practical demands of the system model.

This compromise can be seen in our consideration of repetitive viscosity.
Focusing upon the minimal input sequences as an indicator of viscosity suggests that all actions have an equal status. Such an assumption may clearly be unrealistic, however it avoids the additional complexity of appraising and accommodating the relative status of different inputs and input sequences.

3.5 Example—LaTeX tables

Here the measures of resistance to change are illustrated for a small example of preparing tables in a document mark-up language.
We examine one textual notation for defining tables in documents (namely LaTeX) which is similar in nature to others commonly used, such as HTML [11].
Our formalisation of viscosity is used to compare extending a table of information horizontally (more columns) or vertically (more rows).
The specific LaTeX notation is briefly described, then two types of general modification to a table using a primitive line based editor are assessed.

LaTeX tables The number of columns and their format is defined by an opening parameter list (in the example, this is {l r | c | l l}).
Subsequent rows are separated by the special token `\\', and column entries within a row are separated by the token `&'.
For example:

```
\begintabularlrlclll
\hline
Heena &     & Jim \\
\hline
Jane & Andy &      \\
\hline
Mehmet & Hannah & Sarah \\
\hline
3 & 4 & 77 \\
\hline
\endtabular
```

(Note, `\hline' makes a horizontal rule in the table.)
defines the table:

Heena		Jim
Jane	Andy	
Mehmet	Hannah	Sarah
3	4	77

The two modification tasks we consider are introducing a new row or column of data. Assuming that the current table has n rows and m columns, the user goals we shall consider are:

[*wider*] = ``A column $m+1$ exists''
[*longer*] = ``A row $n+1$ exists''

Modifications are characterised using the above goals and two further goals are used to represent the table contents prior to a modification and the requirement that all cells have a defined format.

[*table1*] = ``The table content includes ... ''
[*allFormatted*] = ``All table cells have a defined format''

Repetitive Viscosity

In terms of our formalisation, the introduction of a new column is represented by the *pre-condition: table1* ∧ *allFormatted* and the *post-condition: table1* ∧ *allFormatted* ∧ *wider*. That is, the table content is not changed, all cells are formatted and a new column exists.

Hence the language of input sequences characterising this change is given by:

$$Lh = (table1 \land allFormatted) \ \mathsf{REP} \ (table1 \land allFormatted \land wider)$$

Similarly, the introduction of a new row is represented by the language:

$$Lv = (table1 \land allFormatted) \ \mathsf{REP} \ (table1 \land allFormatted \land longer)$$

The proposed measure of these two languages to indicate the repetitive viscosity of the respective modifications, is the shortest elements within them.

For the first case *Lh* must include a modification within the tabular parameter list and a modification of at least one of the rows.

By contrast, in the second case *Lv* must include just a new row description.

Comparing *Lh* and *Lv* , *Lv* includes shorter input sequences, hence, the introduction of a new row can involve less work and we interpret it as being less viscous than the introduction of a new column.

Disruption

The assessment of knock-on viscosity in formal terms of disruption requires that we identify other goals that may be influenced by the achieving *longer* or *wider*

For this example, we employ *allFormatted* from above.

When introducing a new row (that is achieving goal *longer*) the row's format is the same as that defined by existing parameter list, hence there is no disruption of *allFormatted* .

By contrast, when introducing a new column (by achieving *wider*) the format of that column needs to be defined in the tabular parameter list.
Hence, if a column is introduced by creating new cells, then the goal *allFormatted* is disrupted and the user will eventually have to attend to updating the parameter list.

In summary, for the goals considered here:

Disruption	
wider DIS allFormatted	when a cell is created
longer	NO DISRUPTIONS

Assuming that lower resistance to change is preferable for authors of tabular information in LaTeX, the measure of repetitive viscosity `favours' vertical extensions to tabular information, as this involves less effort. Similarly, the measure of knock-on viscosity `favours' vertical extensions, since they involve fewer disruptions.

4   A Case Study

This section describes the application of our interpretation of viscosity to a larger scale interactive problem.
We examine the facilities offered by an integrated program development environment (called IPE) in the form of alternative programming languages.
IPE supports a mixed model of software development combining an executable specification language and an imperative programming language.
Our account of repetitive and knock-on viscosity enables the comparison of the two languages in terms of what program modifications they support.

4.1   IPE

IPE is a prototyping environment that enables the construction and validation of software throughout development in an evolutionary manner.
The nature of languages provided in the environment reflects this philosophy.
For each module the user (as program developer) has to select between using an executable specification language or a conventional imperative language.
The executable specification language is ADTSPEC, an executable algebraic language [14], and the conventional implementation language is a modular Pascal, Paradox Pascal [18]. The use of executable specifications enables early feedback on the poorly understood parts of the system to be obtained in a timely and low risk fashion. This is of paramount importance in development because the cost of full-scale production quality system requiring modifications is extremely high [15].

4.2   The Signal Problem

The two languages supported by IPE, ADTSPEC and Pascal, can be individually examined in terms of their suitability in accommodating certain modifications in evolutionary development.
To achieve this our measures of viscosity will be illustrated using a programming problem which has been the subject of empirical studies [26] interpreted in terms of knock-viscosity [25].

The initial problem statement:

A message delivered in a communication line consists of a series of data
digits. These are 1's and 2's respectively. A message is terminated by the
digit 0. Given a message it is required to return:

> (a) the number of 1's in the message
> (b) the number of 2's in the message

Solutions to this in each language are illustrated in figures 1 and 2.
Space does not permit a details explanation of these programs.
It should observed that in the Pascal a significant portion of the program is devoted to implementing the input list as an abstract data type.

```
ADT_MODULE message_definition;
  INTERFACE
    TYPE list;
    CONSTRUCTOR cons(item: integer; next: list): list;
    CONSTRUCTOR empty                  : list;
    FUNCTION   no_of_ones(L: list)     : integer;
```

```
FUNCTION   no_of_twos(L: list)           : integer;

other relevant list ops

SPECIFICATION
  VAR item: integer;
    L  : list;
  EQUATIONS
    no_of_ones(cons(0, L))   = 0;
    no_of_ones(cons(1, L))   = 1 + no_of_ones(L);
    no_of_ones(cons(item ,L)) = no_of_ones(L);

    no_of_twos(cons(0, L))   = 0;
    no_of_twos(cons(2, L))   = 1 + no_of_ones(L);
    no_of_twos(cons(item, L)) = no_of_twos(L);

    other relevant list ops
END.
```

Figure 1: An equational specification (ES1) for the Signal Problem in ADTSPEC.

```
MODULE message_definition;
  INTERFACE
    TYPE list = HIDDEN;

    same function signatures as in ES1
    other relevant list ops

  IMPLEMENTATION
    TYPE list      = ^list_record;
      list_record = RECORD
                  item: integer;
                  next: list
                END;

    FUNCTION cons(* item: integer; next: list): list *);
      VAR new_list: list;
    BEGIN
      new(new_list);
      new_list^.item:=item;
      new_list^.next:=next;
      cons:=new_list
    END;
```

```
FUNCTION empty(* : list *);
BEGIN
 empty:=nil
END;

FUNCTION no_of_ones(* L: list): integer *);
   VAR result: integer;
BEGIN
 result:=0;
 WHILE (L^.item <> 0) DO
 BEGIN
  IF L^.item = 1 THEN result:=result + 1;
  L:=L^.next
 END;
 no_of_ones:=result
END;

 similarly so for no_of_twos
 other relevant list ops
END.
```

Figure 2: An extract of the Signal Problem in Pascal (IM1).

Having specified and implemented the original problem, the next step will be to demonstrate how modifications to the requirements can be accommodated in both paradigms.

We consider an additional emerging requirement (modification~1) and a change to the original requirements (modification~2).

```
ADT_MODULE message_definition;
 INTERFACE

  ...
  FUNCTION longest_ones(L: list): integer;

 SPECIFICATION
  FUNCTION max(item1, item2: integer): integer;
  FUNCTION count_ones(L: list)      : integer;
  FUNCTION without_ones(L: list)    : list;

  VAR ..., item1: integer;

 EQUATIONS
  ...
  max(item, item1)  = IF item >= item1 THEN item
                 ELSE item1;
```

```
count_ones(cons(1, L))   = 1 + count_ones(L);
count_ones(cons(item, L)) = 0;

without_ones(cons(1, L))   = without_ones(L);
without_ones(cons(item, L)) = L;

longest_ones(cons(0, L)) = 0;
longest_ones(cons(1, L)) = max(count_ones(cons(1, L)),
              longest_ones(without_ones(cons(1, L)))
                    );
longest_ones(cons(item, L)) = longest_ones(L);
END.
```

Figure 3: Extract of the modified equational specification (ES2) for the Signal Problem in ADTSPEC.

Modification 1
In addition:

> Calculate the length of the longest sequence of 1's in a given message.

This requirement can be incorporated in the original ADTSPEC specification by the introduction of a further accumulator (see figure 3). The same modification implemented in Pascal (see figure 4) involves fewer operations to be defined, the procedural paradigm enables `counting' and `working down the list' to be combined.

```
MODULE message_definition;
 INTERFACE
  ...
  FUNCTION longest_ones(L: list): integer;

 IMPLEMENTATION
  ...
  FUNCTION longest_ones(* L: list): integer *);
    VAR ones : integer;
      result: integer;
  BEGIN
   result:=0;
   WHILE (L^.item <> 0) DO
   BEGIN
    IF L^.item = 1 THEN
    BEGIN
     ones:=0;
     WHILE (L^.item = 1) DO
```

```
    BEGIN
      ones:=ones+1;
      L:=L^.next
    END;
    IF ones >= result THEN result := ones ;
    END
    ELSE L:=L^.next
  END
  END;
  longest_ones:=result
END.
```

Figure 4: Extract of an implementation (IM2) for the Signal Problem in Pascal.

Modification 2
A change to the original requirements:

A message delivered in a communication line consists of a series of digits. Digits can be either data digits containing either 1s or 2s, or *control digits*.

This change involves adding a new attribute to the representation of a message, indicating the nature of each digit transmitted. Figures 5 and 6 illustrate the required modification in each language.

```
FUNCTION cons(item: integer; it: item_type; next: list): list;
  ...

item_type  = (control, data);
list_record = RECORD
          it: item_type;
          item : integer;
          next : list
        END;

FUNCTION cons(* item: integer; it: item_type; next: list): list *);
  VAR new_list: list;
BEGIN
  ...
  new_list^.it:=it
  ...
END;
```

Figure 5: Changes in data representation in Pascal (IM3).

The ADTSPEC modification, though mechanical, is dispersed and requires more effort. This is because all the equations that explicitly use constructors as full expressions in their arguments need to be updated to incorporate the change in the data structure.

ADT_MODULE message_definition;
  INTERFACE

     ...
    CONSTRUCTOR cons(item: integer; it: item_type; next: list): list;

     ...
  SPECIFICATION
    VAR ..., it: item_type;

  EQUATIONS

     ...
    no_of_ones(cons(0, it, L))   = 0;
    no_of_ones(cons(1, it, L))   = 1 + no_of_ones(L);
    no_of_ones(cons(item , it, L)) = no_of_ones(L);
     ...

END.

Figure 6: Illustration of changes in data representation in ADTSPEC (ES3).

4.3   Repetitive Viscosity

The repetitive viscosity of achieving the example modifications may be expressed formally referring the following goals:

counts = the number of 1's and 2's in a message is computed

seqOnes = the length of the longest sequence of 1's is computed

controlData = some data items may be control digits

In order to realistically apply our formalisation to these examples it is necessary to ensure that the goals used adequately characterise the qualities of the specific programs. Hence, it will be assumed that the goals *counts* , and *seqOnes* embody notions of good programming practice, such as style conventions, the use of `meaningful' identifier names, etc.

The two modifications can be assessed using the languages:

Modification 1
     L1 = *counts* REP (*counts* ∧ *seqOnes*)

Modification 2

$$L2 = counts \text{ REP } (counts \wedge controlData)$$

At best the examples provide an upper bound on elements of these languages, counting the number of line based editor operations necessary to achieve the modifications we have:

Language	Modification 1 $L1$	Modification 2 $L2$
ADTSPEC	≤ 13	≤ 12
Pascal	≤ 26	≤ 5

This indicates that the different languages have differing viscosity based upon the type of modification considered. ADTSPEC appears as less viscous for the emerging functional requirement. Where as, Pascal is less viscous for the change in data representation. Clearly, we have only considered two examples of modification here in order to illustrate the `measure' of repetitive viscosity defined. In general, the formal definition of repetitive viscosity has the potential to enable the rigorous examining and comparison of languages and the types of modification they are amenable to.

4.4   *Disruptions*

Knock-on viscosity is assessed in terms of cases of the property DIS .
Hence, for the two languages ADTSPEC and Pascal we can expect different instances of DIS to hold reflecting inherent complexities of the two languages.

Focusing upon the example modifications we consider disruptions involving programmer goals concerning accumulators and data attributes.
We propose the following general programmer goals:

allInit = ``All accumulators are initialised"

allUsed. = ``All accumulated values are used"

dataDefined = ``No data attribute is undefined"

During development and modification the integrity of evolving software is dependent upon programmers ensuring the satisfaction of goals such as *allInit* , *allUsed* and *dataDefined* .
In addition, we consider the following goals reflecting the modifications examined:

Accum It is recognised that a new accumulator is required for the purpose of counting 1's (in ES2 and IM2):

Accum = ``There is an accumulator for a particular purpose"

Att It is recognised that a new data attribute is required for the purpose of accommodating control data (in ES3 and IM3):

Att = ``There is a data attribute for a particular purpose"

In the case of the language ADTSPEC it can be observed that introducing a new accumulator can involve either: (i) defining how it is to be used, in which case its initial value will still need to be defined, or (ii) defining the accumulated value, in which case its use will still need to be defined.
Alternatively, if an new data attribute is introduced (as in modification~2) the language ADTSPEC requires that the attribute is explicitly introduced in all equations using it.
Hence, introducing the new attribute disrupts is *dataDefined* .

For ADTSPEC:

Disruption	when inserting
Accum DIS *allUsed*	definition of accumulator value
Accum DIS *allInit*	definition of accumulator use
Att DIS *dataDefined*	definition of attribute

By contrast, for Pascal it can be observed that introducing a new accumulator can involve one of *three alternatives*: (i) introducing an update for an accumulator, in which case it still needs initialisation and use, (ii) introducing the initialisation of an accumulator, in which case it still needs to be used, or (iii) introducing the use of an accumulator, in which case it still needs initialisation. If a new data attribute is introduced in Pascal, there is no necessity to explicitly accommodate the new attribute within existing code.

For Pascal:

Disruption	when inserting
Accum DIS *allUsed*	initialisation of accumulator
Accum DIS *allUsed*	update of accumulator
Accum DIS *allInit*	update of accumulator
Att DIS *allInit*	use of accumulator

With no disruptions associated with Att and dataDefined

As with our assessment of repetitive viscosity, the knock-on viscosity encountered by a user of IPE is dependent upon the programming task they are engaged in.

When dealing with accumulators in a problem, the likelihood of encountering knock-on viscosity is lower in ADTSPEC, since fewer instances of disruption exist. However, when managing a change to data representation ADTSPEC incurs knock-on's that are not evident in Pascal.

Consolidating our analysis of these languages with other studies of similar languages, reveals that the examination of individual solution examples can be misleading (see [23]. Analogous examinations of declarative and imperative languages concur with our findings regarding knock-on viscosity, that is those languages classed as declarative (e.g. ADTSPEC and Prolog) generally incur lower knock-on viscosity. However, previous cases also show repetitive viscosity to be generally lower for imperative languages (Pascal and Basic). The likely cause of the high upper bound for repetitive viscosity in modification~1 in Pascal, is that the program (IM2) is a well structured solution and far from the minimal update necessary.

Drawing upon examples of applying our interpretation of cognitive dimensions, there appears to be a tendency for knock-on viscosity to trade-off against repetitive viscosity. Lower knock-on viscosity tends incur higher repetitive viscosity. Extrapolating from this suggests that viscosity is not necessarily avoidable and that any notation may in some way resist the manipulations and modifications its users require. In the following section we draw a similar conclusion from formally examining the interpretations of viscosity developed.

5   Hybrid Tools

The use of our formal interpretations of viscosity has been largely evaluative and applied to partially described systems,e.g. LaTeX tables and IPE. Such illustrations demonstrate the potential utility and validity of our proposed measures. However the more significant feature of formally characterising dimensions such as viscosity is that it enables the predictive assessment of general classes of interfaces [22]. To illustrate this we examine the influence of one frequently used general interface design technique upon system viscosity. The technique considered is the provision of *hybrid tools* which enable users to freely move between two (or more) individual tools for viewing and manipulating the same data. This technique is widely adopted in many popular interactive systems, examples include: the availability of different document views in word processors and the provision of differing views of file systems or complex programs.

A hybrid tool for our example of LaTeX tables can be envisaged that would enable, say, rows and columns to be treated equivalently. An implicit assumption behind such tools is that the benefits of each tool are equally available to users.

$(A \oplus B)$ is a hybrid tool combining tool A and tool B, special user operations are available which make the tool look and behave as A or look and behave as B.

Without detailing the specific characteristics of such tools, we can assess the repetitive and knock-on viscosity of $(A \oplus B)$ based upon the viscosities of the A and B. This yields valuable generic observations about $A \times B$ and the combination of tools it provides.

Our measure of *repetitive viscosity* is based upon the minimal inputs that achieve particular tasks, and thus in the case of $(A \oplus B)$ the minimal inputs will always be the lowest of either A or B. Hence, the repetitive viscosity of $(A \oplus B)$ is always no greater than that of A and that of B. This can be seen for our comparison of ADTSPEC and Pascal: If a hybrid tool existed, effort could be minimised by using Pascal for data modifications and ADTSPEC to specify new functions.

By contrast, *knock-on viscosity*, as measured by disruptions, is not improved, since the disruptions in A and B are union-ed for $(A \oplus B)$. Hence, there are no fewer disruptions in $(A \oplus B)$ than its components. For instance, a hybrid tool for ADTSPEC and Pascal would inherit the disruptions of both languages.

In summary, from inspection we have that:

repetitive viscosity of $(A \oplus B) \leq$ repetitive viscosity of A
repetitive viscosity of $(A \oplus B) \leq$ repetitive viscosity of B

---

knock-on viscosity of $(A \oplus B) \geq$ knock-on viscosity of A
knock-on viscosity of $(A \oplus B) \geq$ knock-on viscosity of B

These observations, concur with our analyses of individual systems indicating how the two notions of viscosity are inter-related. In general, hybrid tools are not a panacea to interface design problems. The strategy of combining tools has certain costs for the user, informally, a combined tool does not by itself guarantee its effective or efficient use. In fact the higher knock-on viscosity for $A \times B$ indicates a higher opportunity for ineffective use through hard to manage changes. Clearly, there are other factors that determine overall tool quality which are not covered here. However, our analysis does reveal a strong dependency between two relevant measures.

6   Conclusion

This paper forms part of an investigation into the formal characterisation of psychologically motivated measures of notations and tools. Two cognitive dimensions concerned with resistance to change have been given a system based interpretations and applied to an example prototyping environment. This work is novel in adopting a strongly cognitive perspective in within a system based framework. In doing so we have addressed a major weakness of cognitive dimensions by proposing its interpretation within an explicit common framework. This treatment of the dimensions enables their precise expositions and also enables trade-offs and comparisons between dimensions to be made. Specifically for the two dimensions considered, we have been able to identify characteristics of trade-offs between them, both using a case study and analysis.

References

[1] P. J. Barnard and M. D. Harrison (1992) Towards a Framework for Modelling Human Computer Interactions", Proceedings International Conference on {HCI}, EWHCI'92 ed J. Gornostaev pp189-196 Moscow:{ICSTI}

[2] T. Berners-Lee and D.Connolly (1995) Hypertext Markup Language - 2.0 Internet-Draft of the International Engineering Task Force

[3] A. J. Dix (1991) Formal Methods for Interactive Systems Academic Press

[4] D. J. Duke and P. J. Barnard and J. May and D. A. Duce(1995) Systematic Development of the Human Interface; Proceedings of APSEC'95: Second Asia-Pacific Software Engineering Conference, IEEE Computer Society Press

[5] D. J. Duke and M. D. Harrison (1995) Mapping user requirements to implementations; Software Engineering Jounal, 10 1 pp13-20

[6] D. J. Gilmore (1997) Cognitive Dimensions as a tool for comparative evaluation; Psychology Department, University of Nottingham

[7] T. R. G. Green (1989) Cognitive Dimensions of Notations; People and Computers V ed A. Sutcliffe and Macaulay; Cambridge University Press pp443-460"

[8] T.R.G. Green and M. Petre (1996) Usability Analysis of Visual Porgramming Environments: a `cognitive dimensions' framework; The Journal of Visual Languages and Computing 7 (2) pp131-174

[9] M. D. Harrison and A. E. Blandford and P. J. Barnard (1993) University of York; The software engineering of user freedom :Amodeus 2 Document

[10] Leslie Lamport (1986) LaTeX: A Document Preparation Language

Addison-Wesley : ISBN 0-201-15790

[11] D. Lavery and G. Cockton and M. Atkinson (1996) Cognitive Dimensions: Usability Evaluation Materials. Deparment of Computing Science, University of Glasgow

[12] R. De Nicola and A. Fantechi and S. Gnesi and G. Ristori (1991) An Action based framework for verifying logical and behavioural properties of concurrent systems: Proceedings of 3rd Workshop on Computer Aided Verification

[13] M. B. Özcan (1993) An Integrated Rapid Prototyping Environment Based on Executable Specifications: UMIST, U.K

[14] M. B. Özcan and J Siddiqi (1996) Interchanging Specifications and Implementations in Evolutionary Prototyping: Software- Practice and Experience 26 (9) pp999--1023

[15] F. Paternò (1995) Proceedings, EUROGRAPHICS Workshop on the Design, Specification, Verification of Interactive Systems, Bocca di Magra, Italy", Springer-Verlag: Eurographics Seminar Series ISBN 3-540-59450-9

[16] S. J. Payne and T. R. G. Green (1986) Task-action grammars: a model of mental representation of task languages: Human-Computer Interaction 2 (2) pp95-133

[17] M. S. Powell (1989) A Program Development Environment based on Persistence and Abstract Data Types: Workshop on Persistent Object Systems

[18] P. Reisner (1983) Formal grammar as a tool for analysing ease of use: some fundamental concepts Human Factors in Computer Systems, ed J. C. Thomas and M. L. Schneider   pp53-78

[19] C. R. Roast (1994) Modelling Interaction Using Template Abstractions, People and Computers IX; ed G. Cockton, S. W. Draper and G. R. S. Weir pp273-284

[20] C. R. Roast and J. I. Siddiqi (1996) , The Formal Examination of Cognitive Dimensions; HCI96 Adjunct Proceedings pp150-156

[21] C. R. Roast and J. I. Siddiqi (1996) Formally Assessing Software Modifiability, BCS-FACS Workshop on Formal Aspects of the Human Computer Interface, Sheffield Hallam University, 10-12 September 1996; Springer-Verlag Electronic Workshops in Computing; ed, C. R. Roast and J. I. Siddiqi ISBN 3-540-76105-5,

URL: http://www.springer.co.uk/eWiC/Workshops/FAHCI.html"

[22] C. R. Roast and J. I. Siddiqi (1997) Usability Requirements as Specification Constraints --- an example of WYSIWYG; IEE Proceedings Software Engineering 144 (2) pp101-110

[23] C. R. Roast and J. I. Siddiqi (1996) Relating Knock-on Viscosity to Software Modifiability; Proceedings of OZCHI 96, Hamilton, New Zealand: IEEE Computer Society Press

[24] J. I. A. Siddiqi and B. Ratcliff (1985) An Empirical Investigation into Problem Decomposition Strategies used in Program Design; International Journal of Man Machine Studies 22 pp77-90

[25] S. Yang and M. Burnett and E. DeKoven and M. Zloof (1995) Representation design benchmarks: a design-time aid for VPL navigable static representations Oregon State University; No TR 95-60-3

[26] C. R. Roast and J. I. Siddiqi (eds) BCS-FACS Workshop on Formal Aspects of the Human Computer Interface, Sheffield Hallam University, 10-12 September 1996 Springer-Verlag, Electronic Workshops in Computing ISBN 3-540-76105-5, URL: http://www.springer.co.uk/eWiC/Workshops/FAHCI.html

[27] A. Blandford and H. Thimbleby (1996) HCI96 Industry Day & Adjunct Proceedings ISBN 1 85924 119 0

Direct Object Manipulation vs. Direct Concept Manipulation: Effect of Interface Style on Reflection and Domain Learning

Kamran Sedighian & Marv Westrom

Department of Computer Science
The University of British Columbia
Vancouver, B.C., V6T 1Z4, Canada
Phone: +1 (604) 261-4667
E-Mail: kamran@cs.ubc.ca

Department of Curriculum Studies
The University of British Columbia
Vancouver, B.C., V6T 1Z4, Canada
Phone: +1 (604) 822-5314
E-Mail: westrom@ubc.ca

This paper investigates the effects of interface style on children's domain learning and reflective thought. It argues that the educational deficiencies of Direct Manipulation (DM) interfaces are not necessarily caused by their "directness", but by their directness towards objects rather than embedded educational concepts. This paper furthers our understanding of the DM metaphor in educational software by proposing a shift of approach from Direct Object Manipulation (DOM) to Direct Concept Manipulation (DCM). A number of pedagogical strategies for supporting the DCM metaphor are offered. Results reported from a study using three variations of an educational software application are used to support these points.

Keywords: Interface, direct manipulation, reflection, children, education, learning, motivation, mathematics, problem solving, human-computer interaction, transformation geometry.

Kamran Sedighian & Marv Westrom

Introduction and Background

Direct Manipulation (DM) refers to systems which allow the user to manipulate the objects on the screen with some kind of pointing device (Shneiderman, 1988, 1993; Norman and Draper, 1986). It stands in contrast to command-based syntax for manipulating objects. As a technique for controlling computer systems, it is widely used in many application areas. The term "direct" has many implications which make the concept of DM very complex (Norman & Draper, 1986). Norman (1986) presents the notion of two gulfs (Gulf of Execution and Gulf of Evaluation) between the computer system and the user which can be bridged by either bringing the system closer to the user or the user closer to the system. Hutchins, *et al.* state that "the feeling of directness is inversely proportional to the amount of cognitive effort it takes to manipulate and evaluate a system" (1986, p. 95). The goal is, therefore, to reduce the distance across these gulfs and thereby minimize the required cognitive effort. It is unclear whether this minimization of cognitive load is desirable only for learning how to use a productivity tool or whether it also applies to the design of educational interfaces.

Recent HCI research in problem solving and learning indicates that interfaces with the lowest cognitive effort are not the most educationally effective (Svendsen, 1991; Holst, 1996; Golightly, 1996). Studies by Svendsen (1991) show that subjects who used a command-based interface learned more than those who used a DM interface. They made fewer errors, required fewer trials, and spent more time per trial. Holst (1996) argues that increasing the users' cognitive load and requiring users to remember, evaluate, and design new courses of action puts them in a better position to make correct decisions. Golightly examines the notion of Indirect Manipulation and argues that "less direct interfaces cause the user to build a more verbalisable and transferable body of knowledge about the domain" (1996, p.37).

The idea that a command-based interface or a less direct interface can enhance learning is important. However, DM is not entirely harmful. It has tradeoffs. One of the main advantages of DM is the notion of "Direct Engagement" (Hutchins, *et al.*, 1986). DM interfaces put users into direct contact with a world of objects, eliminating the need to communicate through an intermediary. This is satisfying to users, whereas a less direct interface may be less motivating. On the other hand, a major disadvantage of DM is that it can support and amplify a user's naive or familiar understanding of a particular domain which misses the potential of the technology (*ibid.*). Therefore, interface designers are faced with the challenge of "providing ... new ways [to think of and interact with a domain] and creating conditions that will make [users] feel direct and natural" (*ibid.*, p.118).

In an educational learning environment, the main goal is to learn a particular domain of knowledge. One would ideally want to immerse users in direct engagement with the concepts of that domain. It is necessary, as far as possible, to enable the user to interact with and think in terms of the concepts being learned rather than the objects that the concepts act upon. So the focus should be shifted from manipulating the objects directly (Direct Object Manipulation) to manipulating the concepts directly (Direct Concept Manipulation). However, since, unlike objects, concepts are abstract entities, this manipulation must be directed at the referents to those concepts – that is, interface elements that represent the structural and semantic properties of the concepts.

The study outlined here is concerned with two main questions: 1) Is a simple shift from DOM to DCM conducive to domain learning and reflection? 2) Are there other pedagogical strategies that would support and enhance the DCM metaphor?

The notion of a "concept" is an unresolved issue in philosophy and psychology (Guttenplan, 1995). Nonetheless, Novak and Gowin (1984) define a *concept* as "a regularity in events or objects designated by some label." They define an *event* as "anything that happens or can be made to happen," and an *object* as "anything that exists and can be observed." (p.4).

A shift from DOM to DCM has certain design implications. One implication is that whereas an ideal DOM interface tries to reduce the semantic distance between the output and the user's mental model, a DCM interface should invite the user to gradually cross this distance and adapt to the semantics of the concepts. Another implication involves the epistemological characteristics of objects and concepts. In most cases, objects represent concrete entities, and consequently require shallow understanding. In contrast, concepts are abstract entities and have depth. Thus, they have to be understood in ever greater degrees in a "progressively differentiated" (Ausubel, 1968, p. 153) manner, i.e., in terms of detail and specificity. Novak and Gowin (1984) state that:

> "[M]eaningful learning is a continuous process wherein new concepts gain greater meaning as new relationships (propositional links) are acquired. Thus concepts are never 'finally learned' but are always being learned, modified, and made more explicit and more inclusive as they become progressively more differentiated" (p. 99).

Another implication is that referents to concepts have to be selected carefully. As stated above, since concepts are abstract entities, DCM involves manipulation of objects representing the educational concepts. The choice of these objects plays an important role in the educational effectiveness of the DCM metaphor. Suitable representations are very important for dealing with and communicating the concepts (Guttenplan, 1995; Polya, 1957; Forman, 1988; Norman, 1993).

A final implication is the requirement for a careful analysis of the way that the learning occurs. Learning can be by trial and error and passive aggregation of information, or it can be through reflective and effortful thought[1] (Hayes & Broadbent, 1988; Norman, 1993). The former can lead to implicit knowledge and the latter to explicit, insightful knowledge. Two methods that can promote reflective thought and insight learning are: 1) inducement of "epistemic conflict"[2] (Forman & Pufall, 1988) in learners, and 2) increasing the cost of interaction and creating constraints for learners (Trudel & Payne, 1995).

The research described here attempts to address the issues related to the design of the DCM metaphor. It compares the educational effectiveness of different interface implementations of a puzzle-solving activity, tangrams – an activity which requires assembling some two dimensional shapes into a given outline. Concepts inherently embedded in this activity are geometrical transformations[3] (i.e., concepts of slide, turn, and flip)[4]. *Super Tangrams* is an interactive version of this activity allowing children to solve tangram puzzles by manipulating on-screen images of the given geometric shapes. Three variations of this program were created: DOM (Direct Object Manipulation), DCM (Direct Concept Manipulation) and DCM+ (Direct Concept Manipulation Plus). In contrast to studies of this nature, each version of *Super Tangrams* was fully polished to give children an impression of a commercial game. This is important to create a realistic rather than a clinical situation for children, and to keep children's motivational needs from interfering with the study.

Super Tangrams: Three Variations

In the DOM version, the user manipulates the geometric shapes directly. The desired outline is presented as a gray area in the centre of the screen, with the available pieces scattered around the periphery (see Figure 1). Buttons on the side allow the user to select flip (horizontally or vertically), rotate (clockwise or counterclockwise), or drag

---

[1] This form of learning is also called "insight" learning.
[2] "Epistemic conflict" is a property of the constructivist theory of learning and refers to an externally induced conflict that prompts a reflective response.
[3] Tangram manipulatives are used for teaching mathematical concepts, including transformation geometry (Russell & Bologna, 1982).
[4] These are terms used in children's mathematics textbooks which correspond to translation, rotation and reflection respectively. To learn each one of these concepts, an individual must develop an understanding of their structural and semantic characteristics. For instance, to formally understand translation, one has to understand that it involves motion along a straight line a certain distance and in a certain direction.

mode. The mode chosen is indicated by the mouse cursor. In flip mode, clicking on any shape will cause it to flip over (horizontally or vertically). In rotate mode, clicking on a shape causes that shape to turn $22.5°^5$ (clockwise or counter-clockwise). In drag mode, the user can simply drag the shape to the desired location. The shapes do not lock into place, but behave much like cardboard pieces. The order of the puzzles is fixed and every puzzle has a fixed score which is added to the users total score when the puzzle is completed. A timer shows elapsed time for every puzzle. The volume of the background music can be adjusted up, down, or off.

In the DCM version, the user directly manipulates representations of the transformation concepts rather than the shapes themselves. The screen has a coarse grid in the background and the concept of 'selected piece' is introduced (see Figure 2). The user chooses a shape (shown by the piece having a different pattern). The operation (*Slide*, *Turn*, or *Flip*) is selected from the buttons on the right and this causes the transformation representation and the ghost image of the shape to appear. For *Slide* (see Figure 4), this representation is a vector showing direction and length. Rather than moving the shape, the user directly manipulates one of three handles on the head, tail, and centre of the vector. Moving either the head or the tail can change the direction or length, causing a corresponding shift in the location of the ghost image. Moving the centre point of the vector moves the whole vector but does not change the ghost image. When the user has the vector set as desired, he or she clicks the *GO* button and the selected shape slides into the ghost image spot. With *Turn* (see Figure 2), the transformation representation is an arc attached to one vertex of the selected shape with moveable centre and endpoint. Manipulating the centre changes the centre of rotation and adjusting the endpoint changes the angle of rotation. With *Flip* (see Figure 3), the representation is a line of reflection with two handles. One handle controls the location of the line of reflection; the other controls the angle of reflection. Since reversing the transformations is not as easy as in the DOM version, an *UNDO* button is added. Furthermore, a *Learn* module is included in case children like to learn about the unfamiliar concepts (for a detailed explanation of *Learn* and its relationship to this project, see Sedighian, 1997).

In the DCM+ version, the user manipulates transformation representations as in DCM except that a number of features are added to DCM to support and enhance it. In order to allow children to interact with the concepts in a progressively differentiated manner while causing cognitive dissonance, the representations fade over three levels of the program. Figures 4 to 6 demonstrate this strategy as applied to one of the transformation concepts: translation. In *Level 1* (Figure 4), children encounter the most generalized notion of translation without having to be concerned with the details and

---

[5] The resolution of the rotation, 22.5°, is the largest setting that will permit all of the required variations to solve the given puzzles.

specifics of the concept. In *Level 2* (Figure 5), the ghost image is not displayed. Consequently children can not rely on the visual feedback they received in *Level 1*; they now have to pay attention to where to position the head and tail of the arrow. In *Level 3* (Figure 6), the tail of the arrow is fixed to a certain coordinate. Therefore, children have to pay attention to the grid and become conscious of the length and direction of the translation vector. This same strategy is applied to the other two transformations but in accordance with their conceptual properties.

A cost of unit operation is placed on children's use of the transformations by the introduction of a *par* notion (min, avg, and max number of moves). The score children receive is a function of the number of moves they make to solve a puzzle -- the fewer the number of moves, the higher the score. In addition, constraints are placed on the transformations that can be used. Therefore, in many puzzles, children can only use a certain transformation (see Figure 3 in which *Slide* and *Turn* are disabled).

Contrary to the accepted belief that problem solving is conducive to learning, Sweller (1988) states that it puts a heavy cognitive load on learners leaving little cognitive resources for learning domain knowledge. To allay this situation and free mental resources so that children can pay more attention to the concepts, several features are added to DCM+. A *Hint* button is added which tells children where certain shapes fit in the outline. In addition, unlike the other two versions, when a shape is moved to a position where it is supposed to be placed, it locks into place, and a happy-face icon appears on the shape. The *Learn* module in DCM+ is expanded to aid children through different levels with their conceptual difficulties.

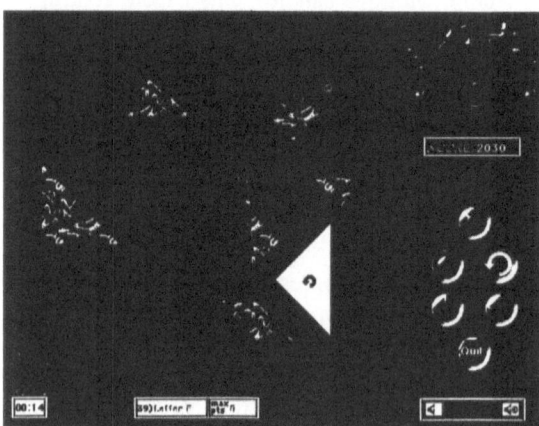

Figure 1: DOM screen showing a counter-clockwise rotation

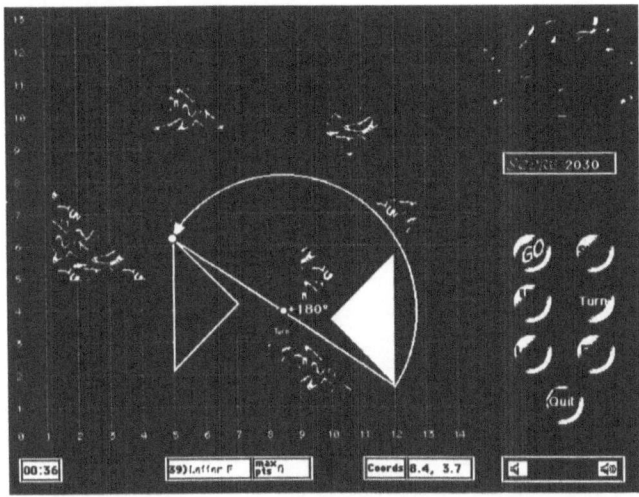

Figure 2: DCM screen showing arc of rotation

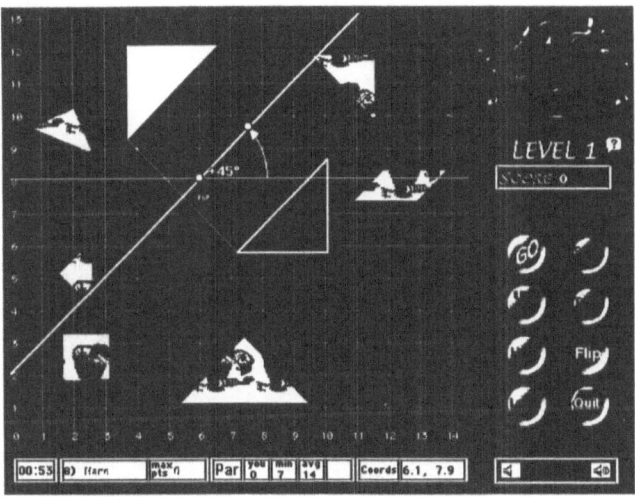

Figure 3: DCM+ screen showing line of reflection

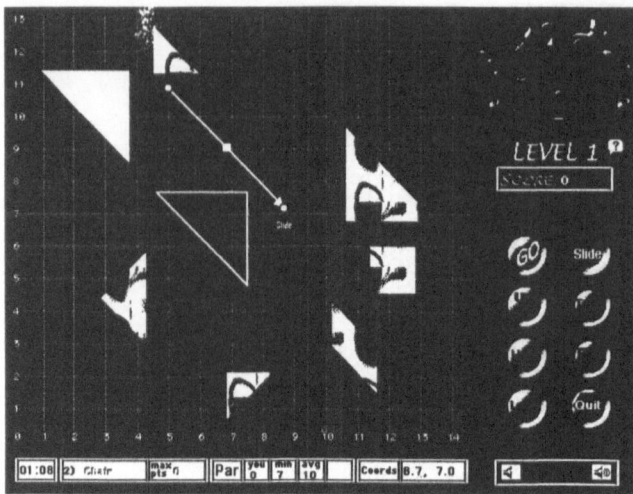

Figure 4: DCM+ screen showing a vector and a ghost image

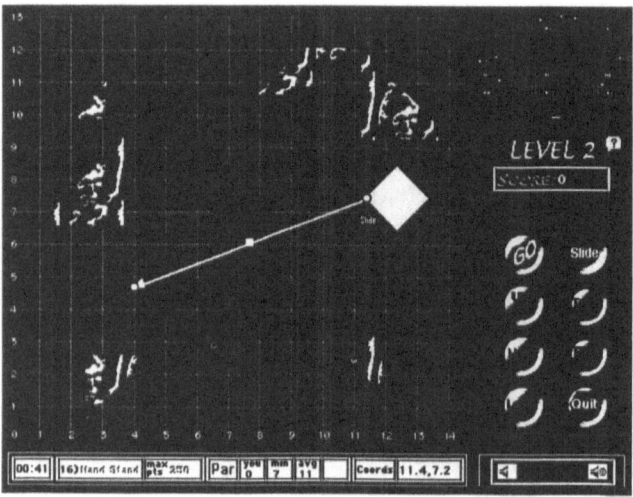

Figure 5: Vector without a ghost image

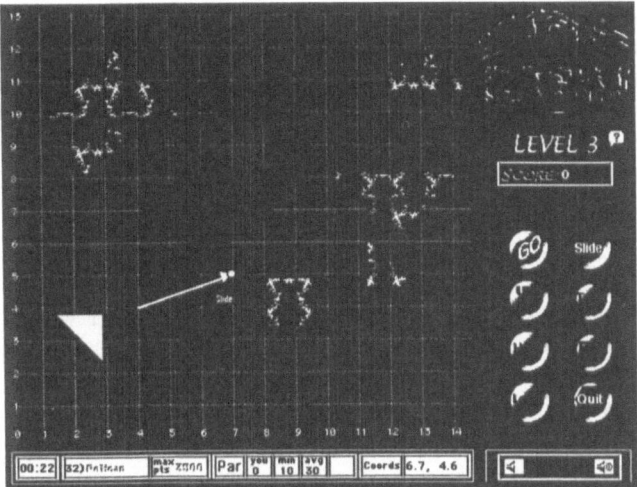

Figure 6: Vector with tail fixed

Study

Subjects

Forty four grade-6 (eleven-year old) children (21 females, 23 males) from two classes of an upper middle-class school (Vancouver, Canada) were used.

Research Setting

A temporary computer laboratory was set up in a small room adjacent to a grade 4/5 class in one of the schools. The two rooms were separated by a partition wall. There were eight Macintosh Performa computers arranged on three long tables, with two or three computers on each table.

Sources of Data

Test

A paper and pencil test was constructed to measure children's understanding of two dimensional transformation geometry concepts. It was a test of their formal, explicit mathematical knowledge, rather than their intuitive, implicit understanding of flip, turn, and slide. Questions were presented in a general format that would be understandable to anyone learning transformation geometry, and not just to users of *Super Tangrams*. The test contained 51 questions of varying degrees of difficulty, ranging from very easy to very difficult questions, 49 multiple choice and 2 that required drawing solutions on the paper. The questions were weighted, with questions requiring a more sophisticated understanding of formal operations having higher values. This test was piloted with two different classes and was validated by two mathematics education experts.

Questionnaire

A paper and pencil questionnaire was given to children. It consisted of a varying number of multiple choice questions about *Super Tangrams*, some questions requiring written comments explaining the choices. The questions varied depending upon the version of *Super Tangrams* used. For example, students who observed ghost images in their version were asked questions about ghost images; others were not.

Video

A researcher videotaped children's interaction with *Super Tangrams*. Videotaping focused on how they progressed through the game, the sort of problems they encountered, what caused confusion, and how they constructed knowledge. Interviews with selected students following the posttest were also videotaped.

Interviews

Clinical interviews were conducted with 20% of students from each group to provide further information about their responses on the tests and questionnaire, and to explain the quantitative data.

Log Files

As students interacted with *Super Tangrams*, it kept a data log of the number of moves, the transformations selected, and the time taken to solve each puzzle.

Design

A quasi-experimental nonequivalent pretest-posttest group design (Schumacher & McMillan, 1993) was used. Subjects were given a pretest, one of three different treatments, and a posttest. The posttest was exactly the same as the pretest. Due to the nature of working with elementary school classes and to prevent contamination, entire classes were randomly assigned to the different conditions (*ibid.*). Subjects were divided into three groups for the DCM+, DCM, and DOM treatments. The DCM+ group (15 students) was drawn from the grade-6 students of a grade 6/7 class. The

DCM and DOM groups were established by randomly splitting a grade-6 class (14 and 15 students respectively). Table 1 shows the distribution of males and females across different groups.

	Males	Females
DCM+	9	6
DCM	6	8
DOM	6	9
Total	21	23

Table 1. Distribution of males and females

Procedure

Consent forms consisting of a sheet describing the software and the project were distributed, and all children were asked to obtain consent from their parents to participate in the study. Only children who obtained parental consent participated in the study.

A researcher visited each classroom afterwards and, in the presence of the teacher, asked the students to write the required paper and pencil tests and answer the questionnaire. Children were told that their achievements on the tests would not affect their mathematics grade at school, and that the purpose of the study was to find out how to design mathematics software that would be enjoyable to children. They were asked not to guess answers to the test questions in order to help researchers understand how to design better educational software.

Shortly afterwards, during a regular mathematics period, students completed a questionnaire measuring their attitudes towards geometry and transformation geometry. They then completed the pretest on transformation geometry.

Students were assigned to work on the computers in pairs. These groupings were made by the students' teachers. They worked on *Super Tangrams* for ten 35- to 40-minute sessions, held on consecutive school days during students' regular mathematics periods. The students were given a brief overview during the first session but thereafter were not given any adult help, except to advise them that the answers to their questions could be found in the program.

After the treatment, all students completed the same questionnaire on attitude to geometry and transformation geometry, and the same test on transformation geometry.

They also completed a follow-up questionnaire asking them about their version of *Super Tangrams*.

Following the posttest, clinical interviews were conducted with 3 students from each group to provide further information about their responses on the tests and questionnaires. The students were selected for their perceived thoughtfulness and ability to communicate. The interviews were videotaped and were 20 to 30 minutes in length. Students were asked to comment on their responses, their answers to test questions, and to events that happened during the experiment. They were shown the other versions of the program, given an explanation, and asked to comment on the differences (how much they thought they would learn, which they liked best, which was easiest/hardest).

Predictions

It was predicted that the DCM+ version would cause more learning and reflection than both DCM and DOM, and that DCM would cause more learning than DOM. It was not clear how much reflection DCM would invoke. Furthermore, it was not clear whether the difficulty involved in solving puzzles in DCM+ would have a negative effect on children's liking of the program or their motivation.

Results

The results are organized into three parts: the influence of interface style on domain learning (transformation geometry), on reflection, and on motivation.

Domain Learning
The test for measuring students' knowledge of two-dimensional transformation geometry is described above. Table 2 shows the means and medians of the pre- and posttests for all three groups. The means and medians for the pretests and posttests for the three groups are close, except for the DCM pretest and the DCM+ posttest.

An analysis of covariance was performed controlling for prior knowledge of transformation geometry, and there was a significant main effect between the groups $(F(2,40)=50.295, p=0.000)$. Tukey post hoc tests were performed to determine where these differences occurred. There was a significant difference between the DOM and DCM groups $(q(2,40)=4.47, p<0.01)$, between DCM and DCM+ groups $(q(2,40)=9.24, p<0.001)$ and between DOM and DCM+ groups $(q(2,40)=13.97, p<0.001)$. Figure 7 compares the pretest and posttest mean scores of the three groups.

	DOM	DCM	DCM+
Pretest			
mean	22.5	22.3	25.0
median	22.0	16.7	25.2
Posttest			
mean	18.9	37.2	76.1
median	18.1	36.5	85.4

Table 2. Means and medians

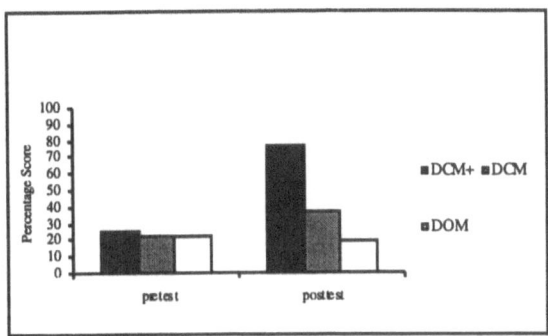

Figure 7: Mean Scores

Reflection

Data was collected for three indicators of reflection. On the questionnaire, students were asked if they had to think hard before moving a piece, and were also asked if it was easier and faster to guess. The number of puzzles solved was used as an indicator -- solving more puzzles indicating more action and correspondingly less time reflecting.

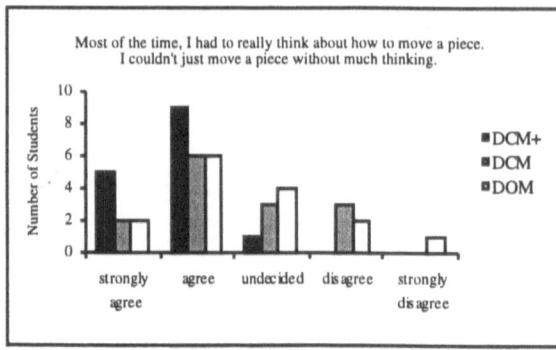

Figure 8: Thinking

Figure 8 compares the three groups' perceptions of how hard they had to think to make each move. Ninety-three percent of students in the DCM+ group agreed or strongly agreed that they could not move a piece without thinking hard. Only 57% of the DCM group and 53% of the DOM group felt this way.

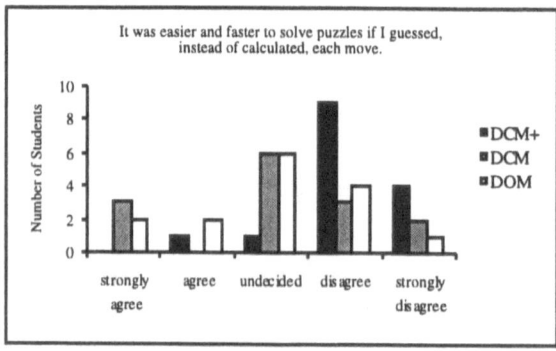

Figure 9: Guessing

Figure 9 compares the three groups' perceptions of the value of guessing. Eighty-seven percent of the DCM+ group did not think guessing was helpful in making their moves whereas 36% of the DCM group and 33% of the DOM group felt that way. In contrast, 27% of the DOM group and 21% of the DCM group apparently felt that guessing was valuable while only 7% of the DCM+ group agreed.

DCM+	31
DCM	70
DOM	77

Table 3. Mean number of puzzles completed

Table 3 shows the average number of puzzles solved by each of the three groups. This information was distilled from the log files. The DCM and DOM groups solved more than twice as many puzzles as the DCM+ group.

Motivation

One of the questions on the questionnaire asked students to rate *Super Tangrams* against other educational computer games they had played. The results are shown in Figure 10.

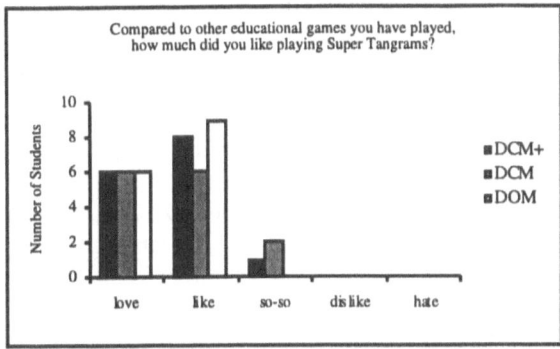

Figure 10: Liking

The children's liking of the three variations seems quite uniform.

Discussion

On the test of domain knowledge, the mean score of the DOM group dropped slightly, the mean score of the DCM group increased 15% and the mean score of the DCM+ group markedly improved by 51%. Clearly the DCM version was more effective than the DOM version, and the DCM+ version was most effective in promoting domain learning. The distribution of scores for DOM and DCM on the posttest are relatively normal while the DCM+ scores are negatively skewed (mean < median, see Table 2);

that is, a majority of the students showed superior knowledge rather than a few students improving dramatically.

The DOM and DCM students did not show a significant difference in the amount of reflection required to progress through the game. This is evident from their own perceptions of how much they had to think and also by the number of puzzles they managed to solve. In contrast, the DCM+ group had perceived their task as requiring hard thinking and discouraging guessing. They managed to solve fewer than half of the number of puzzles solved by the other two groups. Clearly the DCM+ interface style resulted in more reflective thought by the students.

On-site observations and post-hoc interviews added significant depth to these quantitative findings. From the point of view of domain learning, the mere shift from the DOM style to the DCM style had an immediate effect on children's conception of transformation geometry. For instance, in their first encounter with the concept of translation, children using the DCM style would know that translation is along a straight line. In contrast, some students in the DOM group thought of translation as a drag motion, moving curvilinearly on a two dimensional plane. One of the reasons for this was the difference in operational affordances of these interfaces. In the DOM version children would drag an object in any direction they desired, while in the DCM version, once the length and direction of the translation arrow were adjusted, they would click on *GO* and see the selected shape slide on a straight line into the desired spot. In the case of the latter there was a lag between the time children adjusted the parameters of a transformation and the time they clicked on *GO*. This lag time provided children with the opportunity to observe and think about what was taking place on the screen. Differences in understanding between children from these two groups were also observed with respect to the concepts of rotation and reflection.

The enhancements made to the DCM style, resulting in the DCM+ style, added much to the latter's efficacy to support concept development in children. The most immediate effect could be observed in *Level 1*, which was almost identical to DCM, except for two differences: 1) in most puzzles, children could not use all three transformations, and 2) there was a cost of unit operation on the number of transformations they employed. For example, to do a rotation in DCM, many children would perform two operations, a *Turn*, adjusting the angle of rotation, followed by a *Slide*. This, in some cases, meant that they never realized that they could accomplish this task using only one rotation. In contrast, children in the DCM+ group had to discover and be aware that *Turn* accomplished this in one move. Some students excitedly articulated the power of *Turn* when they discovered it (Sedighian & Klawe, 1996b). As for the effect of the cost of unit operation, in some cases students would get annoyed by their partners if they did not pay attention to the *par*, asking them to think and figure out the proper solution lest they lose points. The motivation to complete the puzzle with the fewest number of moves caused reflection and better learning of the concept.

During the study it was observed that the DCM and DOM groups' activities were characterized by much more moving of pieces than the DCM+ group. The DCM+ group's activity was characterized more by pausing, reflecting, and thinking. As children moved to *Levels* 2 and *3*, the progressive differentiation of the concepts, as presented through the fading interface, required them to engage in progressively greater degrees of reflection and reasoning. They had to pay attention to details and specifics of the concepts they were manipulating. This requirement for a greater depth of conceptual knowledge encouraged many children to use the *Learn* module to try to understand the mathematical concepts to avoid making unnecessary and costly moves (Sedighian, 1997).

In the post-hoc interviews, DCM+ students who were shown the DCM version of the program immediately understood how it worked. They observed that the DCM activities seemed much easier than their DCM+ tasks and had the same reaction to the DOM version. They said that it was very easy compared to the DCM+ version. The DCM group found the DCM+ activities more difficult, and the DOM activities easier. The DOM group had difficulty understanding what to do in the DCM+ activities, and felt that the DCM activities were more difficult than their DOM tasks. These findings indicate that different interface styles may influence children's conceptual understanding in a hierarchical manner – the more concept-focused styles encompassing the less concept-oriented ones.

The students reported liking the three versions equally well. Therefore the change of style did not have a negative impact on their motivation and perception of the activity as a whole. Ordinarily, it would be expected that the difficulty of DCM+ would have a negative effect on children's liking of this version compared to the other two. However, their liking of *Super Tangrams* seems quite uniform across these styles. It is noteworthy that during the interviews, when DCM+ students saw the DCM and DOM versions, many stated that they would not find them challenging enough to hold their interest, and that they preferred the DCM+ version.

A final point highlighting the difference between DCM and DCM+ is the inclusion of the *Hint* and the *locking-in-place* features in DCM+. These two features helped children focus more on doing the transformations rather than solving tangram puzzles. In most cases, children using the DCM+ version knew where a shape should be placed; the difficult task was to figure out how to move it there. In the light of this, the tallies, reporting children's perception of how much they had to think to move a piece, take on greater significance. Tangram puzzles can be quite difficult to solve, requiring significant cognitive effort. All three groups were motivated to solve the puzzles, but the DCM+ group had to use considerably more cognitive energy in the solving of their transformation problems. The solving of the tangram puzzles became secondary to making the transformations.

Conclusions

This study specifically addresses the design of educational interfaces. Important questions have to be raised regarding how the DM style should be used in the context of computer-based learning environments. The DM metaphor can be misapplied and misused in the design of educational interfaces. From this study, it can be stated safely that one of the main educational deficiencies of DM is caused by directly manipulating objects rather than concepts. A shift from the DOM style to the DCM style will help learners to interact with embedded educational concepts and acquire domain knowledge.

Hutchins, *et al.* (1986) characterize "directness" in terms of "distance" and "engagement". By "distance" they mean the Gulf of Execution and the Gulf of Evaluation that must be spanned. Accordingly, to create the feeling of directness in users, the challenge of interface designers is to create systems that maximize engagement and minimize distance. These goals apply to DCM-style educational interfaces, with some changes in their characterization. It is still desirable to create a feeling of full engagement for users, but with the world of conceptual interface representations rather than objects. The way in which these representations are operationlized plays an important role in creating conditions that will make learners feel that they are directly involved with the concepts and are immersed in them.

In terms of the Gulf of Evaluation, it is desirable to continue to keep the distance at a minimum so that learners can readily interpret the results of their actions. In terms of the distance across the Gulf of Execution, it is axiomatic that in a concept-centered learning environment there must be an initial distance for the learner to cover with regard to concept acquisition. Moreover, the learner must expect to learn the language of the system rather than vice versa. This kind of distance is expected in a learning environment, and so does not diminish the feeling of "directness" in the learner. This is in contrast to a productivity tool in which the user does not expect to be learning concepts.

In contrast to object-centered systems, concept-centered systems have depth and require special support to promote reflective thought and focus the learner's attention on the concepts being learned. The system must be able to provide appropriate learning opportunities by constantly moving away from the learner, leading the learner to ever greater depths of understanding. This movement is not caused by making the interface more difficult to execute, but by using the interface to require ever higher degrees of understanding of the concept. A well-designed system must constantly recede, maintaining a manageable challenging distance between what the learner knows how to execute and what the learner can still acquire. Further supports can be provided in the form of introducing constraints and/or putting a cost on the use of resources.

The shift of approach from the DOM to the DCM metaphor is not straightforward and requires further study. Research is needed to develop a typology of concepts and investigate how different concepts can be represented and operationalized. Not all concepts can be treated the same, and small changes in treatment can make big changes in learning (Sedighian & Klawe, 1996a; Sedighian & Westrom, 1997).

Acknowledgments

This research is part of the E-GEMS (Electronic Games for the Education of Math and Science) project funded by NSERC, EA Canada, BC ASI, and Apple Canada. Special thanks go to Maria Klawe for her continuous support and guidance.

References

Ausubel, D. P. (1968). Educationa; Psychology: A Cognitive View New York: Holt, Reinhart and Winston

Forman, G. (1988). Making Intuitive Knowledge Explicit Through Future Technology. In G. Forman, & P. B. Pufall (Eds.), *Constructivism in the Computer Age*. Hillsadale, NJ: Lawrence Erlbaum Associates, Publishers.

Forman, G., & Pufall, P. B. (1988). Constructivism in the Computer Age: A Reconstructive Epilogue. In G. Forman, & P. B. Pufall (Eds.), *Constructivism in the Computer Age*. Hillsadale, NJ: Lawrence Erlbaum Associates, Publishers.

Golightly, D. (1996). Harnessing the Interface for Domain Learning. *Proceedings of CHI '96: Conference Companion*, 37-38.

Guttenplan, S. (Ed.) (1995). *A Companion to the Philosophy of Mind*. Basil Blackwell Ltd., UK.

Hayes, N. A., & Broadbent, D. E. (1988). Two models of learning of intreactive tasks. *Cognition*, **22**, 249-275.

Hutchins, E. L, Hollan, J. D., & Norman, D. A. (1986). Direct Manipulation Interfaces. In D. A. Norman, & S. Draper (Eds.). *User centered system design: New perspectives in human-computer interaction.* Hillsdale, NJ: Lawrence Erlbaum Associates, Inc.

Holst, S. J. (1996). Directing Learner Attention With Manipulation Styles. *Proceedings of CHI '96: Conference Companion*, 43-44.

McMillan, J. H., & Schumacher, S. (1993). *Research in Education: A Conceptual Introduction.* New York: HarperColins College Publishers.

Norman, D. A., & Draper, S. (Eds.). *User centered system design: New perspectives in human-computer interaction.* Hillsdale, NJ: Lawrence Erlbaum Associates, Inc.

Norman, D. A. (1986). Cognitive Engineering. In D. A. Norman & S. Draper (Eds.). *User centered system design: New perspectives in human-computer interaction.* Hillsdale, NJ: Lawrence Erlbaum Associates, Inc.

Norman, D. A. (1993). *Things that make us smart: Defining human attributes in the age of the machine.* New York: Addison-Wesley Publishing Company.

Novak, J. D., & Gowin, D. B. (1984). *Learning How to Learn.* Cambridge University Press.

Polya, G. (1957). *How to Solve It.* Doubleday, New York.

Russell, D. S, & Bologna, E. M. (1982). Teaching Geometry with Tangrams. *Arithmetic Teacher*, **30**(2), 34-38.

Sedighian, K., & Klawe, M. M. (1996a). An interface strategy for promoting reflective cognition in children. *Proceedings of CHI '96, Conference Companion: Human Factors in Computing Systems*, Vancouver, 177-178.

Sedighian, K., & Klawe, M. M. (1996b). Super Tangrams: A child-centered approach to designing a computer supported mathematics learning environment. *Proceedings of the 2nd International Conference on the Learning Sciences*, Northwestern University, 490-495.

Sedighian, K. (1997). Challenge-driven learning: A model for children's multimedia mathematics learning environments. To appear in *Proceedings of ED-MEDIA '97: World Conference on Educational Multimedia and Hypermedia*, Calgary.

Sedighian, K., & Westrom, M. (1997). Designing Interactive Educational Software for Children: Some Lessons Learned. Submitted to the *DIS '97 Conference: Design of Interactive Systems*. Amsterdam, Netherlands. August 1997.

Shneiderman, B. (1988). We Can Design Better User Interfaces: A Review of Human-Computer Interaction Styles. *Ergonomics*, 31(5): 699-710.

Shneiderman, B. (1993). Direct Manipulation. In B. Shneiderman (Ed.), *Sparks of Innovation in Human-Computer Interaction*, Ablex Publ., NJ.

Svendsen, G. B. (1991). Influences of Interface Style on Problem Solving. *International Journal of Man-Machine Studies*, 35, 379-397.

Sweller, J. (1988). Cognitive Load During Problem Solving: Effects on Learning. *Cognitive Science*, 12, 257-285.

Trudel, C. I., & Payne, S. (1995). Reflection and goal management in exploratory learning. *International Journal of Human-Computer Studies*, 42, 307-339.

HyperAT: HCI and Web Authoring

Yin Leng Theng, Cécile Rigny, Harold Thimbleby and Matthew Jones

School of Computing Science, Middlesex University, U.K.

We review HCI problems with hypertext, and for authoring World Wide Web documents in particular. We suggest that a framework is required to understand the usability issues, and that these issues cannot be seen as pyschological or computing: they are multi-disciplinary. We discuss HyperAT, a prototype authoring tool, being implemented to test these ideas.

Keywords: "lost in hyperspace", authoring tool, World Wide Web, multi-disciplinary approach

1   The World Wide Web and its problems

When reading or writing a book, the user (reader or author) can use an algorithm for completing their task — for instance, start at page 1, process it, turn to next page, and so on, then stop on the final page. In contrast, there is no algorithm for reading or writing an arbitrary hypertext document that guarantees completion of, or even uniform progress during the user's task. In general, any non-trivial task involving hypertext is impossible to do well, unless computer support manages the task in such a way that a sense of direction can be provided. But this is rarely possible, either because the computer does not know enough about the task, or because the hypertext structure is unknown (as on the World Wide Web). Without a 'sense of progress' a user will never be certain when they are able to stop or when their task is completed, or if they pause, how to resume without repetition; there may always be other pages or other links in the document that need considering. There is a wide range of literature on this topic (e.g., Cockburn and Jones, 1995), though mostly concerned with users' behaviour and performance rather than the causes. For the purposes of this paper, we shall call the problem 'lost in hyperspace' (see Thimbleby, Jones and Theng, 1997 for more details). This paper will first review the problem, survey solutions to the problem, and then discuss our engineering approach to it.

When the World Wide Web (WWW) was developed in 1991, the intention was to link a select group of users such as physicists and engineers at different sites. In three years, it had an estimated 30 million users (Nielsen, 1995a). Today, the

WWW is used by millions of users all across the world. It has affected us directly, or indirectly in almost every facet of our lives, ranging from scientific work to business and education needs. The WWW has changed the Internet to the extent that it has become almost synonymous with the modern use of the Internet.

This paper concentrates on the WWW because it is the largest hypertext ever, and any usability issues are 'scaled up,' affecting millions of users (Maurer, 1996). This view was supported by the results of the 4th WWW User Survey by the Graphic, Visualisation and Usability Center conducted over October/November 1995 (Pitkow and Kehoe, 1995). From a sample size of more than 23 000, the report showed that users suffered different forms and degrees of "lostness": not being able to find a page they know is out there (34.5%); not being able to find a page once visited (23.7%); not being able to visualise they have been and where they can go (14.3%); and not being able to determine where they are (6.5%).

2   Survey of solutions to address the LIH problem on the World Wide Web

Much work has been done to address the "lost in hyperspace" (LIH) problem on the WWW. Some solutions are aimed at helping hypertext users, others are aimed at helping hypertext designers.

2.1   For the hypertext users

*   *Better navigation support mechanisms.* Nielsen (1995b) lists eight navigation support mechanisms that had been implemented in Netscape Navigator, the most popular WWW browser, to help user navigation: (1) using a standard URL notation to go to an absolute address; (2) indicating hypertext links with underlined text or figure; (3) allowing users to return to previously visited nodes using a backtracking feature; (4) allowing users to build a set of direct jumps to favourite places in hyperspace using bookmark; (5) generating a history list to allow users to go back to a list of visited nodes; (6) changing colour of underlined text once the users have seen the destination node it points to; (7) showing prospective view in the footer *before* the user makes the jump; and (8) providing landmark like "Home page" or "What's new?". Maurer (1996) suggests having overview documents to represent the structure of the hyperweb, containing a list of links to other documents, an annotated diagram, map, etc. Cockburn and Jones (1995) propose building a graphical browser that dynamically adapts to, and reinforces, users' browsing actions and users' mental models. Dynamically generated structure maps in the form

of graphical browsers are also suggested: global maps show the entire hyperspace; local maps show the "vicinity" of the current node in terms of hyperlinks to and from other related nodes; and fisheye views focus attention on important nodes by deliberately distorting the view.

* *Search and linking facilities.* Sophisticated search facilities such as keyword search, content search and fuzzy (inexact) search are indispensable for finding specific information once the size of the hyperweb exceeds browsable proportions (Maurer, 1996). Work done includes automating indexes (such as web robots or spiders) to walk the entire server tree.

* *Better adaptive and adaptable facilities.* The lack of support for typed nodes and links limits the richness of information which can be represented. A project, called MacWeb undertaken by Nanard and Nanard (1993), draws upon knowledge-based approaches to address the LIH problem, by extending the hypertext metaphor with typed links and typed nodes to represent knowledge in the hypertext as a semantic network (Clibbon and Callaghan, 1996). This solution provides great potential for building adaptive and adaptable hypertexts, taking into consideration users' needs and browsing patterns. Users can navigate round hypertexts more efficiently with a reduced chance of getting LIH.

2.2 For the hypertext designers

* *More comprehensive style guides.* Style guides describe the design principles and guidelines used to create hyperdocuments on the WWW. Many style guides have been written to help designers produce better, usable hyperdocuments. According to Tilton (1996), users' perception and assumptions about the organisation of the websites can have a major impact on the usability of the page and site design. Therefore, designers need to give users a feeling of knowing where they are. Tim (1995) suggests structuring hyperdocuments using a tree structure, and designers can use this structure to organise files into directories. To help users identify the origin and relationships of WWW pages, consistent and predictable WWW pages should be produced. The essential elements that should appear on each WWW page are (Tim, 1995; Lynch, 1995; Thimbleby, 1995, Tilton, 1996, *etc.*): (i) a meaningful title to occur at the head of the document to identify the content of the document in a fairly wide context; (ii) text-labelled buttons to provide fixed links between a series of pages to bind them into a document, e.g., "Previous", "Next", "Home", "Table of contents" buttons, *etc.*; (iii) links to other related pages in the local WWW site; and (iv) page footer to identify the origin, authorship, author contact information, copyright statement, date of creation and modification. In addition, other elements that are crucial for good WWW page writing include: writing device-independent HTML codes;

combining all the WWW pages into a single document for easier printing; keeping language simple and clear; keeping typographical styles to a minimum; putting in links to explain themselves so that users know where they are going; and keeping WWW pages short ranging from half a A4 page to 5 pages, since scrolling pages can be particularly disorientating as users move through long HTML pages.

- *More powerful programming languages.* All browsers display pages written in HTML. However, HTML does not allow authors to have much control over page and presentation layouts. While HTML provides information about content, style sheets consist of style rules that tell a WWW browser how to present a hyperdocument (Pozadzides and Quinn, 1997). At the time of this writing, Microsoft Internet Explorer 3.0 and 3.01 are the only browsers supporting Cascading Style Sheets, which means that several different style sheets, each with a different order of importance, are combined in order of importance to create a presentation style (Tilton, 1996). Though style sheets are a new development on the WWW and currently are not widely used, Nielsen (1997) predicts that they are the only solution to getting nice presentation with ever-increasing numbers of browsers and display devices. JavaScript, a programming language from Netscape incorporated in their browsers, is also gaining great popularity because users are attracted to fanciful, animation features it can produce on the WWW. There are several features JavaScript can provide for existing websites (Harold, 1996): letting server draw pictures in a window on the client; using graphics primitives to create desired WWW page, putting less load on the server; and allowing more user interaction. Recognising the potential in JavaScript and Style Sheets, the WWW Consortium has defined a new standard called JavaScript Style Sheets.

- *More systematic testing methods.* Tim (1995) advocates carrying out testing on hyperdocuments to ensure that they are well-designed and well-structured. Designers should always proof-read hyperdocuments to avoid making "silly" spelling mistakes. Designers should test-run the hyperdocument using several different client programs to ensure that it has been coded in a device-independent way. Use the server log files to monitor the readership of the hyperdocument. Another way to test the hyperdocuments is to invite feedback from readers.

- *More efficient authoring tools.* HTML documents can be written in any text editor. Many authoring tools have been developed, which can broadly be categorised into commercial tools (e.g., HoTMetaL, Netscape Gold, Front Page, etc.), and research tools. All these efforts suggest that there is a need to provide better editing facilities in authoring tools to help designers produce well-structured hyperdocuments.

So far the solutions discussed above are aimed at improving the performance of the WWW. Due to the exponential growth in WWW usage as well as an avalanche of servers, documents and hyperlinks, there is a grave concern as to how websites can be efficiently maintained. Hence, alternative solutions to the WWW are sought. A well-known example is the development of Hyper-G at the Graz University of Technology. Hyper-G, a second-generation hypermedia information system released in 1994, tries to combine the advantages of the WWW, WAIS (Wide Area Information Service), and Gopher while minimising their disadvantages. Hyper-G claims to have overcome some of the shortcomings of the WWW (Maurer, 1996). Another solution is the development of Microcosm, an open hypermedia system, by the University of Southampton. Microcosm does not suffer from some of the problems of the WWW and has been applied successfully to unstructured hypertexts on the WWW (Hall, Carr and Roure, 1994). The flexibility of Microcosm separating the link structure from the data in the system to enable separate link and data processing, makes authoring easier for designers.

3   Concrete proposals

Although much work has been done to tackle the LIH problem, it still exists (Thimbleby, Jones and Theng, 1997). *Ad hoc* methods of designing, constructing and validating hypertexts are not enough. If users get "lost" in hypertext, designers do too. This suggests that tools for designing hypertext should provide improved support for designers. Nielsen (1996) predicts that due to a change in the dominating styles for websites over recent years, a real HCI contribution essential for web design should consist of further research into these different knowledge areas: (i) knowledge of icon design; (ii) knowledge elicitation to discover appropriate information space structures; (iii) usability testing; and (iv) task analysis techniques. We agree that this is the way forward if the performance of the WWW is to be enhanced. But searching for solutions in isolated disciplines, and recommending them to designers in the hope that they would somehow remember to put them into practice, may not be as simple as it sounds. In practice, many factors could have prevented well-intentioned designers to put these good suggestions into practice. One of which could be that designers may be too overwhelmed, and/or may seemingly do not have the time and capacity to attend to all these authoring details. In order for Nielsen's suggestions to be truly effective and implementable, we should go beyond just providing designers with a list of do's and don'ts. Designers need authoring help. If some of these ideas could be automated so that designers need not worry about their implementation, chances are that better hyperdocuments could be produced since designers would be freed to concentrate on other critical issues that cannot be automated, but require sound human judgement and expertise.

This paper addresses the LIH problem in the WWW by taking a different stance, that is, integrating *proactive, multi-disciplinary* approaches to address the LIH problem with the emphasis of doing things right from the start. By integrating the approaches proposed below, a practical authoring tool called HyperAT for the design and building of usable hypertexts, is developed to test these ideas.

- *Need for good hypertext structure (Approach One).* Owing to the associative relationships that exist between nodes and links in hypertext, it is imperative that these relationships should be correctly captured and represented. Unlike books, there is no universally accepted organisational principles and structures in hypertext. Without which users will have to "guess" the structure of the hypertext, and try to understand what the interface wants to convey. The way the nodes and links within hypertext is structured is dependent upon the tasks users want to perform or try to perform, as well as the functional support provided by the hypertext. Many different approaches have been investigated to find out how best to structure information. Some researchers adopt a prescriptive approach by imposing a simple, regular structure on intractably complex information (e.g., Garzotto *et al* 1991, *etc*). These structures can be linear, hierarchical, and recursive. While hypertext is intrinsically non-linear, some hypertext authoring tools allow extensive use of linear structures, in the form of cards and stacks in HyperCard, or scrolling windows in Guide. Hierarchical structures have also been extensively used by many researchers to organise the contents of hypertexts (Smith and Newman, 1996), since users find them easy to understand (Garzotto *et al,* 1991). To some researchers, this may be forcing structure too early in the design process, which is not desirable (Halasz, 1987). However, a counter-argument is that divergence can be prevented in hypertext, normally the reason for users being LIH, and limitedness of the hypertext structure is a good way to do that (Am, 1994). Several researchers (e.g., Rada and Murphy 1992, *etc*) stressed the need for information in hypertext to be structured in such a way to support users' tasks. The types of information structures that have been investigated are hierarchical structures, network structures and a combination of both. Different information structures support different types of tasks. Mohageg (1992) found that trying to perform searching tasks in a network structure produced a negative effect on task performance. In fact, research has shown that "unfocused browsing or exploratory" tasks are best supported by a network or combination information structure, while "focused browsing or searching" tasks are best supported by a hierarchical information structure (Smith and Newman, 1996).

- *Need for good design guidelines and principles (Approach Two).* Good design takes into account characteristics of the intended users and the work that they do. Therefore, good computer systems are systems that are useful, usable and desirable, that is, people can easily learn, can do things they want to do because of the functions provided, and people like them. Interactive systems require iterative design. Since disorientation can occur in a spatial network of nodes and links, we want to re-look at design issues. We need to ensure that good hypertext design principles and guidelines are incorporated into the building of hypertext in the first place. Much of the work done so far in hypertext design concentrated only on the interface design issues. Design principles and guidelines should go beyond just providing an attractive interface. By "design interface issues," we refer to the information channel that allows the hypertext to explain the internal structure and representation of nodes and links to the user in the simplest and most effective way, and for the user to communicate his intentions and obtain the answer to his intentions. If users were to be helped in navigating hypertext, the user interface needs to be usable. On the other hand, users build models of what is happening in their minds, and they use these models called "mental models" in their interactions. To proceed with their interactions with the hypertext, users expect it to give them cues, otherwise they will need to rely on their prior experiences with hypertexts and computer systems. This in itself is not bad. However, there are occasions when users' prior experiences interfere with their understanding and interactions with the current hypertext they are navigating. To ensure that this does not take place, we should provide users with a clear and unambiguous user interface, reflecting accurately the underlying hypertext structure of nodes and links. Interface design principles applicable to hypertext authoring are: consistency of presentation; minimal mental overload for users; ease of learning and use; good conceptual model of users; well-structured network of nodes and links; and full and continuous feedback to users.

- *Need for an engineering, task-based approach to understand users' needs (Approach Three).* It is well-known that designers often design for themselves unless they are trained to realise that people are diverse, and that users are unlikely to be like them. Solutions to the LIH problem should then address the issues of helping users navigate through conceptual space. We need to have an accurate respresentation of users' behaviour and actions when they perform or try to perform common tasks such as browsing, information search, seeking references and recall. By trying to make sense of what users should do or what they actually do, hypertext authors will at least stand a better chance of producing user-centred hypertexts that will meet users' needs more effectively. Task analysis and cognitive user modelling techniques can be used to help us understand users' behaviour and actions, taking into consideration users' reasoning and learning processes (Theng, Rigny, Thimbleby and Jones, 1996).

4   HyperAT: Implementing the proposals

HyperAT stands for "Hypertext Authoring Tool". HyperAT is a prototype designer tool for authoring hypertext and WWW documents. It is implemented in Macintosh Common Lisp (version 3.9) for PowerPCs. We would like to emphasize that it is not the intention of HyperAT to provide a full range of editing facilities with attractive interface, and HyperAT does not claim in any way capable of competing with commercial tools in this aspect. However, being a research tool, HyperAT aims to investigate facilities not seen or fully exploited in popular commercial tools which we think are crucial in helping designers build more usable hypertexts. HyperAT aims to address the LIH problem by helping designers manage the complexity of the design process without themselves getting "lost", and users navigating the hyperdocuments produced by HyperAT without feeling "lost". We see HyperAT contributing in these areas:

- HyperAT is a practical authoring tool to help hypertext designers build usable hypertexts.
- HyperAT is an experiment in collaborative efforts involving many disciplines.
- HyperAT is an analytical research tool for contextualising and delivering the results of hypertext usability to hypertext designers.
- HyperAT is a preliminary and innovative investigation in cognitive user modelling minimalism in hypertext authoring.

4.1   *General overview*

Figure 1 gives a general overview of HyperAT, its inputs and outputs. Inputs refer to the multi-disciplinary approaches that underlie the design of the authoring and usability components that made up HyperAT. Because the WWW is a special hypertext, these approaches had to be adapted for use on the WWW. Approach One stresses good WWW page structure to help both designers and users. Approach Two examines design guidelines and principles, adapted to good WWW style guides. Approach Three emphasizes the importance of understanding users' browsing needs and the tasks they perform. Outputs are the deliverables produced by HyperAT. Besides providing the basic authoring facilities to produce WWW pages, HyperAT also delivers usability results to designers regarding any usability problems that might be detected during its analysis.

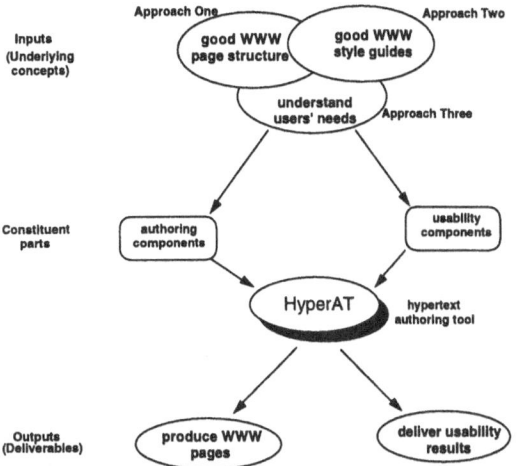

Figure 1: General overview of HyperAT, its inputs and outputs

An understanding of HCI elements essential for any interactive systems is crucial in designing successful interactive systems. In designing the authoring components, we incorporated two underlying design concepts, that is, the need to impose a structure, and the need to incorporate good WWW style guidelines and principles. For the usability components, we incorporated features that help designers to better understand users and their browsing behaviour.

4.2   *Authoring components*

The main objective of HyperAT is to help designers build usable, well-structured hyperdocuments. By that, we refer to a hyperdocument with the following characteristics: (i) no links that go nowhere; (ii) no nodes that are not linked; and (iii) minimum number of links traversed to reach required nodes. The authoring components in HyperAT provide the basic authoring environment for the creation, loading and modification of hyperdocuments. HyperAT's facilities are accessed using a graphical, user-based interface. Hyperdocuments are created via a form-like screen and converted into predetermined HTML format, which can be displayed on the WWW using a WWW browser. Designers can also display graphically both global and local views of the structure of hyperdocuments created. Hard copies of the hypertext structure and the associated HTML coding can be printed and kept for documentation as well as for maintenance purposes. A HTML-editor is also incorporated to provide designers with a menu to write HTML codes, without designers having to memorise the syntax.

Imposing a structure (Approach One)

Despite its broad appeal, one of the limitations of the WWW is that there is no information structuring facilities beyond hyperlinks (Maurer, 1996). Because hierarchies are easily understood and used by both hypertext designers and readers (Tim, 1995, Lynch, 1995), we had incorporated into HyperAT quasi-hierarchical structures as framework for capturing information. HyperAT captures node relationships using a simple parent-child analogy. This simple way of representing node relationships is not only intuitive to designers but powerful in constructing data structures. Node relationships are expressed in terms of the associations between nodes. There are two common kinds of associations between nodes and they are represented in terms of hierarchical and cross-referenced links.

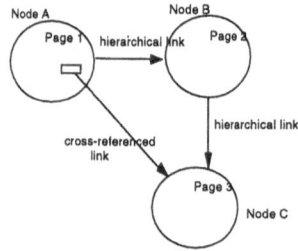

Figure 2: Relationship between nodes A, B and C

Representing these links in HyperAT is simple. Using Figure 2 as an example, the relationships among nodes A, B and C are described by these facts:

- *Fact 1*: "node A is hierarchically linked to node B"
- *Fact 2*: "node A is referentially linked to node C"
- *Fact 3*: "node B is hierarchically linked to node C"

To input information about the nodes, a form-like screen is used to capture information about the nodes. In HyperAT, a node refers to a unit of information representing a WWW page. Each page has the following attributes: file name refers to the name of the HTML document to be created; window name refers to the title of a WWW page; node name refers to the name of a WWW page; icon name refers to any icon file associated with a WWW page; node text refers to the body of text which may/may not contain hotspots or cross-referenced links in a WWW page; neighbour nodes refer to WWW pages referenced by cross-referenced links in the node text; and parent node name refers to the parent of a WWW page. To represent the relationship between node A and node C, we enter into the node text a HTML <a href="c.html"> tag to indicate a cross-referenced link from node A to node C. Figure 3 shows the various input screens recording how these three facts are captured in HyperAT.

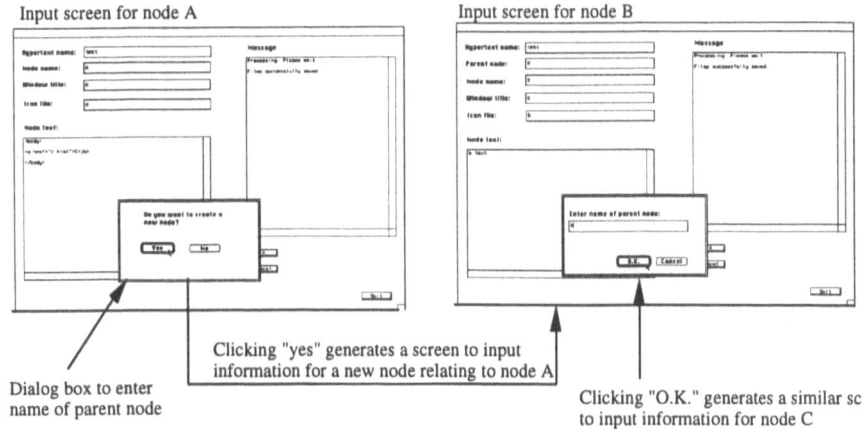

Figure 3: Screen shots to input information on nodes A, B and C

During the conversion of the hyperdocuments into HTML codes, HyperAT also generates a table of contents, a hierarchical representation of the structure of the hyperdocuments, accessible from every page of the hyperdocument, using the "contents" button (Figure 4). A fisheye view of related pages with respect to users' current page, is also provided to help users better understand the structure of the hyperdocument in relation to where they are, thus ameliorating the LIH phenomenon.

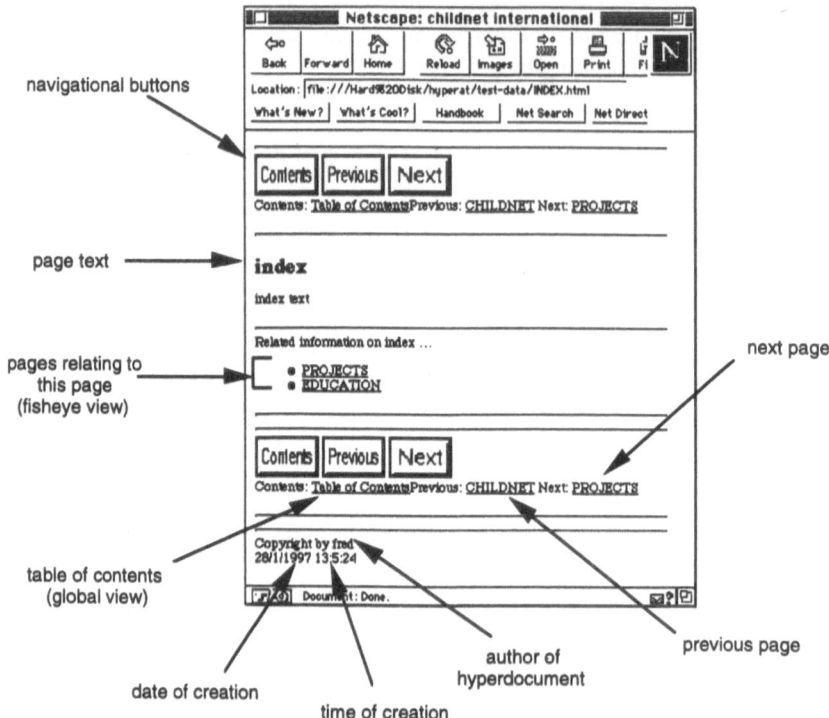

navigational buttons

page text

pages relating to
this page
(fisheye view)

next page

table of contents
(global view)

previous page

date of creation

author of
hyperdocument

time of creation

Figure 4: A sample WWW page generated by HyperAT

Besides providing within HyperAT's authoring environment an automated, hierarchical structuring feature to represent node relationships, we also incorporated other authoring aids. One is a generated trace of created nodes during a HyperAT session to provide useful memory jots for designers, who may be interrupted during the HyperAT session or are simply confused over the nodes created. Another is a generated global map showing the structure of the hyperdocument with its constituent nodes. Clicking onto a node will bring up another map, with that node as the root node, providing designers with a fisheye view cancelling off other details not related to it.

WWW guidelines and principles for better design (Approach Two)

Designing, structuring and maintaining websites is difficult. Not only should designers ensure that websites are structurally sound to prevent users from getting

LIH while surfing the WWW, they have to create websites that are aesthetic enough to attract users. Proper WWW page design is largely a matter of balancing the structure and relationship of menu or home pages and individual content pages or other linked graphics and documents. The goal is to build a hierarchy of menus and pages that is natural and well-structured to the users, and does not interfere with the use of the WWW pages or mislead them (Lynch, 1995). Given that there are potential difficulties in creating WWW pages that are both easy to use and full of complex content, Tilton (1996) proposes that the best strategy is to consistently apply a few basic document design principles in every single WWW page designers create.

We implemented into HyperAT a few established website design principles and guidelines to illustrate that they can be automated in any authoring tool without designers having to worry about their implementation. Figure 4 shows a sample WWW page generated by HyperAT. To ensure consistency of presentation, every WWW page has a standard "look and feel" with navigational buttons at the top and bottom. Each WWW page contains essential elements like the title, author, date and time of creation, button bars which represent fixed links that allow users to move to content page, previous page, or next page. Links to other related WWW pages are also generated for each WWW page so that users can have a better understanding of how they can obtain related materials.

WWW browsers provide users with a prospective view by showing the URL with path and filename in the footer before users make the jump (Jones, 1996). Adopting this idea, HyperAT provides users with prospective information by generating the title of the pages users would move to if they were to click onto the navigational buttons. For example, "previous" and "next" buttons in Figure 4 indicate moving to pages named "Childnet" and "Projects" respectively. These names are more meaningful as they reflect titles of WWW pages, in contrast to the URL's way of naming of pathnames. Because these prospective views that accompany navigational buttons are not hard-coded but automatically generated by HyperAT, no extra effort is therefore required from designers to ensure the inclusion and maintenance of this feature.

4.3   Usability components

In the 'early' years of website design, efforts had been focused on hacking HTML as the main requirement for creating a website, and user interface design is often an afterthought. Nielsen (1996) predicts that web-surfing is dead, with only a few websites visited repeatedly by a substantial number of users. Owing to a change in relationship to web design, there is an increasing need to treat users as individuals rather than a nestful of hungry GET-request users. Usable WWW pages that subscribe to users' needs should be developed. However, this is not a simple task.

Understanding users' browsing pattern and needs (Approach Three)

Designers need authoring aids to help them understand users' needs and browsing behaviour. Tim (1995) suggests carrying out testing on the hyperdocuments produced even though testing takes time. However, the decision of how much testing designers do depends on the quality of the document designers wish to provide. Hence, apart from the basic editing facilities of create, edit and save, embodied within HyperAT is an experimental, authoring testbed which allows hypertext designers to carry out different modes of usability testing on the hyperdocuments created by HyperAT, all within the authoring environment of HyperAT: (4.3.1) structural analysis; (4.3.2) real user evaluation; and (4.3.3) executable user modelling. The ability to toggle between different modes makes testing less cumbersome, and hence more convenient for designers, thereby increasing the chance of creating more usable hyperdocuments. We have implemented the first and second modes of testing in HyperAT, and are exploring the potential of non-human user testing.

4.3.1 Structural analysis

In HyperAT, not only do we want to help designers structure information, we also want them to avoid structural inconsistencies and mistakes. By treating users like computers, we implemented a formal way of analysing the structure of the hyperdocument. HyperAT allows designers to analyse the structure by firstly, performing integrity checks on the nodes and links, and secondly, measuring the complexity of the structure of hyperdocuments. The analysis reflects usability measures for various tasks based on the structure of the hyperdocuments. If the structure of a hyperdocument is inconsistent or too complex, chances are that users would become confused and "lost". This first-cut evaluation of the hyperdocuments alerts designers to take corrective measures as early as possible in the design process before it is too late.

The more complex the structure of the hyperdocument is, the more easily users may feel "lost". In HyperAT, designers can detect structural inconsistencies like missing or inconsistently-named files/nodes. This form of analysis brings to designers' attention "silly" mistakes that can be easily rectified. The simple metrics implemented to measure the complexity of the structure of the hyperdocuments are:

- *No. of nodes*. HyperAT calculates the total number of nodes in the hyperdocuments, together with a listing of all the nodes present. If the number goes beyond a certain value, 10 000 nodes for example, then perhaps the structure may be too complex. Designers may have to decide to reorganise the structure.

- *No. of links per node.* This metric indicates how "busy" the nodes are in terms of the number of links per node, both in-coming links and out-going links. If a node has too many links, then designers might infer that it contains too much information. Perhaps the design decision is to split it into simpler nodes, since good design guideline suggests that nodes should be kept simple.

- *All possible paths from a given node.* Designers can query this information by selecting from a list of nodes. This information provides designers with all possible paths from a given node to all the leaf nodes in the hyperdocument. Designers can find out from this information the number of nodes that has to be taken to reach a leaf node. If the number is too high, then it would imply that the structure is too complex. Designers can perhaps make use of this information to provide more directed navigational help to users.

- *Depth of a structure.* This metric shows the number of levels away from the root node that is present in the hyperdocument. Accompanying this information is a global map of the structure. Clicking onto a node will open up another map which is a fisheye map of that particular node.

- *No. of successors.* This metric isolates those nodes with less than three successors from those with three or more successors. Though the number three may be arbitrary and may vary for different domains, it forces designers to re-think of the structure if too many nodes have more than three successors, violating their design principle to keep structure simple.

4.3.2 Real user evaluation

Real user evaluation is important because hyperdocuments are designed for users and not just what designers think or feel are important. Real users can be employed to evaluate hyperdocuments on the WWW with their transactions logged by the server log files, a view shared by Tim (1995) and Shneiderman (1997). However, Tim (1995) cautions that analysing the server log files takes time, if designers have to do that manually. Therefore, to help designers analyse these log files, HyperAT has a facility that parses and analyses server log files and interprets them, providing designers with useful insights into understanding users' browsing pattern. In HyperAT, we have implemented the following:

- *Frequencies of visits.* This information provides designers with information on the most visited pages to spur them to think of reasons why certain pages are more frequently visited than others. Could it be a case of design flaws? The whole idea about giving designers this kind of information is to bring to their awareness and set them thinking about their designs.

- *Clients' browsing information.* This report provides designers with the browsing path of all clients who visited the websites held in the WWW

server for a particular period. This means that designers can get real users to
browse a website, and then analyse their browsing pattern.

- *Pages visited.* Designers can perform a query to find out information about
  pages visited. The data captured include the time and date of visit, and
  frequencies of visits.
- *Clients visited.* Designers can also query browsing behaviour of a certain
  client.

HyperAT also generates a report to compare users' performance in terms of the
goals satisfied and the number of steps taken to achieve these goals, with the actual
steps based on designers' opinions (Figure 5). If users were taking more steps than
expected, then designers might want to investigate the reasons by re-examining the
structure of the hyperdocument, and/or interviewing the users concerned. In
HyperAT, we have implemented some ideas to demonstrate that analysing the
server log files containing otherwise untappped users' data, can be useful design
aids to pinpoint usability problems, and guide design decisions.

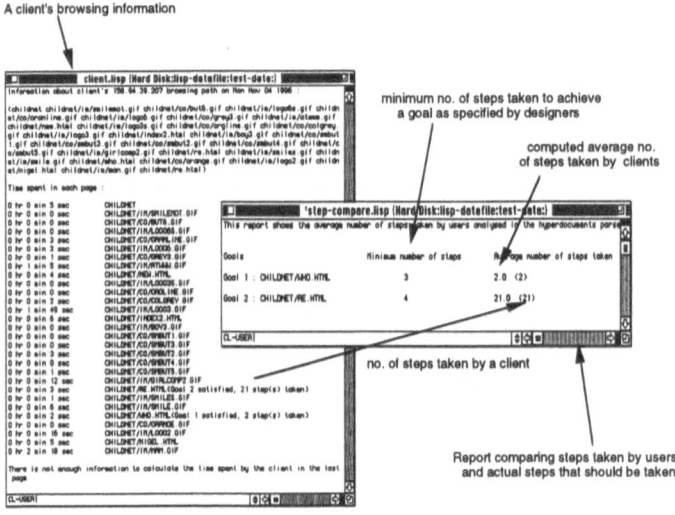

Figure 5: Report comparing steps taken by users and actual steps that should be
taken

4.3.3   Executable user modelling

In user modelling evaluation, we propose incorporating CUM-DesTool into
HyperAT to automate the usability evaluation of hyperdocuments produced by
HyperAT. CUM-DesTool is a tool for running executable user models to pinpoint
potential usability problems for interactive systems (Rigny and Thimbleby, 1996),

so that hypertext designers can make informed decisions based on recommendations suggested for improved design. Executable user models are software agents that simulate real users' behaviour, as well as predict users' performance. They can embed multi-disciplinary knowledge that most designers and most users would not be expected to know or be able to verbalise in their accounts of interaction. They are able to do more exhaustive checking of the hypertext prototypes, long before they have reached a stage where actual human-user interaction would be practicable. Because user models are reusable, it is possible to rapidly simulate large groups of users and obtain useful statistical information. The idea in using executable models achieves a two-fold purpose in rapidly iterating the design process and avoiding many design blunders. However, the reliability and efficiency of the executable user models is very much dependent on the cognitive theories used to generate them (Barnard and May, 1993). It is, therefore, important that the results obtained from simulating executable user models be sufficiently tested for them to be reliable (Wilson and Clarke, 1993).

Preliminary work carried out to investigate incorporating CUM-DesTool into HyperAT demonstrates that it is feasible (Rigny, Theng, and Thimbleby, 1996; Theng, Rigny, Thimbleby and Jones, 1996). Given that HyperAT generates a formal description of the hyperdocument (using HTML format), it is possible in principle to use the description as inputs into CUM-DesTool. All that needs to be done is to define and implement an interpreter to read and parse the description (Figure 6). Since CUM-DesTool and HyperAT are both written in LISP, combining the two tools is only a matter of programming.

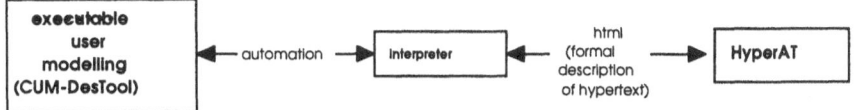

Figure 6: Implementing executable user models into HyperAT

5   Conclusions

Although much research effort has been invested to address the LIH problem, solutions have only been marginal. This paper described HyperAT, a research tool to help designers manage the complexity of the design and validation processes without themselves getting "lost". The approach taken in HyperAT is novel in that we integrated and implemented established HCI elements to ensure proper structuring and presentation of hyperdocuments, as well as to provide different modes of usability evaluation of the hyperdocuments.

Work with HyperAT now involves validating it and the approach it represents with different types of designers (e.g., novice, intermediate, experienced), as well as strengthening the usability environment it can offer to help designers build better, usable and easily maintainable WWW pages.

This paper is based on Yin Leng Theng's PhD research.

References

Am, O. (1994), "Cyberspace and the structure of knowledge,"
    <http://www.hsr.no/~onar/ess/cyberspace_and_the_structure_of_knowledge.html>

Barnard P. J. and May J. (1993), "Cognitive Modelling for User Requirements,"
    In P. F. Byerley, P. J. Barnard & May J. (Eds), *Computers, Communication and Usability: Design issues, research and methods for integrated services*, Elsevier, pp 101-145.

Clibbon, K. and Callaghan, M. (1996), "Beyond Halasz's Hypertext Research Agenda – The WWW?" to appear in Special Issue of *International Journal of Human-Computer Studies on 'HCI & The Web'*, Buckingham Shum, S. and McKnight, C., eds. (forthcoming, 1997).

Cockburn, A. and Jones, S. (1995), "Trails, trials and tribulations: unravelling navigational problems in the world-wide web," *Proceedings of the 5th Workshop on Information Technologies and Systems (WITS '95)*, Netherlands.

Garzotto, F., and Paolini, P., Schwabe, D., and Bernstein, M. (1991), "Tools for designing hyperdocuments," In Berk, E. and Delvin, J. (Eds.), *Hypertext/Hypermedia Handbook*, McGraw-Hill.

Halasz, F.G. (1987), "Reflections on NoteCards: Seven issues for the next generation of hypermedia systems," *Proceedings of Hypertext '87*, pp. 345-365, ACM Press.

Hall, W., Carr, L. and Roure, D.D. (1995), "Linking the WWW and Microcosm," *BCS Workshop on New Directions in Software Development*.

Harold, E.R. (1996), "The comp.lang.java FAQ List,"<http://sunsite.unc.edu/javafaq/javafaq.html>

Jones, M. (1996), "Uniting Authors and Readers – Active Links on the World Wide Web," *APICHI96 Conference Campanion*, pp. 77–81.

Lynch, P. J. (1995), " Yale's World Wide Web Style Manual," <http://info.med.yale.edu/caim/manual-1.html>

Maurer, H. (1996), *HyperWave: The Next Generation WEB Solution*, Addison-Wesley.

Mohageg, M. F. (1992), "The influence of hypertext linking structures on the efficiency of information retrieval," *Human Factors*, **34** (**3**), pp. 351-367.

Nielsen, J. (1997), "Trends for the web in 1997," Jakob Nielsen's Alertbox for January 1997, <http:www.useit.com/alertbox/9701.html>

Nielsen, J. (1996), "Relationships on the Web," Jakob Nielsen's Alertbox for January 1996, <http://www.useit.com/alertbox/9601.html>

Nielsen, J. (1995a), *Multimedia and Hypertext: The Internet and Beyond*, AP Professional.

Nielsen, J. (1995b), "Navigation features in Netscape 1.1," Jakob Nielsen's Alertbox for July 1996, <http://www.useit.com/alertbox/9507.html>

Pitkow, J. and Kehoe, C. (1995), *GVU's WWW 4th User Surveys*, <http://www.cc.gatech.edu/gvu/user_surveys/survey-10-1995/>

Pozadzides, J. and Quinn, L. (1997), "Cascading Style Sheet Quick Tutorial," <http:www.htmlhelp.com/reference/css/quick-tutorial.html>

Rada, R. and Murphy, C. (1992), "Searching versus browsing in hypertext,"
Hypermedia, **4(1)**, pp.1-30.

Rigny, C., Theng, Y.L. and Thimbleby, H. (1996), "Cognitive user models as design aids," *HCI'96*, pp. 139 – 149, U.K.

Rigny, C. and Thimbleby, H. (1996), "CUM-DesTool: applying executable user models for designing interacting systems," *HCI'96 Adjunct Proceedings*, pp. 145–149.

Shneiderman, B. (1997), "Designing information-abundant websites: Issues and Recommendations," to appear in *International Journal of Human-Computer Studies (1997)*.

Smith, P. and Newman, I. (1996), "Applying usability research to the Web: Virtual hypermedia domains and virtual search hierarchies," to appear in Special Issue of *International Journal of Human-Computer Studies on 'HCI & The Web'*, Buckingham Shum, S. and McKnight, C., eds. (forthcoming, 1997).

Theng, Y.L., Rigny, C., Thimbleby, H., and Jones, M. (1996), "Cognitive task graphs and executable user models for better hypertext," *APCHI'96*, pp. 421–433.

Theng, Y.L., Rigny, C., Thimbleby, H. and Jones, M. (1996), "Improved conceptual design for better hypertext," *HCI'96*, pp. 181 – 188.

Thimbleby, H. (1995), "Middlesex University Style Guide," <http://www.cs.mdx.ac.uk/esrc/style.html>

Thimbleby, H., Jones, M. and Theng, Y.L. (1997), "Is 'lost in hyperspace' lost in controversy?" *Hypertext'97*, poster presentation, Southampton (U.K.).

Tilton, J. (1996), "Composing good HTML," <http://www.cs.cmu.edu/~tilt/cgh>

Tim, B.L. (1995), "Style Guide for Online Hypertext," <http://www.w3.org/pub/www/provider/style/all.html>

Wilson, F. and Clarke, A. (1993), "Evaluating system design realisations," In P. F. Byerley, P. J. Barnard & May J. (Eds), *Computers, Communication and Usability: Design issues, research and methods for integrated services,* Elsevier, pp 379–411.

Separating User Knowledge of Domain and Device: A Framework

Peter Timmer and John Long

Ergonomics and HCI Unit, University College London,
26 Bedford Way, London, WC1H 0AP.
Phone: 0171 380 7777 ext. 5304
Email: p.timmer@ucl.ac.uk

Ergonomics and HCI Unit, University College London,
26 Bedford Way, London, WC1H 0AP.
Phone: 0171 387 7557
Email: j.long@ucl.ac.uk

A framework for modelling user-device interaction is presented. Models constructed with the framework explicitly separate 1) what the operator knows about the work (domain) being carried out, from 2) what the operator knows about the state of the devices used to carry out that work. Using an illustration from Air Traffic Management (ATM), the value of such separation is shown, for the diagnosis of operator behaviour that leads to system ineffectiveness. The design implications of using such worksystem models, in conjunction with domain models, are discussed.

Keywords: Mental representation, Domain, Problem diagnosis, Air Traffic Management.

1   Introduction

Interest in 'domains' is growing within the Human-Computer Interaction (HCI) community: domain knowledge (Sutcliffe, Benyon & van Assche, 1996); domain analysis (Dowell, Salter & Zekrullahi, 1995); domain-oriented environments (Fischer, 1993); and domain model integration (Timmer & Long, 1996). This trend accompanies a move away from issues of design for 'usability', towards a view of design for 'effective systems'. For example, Fischer is not so much interested in developing a 'usable' domain-oriented kitchen design environment, as a design-environment that supports the user in designing better 'quality' kitchens (albeit without experiencing usability problems during the design process). The distinction is thus that, on the one hand there is a human-computer worksystem that interacts, and on the other a domain of objects (examples of objects being: kitchen designs; text documents; or aircraft) that are transformed as a consequence of worksystem interaction. Given that we can express the 'quality' of a designed kitchen (in terms of how easy it is to clean; how safe it is for young children to play in; or whether or not it makes best use of limited space), so we can conclude that human-computer worksystems should not only be 'usable', but support the performance of high quality work (i.e. work that is of a desirable quality). Establishing the quality of the work carried out by a worksystem is the activity of domain analysis. Such analysis requires domain knowledge (about the attributes e.g. of a kitchen design). Resultant domain models need 'integration' with other models of human-computer interactions, to support designers in the diagnosis of poor quality work in terms of particular sequences of interaction. While none of the above is new (Rasmussen & Vicente, 1990; Woods & Hollnagel, 1987; Moray, Lootsteen & Pajak, 1986), the growing interest in 'domains' seeks to develop more explicit and more formal techniques for analysis and modelling etc. than have been used before.

This paper presents a framework for modelling user (hereafter called 'operator') mental representations. The framework is illustrated using a simplified simulation of the domain of Air Traffic Management (ATM). Mental representations are taken to be synonymous with operator 'knowledge' or 'what the operator knows'. Models of operator mental representations, and how they are altered during interaction, especially by device feedback, are of value in the diagnosis of design problems - or why particular interactions failed to result in work of the desired quality. The main aim of this paper, however, is not to re-assert the acknowledged value of such models, but rather to claim that mental representations are of different classes. Further, an important class distinction is between representations of the domain, and representations of the state of the devices used to carry out work on objects in that domain. The illustration provided here distinguishes 1) what the operator knows about the aircraft (domain objects) under their management (that is their safety, fuel consumption, progress to plan etc.), from 2) what the operator knows about the condition of the devices used to manage that domain (e.g. an aircraft's altitude, as shown on a flight strip, may no longer be accurate as an intervention to change that aircraft's altitude may have just taken place, hence the strip's altitude data field needs updating). In ATM, this distinction is of particular importance as the ATM domain is not directly observable, indeed the operator constructs a mental representation of the state of the domain (relative positions of aircraft to each other) purely by reference to the available worksystem devices. Knowing that there is a discrepancy between the actual state of the ATM domain, and a device's representation of the state of the domain is, therefore, important for carrying out effective work.

1.1 Common Elements of Operator Modelling Frameworks in HCI

The HCI and process control literature contains a wide variety of operator modelling frameworks. Such frameworks may be characterised as having five common elements, which are used to illustrate the framework proposed here.

First, operator modelling frameworks presume an operator '**mental architecture**'. Such an architecture is comprised of an explicit set of mental representations and processes that make operator mental behaviour possible. Such HCI architectures include: Soar (Newell, 1990); ACT-R (Anderson, 1993); ICS (Barnard & Teasdale, 1993); and COSIMO (Cacciabue, Decortis, Drozdowicz, Masson & Nordvik, 1992).

Second, operator modelling frameworks presume a set of **modelling procedures**. These procedures exist to support model construction, with the given architecture; and to ensure models 'run' (if computational, e.g. Soar), or are consistent, if paper-based (e.g. KLM (Card, Moran & Newell (1983))). An example procedure would be the re-specification of knowledge as production rules (in Soar).

Third, a framework imposes upon models (constructed with that framework) a **representational format**. Possible formats include: paper-based grammar expressions (Reisner, 1984); numerical values (Card, Moran & Newell, 1983); or a code-based output from an executed programme (Blandford & Young, 1993).

Fourth, a framework presumes a specific **scope** (which may be constrained by the architecture and procedures). Blandford & Young's problem-solving process descriptions, and the necessary level of detail required of knowledge specifications to run a Programmable User Model (PUM), restrict the scope of a Soar-based PUM modelling framework. At present, such a framework is appropriate for generating predictions about human mental behaviour for small, well defined problem-solving tasks (Rieman, Lewis, Young & Polson, 1994).

Fifth, frameworks presume a **purpose**. The common distinction here is between the description or prediction of operator (physical and mental) behaviour. Although presented last, it should be the purpose above all that guides the modeller in selecting an appropriate modelling framework for their particular purpose.

1.2 Programmable User Models (PUMs)

Given the five common elements, a single computational (in contrast to paper-based) framework will now be described - the framework for constructing (putative) Programmable User Models (PUMs) (Blandford & Young, 1993).

A recent trend in cognitive modelling has been towards the computationally 'runnable' operator model (Young, Green & Simon, 1989). Runnable operator models (of which a PUM is an example), are intended as a future tool to be developed. Blandford and Young present a "concrete demonstration of what a PUM might 'look like'". The PUM's framework uses Soar for its mental architecture. Soar embodies specifications of control structures that manage mental processes, such as problem-solving. A range of framework procedures are necessary for PUM construction. Procedures include: knowledge analysis 'about the device and task'; and specification of the results of that knowledge analysis in an Instruction Language (IL). The representational format of constructed models is as printable files of code. Organisation of Soar's control structures, such as heuristics for carrying out means-ends analysis, makes use of this PUM's framework complex - which may be considered as configuring the Soar framework. The scope of a the putative PUM's framework is the prediction of problem-solving mental behaviour, involved in carrying out a specified task. A purpose for PUM construction may be the prediction of mental 'problem-solving' behaviour, given a system specification. As such, a PUM would be a tool for simulating human behaviour with a device, and would make possible the early evaluation of system design specifications, prior to implementation, and in the absence of human operators. Blandford and Young emphasize the separation of knowledge about 1) how the simulated operator solves the problem, from 2) what the operator knows about the task. Domain knowledge, as characterised in this paper, exists implicitly embedded in the task description.

1.3   Air Traffic Management (ATM)

As stated earlier, the framework for modelling classes of operator mental representations presented here will be illustrated with reference to a simplified simulation of the ATM domain which will now be described together with its simulated ATM worksystem. The ATM domain consists of aircraft traversing airspace. Components of the ATM worksystem are an operator interacting with a set of devices (a radar and Flight Progress Strips (FPSs)). By interacting with the radar, the operator may change the altitude and speed of aircraft under management (there was no radio telephone, interventions being initiated by pull-down menu options). The quality of work carried out by the worksystem is expressed in terms of the safety and expedition (fuel use, progress to flight plan etc.) of aircraft under management - values for safety, for example, being a function of the relative positions of aircraft to each other. The framework supports the construction of 'descriptive' models of ATM operator-device interactions. A model of the domain (Dowell, 1992) measures the quality of work carried out as a consequence of those interactions.

Models of ATM worksystem (operator-device) behaviour make particular reference to classes of operator mental representations, and mental processes that 'behave' (or operate upon) those representations. Worksystem models are then used, in conjunction with domain models, to express system effectiveness (see framework 'purpose' (Section 5)). Separation of operator mental representations of domain and devices, in conjunction with a domain model, permits description of: the actual state of aircraft from moment to moment (from the domain model); the operator's representation of the state of that domain (often termed the operator's 'picture' or mental model); and the operator's mental representation of how well the devices used in management represent the domain.

Having emphasised the importance of separating mental representations of domain and device, a framework for achieving this separation will be briefly described. Then a model is presented to illustrate how the framework is operationalised. Last, an example demonstrates the importance of separation, in diagnosing ineffectiveness of system performance.

2 Framework for Modelling Operator Mental Representations

The proposed framework will now be described, using the five components identified earlier. While the need for modelling separate classes of mental representation has already been made, its should be underlined that the framework models more than representations. Essentially the framework is intended for modelling worksystem behaviour, a by-product of its use being models that provide a separated account of 1) the operator's 'picture' of the domain, and 2) the operator's knowledge (of the accuracy) of device representations of the state of the domain. Within a worksystem, the distinction already made, between on the one hand the operator, and on the other the devices with which the operator interacts, is maintained. Before discussing framework components, the scope of the framework will be briefly described, and the type of data needed for modelling with the framework will be characterised.

2.1 Scope of the Framework

The framework is used to construct descriptive (as opposed to predictive) models of observed data, over a range of ATM scenarios (having different levels of traffic density). The framework captures data concerning operator mental representations, mental behaviour and physical behaviour. Such models require a rich set of data for construction: head movements; hand movements; and an accompanying concurrent verbal protocol for inferring mental behaviour. The purpose of this paper is to illustrate separation of mental representations using the ATM domain, since the framework has been constructed to model such data. Thus, while a generalised framework for modelling other domains may be possible (requiring some re-configuration of the framework) the proposed framework should be considered appropriate at present for modelling simulated ATM worksystems.

2.2   Operator Mental Architecture

The framework's mental architecture has been derived from a computational architecture, 'the framework for induction', (Holland, Holyoak, Nisbett & Thagard, 1987). In contrast to the induction architecture, the proposed architecture is specified as a paper-based diagram (like the Model Human Processor of Card Moran & Newell (1983)) with textual descriptions.

The operator mental architecture distinguishes four classes of mental structure: storage; process; transducer; and representational. Three major storage structures are specified: long- term memory (LTM); working memory; and a goal store, accommodating a single active goal. Eleven process structures are loosely associated with particular storage structures: 'decay' and 'store' in long term memory; 'form', 'pop', 'suspend' and 'reactivate', for goal management in the goal store; and higher level processes of 'categorise', 'problem-solve' and 'evaluate' in working memory. A single mental processor is assumed, hence models show operator behaviour as a serial stream. An input transducer, with an associated 'encode' process, maps environmental stimuli into a mental code. An output transducer, with an 'execution' process, maps an action specification into physical behaviour. A set of arrows connect process structures, detailing pathways through the architecture. These pathways constrain which processes may follow other processes. For example, the architecture assumes that categorisation of a stimuli always follows encoding.

Mental representational structures take the form of mental categories and category instances. Figure 2 shows a hierarchy of mental categories, used in modelling an operators 'picture' of the domain. Categories in the hierarchy are particular to ATM in that they reflect the different states that aircraft under management may assume. By encoding two radar traces close together, and at the same altitude, the operator's representation of the domain may be updated to reflect two 'unsafe aircraft' under management. An intervention may follow, the consequences of which are to make the two aircraft safe (by changing one aircraft's altitude). Encoding the changing altitude values on the radar will likewise lead to the mental representation of those two aircraft (as instances of unsafe aircraft), changing to reflect the fact that they are now safe, and instances of, for example, 'Active Safe Aircraft'.

Reconfiguring the framework for modelling a worksystem addressing another domain would necessarily require a different set of categories in LTM, categories that reflect the different possible states of the objects being transformed by that worksystem operator. In this framework, the hierarchy of categories reflects a constrained set of possible operator representations, reflecting aircraft states in the domain. The hierarchy itself is derived from instructional material which operators read before interaction. Within the hierarchy the highest level category is that of an ATM aircraft category. Such an aircraft has attributes of a call sign, exit altitude etc. Within this hierarchy of mental categories an 'Active' aircraft is distinct from an 'Incoming' aircraft category. The operator can judge whether an aircraft under management is 'Incoming' or 'Active', by examining the radar. If a trace for that aircraft is detected, it is active, otherwise it is incoming. As the states of aircraft in the domain change, (for example, from being incoming (aircraft) to active (aircraft) and then to becoming unsafe (aircraft) etc.), operator mental representations for those aircraft should also change by encoding values for those aircraft, displayed on worksystem devices. Categories are commonly distinguished by the range of values an attribute may take. An aircraft travelling at 230 knots and altitude 120, may be categorised as 'Active Safe Unexpeditious (Speed) Aircraft'. The aircraft is considered unexpeditious (which is undesirable) because its speed is excessively slow, which leads to a high level of fuel consumption.

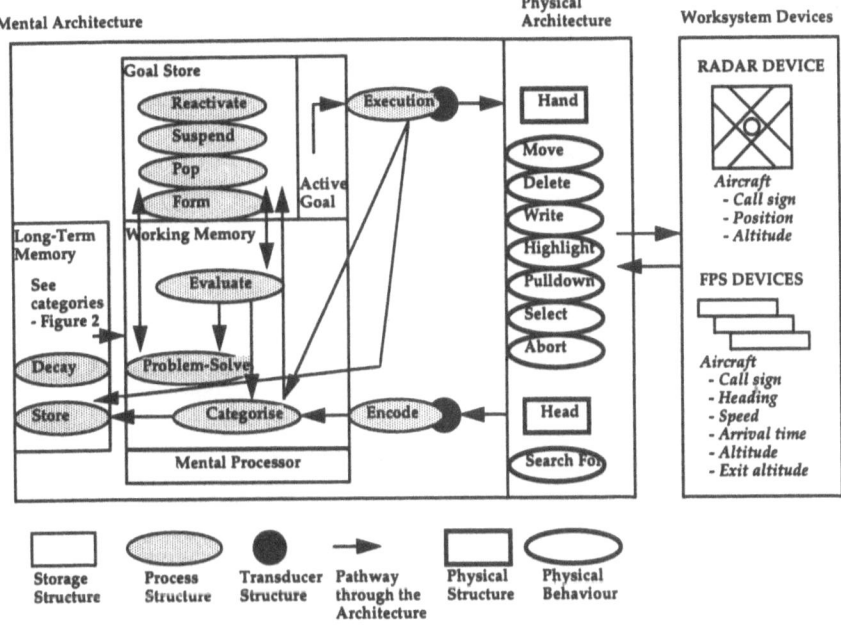

Figure 1: The assumed mental and physical architecture of the operator, plus interactive devices included within the framework.

The operator will be expected to alter that aircraft's speed to satisfy ATM operational goals concerning fuel consumption, i.e. transform that aircraft into an instance of category 'Active Safe Expeditious Aircraft', by allocating that aircraft a speed of 720 knots as soon as possible. Mental categories (of safety and expedition) may be combined. Operator mental representations (categories) also exist for the radar and Flight Progress Strip (FPS) devices in the worksystem. FPSs can be of three types: 'FPS (Entry)'; 'FPS (Intermediate)'; and 'FPS (Exit)' (see Section 2.4). Data displayed on an FPS may be changed as a consequence of operator physical behaviour (see Section 2.3), as data are written on, and deleted from, FPSs as interventions are made.

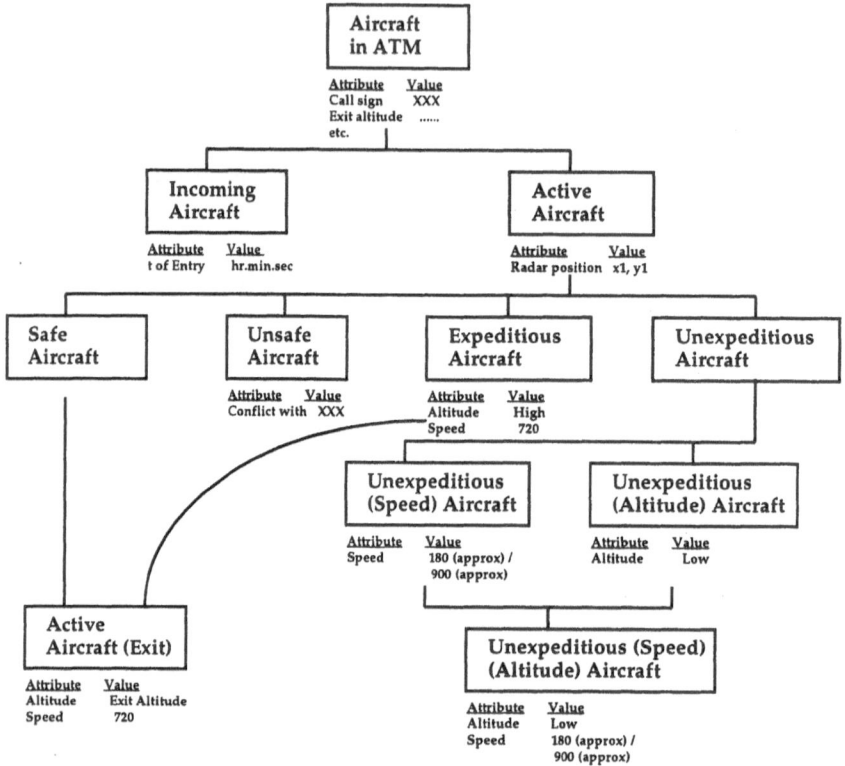

Figure 2: Mental categories used for representing the ATM domain.

Mental representations of the configuration of FPS devices change, as a consequence of such physical behaviour. Following an intervention concerning an aircraft's altitude, the operator will be aware that an aircraft's active FPS is out of date, and form a goal to change the altitude data field on the FPS. If this is performed quickly, the device data then correspond with the state of the domain. If the operator is slow to form such a goal, as a consequence of high workload, the goal may not be formed, the data field remains unchanged, and hence the device representation of the state of the domain is erroneous.

2.3.   *Operator Physical Architecture*

In modelling the ATM operator's physical behaviour, attention needs to be paid to two physical structures - the operator's head and hands. Each physical structure may exhibit a range of physical behaviours. The hands may: 'move' the positions of FPSs on a board; 'delete' or 'write' to data fields; 'highlight' aircraft on the radar; 'pulldown' and 'select' menu options; or prematurely 'abort' one of the mentioned behaviours prior to action completion. Such physical behaviours bring about changes in the configuration of worksystem devices. The head has more limited behaviours of interest, a single 'search for' behaviour that accounts for the operator referring to particular data fields during interaction.

2.4   *Worksystem Devices*

The ATM worksystem possesses two classes of device, a set of FPSs and radar. FPS devices may be of three types: FPS (Entry); FPS (Intermediate); or FPS (Exit). For each aircraft under management, one of each FPS type exists. An operator is provided with all FPSs associated with a particular aircraft prior to that aircraft's arrival on the sector. Figure 3 shows the data fields displayed on each of the different FPS types. When an aircraft arrives on the sector, at its entry beacon, the aircraft's FPS (Entry) device contains relevant data concerning its entry state. All aircraft pass through beacon Delta (_), (see Figure 4), FPS (intermediate) is used for management of air traffic at this beacon. When an aircraft reaches beacon Delta that aircraft's FPS (Intermediate) device becomes relevant, and data from the FPS (Entry) must be copied to the FPS (Intermediate). When aircraft exit beacon Delta they necessarily approach their third and final (exit) beacon. The FPS (Exit) then becomes relevant, containing data detailing the desired exit state of that aircraft. Data fields on all types of FPS are manually updated (by operator physical behaviour) as interventions to aircraft speed or altitude are made. Most frequently, operators copy altitude and speed data from FPS to FPS as aircraft progress across the sector.

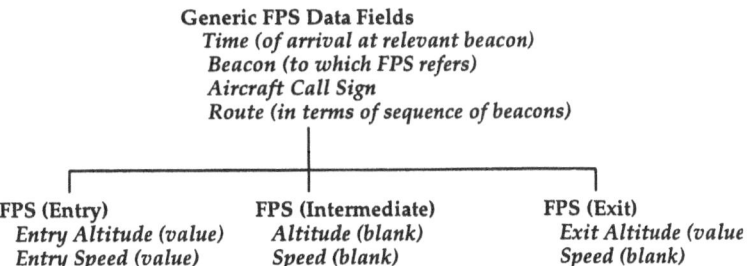

Figure 3: Data fields shown on different types of FPS device. Top of the hierarchy shows data fields shown on all types of FPS (generic data fields).

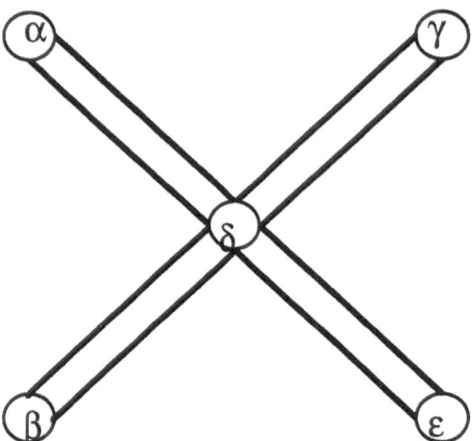

Figure 4: Radar device display of a managed sector.

The radar device (Figure 4) shows the airspace being managed, including beacons and airways between beacons. Beacon positions demarcate the boundaries of the managed sector, within which aircraft traces are shown. These traces correspond to the relative three-dimensional positions of aircraft on the sector. Call sign and altitude data fields are displayed. A menu bar provides a set of pulldown menu options, for carrying out interventions. Before allocating an aircraft a new speed or altitude, the radar trace, that corresponds to that aircraft, must be highlighted on the radar device.

3   Famework Procedures and Modelling Methodology

Data concerning operator interaction with ATM devices are recorded onto video. Embodied in the radar device is the aforementioned ATM domain model which logs the consequences of operator interventions, in terms of the effects each intervention has on aircraft safety and expedition. Thus, while the framework can be used to model the operator's mental 'picture' of the domain, constructed by reference to worksystem devices, the domain model records the actual state of that domain. Video cameras record: head movements; hand movements; verbal protocol trace; alterations to FPS data fields and position; and radar display. The worksystem task involves managing between seven and nine simulated aircraft over approximately a 45 minute time period.

A number of procedures exist for model construction. Two examples of such procedures are rules for data-to-model inference (below), i.e. the translation of overt behaviour into a model. These rules are important to ensure consistency within and between models.

(1) If a hand movement, to an FPS data field is evident, with associated head movement, but without accompanying verbal trace, then infer the data field value has been mentally represented by the operator.

(2) If a data field is searched for again, shortly after an initial reference, then infer that the initial mental representation has decayed.

The framework for modelling operator mental behaviours has procedures to extract the following separate sets of information from the data: worksystem goals; a set of mental representations and processes associated with goal achievement; transformations of individual mental representations of the domain objects (aircraft), as a consequence of the aforementioned mental behaviour; transformations of mental representations of worksystem devices (as a consequence of mental behaviour); changes to the information displayed by devices.

4   Framework Representational Format (Part of a Model)

To illustrate the representational format the framework imposes upon constructed models, an example of part of a model is presented. Figure 5 shows three simple sets of worksystem behaviours: (1) an operator becoming aware of an aircraft's arrival on the managed sector; (2) the operator then updating their FPS (Entry) for that aircraft in consequence; (3) the operator giving the recently arrived aircraft a pre-established new speed of 720 knots.

Five columns present textual descriptions, using a modelling syntax, for: worksystem goals; operator behaviour; operator mental representations of the domain; operator mental representations of the interactive devices; and the actual state of the devices. This model commences with the device entry, 'Radar/Alpha, show, PIN', which means that a new aircraft has become visible on the radar, at beacon Alpha, with a call sign 'PIN'. The operator behaviour column then shows that the operator searches the radar at Alpha ('SEARCH FOR: PIN, Radar/Alpha'), encodes the trace and categorises that trace as aircraft PIN. This series of mental behaviours is dictated by the operator mental architecture (section 2.2). The arrow from the 'Encode: PIN' behaviour indicates that this particular mental behaviour changes the operator's mental representation of the domain. PIN is now active and located at beacon Alpha. Recategorisation of PIN occurs, as an 'active aircraft', based upon the encoded trace. Establishing the presence of PIN also transforms mental representations of interactive devices. Encoding PIN at Alpha changes the operator's mental representation of the radar device. It is updated to reflect the fact that whereas before PIN was not visible on the radar,
now it is visible at Alpha. Likewise, establishing PIN as an active aircraft results in the representation of PIN's FPS (Entry) status, (which reflects the fact that PIN is an 'inactive' aircraft), being tagged as out of date ('old').

As a consequence of the above, a second goal is formed (2), that the position (status) of PIN's FPS (Entry) on the FPS board needs amending. Once this is carried out (2), worksystem devices correspond with the operator's mental representation of the domain, i.e. PIN is active and PIN's FPS (Entry) device reflects this fact. It is assumed that upon inspection of an FPS the operator encodes and mentally represents data fields that correspond to that aircraft's speed and altitude. Hence, as a consequence of PIN's FPS (Entry) being encoded, PIN's speed and altitude are mentally represented. PIN is subsequently recategorised from being 'active' to being unexpeditious with respect its speed (it's travelling at 900 knots when desirable cruising speed is 720).

The physical behaviour of 'Moving' the position of PIN's FPS (to reflect the fact that PIN is active on the sector) results in an updating of the operator's mental representation of the PIN FPS (Entry) device position. The FPS's position is no longer out of date. The change in FPS position is also reflected in the fifth column, a change in actual device configuration.

In the third sequence of behaviour (3) PIN, currently travelling at an undesirable 900 knots, is assigned the goal speed 720. PIN's radar trace is first highlighted, then a menu pulled down and the 720 value selected. In consequence, PIN is recategorised as having a 'changing' speed, and no longer travelling unacceptably fast. PIN is therefore an instance of the category 'Active Safe Expeditious Aircraft' (see figure 2). The physical behaviour of selecting PIN on the radar is reflected both in the operator's mental representation of the radar device configuration, and in the device model. In a similar manner to the first behaviour sequence, changing PIN's speed updates the operator's representation of PIN's FPS (Entry) device to reflect the fact that the FPS states PIN's speed to be 900, whereas now PIN is travelling at 720, and therefore the speed data field needs to be changed.

5   Framework Purpose: Problem Diagnosis in Design

This partial model (figure 5) demonstrates: how the mental and physical architecture and device component are operationalised within the framework; how a constructed model separates domain and worksystem representations; and how representations change as a consequence of physical and mental behaviours. Such a worksystem model, when considered in conjunction with a domain model (recording an intervention's effect upon: aircraft safety; fuel consumption; and time to progress across the sector), supports diagnostic reasoning in a design process. An example of this purpose, diagnostic reasoning in design, will now be illustrated.

A domain model, studied after a particular interaction, records that an aircraft BAN, consumes 70% more fuel than is desirable, and crosses a sector in 13.5% less time than it is scheduled to take. Such aircraft management quality (on the behalf of a worksystem) is considered an instance of ineffective system performance. While the greater speed assigned to BAN reduces flight time, aircraft arrival times at beacons, and hand-over times to other en-route operators (managing different sectors) are planned for reasons of operator workload management, landing time management etc. Greater speed, in this instance, also has a large effect on fuel consumption, and hence airline running costs.

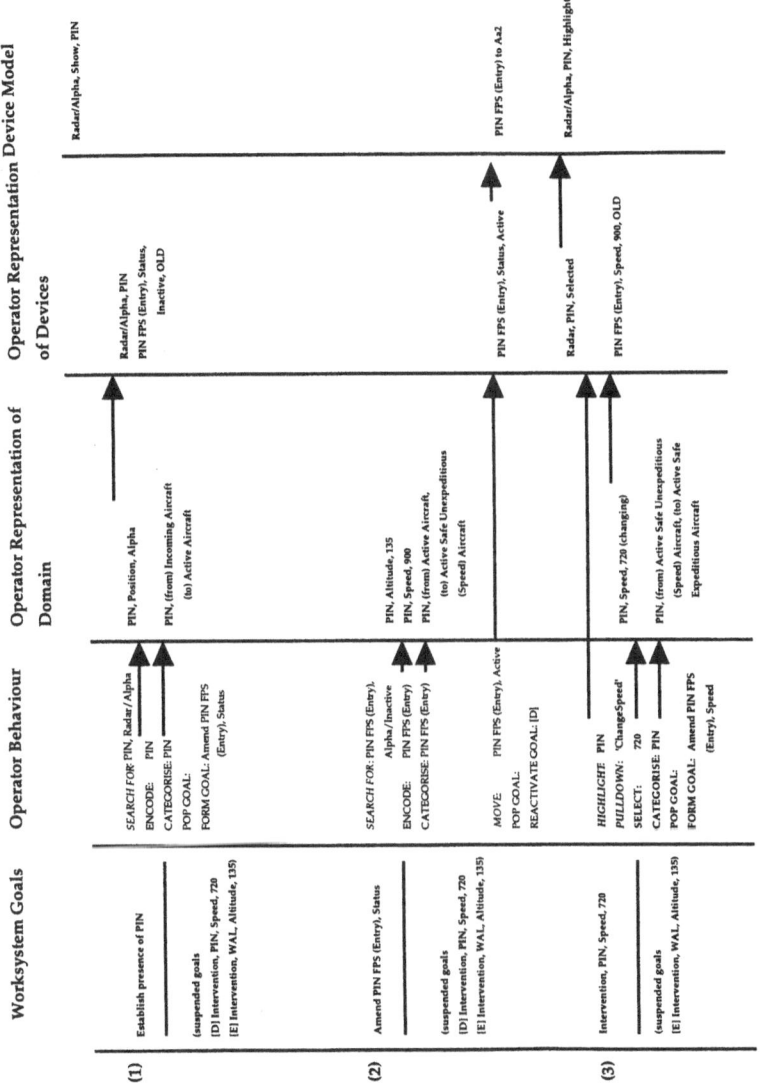

Figure 5: Part of a model constructed with the framework

A worksystem model of the interactions that resulted in such undesirable levels of work quality will now be examined. The model shows that a local safety conflict between BAN and another aircraft, flying across BAN's flight path at the same flight level, led to an operator decision to speed BAN up to 900 knots, from a goal speed of 720 knots. This speed intervention is the origin of the poor task quality shown by the domain model. The intervention resulted in BAN reaching the 'projected' point of conflict early, and thus resulted in the maintenance of aircraft safety. However, the worksystem model shows that the operator failed to carry out the FPS update procedure, to amend BAN's FPS (Entry) speed value to 900 after the intervention. This failure was in part due to a requirement that another conflict between aircraft be resolved. Prior to this speed change, BAN had been flying at a high altitude (which is desirable), and at 720 knots (which is goal speed). BAN was mentally represented as an instance of the category 'Active Safe Expeditious Aircraft'. Following the intervention, BAN was mentally represented as an instance of the category 'Active Safe Unexpeditious (Speed) Aircraft'. When BAN's FPS was next referenced by the operator, the mental representation of BAN, as 'Active Safe Unexpeditious (Speed) Aircraft', had decayed. BAN's decayed mental representation was thus replaced with one that inaccurately reflected BAN's state in the domain, but concorded with the incorrect device speed value of 720. BAN was thus mentally represented as an 'Active Safe Expeditious Aircraft' in its goal state. As the speed of aircraft is not explicitly displayed by the radar, but may only be queried via menu selection, the worksystem model shows the operator never queried BAN's out of date speed value. This erroneous device data field (for speed) was never thereafter corrected. In consequence the incorrect speed value supported the continued miscategorisation of BAN, as in a goal state. Subsequently, no further intervention was made with the aircraft, and it progressed across the sector at 900 knots. This progression rate resulted in poor task quality. Given the number of aircraft managed, and the rate at which speed and altitude values change, mental representations of aircraft categories decay rapidly. Erroneous device data fields thus have the consequences described. It is due to this rapid mental representation decay that the operational procedure, of updating FPSs soon after intervention, is employed.

It can be seen from the above example, that reasoning about system effectiveness requires consideration of both the behaviour of a worksystem, and the consequences of domain object transformations. In the BAN instance, the model supports the diagnosis of a number of worksystem contributions to poor performance. Rapid decay in operator mental representations of aircraft states, linked to a procedure that does not require the operator immediately to update the FPS (but at some convenient time soon after intervention) led to the erroneous FPS data field being sustained during a management scenario. This outcome, coupled with the fact that the radar device does not explicitly represent aircraft speed, resulted in the operator failing to query the old speed value, as it was a desirable goal state for an aircraft. The worksystem model, therefore, supports a process of diagnosing the origins (in terms of mental representations) of undesirable worksystem behaviour. Such a record of operator-device interaction with an existing system is likely to be of value in the subsequent design process of reasoning about the prescription of device functionality, to solve the problem diagnosed.

6 Conclusions

Operator modelling frameworks occupy an important position in the literature. This paper presents a set of elements common to all such frameworks, and characterises the presented framework in terms of these elements, and other published frameworks. The framework for modelling operator mental behaviours has a wider scope than just operator behaviour. It is a framework for modelling worksystem behaviour, with particular concern for operator mental representations. With respect to identified elements, an explicit mental and physical architecture is presented with an account of worksystem devices. Examples of modelling procedures are given and a representational format provided. The framework has an established scope, and the purpose of constructing such models is demonstrated with reference to a design process of diagnosis. The value of separating operator mental representations of domain and device is illustrated. An example shows how it is possible to trace back (diagnostically) an instance of poor quality work to a mis-match between a) an operator's mental representation (or 'picture') of the state of a domain, and b) the actual state of the domain under management. The origins of the mis-match lie with an erroneous device representation used in the construction of a). Important emphasis is placed upon the use of a model of the domain, in conjunction with a worksystem model, to realise this purpose. The domain model informs the designer about those parts of the worksystem model to be considered when identifying the reasons for undesirable task quality. Without a domain model, the worksystem model is merely an account of worksystem behaviour.

References

Anderson, J.R. (1993) Rules of the mind. Hillsdale, NJ: Lawrence Erlbaum Associates.

Barnard, P.J. & Teasdale, J.D. (1993) Affect, Cognition and Change: Re-modelling depressive thought, Essays in Cognitive Psychology Series, Hove: Lawrence Erlbaum Associates.

Blandford, A. & Young, R.M. (1993) "Developing runnable user models: separating the problem solving techniques from the domain knowledge", in People and Computers VIII (Proceedings of the HCI'93 Conference)", eds. J.L. Alty, D. Diaper & S. Guest, Cambridge University Press, 111-121.

Cacciabue, P.C., Decortis, F., Drozdowicz, B., Masson, M., & Nordvik, J-P. (1992)
"COSIMO: A cognitive simulation model of human decision making and behaviour in accident management of complex plants". IEE Transactions on Systems, Man and Cybernetics, 22 (5), 1058-1074

Card, S.K., Moran, T.P. & Newell, A. (1983) The psychology of human-computer interaction. NJ: Lawrence Erlbaum Associates.

Dowell, J. (1992) "Domain analysis of air traffic management", in Proceedings of the International Conference on Information Decision Action Systems in Complex Organisations, University of Oxford. IEE: London.

Dowell, J., Salter, I. & Zekrullahi, S. (1994) "A domain analysis of air traffic management work can be used to rationalise interface design issues", in People and Computers IX (Proceedings of the HCI'94 Conference), eds. G. Cockton, S.W. Draper & G.R.S. Weir, Cambridge University Press.

Fischer, G. (1993) "Beyond Human Computer Interaction: Designing Useful and Usable Computational Environments" in People and Computers VIII (Proceedings of the HCI'93 Conference).

Holland, J.H., Holyoak, K.J., Nisbett, R.E. & Thagard, P.R. (1987) Induction, processes of inference, learning and discovery. MIT Press.

Moray, N., Lootsteen, P. & Pajak, J. (1986) "Acquisition of Process Control Skills, IEEE Transactions on Systems, Man and Cybernetics, Vol SMC-16, No.4, July/August.

Newell, A. (1990) Unified theories of cognition. Cambridge, MA: Harvard University Press.

Rasmussen, J. & Vicente, K.J. (1990) "Ecological Interfaces: A Technological Imperative in High Tech Systems?", International Journal of Human-Computer Interaction, 2 (2), 93-111.

Reisner, P. (1984) "Formal grammar as a tool for analysing ease of use: some fundamental concepts", in Human Factors in Computer Systems, eds. J.C. Thomas & M.L. Schneider, NJ: Ablex.

Rieman, J., Lewis, C., Young, R.M. & Polson, P.G. (1994) ""Why is a raven like a writing desk?" Lessons in interface consistency and analogical reasoning from two cognitive architectures", in Proceedings of CHI'94: Human Factors in Computing Systems, eds. B. Adelson, S. Dumais & J. Olseon, ACM Press, 438-444.

Sutcliffe, A.G., Benyon, D. & van Assche, F. (eds.) (1996) Domain Knowledge for Interactive System Design. Chapman & Hall.

Timmer, P. & Long, J. (1996) "Integrating domain and worksystem models: an illustration from air traffic management", in Domain Knowledge for Interactive System Design, A.G. Sutcliffe, D. Benyon & F. van Assche (eds.), Chapman & Hall

Young, R.M., Green, T.R.G. & Simon, T. (1989) "Programmable User Models for Predictive Evaluation of Interface Designs" in Proceedings of CHI'89: Human Factors in Computer Systems, eds. K. Bice & C.H. Lewis, ACM Press.
Woods, D.D. & Hollnagel, E. (1987) "Mapping cognitive demands in complex problem-solving worlds", International Journal of Man-Machine Studies, 26, 257-275.

Eliciting Information Portrayal Requirements: Experiences with the Critical Decision Method

William B.L. Wong, Philip J. Sallis and David O'Hare

Department of Information Science
University of Otago
PO Box 56 Dunedin
New Zealand
Phone: 64 - 3 - 479 8322
64 - 3 - 479 8143
Fax: 64 - 3 479 8311
e-mail: william.wong@stonebow.otago.ac.nz
e-mail: psallis@commerce.otago.ac.nz

Department of Psychology
University of Otago
PO Box 56 Dunedin
New Zealand
Phone: 64 - 3 - 479 7643
Fax: 64 - 3 479 8335
e-mail: ohare@psy.otago.ac.nz

This study is part of research that is investigating the notion that human performance in dynamic and intentional decision making environments, such as ambulance dispatch management, can be improved if information is portrayed in a manner that supports the decision strategies invoked to achieve the goal states of the process being controlled. Hence, in designing interfaces to support real-time dispatch management decisions, it is suggested that it would be necessary to first discover the goal states and the decision strategies invoked during the process, and then portray the required information in a manner that supports such a user group's decision making goals and strategies.

The purpose of this paper is to report on the experiences gleaned from the use of a cognitive task analysis technique

called Critical Decision Method as an elicitation technique for determining information portrayal requirements. This paper firstly describes how the technique was used in a study to identify the goal states and decision strategies invoked during the dispatch of ambulances at the Sydney Ambulance Co-ordination Centre. The paper then describes how the interview data was analysed within and between cases in order to reveal the goal states of the ambulance dispatchers. A brief description of the resulting goal states follows, although amore detailed description of the goals states and their resulting display concepts has been reported elsewhere (Wong et al.,1996b)t. Finally, the paper concludes with a set of observations and lessons learnt from the use of the Critical Decision Method for developing display design concepts in dynamic intentional environments.

Keywords: display design, cognitive task analysis, Critical   Decision Method, ambulance dispatch management.

1   Introduction

Designing computer displays that support diagnosis and control of real-time and dynamic processes is more than just presenting the data model in a form that supports the work flow of the process operator. To enable effective diagnosis, researchers have found a need to portray the information in a manner that supports the achievement of higher order constraints and operator goals (Kaempf et al., 1996; O'Hare et al., 1994; Pawlak et al., 1996;Rasmussen et al., 1995; Vicente et al., 1995; Woods,1995). This finding is particularly significant in situations where the operator is performing at the extremes of his or her performance envelopes. Such conditions are typical of naturalistic decision making environments where time is constrained, information is incomplete and uncertain, decisions are inter-dependent, and where the stakes are high (Brehmer, 1990; Cannon-Bowers et al., 1996; Orasanu et al., 1993; Skriver,1996; Zsambok et al., 1992)t.

This paper reports on the use of the Critical Decision Method (Klein et al.,1989)t to identify goal states and the decision making strategies invoked during emergency dispatch management. This is the second time this technique has been used in this manner. The outcome of the first investigation has been reported in (Wong et al.,1995)t. In the current study, five dispatchers from the Ambulance Co-ordination Centre of the New South Wales Ambulance Service in Sydney, Australia, participated in the study. Detailed descriptions of the goal states and resulting display concepts have been reported elsewhere (Wong et al.,1996b)t.

The Sydney Centre is responsible for co-ordinating the movements of two rescue helicopters and about 130 ambulances deployed across 45 stations in an area of

approximately 14, 000 square km of 4 million people. In addition to routine jobs like patient transfers, the Centre responds to 295,000 *emergency* calls annually.
The rest of this paper will describe the Critical Decision Method, and how it was used to model and understand the model of goal states and decision strategies which were then used to develop display concepts. Finally this paper will report on the lessons learnt from this experience.

The Critical Decision Method

The method used in the study is known as the Critical Decision Method or CDM (Klein et al.,1989)t. It is a retrospective cognitive task analysis interview technique and an approach to analysing the data. This method has been used for eliciting expert knowledge (Militello et al.,1995)t, decision strategies and cues attended to, and system in naturalistic decision making environments design (Militello et al., 1995;Kaempf et al., 1996; Miller et al., 1992)t.
The technique relies on participants recalling a particularly memorable incident they had experienced in the course of their work. Participants are probed to identify the decisions that they made and how these decisions were made. The amount of information elicited was found to be of sufficient detail to determine the strategies used in making these decisions, the cues attended to, the reasons for performing particular actions, and the goals they were trying to achieve. For instance in this study, participants were able to recall the number of ambulances dispatched, the sequence in which the ambulances were dispatched, the stations from which theambulances came, or what happened when there were not enough ambulances.

Conducting the Interviews

Five dispatchers, each with between 5 to 9 years of experience in dispatch management were interviewed in this study. Each interview lasted about an hour and each session was tape recorded. The tapes were subsequently transcribed resulting in a very large and rich data set for qualitative analysis. The interviews were organised into the following four parts:

  a.   Describe the incident and identify functional processes.
  b.   Organise the incident on a timeline.
  c.   Probe to understand the processes.
  d.   Compare performance with novice or expert

The rest of this section will briefly describe what these parts addressed during the interviews.

Describe the incident and identify functional processes.

In this first part of the interview, participants were asked to think back to a particularly memorable resource allocation incident in which they were involved. Once an incident had been agreed upon, the participants were then asked to briefly describe what the incident was about, when the incident occurred, and what the general situation was like at that time. e.g. a major motor vehicle accident that occurred on the Princess Highway near Lakehurst on the outskirts of Sydney. The caller reported that many people were injured and trapped in the wreckage. A major incident likethis suggested that a number of ambulances would be required to attend to the accident, posing a significant resource allocation challenge, forcingthe dispatcher to operate at the limits of his or her performance envelope.These are the situations that would provide useful insights into the dispatch management decisions.Furthermore an actual situation also provided a context to ask subsequent questions and to understand the events that occurred at that time.

Having some idea of the incident, the next step is to ask the participant the following question, "If I were there with you when that yellow slip arrived in your conveyor belt, what would I see you do and hear you say?". This question was found to be more useful to start the participant off to identify the functional processes, tasks, actions and decisions than a question like, "Please tell me what happened when the yellowslip arrived".

During the interview the information was written down on Post-It™ papers, and randomly stuck on an A3-size sheet. The objective here was to identify the processes and not the sequence. Attempting to put thePost-It™ papers in the proper sequence at this stage would require additional questions to be asked and would distract the participant as he or she attempted to recall the sequence rather than concentrating on recalling the processes, events and decisions. Additional probes used during this stage included what did you write down? what charts were you looking at? and what actions or options were youconsidering? These probes were used to identify some of the information that was used by the participant during each process or decision.

Organise the incident on a timeline

In the second stage of the interview, the participants are then invited to help sequence the events and decision points by re-arranging the Post-It™ papers. As they re-arranged the Post-It™ papers, the participants would remember other details which would then be added to the diagram, e.g. any information that was used or referred to, people or agencies contacted. The Post-It™ papers were re-arranged until the participant believed that the diagram appropriately represented the situation at the time of the incident. Thenext stage is to probe the participant for more details concerning each major decision point.

Probe to understand the processes.

At this stage, the participant together with the researcher would identify the major decision points. The following probes were then used to elicit more detail about each of these decision points. The probes addressed the cues used or attended to, the knowledge needed to make that decision, the way in which the information was presented, the appropriateness of the information format, the goals, what situation assessment was made, what options were considered and the basis for the final choice, what-ifs, and what additional training or knowledge or information would have been be useful in that situation.

Compare performance with novice

In the fourth and final stage, the participants are asked to give their opinion on the expected performance of a less experienced dispatcher when faced with the same situation. This final question seeks to identify the mistakes that would have been made by a less experienced dispatcher, or the information that might have been missed or events mis-interpreted. It was anticipated that the answers from such a question would identify shortcomings in training or the system itself.

Approach to the Data Analysis

This section will describe the procedure taken to systematically extract the goal states and decision strategies from the interview transcripts. The analysis framework was based on the relationship between cues, the situation assessment that was derived from the cues, the actions taken, the rationale for the actions, and the purpose those actions served. Key features of the decisions and decision strategies were extracted from each interview and integrated into a model of a dispatcher's decision goals and strategies.

The transcripts and other data collected during the interviews are analysed in the five stages as illustrated in Figure 1 and is discussed below.

Stage 1: The Decision Flow Chart

From the Post-It™ paper analysis of the decision process documented at the interview, a decision flowchart is developed which extracts the key decision points and the considerations and the thinking necessary for the interviewee to reach a conclusion. Part of such a Decision Flow Chart is illustrated in Figure 2.

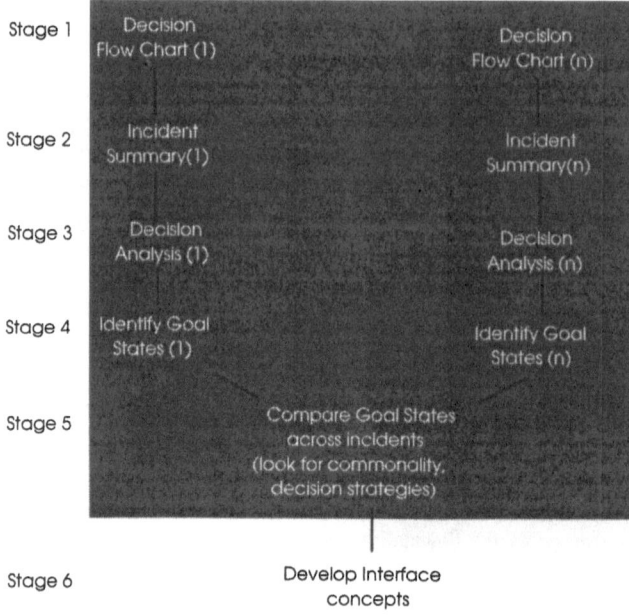

Figure 1: Stages in the Analysis of Incidents Using the Critical Decision Method

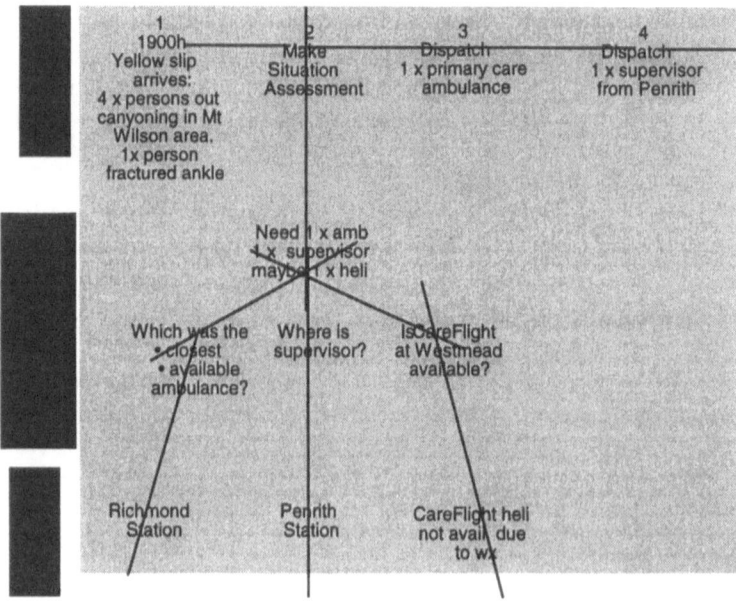

Figure 2: An example of a Decision Flow Chart showing the components of the chart

A decision point is an activity where the operator needs to make a decision about a situation or action. These decision points are drawn along a horizontal timeline and are numbered from left to right to facilitate the reading of the chart. Events that occur in between decision points are also represented in the same way. Events are included as they provide the reader with a context of the situation which is useful for interpreting or appreciating the considerations or actions taken.

The considerations and thinking that arise from each decision point are drawn downwards from a decision point. This progressively depicts how the various aspects of each decision point are considered. This progressive decomposition of the considerations is called "progressive deepening" (Thordsen et al.,1990)t. It is a useful way of depicting the depth and complexity of the decisions being made.

Although this progressive deepening of decisions appears as a tree, it is not a decision tree in the sense that each branch represents the outcomes of a yes-no decision. Instead each branch indicates the factors that were considered and how that consideration was developed and concluded.

The final level of the chart represents the outcomes of the considerations, i.e. which choices were made, or what was concluded after evaluating the issues. The decision flow chart does not include the cues used or associated with each decision point. The analysis of cues is performed after summarising the incident.

Stage 2: Incident Summary

Based on the Decision Flow Chart and further readings of the transcripts, the incident is then summarised by describing what is thought to have happened at each decision point. This description provides the reader with additional details that cannot be easily captured in the Decision Flow Chart. See Figure 3.

Stage 3: Decision Analysis

Each decision point was analysed to identify the Cues, Sass (Situation Assessments) and CoAs (Courses of Action). This section will first define cues, situation assessments and courses of action, and then discuss the cues analysis process, and explain how the Decision Analysis Tables are to be interpreted.

Cues

Cues are factors considered in order to make an assessment of the situation. Cues are information stemming from events or actions that initiate consideration about a particular occurrence. E.g. the yellow emergency request slip that arrives in the conveyor belt is a cue that initiates a series of actions that result in the dispatch of emergency vehicles.

Cues may take the form of:

a. information collected from various display sources like a vehicle status board.

b.   information obtained from communications sources, like the phone or radio communications.

c.   information that may have been derived from other cues.

d   information contained in the spatial arrangement of physical objects, e.g. job slips taken out of the status board and placed on the right-hand side of the desk indicate these are jobs where the vehicles have reached their destinations (e.g. hospital) and are or will be returning to their stations.   This is an indication of their availability (Hoc,1995)t. Another example is the arrival of a yellow slip in the conveyor belt signals the start of an emergency incident.

Incident Summary
Princess Highway Incident, November 1995

1.   Booking staff at the Sydney Coordination Centre received the call. A serious MVA (motor vehicle accident), numerous persons injured and trapped. The accident had occured on the Princess Highway at Lakehurst. As people were injured, the call-taker recorded on the yellow emergency slip and passed it to the South Area Coordinator through the conveyor belt.

2.   South Area Coordinator's initial response: Dispatch one paramedic car (Caringbah), one general duties car (Hurstville), and one supervisor (who is also a paramedic from Rockdale) to the scene according to standard procedures. The coordinator also instructed the first vehicle on the scene to provide a report on the severity of the the situation.

3.   The coordinator then informed the Floor Supervisor of the accident, who then ' decided to initiate the Police Rescue.

4.   Received initial report came from the Caringbah and Hurstville vehicles who were first on scene: "The initial report was three or four people trapped and two or three other minor patients outside the vehicle."

Figure 3: Part of an Incident Summary

Situation Assessment (SA)and Course of Action (CoA)

A Situation Assessment (SA) is the outcome of an appraisal of the information that describe a situation. It represents the appraiser's understanding of the situation before him. The SA should clearly describe the elements of the situation as they are, i.e. the *who, what, where, when,* of the incident and help him make decisions about the resources to send, which represents the Course of Action or the plan he or she develops once he or she has understood the situation and its implications.

For example,   in one incident there was a casualty with a compound fracture of the right ankle.   The casualty is three hours walking time into the bush. The accident had occurred several hours ago, but the person who raised the alarm had only just been able to contact the emergency services. While the casualty is seriously injured, his injuries were not considered life-threatening. Coupling the above information with the dispatcher's knowledge of the area, the dispatcher concluded that the terrain will be difficult to access and also to extricate the casualty. From his experience, a rescue helicopter with a special casualty access team would be appropriate, but if that was not available, the situation could become a protracted incident extending over many hours. The operator's understanding of the local geography also helped him determine that the Richmond ambulance station is closest to the incident site.

This decision process modelled during the investigation appears consistent with the Recognition-Primed Decision model (Klein, 1993)t. The RPD model explains that decisions in the real-world are not made in the classical decision-making manner where many options are derived and then evaluated and finally one is selected. Instead, based on the decision maker's understanding the situation, he develops a course of action, modifies it until the decision maker believes it is capable of achieving the goals governing the situation. He then implements the action.

The Decision Analysis Table

The Decision Analysis Table is illustrated in Table 1. Each key decision point is investigated to identify the cues that triggered the event or that were attended to during that event. The next step is to identify what were the other information and factors considered or had influenced the interpretation and assessment of the state of the situation.

CUES	SIT. ASSESSMT	ACTIONS	Why?	What for?
<u>Yellow slip on conveyor belt</u>	• An emergency.	• Pick up slip. • Read contents / details of the job. • Assign job number.	SOP – To determine nature of problem, and location of problem.	To determine what resources are needed – how many and what types. *(Determine what resources are needed)*

Table 1: Decision Analysis Table for Reporting the Analysis of Cues, SAs, and CoAs.

The situation assessment resulting from that appraisal process is next identified. The courses of action that resulted from that situation assessment is also determined. To gain a better understanding of the courses of action adopted, it is also necessary to identify the rationale for that course of action, and the higher

purpose that the action was to achieve. This information may provide insights
about how the decision strategies invoked by the dispatcher used the information
provided by the cues and the factors. This process is illustrated in Fig 4.

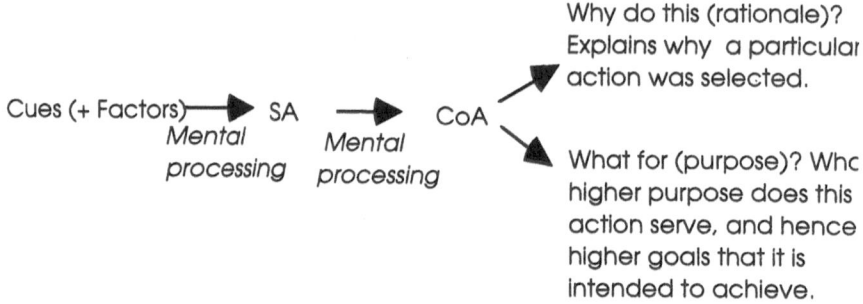

Figure 4: The Decision Analysis Process.

Stage 4: Identify Goal States

The goal states in each incident were identified through the analysis of cues,
situation assessments, and courses of action reported in the Decision Tables. The
analysis of goal states involved two steps:

    a.   Extraction of goal states and their statements of purpose from
            individual incidents,

    b.   Comparison of identified Statements of Purpose,

Extraction of goal states and their statements of purpose

An example of how the goal states for individual incidents were extracted is shown
in Figure 5. It lists the goal states and the statements of purpose extracted from
the Cowan Railway Station incident.

Table 5 Cowan Railway Station Incident	
Goal States	**Statements of Purpose**
Maintain situation awareness	To determine the nature of the emergency.
	" A snapshot picture so that you know what's available, know what to send." (115)
Get resources moving	To get a vehicle to the scene ASAP.
Planning resource to task compatibility	To minimise disruption to on-going activities.
	To enable re-deployment of vehicles to reinforce depleted areas (11-13).
	"The goal would be to send the correct amount of ambulances to cope with the situation withou shortfaling the area that aren't involved."(36
	"You don't want to send everything out of one

Figure 5: Sample Goal states and Statements of Purpose

The goal state represents what the dispatcher was attempting to achieve in order to adequately perform his or her dispatch task. The goal states are inferred from the statements of purpose reported by the interviewee. The statement of purpose indicates what the a dispatcher was attempting to achieve during a particular decision or task. At times these statements are very clear and may be found in a single sentence. However, more typically, the purpose of a set of actions spans several sentences or text units. As such the purpose has to be interpreted within the context of the discussion. Once this has been interpreted, this statement is written in summary form and documented in the *"What for"* column of the Decision Analysis Table.

Comparison of Statements of Purpose Across Cases

This is an intermediate step. It involves bringing together all the statements of purpose into a format that facilitates inspection for commonalties. The common statements of purpose are then identified and grouped. This is illustrated in Figure 6.

	Cases		
	Princess Highway	Westfield's	Botany Bay
	To determine nature of incident.	To determine nature of incident.	To determine nature incident.
	To determine what (relevant) resources are available and where they are.	Make colleagues aware of the potential disaster by shouting across the room.	Keep track of all othe activities going on at same time to enable planning and re-deployment of resou as the situation chan
	Monitor transfer of patients to hospital to track where each patient and ambulance is. (Also so as not to overload a single hospital in event of major incidents.)	To develop a mental map of where each unit was in relation to the incident in the next 10 minutes.	To keep track of pati being transfered to hospital "... so that w won't have a terrible overload all at one hospital" (102)
ponse of ies as dditional eing re-	To get medical aid to the scene ASAP	To get a vehicle on the scene ASAP to: a. start treatment b. get initial report	

Figure 6: Sample segment of the format used to compare statements of purpose

Stage 5: Compare Goal States Across Cases.

Once common statements of purpose have been identified and grouped, each group is then given a short meaningful description that attempts to capture the essence of the goal the dispatcher was trying to achieve. This is illustrated in Figure 7. Through this analysis, the goal states of the dispatch management process are identified. The next section briefly describes what these goal states are.

			Cases
Goal States	Mt Wilson	Princess Highway	Westfield's
		so as not to overload a single hospital in event of major incidents.)	
Get resources moving	To get initial response of required resources moving as soon as possible while additional resources are being considered and re-deployed.	To get medical aid to the scene ASAP	To get a vehicle on the scene ASAP to: a. start treatment b. get initial report

Figure 7: Grouping and naming of Statements of Purpose.

The Results: Goal States of the Dispatch Management Process

Goal states are the higher-order constraints that the dispatcher must attempt to achieve in order for the process to operate at an acceptable level of performance. The study resulted in the identification of five goal states. These goal states together with the strategies invoked and an appreciation of the situational factors involved should then drive the design of the display formats. For completeness, these goal states are briefly described below but see (Wong et al.,1996b)t Wong et al., 1996b, for more details on the design concepts.

(1)   Notification of emergencies

This goal state represents the need to be notified quickly of any emergencies. In this study, the dispatchers were notified by the emergency yellow job slip arriving in their respective segments of the conveyor belt system. This segment is immediately next to where they are seated. Because of the way the conveyor belt is made, job slips arriving in the respective segments were heard to make a scratchy noise which serves to alert the dispatcher to its presence. However, this method of notification was also observed to have gone unnoticed because of ambient noise or due to the dispatcher attending to other competing activities. Notification designs need to overcome these situational factors.

(2)   Maintain situation awareness

Display designs for situational awareness need to portray information such that it enables the dispatcher to develop and maintain a highly dynamic mental representation of critical aspects of the environment so that he or she may effectively

   a.   Co-ordinate activities within and between boundaries What is going on in one region may affect outcomes and resource allocation in another region
   b.   Globally optimise the use of resources What resources are available globally before planning deployment of vehicles in a major incident. This includes knowing what jobs are outstanding so as to trade-off emergency and medical cases, and also to balance the ambulance coverage of the immediate area.
   c.   ensure compliance to instructions Following up of decisions to ensure that assigned tasks are being implemented, and to monitor if is performance is in line with goal expectations. The information that is communicated is information about the status of these decisions rather than resource-type information

(3)   *Planning resource to task compatibility*

This goal state requires the dispatcher to determine what the needs of a situation are, and to find an appropriate match between available resources and these needs. Achieving this goal involves the following tasks:

a.   Locating available resources. In one case, the dispatcher had to refer to multiple sources of information in order to locate and assemble specially trained personnel into a SCAT(Special Casualty Access Team) team. Having identified the SCAT officers, the dispatcher then had to determine which of these officers were closest to the accident scene. Becuase the appropriate officers were part of separate double crews at two different stations, these crews had to be dis-banded in order to establish one SCAT Team.

b.   Translating the need into resources to send. Part of planning. The dispatcher has to translate what has happened into the number of resources to send. Receiving accurate information about the incident is very important to organising an appropriate response to the incident. However this cannot be gauranteed, but the interpretation errors can be reduced by reducing the number of people an in-coming call has to go through before a decision is made.

c.   Minimise disruption to on-going activities.   One major consideration that influences the number of ambulances to send is the concern with sending too many ambulances as excess vehicles become unavailable to other incidents. Over-estimating the number of ambulances needed during periods where resources are stretched may require pulling ambulances off other less life-critical but necessary jobs, or delaying them, to the inconvenience of the patients.

d.   Planning ahead. Two planning horizons: In real-time planning the concern is with which ambulance is to be sent now or in the immediate future to an incident; and planning ahead involves predicting what the future state of the ambulances will be and to match that to a forecasted set of activities.

e.   Planning to fill gaps in ambulance coverage. Ambulance coverage in an area could be badly depleted such that it may take an unacceptably long time for an available ambulance to respond to an emergency. Such depletions are called 'gaps' or 'holes' in the coverage. To fill these gaps, ambulances from neighbouring areas are usually re-deployed to cover the gaps, called 'balancing the region'.

The display concept needed to support this goal state requires to display more than just the status and location of the ambulances at the time of request, but it needs to also present information about their planned future taskings to allow these factors to be taken into consideration.

(4)   *Speedy response*

Another goal state of the ambulance dispatch process is that of attaining a speedy response to emergency calls. The Co-ordination Centre has a requirement for a vehicle to be on the road within three minutes of receiving the emergency call. In all cases interviewed, all dispatchers were concerned with getting medical aid to the scene as soon as possible in order to start initial treatment, and to receive an initial report about the severity and extent of injuries at the accident.

(5)   *Maintain history of developments*

Although reported in only two of the five interviews, the need to maintain a history of what had happened cannot be overlooked. The main use of these histories is to assist legal investigators re-construct events from job slips and other operational documents in order for investigators to determine what had happened and when it happened. While an important goal in itself, it is not considered directly relevant to the design of how information should be portrayed in dynamic decision making environments.

Lessons Learnt

In reflecting upon the procedure employed in this investigation, the following lessons were learnt.

Goal States and Display Concepts.

The identification of the goal states is a critical step towards the development of display concepts that support decision making.   Decisions are not made in isolation but within the context of a situation such that the resulting actions may satisfy the over-riding goals. As goals may be achieved in a variety of ways, it is necessary to consider the design of displays together with the decision strategies invoked by the dispatchers. The decision strategies then guide and constrain the development of display concepts aimed at supporting specific goal states.

Goal states are not obvious.

Dispatchers do not explicitly think about all the goal states they are trying to achieve. They need to be drawn out. Simply asking why he or she acted in a particular manner only provides the immediate reason for the action or decision, e.g. it could be standard operating procedures. The dispatcher has to be probed further to reveal what, for example, is the purpose of that standard procedure. In other instances, the purpose of a set of actions had to be inferred during the data analysis phase as the dispatchers were unable to articulate it clearly, or were not explicitly aware that they are attempting to serve that purpose.

Cues analysis and perceptual organisation.

The cues analysis does not reveal the perceptual order or arrangement of the data on a display. The analysis only indicates what cues were used or attended to, and how individual cues logically relate to one another. Although some research is being conducted into a formal method for how these cues should be perceptually organised on a display (Wong et al.,1996a)t, display concepts at the moment are still determined through a combination of researcher's appreciation of the decision strategies and goal states, and his experience.

Behavioural and Cognitive Task Analysis.

A strictly behavioural approach to task analysis would not have identified the ways by which dispatchers considered the information or the ways in which decisions were made. The cognitive task analysis approach focused on *how* those decisions were made rather than on just what decisions were made and the information needed. While is may be argued that a good behavioural task analysis could reveal such insights about the decision process, that is not its purpose nor are its tools designed to elicit such information. Whereas it is more probable that a well executed cognitive task analysis would reveal those specific insights. The difference between the two approach lies in the skilful application of the cognitive probes. From experience, simply asking "What did you think about at this decision point?" had resulted in a blank face. Cognitive probes need to be phrased in a manner that help the interviewee tangiblise the process of thinking about a decision. When appropriately applied, the cognitive probes provided valuable insights into the way dispatchers thought about the decision process, how the information cues influenced the decision process, and how well the information is organised or presented to support the decision, e.g. did the dispatcher actively search for the cue or was the cue present in a readily accessible location or format.

Selecting incidents.

It is worthwhile spending a few minutes at the start of the interview determining whether the incident being considered by the interviewee is appropriate before proceeding with the interview. In determining this, we need to appreciate the scope of the incident, e.g. was it a single incident or many incidents spread over a long-time period, and what was the interviewee's involvement in the incident, i.e. was the interviewee the main co-ordinator or did he or she help another co-ordinate the incident. There will be a difference in the information recalled because of the different perspective, e.g. a supervisor who helped co-ordinate the incident would not remember the specific planning and movement of vehicles under the control of the co-ordinator who actually controlled the incident.

Visualisation of the decision process.

The use of sticky PostIt™ papers was found to be very useful in encouraging interviewee participation and in setting them at ease. Recording the processes and functions down without concern for the sequence they occurred at the start allowed the interviewee to concentrate on what happened. The Post-It™ papers could then be quickly re-organised in the proper sequence once all the main functions were documented. At this stage, more details could then be elicited, using the properly sequenced Post-It™ papers as a framework for investigating each decision point.

In Conclusion

The investigation has provided many useful insights into the use of the CDM. The study has also suggested the need for further adaptation or extension of the method so as to allow its outcomes to be used directly and objectively for the perceptual organisation of display designs.

Acknowledgments

We would like to thank Mr Peter Payne, Communications Superintendent, Mr Alan Reinter, Senior Supervisor, Mr Stuart Greenshields, Supervisor, and staff of the Ambulance Co-ordination Centre, Ambulance Service of New South Wales, Sydney, for giving us many hours of their time and co-operation without which this study would not have been possible.

References

Brehmer, Berndt. (1990). Strategies inreal-time, dynamic decision making. In R. M. Hogarth (Ed.), <u>Insightsin Decision Making</u>, (pp. 262 - 279.). Chicago: University of ChicagoPress.

Cannon-Bowers, Janis A., Salas, Eduardo, &Pruitt, John. (1996). Establishing the boundaries of a paradigm fordecision-making research. <u>Human Factors,</u> <u>38</u>(2), 193-205.

Hoc, Jean-Michel, Cacciabue, Pietro C., andHollnagel, Erik. (Ed.). (1995). <u>Expertise and Technology: Cognitionand Human-Computer Interaction</u>. Hillsdale, NJ: Lawrence ErlbaumAssociates, Publishers.

Kaempf, George L., Klein, Gary, Thordsen,Marvin, & Wolf, Steve. (1996). Decision making in complex naval command andcontrol environments. Human Factors(Special Issue).

Klein, Gary A. (1993). A Recognition-PrimedDecision (RPD) Model of Rapid Decision Making. In G. A. Klein, J. Orasanu,R. Calderwood, & C. E. Zsambok (Eds.), Decision Making in Action:Models and Methods, . Norwood, NJ: Ablen Publishing Corp.

Klein, Gary A., Calderwood, Roberta, &Macgregor, Donald. (1989). Critical decision method for elicitingknowledge. IEEE Transactions on Systems, Man and Cybernetics, 19(3),462-472.

Militello, Laura, & Lim, Leona. (1995). Patient assessment skills:Assessing early cues of necrotizing enterocolitis. The Journal ofPerinatal and Neonatal Nursing, 9(2), 42-52.

O'Hare, D., Wigins, M., Batt, R. , & Morrison, D. (1994). Cognitivefailure analysis for aircraft accident investigation. Ergonomics, 37,1855-1869.

Orasanu, Judith, & Connolly, Terry. (1993).The re-invention of decision making. In G. A. Klein, J. Orasanu, R.Calderwood, & C. E. Zsambok (Eds.), Decision Making in Action: Modelsand Methods, . Norwood, NJ: Ablen Publishing Corp.

Pawlak, William S., & Vicente, Kim J. (1996).Inducing effective operator control through ecological interface design.International Journal of Human-Computer Studies, 44, 653-688.

Rasmussen, Jens, & Pejtersen, Annelise Mark.(1995). Virtual Ecology of Work. In P. H. John Flach, Jeff Caird, and KimVicente (Ed.), Global Perspectives on the Ecology of Human-MachineSystems, (Vol. 1, pp. 121-156). Hillsdale, NJ: Lawrence Erlbaum Associates, Inc.Publishers.

Skriver, Jan. (1996). Naturalistic decisionmaking. Report on the NDM Panel discussion held at the 1996 AnnualConference of the Psychological Society. The Psychologist(July 1996),3321-322.

Thordsen, Marvin, Galushka, Joseph, Klein,Gary A., Young, Saul, & Brezovic, Christopher. (1990). A knolwedgeelicitiation study of military planning (Technical Report 876): United States Army Research Institute for theBehavioural and Social Sciences.

Vicente, Kim J., Christoffersen, Klaus, &Pereklita, Alex. (1995). Supporting operator problem solving throughEcological Interface Design. IEEE Transactions on Systems, Man, andCybernetics, 25(4), 529-545.

Wong, William B.L., O'Hare, David, &Sallis, Philip J. (1996a). Experimental Transformation of a CognitiveSchema into a Display Structure. Paper presented at the The First Asia Pacific Conference on Computer HumanInteraction APCHI '96, Human factors of IT: Enhancing productivityand quality of life, Singapore, pp. 455-468.

Wong, William B.L., O'Hare, David, &Sallis, Philip J. (1996b). A Goal-Oriented Approach for DesigningDecision Support Displays in Dynamic Environments. Paper presented at theOzCHI '96, The Sixth Australian Computer Human Interaction Conference, Hamilton,New Zealand, pp. 78-85.

Wong, William B.L. , Sallis, Philip J. , & O'Hare, David. (1995).Information Portrayal for Decision Support in Dynamic IntentionalProcess Environments. Paper presented at the OZCHI '95, The Fifth Australian Conference on Computer Human Interaction,University of Wollongong, Wollongong, Australia, pp. 43-48.

Woods, David D. (1995). Toward a TheoreticalBase for Representation Design in the Computer Medium: EcologicalPerception and Aiding Human Cognition. In P. H. John Flach, Jeff Caird, andKim Vicente (Ed.), Global Perspectives on the Ecology of Human-Machine Systems, (Vol. 1, pp.157-188). Hillsdale, NJ: Lawrence Erlbaum Associates, Inc. Publishers.

Zsambok, Caroline E., Beach, Lee Roy, &Klein, Gary. (1992). A literature review of analytical andnaturalistic decision making (Final Technical Report): Research, Development, Test and EvaluationDivision, Naval Command, Control and Ocean SurveillanceCentre.t

Author Index

Keyword Index